B Baker
Kirkland, Kate Sayen
Captain James A. Baker of
Houston, 1857-1941

$30.00
ocn771425999
1st ed.   12/05/2012

Captain James A. Baker
of Houston, 1857–1941

RICE UNIVERSITY
100 YEARS
1912 · 2012

Captain James A. Baker of Houston, 1857–1941

KATE SAYEN KIRKLAND

FOREWORD BY

James A. Baker, III

Texas A&M University Press
College Station

LIBRARY OF CONGRESS CATALOGING-IN-PUBLICATION DATA

Kirkland, Kate Sayen, 1944–

Captain James A. Baker of Houston, 1857–1941 / by Kate Sayen Kirkland ; foreword by
James A. Baker, III. — 1st ed.

p.   cm.

Includes bibliographical references and index.

ISBN 978-1-60344-800-0 (cloth :alk. paper) — ISBN 1-60344-800-4 (cloth : alk. paper) —
ISBN 978-1-60344-797-3 (e-book) — ISBN 1-60344-797-0 (e-book) 1. Baker, James Addison, 1857–1941.
2. Lawyers—Texas—Houston—Biography. 3. Bankers—Texas—Houston—Biography. I. Title.

KF373.B295K57 2012

340.092—dc23

[B]   2011053004

Jacket photo: Captain James A. Baker. *Private Collection.*
Frontispiece: Captain Baker, 1930s. *Private Collection.*

For John David Kirkland, who inspired me
(June 6, 1933–January 21, 2008)

Genius is the capacity for hard work.
—*Maxim of Judge James Addison Baker*

Work hard, study and apply yourself closely, stay on the job,
and keep out of politics.
—*Advice of Captain James Addison Baker*

Prior preparation prevents poor performance.
—*Adage of James Addison Baker, Junior*

Nothing is worth having that you don't have to work for.
—*Creed of his father and grandfather, Secretary James Addison Baker, III*

Contents

Illustrations

Foreword

JAMES A. BAKER, III

As a child growing up in Houston, I was consistently reminded of my grandfather. I could not go very far in my hometown without seeing places that had been touched by his guiding hand. Close to my childhood home on Bissonnet Street was Rice University, which Captain Baker played a critical role in establishing. When I went downtown to see a movie or go to church, I would pass by buildings he had helped finance. And when I played tennis, I often did so at the Houston Country Club, which benefitted from his early direction. Houston in the first half of the twentieth century was built by towering individuals like Jesse Jones and Will Hogg. As the head of the city's premier law firm, the founding chairman of Rice University, and a leader in Houston's banking industry, Captain Baker defined integrity. These iconic figures envisioned Houston as a great city and worked throughout their lifetimes to make that dream come true. From my earliest memories, I was surrounded by the product of my grandfather's energy.

Of course, being the captain's grandson came with certain responsibilities. It meant living up to high expectations when it came to hard work, to seriousness, to toughness, and to fairness. Grandfather was a man of genuine authority who maintained a dogged determination to achieve the aspirations that he established for himself, for his family, and for his city. And if I didn't always appreciate the example that Captain Baker set, my father, James A. Baker Jr., and my mother, Bonner Means Baker, were there to remind me of it—not only while he was alive, but also long after he passed away on August 2, 1941. I can't remember how many times they looked me squarely in the eye and said, "Jimmy, you have quite a legacy to live up to."

As a result, it is especially rewarding for me to read this book that Kate Kirkland has written about my grandfather. She discovered parts of his rich history that I never knew, and some that I have long forgotten. Kirkland explains Captain Baker's role in the creation of Memorial Park. She recounts how Captain Baker helped his wife, Alice Graham Baker, establish the Houston Settlement Association, a volunteer organization that today is known as Neighborhood Centers Inc. And she includes the text of the very last letter that Captain Baker wrote before he died—a letter which he sent to me when I was only eleven years old, after I had passed my swimming test at a Texas Hill Country summer camp. Kirkland's book, *Captain James A. Baker of Houston, 1857–1941*, is a well-researched biography of a man whom, as she writes, "men and women turned to when they wanted a project to succeed."

But Kirkland's book is much more than the tale of an influential man. It is a story about Houston during the first half of the twentieth century, when the foundation was laid for its transformation into the international powerhouse that it is today. Perhaps most importantly, it is a story that provides a lesson about what it took, and still takes, to create a great community. As she writes, "Captain Baker lived in an era when loyalty to friends and family, courtesy to others, and duty to community defined a successful life. He searched for excellence because he wanted to do his best for those who relied on him." The legacy of Captain Baker and the other civic titans of his era is an important one because they were just as concerned with building a great city as they were with amassing great fortunes. By preserving the history of Captain James A. Baker, Kate Kirkland has done a real service to the memory of the man and the city he loved so much.

Captain James A. Baker
of Houston, 1857–1941

October 1912

CAPTAIN JAMES ADDISON BAKER and his fellow trustees chose October 12, 1912, to inaugurate the William Marsh Rice Institute for the Advancement of Literature, Science, and Art. Board Chairman Baker and founding President Edgar Odell Lovett invited international luminaries from academia, government officials from the state of Texas, and regional leaders from business, banking, legal, and civic organizations to Houston to launch the fledgling university. That fall Houstonians and their guests who braved the mile-long muddy track extending south of downtown suddenly beheld "an extraordinary spectacle, as of palaces in fairy-story . . . brilliant, astounding, enduring: rising out of the barren brown prairie which extended, unbroken save for a belt of trees, to the horizon." Walls of salmon-hued brick and pillars of white, gray, and purple marble appeared "complete and magnificent, to face the setting sun" and define the Rice Institute Administration Building and Sallyport.[1]

For twenty years Houston's civic leaders and journalists exchanged rumors that millionaire entrepreneur William Marsh Rice had endowed an institute for advanced education in his adopted city. Impatient to enjoy what promised to be a civic asset of extraordinary magnitude,

Illustration: Administration Building, October 1912. Early Rice Collection, Woodson Research Center, Rice University.

some asked Rice why he did not begin building this seat of learning during his lifetime. After the donor's death on September 23, 1900, others grumbled that the old man's hand-picked board of six trustees, led by attorney James A. Baker, was taking far too long to satisfy expectation. In September 1912, critics received their answer as the entire city prepared for a magnificent Academic Festival of celebration.

Fifty-nine students registered for entrance tests and picked up class schedules on September 23, the twelfth anniversary of Rice's death. Three days later, Edgar Odell Lovett challenged these pioneers and his twelve carefully chosen faculty colleagues to embark with him "in high and noble tasks" and to "hold one faith" with him—"that it is possible to learn and that it is also possible to teach."[2] The Thursday morning meeting in the Faculty Chamber, as the Founders' Room was then called, was impressive: trustees, faculty, and Houston's business, religious, and political leaders applauded as students entered the hall. President Lovett clasped the hand of each undergraduate, and his voice trembled momentarily as he began to explain the momentous task confronting the men and women in the room.

Inspiring and personal as was this ceremony, President Lovett and Board Chairman Baker had something much grander in mind to memorialize William Marsh Rice and secure his vision in the international firmament of higher education. As Lovett addressed the students that September morning, scholars and dignitaries from across the United States and around the globe had begun the long, slow journey by ship and rail to Houston, "an overgrown commercial village," of eighty thousand residents, few of whom had experienced formal university classes themselves.[3]

Chairman Baker and President Lovett planned the academic festival that would launch their Institute carefully because they believed attention to detail would reap invaluable public relations rewards. Citing the model of Princeton College's 1896 Sesquicentennial, Lovett proposed a conference of scholars who would bring formal greetings from world centers of advanced learning and whose lectures would affirm the birth of a new academic star. Baker knew an internationally acclaimed institute of higher education would change the face of Houston, and he made sure local and state political, business, and social leaders participated fully in the Institute's inaugural weekend.

At a special meeting of the Institute Board of Trustees on May 2, 1912,

Chairman Baker, Vice Chairman James Everett McAshan, the founder's nephews, William Marsh Rice II and Benjamin Botts Rice, President Lovett, and Secretary pro tem Arthur B. Cohn voted to observe a formal opening Thursday through Saturday, October 10–12, 1912. They decided to invite delegates from "celebrated" universities, colleges, scientific foundations, and learned societies to be their special guests, and they agreed to ask several internationally renowned scholars to present lectures that would be published later in commemorative volumes. Each inaugural lecturer would receive $1,000 and be entertained by the city's premier hosts.

During the annual meeting of the board on May 21, Baker grilled the architect and contractors about their progress, demanding "verbal expressions to the board in open meeting" that the buildings would be ready when students matriculated on September 23. As soon as the contractors left the meeting, Baker told architect William Ward Watkin to spare no effort to finish the buildings, even if he had to hire extra men and work overtime. The chairman instructed Watkin to report to the board "at least once every two weeks until completion."[4]

In July President Lovett visited Captain Baker and his wife Alice at their Bass Rocks summer home in Gloucester, Massachusetts. During a three-day sojourn Lovett and Baker hammered out details of the October festival.[5] Lovett, an established if youthful professor at Princeton when he received the call in December 1907 to build Rice Institute, had spent the intervening years traveling the globe to introduce academic institutions and learned societies to the new university being planned in remote Houston, Texas. From his wide acquaintance, Lovett now chose six savants to present lectures in person and asked six other scholars to provide lectures that would be included in later publications. Mindful of Princeton's sesquicentennial example, Lovett also secured prominent religious leaders to bless the events and invited Henry Van Dyke, a popular Presbyterian theologian, author, and Princeton professor of English Literature, to compose a celebratory ode. Baker extended invitations to Texas' governor, Houston's mayor, the chief justice of Texas' Supreme Court, the city commissioners, and the Houston Chamber of Commerce. Mrs. Baker, long active in civic projects, ensured widespread local support by recommending that the leaders of Houston's church and community boards and programs be included as members of the reception committees. Mrs. Lovett, at her husband's suggestion, tried to "brush up on French during the summer" because several dignitaries spoke no other language.[6]

Their planning complete, the Bakers sailed to Germany for six weeks at a spa while Lovett returned to Houston to issue invitations and oversee preparations. A "corps of stenographers and clerks" toiled for weeks at the Institute offices to prepare more than one thousand invitations from "The President and Trustees of The Rice Institute of Liberal and Technical Learning." The committee dispatched oversized calfskin invitations—embossed with the Institute's seal, rolled in scrolls tied with blue ribbon, and placed in shellacked wooden cylinders—to every university and learned society in the world. Individuals received large engraved invitations, and all attendees were sent a packet of engraved cards to twenty-one specific events.

Response was immediate. Thoughtful messages of congratulation poured into the city; some were engraved on heavy paper or inscribed on parchment, many were later framed for the president's office. Newspapers estimated that delegates from "about 175 universities, colleges, societies and academies" would attend the festival and noted that Australia, the Philippines, South Africa, and Sweden were sending representatives.[7] The presidents of Johns Hopkins, Stanford, Tulane, Vanderbilt, the Massachusetts Institute of Technology, the University of Chicago, the University of North Carolina, and the University of Texas led a parade of deans and faculty members from every important United States institution of higher learning.[8] All guests received passes to enjoy the Houston Country Club and its golf course and the downtown Houston and Thalian clubs, although when these visitors would find time to relax remains a mystery. No sooner had the delegates debarked at the train station than they began a grueling schedule of activities. Temperatures registered in the nineties, with soothing seventies at night and a pleasant breeze on Saturday for the presidential address.

On Thursday October 10 at 8:30 a.m., Captain Baker and the Trustees of the Institute welcomed guests to the first event—an informal breakfast for 150 at the elegant Bender Hotel. Afterwards, a fleet of autos carried diners to the campus. Attendees entered the Faculty Chamber, resplendent with a "frieze of . . . flags and banners of the nations of the earth." Above the rostrum floated the gray and blue standard of the Institute surrounded by huge American flags. Texas Governor Oscar Branch Colquitt and his staff "in full dress regalia" passed down the center aisle "amid gloved applause." More glorious still was President Lovett, appearing "in his silken robe of black, with the cape of gray and blue, while a ribbon of purple stretche[d] across his breast." Professor Hugo de Vries of Amsterdam "had the appearance of a prophet" in his black robe and orange cape, while Professor Senator Vito Volterra of Rome "was resplendent in a robe of wonderful yellow contrasted with scarlet." Other participants wore conventional morning dress of vest, swallow-tailed coat, and starched collar that must have been stifling in the ninety-degree heat.

The board, faculty, students, and leaders of Houston's social, educational, religious, and business life settled on the oak benches for two hour-long presentations, one by Professor Rafael Altamira of Madrid, who discussed the history of human progress, and the other by Professor de Vries, who spoke about geographical botany.[9] Lectures by Professor John Mackail of London on poetry and Professor Frederik Carl Størmer of Christiania on "cosmical physics" were read by title. Two court reporters from New Orleans attended every event to record the speeches in English or in French, as required by the speaker, although some participants spoke so fast on such esoteric subjects that the reporters could not keep up.[10]

Following the speeches, guests once again climbed into waiting automobiles and rumbled back downtown to the Banquet Hall of the City Auditorium, where Mayor Horace Baldwin Rice and the city commissioners entertained the crowd. Mayor Rice, another of the founder's nephews, served as master of ceremonies at the 1:00 p.m. meal and introduced Chairman Baker, "a gentleman of high standing in this community, who has done a great work in its behalf." Baker offered his guests "a cordial welcome, not only to the halls and home of the new institution, but also to the homes and hearts of the people of the whole city of Houston." In his brief remarks, Baker praised the "magnificent generosity" of William Marsh Rice and invited all present "to come and drink from the fountains of knowledge which have been provided for this festal occasion." Governor Oscar B. Colquitt then greeted the delegates, who responded with ten "apologies" or toasts from regions of the world or areas of learning. William Henry Carpenter, Provost of Columbia University, offered a summary: "here is a gathering from the ends of the earth for a purpose that is broader in its intention and its results than any other—the common purpose of education."[11]

Faculty Chamber, Opening Lectures, October 1912. Early Rice Collection, Woodson Research Center, Rice University.

At 3:00 p.m. delegates returned to the handsome faculty room where Professor Emile Borel of Paris spoke on molecular theory and philosophy Professor Sir Henry Jones of Glasgow discussed "the present problems of reflective thought." Offerings by Senator Benedetto Croce of Naples on the problems of art and criticism and by Privy Councilor Baron Dairoku Kikuchi of Tokyo on the introduction of western learning to Japan were read by title. At 5:00 p.m. participants adjourned to the Academic Court of the Administration Building for an informal public garden party and an opportunity to meet "large numbers of Houstonians" anxious "to show their appreciation" to the visitors. Institute gardeners had transformed the construction site with hastily planted shrubs and potted plants. "Prettily arranged tea booths" dotted the "lingering summer" scene. Mrs. Baker, trustee wives, faculty wives, and Rice family members served as hostesses, assisted by the wives and daughters of Houston's leading families.[12]

At 8:30 that evening, Professor de Vries presented a public, illustrated lecture on the "Ideals of a Naturalist" at the Majestic Theatre. At 9:30 p.m.

Captain and Mrs. Baker hosted a reception to honor nearly one hundred guests of the Institute at their home, 1416 Main Street. Mrs. Baker had decorated the downstairs rooms with home and foreign flags, pennants from various colleges, and "flowers in profusion."[13]

Activities resumed at 8:30 a.m. on Friday October 11, when the Houston Chamber of Commerce hosted another informal breakfast at the Bender Hotel. Dignitaries again gave speeches of welcome, and cars again transported the 150 guests to the Faculty Chamber for two more lectures. Chemistry Professor Sir William Ramsay of London spoke about "modern views concerning atoms and molecules." Professor Senator Vito Volterra memorialized the mathematical work and scientific influence of the recently deceased Henri Poincaré, whose lectures on the philosophy of the sciences were later included in the commemorative *Book of the Opening*.

The founder's most politically connected nephew, Jonas Shearn Rice, and his wife then welcomed guests of the Institute to a luncheon at the Thalian Club. After lunch the Kneisel Quartet of New York performed in concert at the Majestic Theatre. That afternoon Baker's law partner Edwin Brewington Parker and his wife Katharine, a noted amateur musician, entertained at The Oaks, their beautiful seven-acre estate. At 8:30 p.m. participants and their wives returned to the faculty room for a chamber concert by the Kneisel Quartet. The Board of Trustees provided supper at the Residential Hall dining commons, and President Lovett served as master of ceremonies for the evening.

As the meal began, diners found a whole grapefruit sitting before them; when they experimented with the straw that punctured the top, they discovered that several unnamed liquors augmented the juice, a touch that lightened the mood and amused the guests. President Lovett introduced eight visiting scholars, who offered toasts on behalf of their disciplines. Following these speeches, some mercifully shortened because the hour was late, Sir William Ramsay unexpectedly stood a second time to wish President and Mrs. Lovett "many long and happy years" at Rice. Replying that he was "deeply touched," Lovett turned attention to the last speaker, design architect Ralph Adams Cram, who, Lovett explained, deserved applause for creating the Institute buildings.[14]

A youthful Julian Huxley, one of Lovett's recruits for the Rice faculty, described the scene: "Cram rose to his feet, produced an enormous roll of typescript from his pocket and proceeded to read implacably on.

After twenty minutes, [Lady Ramsay] could stand no more: 'Oh, I am so tired! . . .' she said, and let her head fall forward on to her hands on the table." Cram continued to his final pronouncement that "Art is the measure of man," and Lovett released the satiated guests well after midnight by wishing them "sound slumber and sweet dreams."[15]

Saturday October 12 dawned with a northerly breeze to freshen the air. Automobiles, buggies, and "every outbound car of the traction company" deposited hundreds of guests at the Institute gates on Main Street. No indoor space could accommodate the audience, which formed a large semicircle that filled the entire Academic Court south of the Administration Building. A speakers' platform of paneled oak surrounded by palms stood immediately before the bas relief of "Inspiration" on the Administration Building's south façade.

Board members, lecturers, faculty, delegates, and students assembled at 9:30 a.m. in the South Hall of the undergraduate Residence complex. After some confusion, delegates organized themselves in order according to founding date of the institution each represented, with the University of Paris delegate taking first place and representatives of newly organized Reed College (1908) and Will Hogg's organization to support Texas' institutions of higher education (1911) following at the end of the line. The fine granite gravel ordered for the Institute's roads and pathways had not arrived, and the academic parade proceeded slowly along a roadway of rough stones. Led by Houston's Municipal Band playing a medley of American airs, the dignitaries followed Dr. Lovett with poet laureate Henry Van Dyke. Next came Captain Baker with Texas Chief Justice Thomas Jefferson Brown, followed by Thomas Frank Gailor, Bishop of Tennessee, walking alone; then came trustee James Everett McAshan escorting Dr. Charles Frederic Aked, and the remaining trustees and lecturers, who proceeded to the speaker's platform. Delegates, faculty, and students moved with them from the South Hall entrance to the walk at the south end of the Administration Building and took their seats between the audience and the speakers.

When everyone had settled in place and a mother had found her lost child, Dr. Robert Ernest Vinson intoned the invocation and read selections from the Bible. The Houston Quartette Society, directed by Hu Huffmaster and accompanied by the Municipal Band, performed Palestrina's "Veni Creator Spiritus." Henry Van Dyke then rose to recite his inaugural poem, "Texas, A Democratic Ode," in a clear voice. His performance was followed by Chief Justice Brown's address "On Education and the State" and the comments of Bishop Gailor about "The Church and Education." The arts, the law, and faith had been well-represented; now the audience turned rapt attention to the final and most important words of the day as Edgar Odell Lovett moved toward the podium to explain his mission for the new institution.

Lovett's address appeared in the press several times, and he expanded his remarks for the *Book of the Opening*, but "the words of unforgettable beauty" he spoke that Saturday morning guided his path as president for thirty-five years. Mindful of the date, October 12, Lovett introduced a theme he would return to repeatedly: like Christopher Columbus, the founders of Rice Institute were embarking on an adventurous journey of discovery, a journey that would demand hope and strength and courage and clear thinking and resolve if they were to reach their destination. While the university's purposes were manifold, at its heart lay twin objectives: to send "forth constant streams of liberally educated men and women to be leaders of public opinion in the service of the people" and to become "a great storehouse of learning, a great bureau of standards, a great workshop of knowledge, a great laboratory for the training of men of thought and men of action." Scholarly research, Lovett explained, would be critical because "an inquiring mind is the safest guide for an inquiring mind." Lovett closed his remarks by telling the "Ladies and Gentlemen of Houston" that the walls and towers of the Rice Institute belonged to them. Lovett saw a long line of trees connecting factory and counting house to the college community "with the happy homes of Houston lying in between," and he invited everyone present and the generations that would succeed them to find on the Rice campus "a temple of wisdom and sanctuary of learning," a retreat where they might contemplate "a great pageant that moves from the living past through the living present into the living future."[16]

The audience greeted Lovett's "Meaning of the New Institution" with enthusiastic applause. Immediately, choir voices recited the One Hundredth Psalm, and Dr. Charles F. Aked pronounced the benediction. The delegates then recessed to the cloister of the South Hall for official photographs. The Gaumont Company of New York had sent a special representative to "make motion films" of the ceremonies and record Houston's most historic event since the city's founding.

Six congratulatory speeches awaited luncheon attendees at the Institute Commons at 1:00 p.m. Professors Ramsay and Borel spoke for foreign universities; Dean William Francis Magie of Princeton represented schools of the East; William Holding Echols from the University of Virginia spoke for Southern schools; while President Harry Pratt Judson of the University of Chicago upheld Northern principals; and Sidney Edward Mezes, President of the University of Texas, championed the West. Greetings from across the globe completed the formal ceremonies. Guests then packed their suitcases for an overnight in Galveston and boarded cars for a drive to the Houston Country Club where President and Mrs. Lovett crowned the social activities with a farewell reception from 4:00 until 6:00 p.m. Mrs. Lovett estimated that "between 600 & 700 people . . . full of enthusiasm for everything" paid their respects to the "most interesting" Institute guests.[17] Members of the Board and their wives, members of the faculty and their wives, seventy prominent Houston couples, and ten single ladies of distinction, all of their names listed several times in Houston newspaper articles, assisted the Lovetts as hosts.[18]

Baker, for thirty years a lawyer for several of Houston's seventeen railroads, had chartered a special train to carry guests to the Hotel Galvez in Galveston where the trustees had booked rooms for "a splendid termination of the festivities." Much to everyone's relief, no program of any kind accompanied the informal Shore-supper and Smoker served on the hotel's veranda; soon guests slipped away to their rooms for "a splendid night of rest." Mrs. Lovett noted that the weary travelers enjoyed the meal and awoke "greatly refreshed" by the soothing sea air.[19] The Academic Festival had come to a happy close.

On Sunday Baker and Lovett sought blessings of a different kind. Churches all over the city joined their choirs under Hu Huffmaster's direction as over four thousand people gathered in the City Auditorium for an ecumenical service. A chorus of "Oh God Our Help in Ages Past" was followed by President Lovett's invocation and Henry Van Dyke's prayer and Bible reading on the theme of love. Dr. Charles Aked, pastor of the First Congregational Church of San Francisco and one of the era's most powerful and popular orators, began a long discourse on ways Rice Institute would produce more good men and more good women.

He lauded President Lovett as "the practical statesman and the visionary combined."[20] In closing, Aked spoke on behalf of the people as he dedicated Rice Institute "to letters, science and art, to the service of the commonwealth of Texas, to the material progress of the South, to human improvement for the earth, and to the greater glory of God."[21] Hymns, "America," and Dr. Aked's benediction completed the service. A reporter noted with approval that although a late train from Galveston caused a delay, the audience "waited patiently . . . and there was not a ripple of applause," but instead "the sacredness of the occasion seemed to hold all in its spell."

Only one event remained. As admiring visitors boarded trains for their journeys home, Houstonians poured into the First Presbyterian Church for a special 7:30 p.m. service. "Every pew was occupied in the main auditorium, aisles were crowded, the Sunday school room behind the altar was filled, every door, window, hallway, niche, and corner within hearing distance of the speaker was jammed tight so that people could neither get in nor out . . . Hundreds were turned away in disappointment."[22] Following a special musical program of choral and solo works, Henry Van Dyke gave "one of the simplest, easiest understood, and most unique [sermons] ever heard from a Houston pulpit." The "profound" lesson addressed to the students admonished them "to reap the benefits of the Rice institute" and "to resolve to do everything well . . . to play with all their hearts and to work with all their hearts."[23]

Captain Baker recognized Rice Institute's inaugural Academic Festival as a culmination and a beginning. For twenty-one years, he had held in trust another man's vision for an institute of literature, science, and art. He had fought those who would derail William Marsh Rice's intentions; he had given form to a donor's vague aspirations; he had found a young leader who would breathe life and purpose into the bricks and mortar of a nascent university. He had taken a bold stand for excellence, for international acclaim, and for broad-based inclusivity. As Captain Baker sat on the speakers' platform in his light summer suit and tight-fitting bowler hat, arms solemnly crossed, he could listen with pride to Edgar Odell Lovett, who assumed the mantle of leadership that Saturday morning. The beautifully orchestrated festival bore the marks of a partnership being forged between board chairman and university president: it highlighted the Institute's aspirations, featured Houston's strengths, and affirmed Baker's actions. Yet, on that Saturday morning, Baker's

stance at the helm of an aspiring seat of high learning was only beginning. For three more decades he would shape the Institute's destiny and
support its president.

*   *   *

In the early twentieth century, Houston's visionary civic leaders imagined a great industrial city rising along the banks of Buffalo Bayou. The
progressive community they envisioned would be a gateway to the West
and a transportation hub to the world that rivaled established urban
centers on the East and West coasts. Investors would build a strong
economic foundation, municipal officials would protect the quality of
life for all, and citizens would develop cultural and service institutions
that defined urban excellence. Captain James Addison Baker, lawyer,
banker, and civic steward, had the means to nurture these aspirations.
As chairman of the board of Rice Institute, he controlled the great fortune amassed by William Marsh Rice. How did the Captain's ambition to
build a modern commercial city strengthened by a vibrant community
of scholars change the trajectory of Houston's development? Who was
this man trusted by so many to steer a sure course?

CHAPTER ONE

Family Roots

TREKKING TO TEXAS in the 1850s guaranteed danger, discomfort, and bad food. Travelers from the 1820s to the 1850s tell the same story. The journey was long—weeks, or even months—and arduous. Pioneers from Europe or states east of the Mississippi traveled down rivers by flat boat and unstable paddle-wheelers or overland on coal-fired rail cars, mule-drawn carts, and horseback. Many crossed the Gulf of Mexico from New Orleans to Galveston, enduring turbulent seas and shipwreck. Public accommodations were filthy, and lodgers often shared bug-infested beds with strangers of dubious honesty and cleanliness. Camping under the stars frequently provided the only resting place. Worst of all was the food—usually fried, largely corn meal mixed with water, and almost wholly lacking in fresh fruit or vegetables. Roads were little more than rutted cattle trails, muddy and impassable after rain or choked with dust in the fierce summer sun. But the trek promised vast plantations of cheap land, open-ended opportunity for entrepreneurs, and a population thirsting for the civilizing expertise lawyers, doctors, teachers, and clerics would bring to a sparsely settled landscape.

Illustrations: James Addison Baker, Rowena Crawford Baker, 1860s. Private Collection.

ANTEBELLUM IMMIGRANTS

Neither James Addison Baker nor Rowena Beverly Crawford left a record of their journeys to Huntsville, Texas, where they would meet, marry, and raise a large family that would include their son and future Houston civic leader Captain James A. Baker. Contemporary travel accounts make it possible to imagine their experiences. Rowena arrived first. Daughter of the Rev. Beverly Crawford and his wife Anna Bland McRobert, Rowena was born in Alabama on April 8, 1828. For four generations, Crawford and McRobert forebears had supported higher education and ministered to Presbyterian flocks in Prince Edward County, Virginia. Bland ancestors had arrived in Virginia in 1654 and established Westover Plantation and Blandford there in the seventeenth century. Rowena was a well-educated young woman who immigrated to Huntsville, Texas, to teach in the town's Female "Brick" Academy. Her mother's sister, Elizabeth McRobert, had settled in Huntsville in 1849, where her Presbyterian evangelist husband Daniel Baker was organizing Austin College, a Presbyterian institution founded that year.[1] The Bakers—no relation to James Addison Baker—invited Rowena to join them on their journey, offered her a home, and probably helped her obtain her teaching position. Rowena was quickly named Female Academy principal, a post she held until her marriage.

James Addison Baker traveled to Huntsville in April 1852 when "every variety of flower" danced across the widespread prairies and fields, "presenting a scene calculated to awaken a passion for natural objects."[2] After the death of his first wife, Caroline Hightower, Baker left rural Lauderdale County in the northwestern corner of Alabama and moved to Huntsville at the request of Hightower family members who had established businesses and purchased property there in the 1840s. Baker probably began his journey by catching the Memphis & Charleston Railroad, which had been chartered in 1846 and was still under construction near the two terminal cities. In Memphis he probably took passage on a paddle-wheel steamer headed down the "seething turbid water" of the Mississippi to New Orleans.[3] River travel was reasonably fast and far easier than trudging overland through forests, swamps, and sparsely settled lands. Accommodations varied from fairly comfortable to precarious, depending on the size and stability of the vessel. Many male passengers whiled away the hours with a perpetual poker game. Fights among passengers, fires in the engine room, and treacherous shoals in the river made each voyage a memorable adventure. Passengers going to interior Texas towns usually debarked at the point where the Red River joined the Mississippi. They then began the slow, treacherous journey up the Red River on small boats, "scows in build, perfectly flat, with a pointed stem and square stern."[4] In Natchitoches Parish, Louisiana, travelers purchased horses or mules and carts for the overland trip to the Sabine River crossing into Texas and on to Huntsville, a distance of nearly two hundred miles. To make the journey even more toilsome, mules ambled slowly, ferry captains overcharged, and frequent delays were standard. One diarist noted that he and a companion arrived at the 10:00 a.m. boat at 2:00 p.m. Told to board quickly because the crew was departing immediately, they hastily loaded their luggage and waited another five hours.[5]

Yet immigrants poured into Texas, felling forests, fencing prairies, and planting farms. Educational missionary and memoirist Melinda Rankin spent a year in Huntsville, taught at the Female Academy with Rowena Crawford, and then embarked on a twenty-year crusade to educate Mexican Indians. Although Rankin envisioned Huntsville as desolate and miserable,[6] she was pleasantly surprised to discover "a town of growing importance" where one thousand residents showed "unparalleled energy and public spirit."[7] Valleys of the region were "as rich and beautiful as it is possible to conceive over which nature has . . . spread her emerald carpet of grass" and "present[ed] greater inducements to the emigrants than, perhaps, any portion of our country."[8] The town's "concentration of talent, enterprise and morality" made Huntsville an ideal settlement.[9]

Pleasant and Ephraim Gray, natives of Huntsville, Alabama, had established an Indian trading post near the Trinity River about 1835 and named the hamlet for their former home. Rich soil and easy communication along the river quickly attracted planters and merchants, "men of wealth, talent and influence" from Alabama, Mississippi, and Tennessee.[10] By 1850 Huntsville had established the four pillars of its future economy: the town was a mercantile center; it became county seat of Walker County on April 1, 1846; in 1847 legislators located the State Penitentiary there; and its citizens supported several educational institutions. Set amid rolling hills surrounded by open prairies and forests of pine and hardwoods, the Huntsville area was well-watered by many creeks and connected to Gulf ports by the Trinity River. Corn and cotton were the primary commercial crops, but the rich loam of creek and river beds also yielded bushels of berries, apricots, peaches, and grapes throughout the summer. Moderate year-round temperatures, ample rainfall, springs of pure water, and abundant fish and game supported a prosperous town by 1850. Two hotels housed visitors: the Globe, whose dining room menu boasted produce from the owner's farm, and the Keenan House, which advertised large and roomy stables and good servants. The saloonkeeper, a local merchant, promised "choice liquors" from New Orleans, Galveston, and Houston.[11] Despite these amenities, and several newspapers and schools, Huntsville lost the competition to become the Texas state capital when Austin, located in the rugged Hill Country, won more supporters in statewide polling.[12]

In keeping with nineteenth-century westward migration patterns, James Baker left family members in northern Alabama when he emigrated to Texas. Baker was born in Madison County near Huntsville, Alabama, on March 3, 1821, the eldest son of Elijah Adam and Jane Saxton Baker. Elijah and Jane, natives of North Carolina who proudly traced their ancestry to Presbyterian Scotland, had married about 1820 and moved to rural northern Alabama. In 1826 Elijah received a land grant about twelve miles west of Florence, seat of Lauderdale County, Alabama. There he and Jane established a plantation near Gravelly Springs and raised nine children. The five boys, James (b. 1821), John (b. 1826), Gabriel (b. 1829), Andrew (b. 1836), and Elijah Matthew (b. 1838) grew to adulthood and migrated to Huntsville, Texas. Mary Jane (b. 1823) married a local plantation owner James Wilson Carroll in 1842 and died near Gravelly Springs in 1863 after the birth of her ninth child. Three other Baker girls died in childhood. Elijah prospered by expanding his land holdings into northeastern Mississippi and operating a blacksmith's business. After Elijah's death in 1845, Mary Jane and James Carroll, administered her father's estate for several years. Elijah's widow Jane married Samuel Croft on January 8, 1848. Croft died six years later (January 1, 1854), and Jane married Jabez M. Cobb in 1857. By the early 1860s, Jane was widowed again.

The Bakers must have valued education and found some way to secure teachers for their children, because one son became a lawyer, two practiced medicine, and two engaged in business. Sparsely populated northern Alabama failed to provide opportunities for these gifted young men, who prospered in Texas. In 1839 eighteen-year-old James left home to teach school. This career was short-lived, and by 1841 he was clerking in the chancery court and reading law with Samuel W. Probasco, an

Ohio native who practiced in Florence. James was admitted to the Alabama bar in 1843, joined Probasco as partner, and at the older man's unexpected death in 1845, inherited his clients. Some years earlier Probasco
had married Catherine Hightower (b. 1811), daughter of the prosperous
Hightowers who left Alabama for Texas in 1841. Catherine had taken
charge of her sister Caroline, fifteen years her junior and considered too
frail for the uncertainties of frontier life. As a close friend of the Probasco
and Hightower families, James was well-acquainted with the slim, pretty
Caroline, and the couple married on May 30, 1849. By January 1852 death
had claimed the delicate woman, and James was left a childless widower
at age thirty-one with no particular reason to remain in Alabama.[13]

The Hightowers urged Baker to join their family group, and he left
for Texas in April 1852. Not long after his arrival in Huntsville, the senior
Hightowers died. Once again, James acquired family business and social
acceptance when he and John Hightower were named administrators of
the Hardy Hightower estate sometime before July 1853. The estate was
considerable because Hardy and his wife Harriett were prominent slaveholders who had accumulated land, run a plantation, and started a mercantile business. For the twenty years James Baker remained in Huntsville, he followed the Hightower example, practicing law, purchasing
land, building a business, and serving community interests as a popular
civic leader.

It is not clear when James's brothers joined him in Texas or whether
John, who was twenty-six when his brother emigrated, traveled with him
to learn about opportunities that might benefit other family members.
Good reports quickly reached Alabama. James had established his legal
practice, had begun to invest in his new hometown, and had joined the
local Masons. Fellow Masons—including former President of Texas
Sam Houston, Texas Governor George T. Wood, and Texas historian
and attorney Colonel Henderson Yoakum—elected Baker Grand Master of Forest Lodge #19 in 1853, 1854, and again in 1858. On January 23,
1857, the James A. Baker 202 Lodge was chartered in New Hope, Texas, in
his honor, quick recognition for a newcomer. By 1857, when their father
Elijah's will was belatedly probated, brother Gabriel (Gill), trained by
Lauderdale County physician James Kyle, had established his practice
in Huntsville, and brothers Andrew and Elijah Matthew (Matt) were
working in a grocery there. Before the Civil War ended, John, who completed medical training in Nashville in 1861, and their mother, Jane Baker

Croft Cobb, had joined the family group, which then included wives and children.[14]

ROWENA AND JAMES

Although he worked hard to build his law practice, administer the Hightower estate, and maintain mercantile partnerships, James did not neglect his personal life. Soon after his arrival, the friendly widower sought an introduction to Rowena Crawford, the lively young lady who lived with the Daniel Bakers and ran the local Brick Academy for female students. By June 1853 a romance between the accomplished attorney and capable educationist had progressed to the proposal stage, when a moment of restraint overcame the advocate. Perhaps in the guise of overseeing Hightower and Baker business in Lauderdale County, Alabama, James traveled to Raleigh, Tennessee, near Memphis, to meet Rowena's mother, the widowed Anna McRobert Crawford. After visiting with her and receiving two bottles of cordial and other gifts for Rowena, James departed without discussing his reason for coming—"to consult with [her] upon the propriety of... addressing Miss Rowena, and if consistent with your pleasure, to obtain your approbation of my suit," as he confessed in his delightful thank-you letter of June 22. James noted that Mrs. Crawford "may think it a little strange that I did not mention [this important communication] in person," but he "had not then asked permission directly of Miss Rowena to do so; and secondly, the short time I had to stay, would have given the whole, too much the air of a common business transactional—thereby seemingly divesting the subject of that importance and consideration that properly belonged to it."

Something about Mrs. Crawford's reception in Raleigh must have encouraged the reticent admirer; back in Huntsville, James immediately asked Rowena if she would permit him to ask her mother for permission to pay his addresses to her. Rowena not only approved his letter to her mother but also sent one of her own. If Mrs. Crawford saw the delightful humor of the couple's convoluted logic, she did not confess; instead, she readily granted permission for this courtship to proceed. James and Rowena settled things quickly, each writing to Mrs. Crawford again. Her August 29 response to these letters was ecstatic: "My beloved child," she began, the contents of Rowena's letter "afforded me the sweetest pleasure because I learned that you were happy and you know that the great desire of my heart is to see my children happy." She praised her future son-in-law, said she believed the two were "suited to each other, [which] is essential to happiness in married life," and asked her daughter to "tell Mr. Baker that I am very much obliged to him for his interesting letter and for his affectionate solicitude for me." She added that she had just returned from Memphis, where she "heard great praise" about Rowena's fiancé.[15]

On September 27, 1853, Rowena's cousin William M. Baker, son of Daniel and Elizabeth McRobert Baker and pastor of the First Presbyterian Church of Austin, united the happy couple in marriage at the residence of Dr. Charles Grandison Keenan, as witnessed and recorded by Walker County Clerk John W. Davidson.[16] Apparently the newlyweds' affectionate solicitude toward family members faltered during the honeymoon phase because Mrs. Crawford penned a plaintive note from Raleigh on October 20, 1853: "I have received no letter from you my dearest Row since you were married." She hoped that "love till they die" would "be the case with you and the dear man on whom you have bestowed the treasure of your love. . . . Give my love to him and tell him he is already to me a dear child and may God bless you both is my constant prayer."[17]

Family, law, and education would define the marriage that began with such loving support. Following proper nineteenth-century custom, Rowena resigned her post as school principal, because managing a household and rearing a family, as much as running a school, were considered full-time occupations, but her interest in education never wavered. Her letters paint an affectionate, capable, and articulate woman with a keen sense of humor and strong moral compass—a good partner for a man who traveled the wilds of Texas to practice law and build his business. Rowena endured long separations during which she made decisions about house improvements, managed farm properties, rented slave labor from family friend Sam Houston, and tended her vegetable garden and fruit trees. These absences caused her "much pain." In one two-week period when James was in San Antonio, La Grange, and Seguin—"the longest two weeks of my life"—eight letters do not suffice to explain how much she missed her Dearest Husband and wished Aladdin's Lamp could transport them "to enjoy each other's society." Letters from James to My Dear Wife were usually briefer, recorded fatigue from long horseback rides, warned of Indians, and inevitably ended by wishing he were at home. By March 14, 1855, home also included a "dear little boy," Beverly Crawford Baker. Beverly proved to be a sickly child who

Courthouse Square, Huntsville, Texas, ca. 1870. Walker County Treasures Collection of the City of Huntsville. Supported by a Tex-Treasures grant from the Texas State Library and Archives Commission and by the Walker County Genealogical Society.

died June 13, 1856. Not quite seven months later James Addison Baker junior was born on January 10, 1857. The second Baker child, called Jimmie by family members throughout his life, would drop junior from his signature after his father's death and be known to contemporaries and posterity as Captain James A. Baker. The new baby's birth must have been bittersweet, although Rowena later wrote to her grown son that his arrival was "doubly welcome & . . . a token of [God's] love."[18] The Bakers' first daughter, Mary Susan (Minnie), arrived on May 13, 1858, and proved a plucky playfellow for the older brother she called Buddy.

James Addison Baker built a reputation as a lawyer quick to recognize talented colleagues. Samuel Probasco had taught him well, and his partner in Alabama, Richard Wilde Walker, later served as an Alabama legislator, as associate justice of the Alabama Supreme Court, and as senator for Alabama in the 1864–1865 Confederate Congress. When Baker arrived in Huntsville he associated with the town's most established lawyers. After the Civil War, he and Judge James M. Maxey formed a partnership with offices in a vine-covered, columned building on the corner of the courthouse square. From time to time Baker also tried cases with his nephew John D. Hightower. As a county seat and thriving market town, Huntsville produced enough legal business to attract several capable lawyers, but not enough to support them all comfortably. Typical of most frontier lawyers, Baker augmented his income with business and agricultural enterprises. Because clients lived miles from town and because state and federal judicial districts covered business in several sparsely populated counties, Baker frequently packed clothes and legal papers into his saddle bags and rode long distances to consult clients and try cases. Walker County records show he handled real estate deals, secured land titles, collected debts, wrote wills, administered estates, and acted as guardian for minor children. Many of the cases he brought to court involved disputes about land and slave ownership. Baker also accepted railroad work when the new mode of transportation began to push rail lines further into the state. Railroad litigation involving rights of way as well as injuries suffered by construction workers, passengers, passersby, and livestock provided steady legal business and enhanced Baker's reputation in the southeastern section of the state, where the companies built their headquarters.[19]

Land was the principal source of wealth in antebellum Walker County, and landholders held "the chief power in the state."[20] Agricultural products were the main exports; on the eve of civil war, Walker County landowners produced about 12,000 bales of cotton and over 315,000 bushels of corn. Most farmers (232 of 349 families) worked farms smaller than fifty acres; only twelve plantations exceeded 500 acres, and only 20 percent of slaveholders owned more than twenty slaves. County records suggest that the Bakers owned several town lots, as much as 600 acres of land in the county, and a number of slaves. Cash was in short supply; loans typically commanded 12 percent interest, and borrowers used complex arrangements involving slaves, slave labor, and land as collateral. As an attorney, Baker frequently mediated these business arrangements; as an entrepreneur, he guaranteed loans and traded services for property. The Hightowers had amassed extensive landholdings before their deaths and had operated a general store, one of several that thrived in Huntsville. Like Huntsville's better known mercantile, Gibbs Brothers & Co., Hightower & Co. was a family business that sold everything from food and clothing to agricultural equipment and seeds. These stores

brought a taste of luxury and fashion to a frontier world lacking manufactured products and financial resources. Local storekeepers were the
only "bankers" in town; they made loans, promoted the local economy,
and supported civic clubs, schools, and churches. Cash, goods, and services were acceptable forms of payment, and storekeepers frequently
signed promissory notes to help farmers survive from planting season
to harvest time. As factors, these storeowners transported and marketed
crops to commercial suppliers in Houston and Galveston or further
afield in New Orleans or New York, cities where the shopkeepers maintained their own banking arrangements and traded for the merchandise
displayed on their shelves. James brought his legal expertise to the Hightower business, and by 1860 his younger brothers Andrew and Matt had
joined Hightower, Baker & Co.[21]

"A TRULY *HIGHER* EDUCATION"

Family ties and economic opportunity brought Rowena Crawford and
James Baker to Huntsville, but advocacy for education and acceptance
of Daniel Baker's evangelical Presbyterian faith sustained their cultural
life for two decades there. The Brick Academy that Rowena supervised
from 1849 until her marriage in 1853 had been built of locally made brick
on land donated by Pleasant Gray in 1842. The two-room schoolhouse
was warmed by large fireplaces in each room and was financed by voluntary contributions from townspeople. Its charter stipulated that the
Brick Academy was nondenominational and "open for the use and benefit of all." Until the Huntsville Male Institute was chartered in March
1845, Brick Academy teachers taught boys in one room and girls in another. No record of Brick Academy curriculum remains, but many towns
in Texas sponsored male and female academies, which expanded the
elementary learning provided by parents or church schools and offered
the highest level of formal education attained by most mid-nineteenth-
century Texans. Girls read classic literature and learned to paint and
play musical instruments; ladylike deportment and moral fortitude
complemented training in domestic arts so graduates could better raise
their families and serve their communities.[22] By 1854, when the Andrew
Female College, sponsored by the Texas Conference of the Methodist
Church, opened its doors in Huntsville, the Brick Academy had closed.

Rowena continued to mentor female students by inviting girls from Andrew Female College to board at the Baker home.

Huntsville's male and female academies resembled the 6,085 privately funded academies founded in the early nineteenth century to serve children in all parts of the young nation, where no publicly funded education systems existed until the late 1800s.[23] These academies taught basic skills, preached civic responsibility, and provided a modest understanding of literature and the arts, but Austin College, founded in Huntsville in 1849, had much higher aspirations to train men for the Presbyterian ministry and other professions. Presbyterians of the era firmly believed their flocks could only receive salvation through the efforts of an educated minister who should be the most learned citizen in town, and they prized education highly.[24] Midcentury Presbyteries believed they were called to educate and uplift the sparsely settled outposts of Texas and to combat the Roman Catholicism of Texas' Spanish and Mexican heritage.

The opportunity to evangelize a new country coincided with a schism in the denomination as Cumberland Presbyterians softened Old School Calvinism by declaring Christ had died for all mankind, not just for a chosen few; they also insisted that sinners would not suffer eternal damnation, that infants who died without baptism were saved by Christ, and that the spirit of God operated on daily life.[25] A year after Texas independence and the new government's promise to protect all religious beliefs, three Cumberland Presbyterian ministers and an elder formed the first Texas Presbytery in November 1837. On June 2, 1838, twenty-two people, including two African American slaves, founded the first Old School Presbyterian church near San Augustine. During the next decade Episcopalians, Methodists, Baptists, and Disciples of Christ vied with Presbyterians for parishioners and traveled itinerant preaching circuits in the state. Cumberland Presbyterians built the first church in Huntsville in 1850. Baptists built the second church there, and in 1855–1856 Old School Presbyterians built the third church, which they called the First Presbyterian Church. Daniel Baker and James Baker both affiliated with First Presbyterian.

Daniel Baker, one of the era's most charismatic clergymen, was born in 1791 in Midway, Georgia, where his father served as deacon. The future evangelist was graduated with honors from Princeton College in 1815 and was ordained three years later after receiving a Doctor of Divinity degree.[26] Following a preaching tour in western Virginia that gave him "a hankering after a missionary life," Baker accepted a pastor's post, married, and began his family, but the missionary call remained strong. Soon Baker was traveling across the South, an energetic figure whose "voice was strong and clear, . . . his utterance easy and fluent, his manner very earnest and animated."[27] In the 1830s, Baker accepted an appointment by the Board of Missions of the Presbyterian General Assembly to be missionary agent in Texas, empowered "to preach the Gospel" and "to organize churches wherever he may think it expedient."[28] He sailed for Galveston in 1840 and celebrated the first Presbyterian communion and first Protestant baptism in that city. Wherever he traveled, Baker met local leaders and debated the importance of establishing a Presbyterian college in Texas to "raise up preachers among ourselves."[29]

In April 1848 Daniel Baker returned to Texas as financial agent for the college project. He visited sites, held revivals, and converted local residents as he inspected their towns. In Huntsville, Baker discussed placing a college there with lawyer, legislator, and West Point graduate Henderson Yoakum, who realized an institution of higher education would benefit the town. Although he was a Methodist, Yoakum rallied his fellow citizens at a public meeting and raised $8,000 in subscription pledges. Baker convinced the Presbytery to locate the state's first Presbyterian college in Huntsville and asked Henderson Yoakum to prepare a charter adapted from documents granted in the previous century to Princeton and Yale colleges, both founded to train men for the ministry. He named the new institution for Stephen F. Austin, whose sister Emily Austin Perry and brother-in-law James Franklin Perry Jr. had pledged their financial support to a Presbyterian college.[30]

As soon as he secured legislative endorsement for the college, Daniel Baker moved his family to Huntsville and appointed a board of trustees that included Henderson Yoakum and Sam Houston. Mississippi pastor Dr. Samuel McKinney, a graduate of the University of Pennsylvania, accepted the job as president and joined the first trustees' meeting on April 6, 1850. McKinney served as Austin College president for three years. In 1853 Baker took charge as president and added administrative and fundraising duties to his evangelical preaching. In the decade from 1848 until his death December 10, 1857, Baker raised over $100,000 for the fledgling college by traveling throughout Texas and the South on speaking tours to extol the college's success and importance. Baker's death threatened the school's academic and financial standing. The board struggled to find a replacement and finally appointed a faculty member to lead the school.[31]

As an elder of the First Presbyterian Church of Huntsville, a friend of Henderson Yoakum, and a relation by marriage of Daniel Baker, James Addison Baker was a natural choice for leadership of the town's most important civic institution, and in 1854 he joined his friends on the board of Austin College. His first four-year term (1854–1858) was followed by board service from 1864–1867 and again from 1873–1876. In June 1854 James Baker represented the trustees at a statewide Education Convention that was held in Huntsville at Daniel Baker's suggestion. Although bad weather hindered travel over flooded streams and roads, forty-nine delegates from around the state gathered to discuss education reforms and curricula, state funding for colleges, and possible accreditation for secondary schools. In 1856–1857 Baker filled the treasurer's post at the college but refused the $100 salary voted for the position. Striving to provide "a truly *higher* education" for Texans, Baker and board member John Hume told fellow members at their meeting on May 28, 1856, that the board should authorize a broader curriculum and an immediate appointment to the vacant chair in foreign languages.[32] During his tenure, Baker served on the Executive, College of Officers, and Finance committees.

In 1854 Austin College trustees began debating the idea of starting a law department. In an era when most aspiring lawyers gained legal knowledge by apprenticing themselves to established attorneys, no law school existed in Texas, but Henderson Yoakum and Sam Houston wanted to develop a legal department for their school. The executive committee of the board appointed three lawyers—Yoakum, James A. Baker, and Texas Supreme Court Justice Abner Lipscomb—to study the feasibility of a new department and make a formal recommendation to the board. After considering likely financial resources and studying the costs associated with developing a library, building classroom space, and hiring faculty, the lawyers surprised no one by announcing that Austin College should offer a law curriculum.

On March 17, 1855, the board officially sanctioned the department and a two-year curriculum comprising two four-week semesters each year. Royal T. Wheeler, who had been a district attorney and district judge during the Republic and was a sitting associate justice of the State Supreme Court (then a part-time job), was appointed professor. Henderson Yoakum became assistant professor and secretary of the department.

Classes began in June 1855 with nine students; the school granted four degrees in 1856 and one in 1857. But the department struggled financially, and fees did not cover Wheeler's salary and the required law books. On November 30, 1856, the department lost its most zealous spokesman when Henderson Yoakum died unexpectedly. Judge Wheeler, named Chief Justice in 1857, accepted an offer to teach at Baylor College's newly formed, full-fledged law school, and he decamped to Waco that year. With no faculty and no fund-raiser, the department closed.

Pestilence bracketed James Baker's second term as trustee, as Austin College struggled to retain a dwindling enrollment in the aftermath of the Civil War. Smallpox in the spring of 1864 and an 1867 yellow fever plague that decimated the population brought death to supporters and students. When the town's citizens refused to allow the International and Great Northern Railroad from Houston to Central Texas to lay tracks through the town, they sealed the college's fate. Students from other parts of Texas could not travel easily to Huntsville, the town's economy soured, and families moved away to cities they perceived to be healthier or more prosperous. Austin College President Samuel Luckett began to discuss finding a new location for the school.

Asked to return to the board for a third term in 1873, James Baker opposed moving the campus, but he himself had left Huntsville the year before to practice law in Houston. In 1874 a special board committee recommended that the college choose another location that could offer better financial support and railroad access. On July 6, 1876, Baker resigned from the board, and in 1877 Austin College sold its campus to the citizens of Huntsville and moved to Sherman, Texas. Despite these setbacks for privately funded higher education, Huntsville citizens did not abandon higher education as an important economic and cultural resource for their town. In 1879 when the state legislature decided to establish a normal school—or teachers' college—the town formed a committee to lobby for Huntsville as the perfect location. Citizens argued that the Austin College campus, which the town had consigned to the trustees of struggling Andrew Female College, could serve as a memorial to Sam Houston. By the fall of 1879 Sam Houston Normal School under Principal Bernard Mallon had absorbed the assets of both earlier institutions and was ready for business.[33] The publicly funded institution became Sam Houston State University in the twentieth century.

As an elder of the First Presbyterian Church, James Baker took his fund-raising duties seriously. He and John Besser, the Superintendent of the Texas Penitentiary, donated money for the bell that was placed in the church steeple in 1856; the bell continued in use through several church reconstructions. After the Civil War, Baker expanded his service to help the African Methodist Episcopal Church in Huntsville as attorney and trustee. He arranged a loan of $50 in gold for the purchase of Lot 225, Block 27 so the congregation could construct a church. When the debt had been repaid in 1875, Baker handed title to the land and church to the congregation and its trustees.[34]

SEPARATED BY WAR

By 1860 James and Rowena Baker could look with pride on their accomplishments. James's reputation as an honorable and conscientious lawyer, a fair business partner, and a loyal friend provided a comfortable living for his family. On his frequent absences from home, he could rely on his "dear wife to spare no efforts to promote our mutual interest in all things,"[35] manage their farm, and nurture their growing family, for Rowena had created a domestic landscape of home and garden that James assured her satisfied him completely. Their affectionate partnership would soon be tested. That year James announced his candidacy for office and was elected to the state legislature. Huntsville was embroiled in the national debate that threatened schism and war. The town's leading citizen, Governor Sam Houston, fought hard to preserve the Union, famously warning his fellow Texans that the North was "determined to preserve this union" and would "move with the steady momentum and perseverance of a mighty avalanche" to "overwhelm the South."[36] Texas repudiated Abraham Lincoln's candidacy in the November 1860 election, voted to secede from the Union on March 2, 1861, and joined the Confederacy on March 5. Texans removed Governor Houston from office on March 16 and replaced him with South Carolina native Francis R. Lubbock (1861–1863); even many Huntsville friends reviled the liberator of Texas when he returned home.

James Baker made clear his sentiments. Now forty years old and the father of three small children, Jimmie, Minnie, and Baby (Anna Bland, born September 13, 1860), he resigned his legislative seat and in October 1861 signed on as a private in Captain James Gillespie's company of Huntsville volunteers. During his six-month enlistment, James was assigned to Galveston, under blockade since July 2, 1861. James's younger brothers Andy and Matt enlisted in February 1862 and requested "more action" than Texas provided.[37] Huntsville was "practically depleted of its able-bodied men" because the town supplied troops for the defense of Galveston and for the 4th and 5th regiments of John Bell Hood's Texas Brigade, sent to the Virginia theater.[38] Both Rowena and James saw his war service as "a duty that [he] should discharge," and James noted with understanding, "I am pleased to hear that you are bringing all your philosophy to bear in regard to my absence. It is no less painful to me than to you and certainly very great deprivation." Despite uncertain mail delivery, James and Rowena wrote to each other several times a week during their six-month separation. Their lively letters provide vivid details of life at home and in camp and illuminate a loving, enduring marriage.

In November James found camp life quite dull and uneventful although he believed "Gillespie's company is the finest in the regiment . . . [and] our men are learning fast and improving every day." He repeatedly assured Rowena that no attack was imminent and made light of hardships; camp, he told her, was comfortable with plenty of "bed cloths," a stove, six or seven soldiers to a tent, and a slave named Bill to cook and wash for his group. By February 1862 James did confess that the "living now is not enriched with much variety—only meat and bread and barley coffee and molasses—this no doubt is far better than many troops are now having—in other parts of the Country." Although the Galveston blockade severely curtailed Texas commerce, watchful Confederate troops saw little action; Baker was no longer with the army on October 8, 1862, when Federal forces briefly captured the city, only to be forced off the island again on January 1, 1863. Federal ships harassed commercial shipping but never completely controlled the coastline, and Galveston was the only major southern port still flying the Confederate flag at the end of the war.

Most of James's letters describe the weather, reassure Rowena about his health, or discuss farm management problems. He told Rowena no letter can be too long: "Your longest is short to me. Every little thing and circumstance from home interests me, however trivial or unimportant it may seem to you." He also promised his dearest wife that "I have been and will be entirely candid with you about all matters" concerning military maneuvers and camp conditions. James sent her shoes and salt purchased in Houston and told her not to "feel desponding" about Confederate losses in February 1862. "You must remember our long list of uninterrupted victories prior to our recent reverses and it would perhaps be presumptuous in us to expect our forces to march on Conquering and to Conquer enemies superior to us in numbers and all of the paraphernalia of war, without any reverses at all." He concluded that setbacks in Tennessee and Kentucky "will arouse the entire South and such numbers will be thrown on the enemy that ere long a yankee [sic] victory will, to him, be but the precursor of utter defeat, ruin, and devastation."

Rowena numbered her letters and by November 29, 1861, had sent at least twenty-eight. At first she tried to carry on as usual, describing day-to-day life at home and in the community. By November Rowena's letters no longer hid the home-front changes. She felt lucky because she had "an abundance of everything that is needful," unlike families who were "left with nothing for a support except what they can make by their own exertions." Women had formed sewing groups to fabricate uniforms for Huntsville regiments but did not have enough buttons and trim to finish the coats. By the spring of 1862 Rowena was selling the Bakers' cotton crop to the penitentiary, where prisoners manufactured cloth for uniforms, although many purchasers complained the prison overcharged for the finished product. Food shortages, high prices, and erratic mail delivery thread through the correspondence as Rowena directed workers to douse fires, orchestrated planting and harvest seasons, and assisted ailing neighbors. She described servants who had succumbed to fevers or lost young children and praised the hard work of the family's most important slave, Silas, who was resourceful, reliable, and willing to undertake new tasks. Rowena repaid his loyalty to the family throughout the war by showing concern for his welfare; when Silas was ill she reported anxiously to James that the doctor, also sick, had been unable to pay them a visit. Quite early in the conflict it was impossible to find luxuries like coffee and difficult to acquire necessities like salt, used in food preservation. Few doctors remained to care for the civilian population, and little could be done to help women preparing for childbirth. Rowena and her friends shared responsibilities as they gathered army supplies, cared for children, and nursed neighbors. Many families sheltered refugees, white and black, from Confederate states east of the Mississippi.[39]

Most of all, Rowena and the children missed James: "The reception of your letters is the only thing that mitigates the pain of your absence, and receiving one letter only makes me the more eager to receive another. It is like good news from a far country and like . . . green spots in a desert and like water to a thirsty traveler for a loving wife to receive affectionate letters from an absent Husband, and were it not for those tokens of love that come so regularly I think your absence would be insupportable." By November 30, 1861, mail delivery stabilized enough for James to promise he would write twice a week so that Rowena could expect letters on Tuesday and Saturday. Despite these assurances, letter delivery often took two weeks, and on December 9, 1861, Rowena noted that Huntsville had no newspaper or telegraph service to provide news.

In her December 12 letter, Rowena told James that the children were very excited about his promise to bring them a dog. Minnie, she said, "is very much delighted at the prospect of having a dog of her own for you know Jimmie is very much inclined to appropriate everything and Minnie is disposed to yield superiority to him on the grounds on which he presses his claims that he is one of the Lords of creation. As he is the oldest he of course leads in their plays, and of course selects masculine plays such as having stages and horses. And whenever Minnie does not please him or he is inclined to be overbearing he will say, 'Minnie Girls don't have stages . . . or dogs . . . or whips . . . or hammers.'" Apparently Minnie "retaliates very roguishly" by informing him that Mama will make her some pants "and then I will be a boy." On Christmas Eve 1861 Rowena contrasted the day with the same time the year before, noting it was the first Christmas Eve she and James had spent apart since their marriage. Yet Rowena concluded that her life could be "much worse," and she was "rather disposed to bless the Lord for all his goodness than to repine at the hardness of my lot."

James wrote loving and sensitive letters to his children. He always asked Rowena about the baby and enclosed tiny notes to Jimmie and Minnie, written with simple words to reassure them of his love or describe the dog he had bought for them. The children in turn dictated letters to their mother, who wrote down their words and sent them on. One letter, saved by the family since 1862, reads: "My dear Papa. Mama told us you wrote to her you were well. And your little children are very glad. I got a bouquet for you and Mama says she will send it with my letter. Papa please write to me the next time you write to Mama. Papa I send you a kiss. Your little boy, Jimmie." The rose petals, dried and slightly crushed, are enclosed with the letter still.[40]

When James had been away only a short time, Jimmie expressed fear his father would be killed. Rowena described the scene in detail for the absent father: she assured Jimmie his father would not be hurt and told him to pray for his father. Hearing these words, Minnie "came and prayed for her papa," too. James usually asked his son, "How is Pa's boy," and closed his letters by urging Jimmie to "Be a good boy and keep your dear Mama and sisters for your Dear Papa." He also asked three-year-old Minnie, "Pa's little girl," to "keep your dear Mama and buddy [Jimmie] for your dear Papa."

James quickly realized that soldiering, especially the inactive defensive service at Galveston, suited neither his temperament nor his talents, and by November 1861 both he and Rowena were looking forward to the end of his six-month engagement. Although at first James was not sure of his course, he promised Rowena he "will not make any arrangement for other, or further service without consulting you upon the subject—for you know that I always like to consult my wife and have her opinion in regard to all things of so much importance." As James pondered the future, a new path opened unexpectedly; Judge Edward Albert Palmer of the 7th Judicial District died suddenly on January 21, 1862, while trying a case in Houston.

During his encampment, James made frequent trips to Houston and was well aware of conditions there. The city's commerce had been weakened by the blockade; prices were high; and essential goods, previously imported from northern industrialized states, could not be found. Judicial proceedings had been sharply cut back. When hostilities flared in 1861, Harris County lawyers asked the court to grant continuances in civil cases for the duration of hostilities, so no civil trials had been held for months. Judges heard criminal trials only if the defendant could not make bail. The state legislature had stayed the statute of limitations on all contracts until the war ended, so loan payments went unpaid and debts uncollected. Despite these problems, on February 5, 1862, Governor Lubbock called for a special election on March 10, 1862, to fill Judge Palmer's seat. On February 7 James wrote Rowena about the possibility of running for judge himself. The 7th District was large and comprised Galveston, Harris, Montgomery, Grimes, and Walker counties. Grimes, with its county seat at Anderson, was the most populous county, but Baker was familiar with the territory and had friends and clients throughout the district.

While Rowena was in Huntsville worrying about her husband's severe cold and wishing he would return home so they "could once more spend some happy time together," James was preparing a campaign strategy. On February 14 announcements appeared in the *Houston Tri-Weekly News* and the *Galveston Weekly News*: "We are authorized to announce Jas. A. Baker, Esq., of Huntsville as a candidate for a [*sic*] judge of the 7th Judicial District."[41] By filing day February 20, three men had declared their availability: James A. Baker of Walker County, R. Theodore Smythe of Grimes County, and Matthew A. Dooley of Harris County. On February 26, James told Rowena that his cold, the most "severe" he remembered, was better but that he had been "troubled with the 'Blues'—and with the prospect of nothing to do—no excitement of any kind," making "the privation of home and all its endearments much more." The tone of his letter then changed as he addressed his sense of the forthcoming election. He had not decided what he would do after the election, "for indeed I am not sanguine of my election. Judicial office, in my opinion, should not be canvassed for as political offices usually are." He pointed out that duties in camp made campaigning almost impossible, but he planned "to have my tickets distributed at the various boxes on the day of election." He had also heard that his opponents were circulating a rumor he had abandoned his law practice. "Of course," he concluded, the rumor "is done to injure me and I am very much dependent for success upon the interest my friends may [exert] for me in the different parts of the district."

As the March 10 contest drew near, James and Rowena felt mounting excitement and commitment to his victory. James confided on February 28 that he was "beginning to feel great interest" in the election although he still thought "it is very doubtful and I confess I don't like to be beaten. Let this expression, however, remain between ourselves. If I should be elected I cant [*sic*] qualify before the middle of May." Rowena responded that "Everyone I have heard speak of [the election] seems to be confident of your success as a candidate." A March 3 letter shows how closely Rowena had been following the campaign. She added "a little sheaf" of comments she had gathered delineating misstatements of Baker's opinions, and she suggested that "perhaps you could give your friends a hint of [these misrepresentations] or even put an advertisement in the papers contradicting it. I only want you to know these things, and then I leave it all to your good judgement [*sic*], as to what is the best course to be pursued. I don't wish to advise for I know your judgment is better than mine. However matters may terminate in regard to it, I will be content as long as I have my husband left to me." Despite the war, there was clearly some campaigning and editorializing on behalf of the three candidates.

James had reason to be concerned about his opposition since he could not leave his army post in Galveston to campaign. R. Theodore Smythe owned a plantation near Plantersville, where he also maintained a law office. Born in Virginia in 1819, he had moved to Texas in the late 1840s. By 1860 his home and real property were listed at $12,490 in census documents. Matthew A. Dooley was a native of Pennsylvania who had lived in New Braunfels for many years and spoke German. As one of three attorneys in Comal and Bexar counties who knew Texas law, he had acquired a following among German immigrants when he moved to New Braunfels to teach them basic legal principles and handle their legal business. He had served as County Judge of Comal County and was the wealthiest of the three candidates. His ability to speak German helped his candidacy in Houston, where 60 percent of the citizens claimed Bavarian, Austrian, or Saxon ancestry.

Record-making rain and flooding and sluggish communication hampered the campaign, but the tally on election day was decisive and thrilled the Bakers. "The result of the election at Huntsville . . . was certainly very gratifying to me. It is to me a matter of great congratulation to know that I stand so fair among those who know me best—particularly when I am absent & have no opportunity of urging or defending my claims." When the secretary of state counted all the votes, the results were clear: Baker 1,095, Dooley 714, and Smythe 538. Baker carried Galveston, Grimes, and Walker counties (all but seven votes in his home county); Dooley swept Harris County; and Smythe was victorious in Montgomery County.[42] The soldiers, James noted, "gave me a most cordial and almost unanimous support." He also confided to Rowena that he believed his actions "greatly contributed to my present success. My resignation of my seat in the Legislature and my declining office in the Service have been of service to me in this election—and as I have said before I still have no regrets for the past." He had been able to present himself as a common soldier untouched by political influence.

WARTIME JUDGE

In late March 1862 James received an honorable discharge from the Confederate army, although he remained in the Galveston-Houston area

Harris County Courthouse, 1869. Courtesy of Baker Botts L.L.P.

through April watching his regiment dwindle.[43] While boarding in a private home in Houston, James wrote of an illness that so alarmed Rowena she caught the next stage going south because she well understood "the importance, the very great importance of good nursing." The stage, crammed with nine passengers inside and two or three on top, missed the "connection for the cars [train] from Navasota." Only after a chance meeting with a friend who assured her James was greatly improved did Rowena return home, where sick children and in-laws demanded her attention. Apparently James's commission as judge did not arrive in time for him to hear cases during the spring session in May 1862, and for most of the spring and summer months James was back in Huntsville, much to his wife's relief.

Rowena's anxiety during these uncertain months was not due only to an absent husband, short supplies, and repeated bouts of illness among members of her household. Although her mother had moved from Memphis to her daughter Mary Crawford Smith's Walker County plantation in 1860, James's mother, Jane Baker Cobb, was still in northern Alabama, where there was serious fighting along the rivers.[44] In 1862 Rowena's sister-in-law Julia Baker suffered a very difficult pregnancy and needed special care, and in March of that year her sister Mary Crawford Smith almost died in childbirth. While struggling to support Julia and Mary, Rowena herself was pregnant during the summer and fall of 1862 and by December 11 was "very closely confined at home." And with good reason: on January 26, 1863, twins Jane and Jeanette arrived, fortunately while their father was at home to help with the household.

Correspondence and court records show that James heard cases in Houston for the fall term of the 7th District Court during the first two weeks of December 1862. The handsome two-story brick courthouse, with a basement that served as a guardhouse for Yankee prisoners during the war, had been built just before hostilities erupted. In late April 1863 James returned to Houston for the spring term, but Rowena's letters to him underlined troubles at home. Not only were pen, ink, and paper hard to find, but also "so much sickness is abroad in the land" that she could not find a healthy doctor to prescribe for Silas and felt an "unusual degree of anxiety about" her husband since he left home. In an attempt to reassure James on May 5, Rowena told him everyone was well and Silas was back in the field but that she "cannot collect [her] thoughts when the babies are crying" so she must end her letter. Just as the spring court session was closing, Rowena began a short letter on Sunday May 11 to tell James one of the babies had suffered with fever for four days before a physician could examine her that night. Interrupted by Dr. Markham's visit, Rowena concluded the note with his diagnosis: "our baby is very sick, my dear come as soon as you can, but I know you will do that." Little Janie, as her tombstone reads, died only days after Rowena dispatched her urgent plea.

In December 1863 Judge Baker returned to Houston for the fall term, which opened Wednesday December 2, when grand jurors and petit jurors were summoned. The next day any jurors who had failed to appear for jury duty were fined $100 or had to show cause why they were not present. During the next several days, 107 cases were brought before the judge, but 93 were continued—to be heard at a later time. Several defendants pled guilty and accepted a fine, and most cases concerned gambling, robbery, and theft of a horse—a serious offense. On the last day of the session, Monday, December 14, Judge Baker set down bail requirements, and the Grand Jury presented indictments. Twenty-four names were drawn to serve as petit jurors during the spring term. Bail amounts varied: $2,000 for swindling; $1,500 for theft of a horse; $1,000 for assault with intent to murder or cattle theft; $500 for unlawful lumber cutting, bribery, or harboring a runaway slave; $300 for keeping a disorderly house; and $100 for unlawful gaming.[45]

Judge Baker also held court in Houston from May 2–14, 1864. On Monday the grand jury was called, and the criminal docket was set for Thursday. Little other business was done, and when Thursday came most criminal cases were continued. Parties in a probate case waived a jury trial, and in the case of *Texas v. Vick Martin*, who was accused of keeping a disorderly house, the jury found the defendant not guilty. On Wednesday, Austin, a slave, was indicted by the grand jury for murdering another slave. He pled not guilty, and the trial was set for Saturday. On Saturday Austin and his lawyer appeared in court, and Judge Baker empanelled a twelve-man jury. Jurors could not reach a verdict, and the judge declared a mistrial. On May 20, the last day of court, twenty-four men were selected to form a jury pool for the next session.[46]

No record of a fall 1864 session appears in court records or Baker family correspondence, and it is probable that court did not meet again until June 1, 1865, when Baker, in Houston, announced that "the Civil docket and the criminal will be called for trial and disposition in full, as in ordinary times."[47] With the surrender of Robert E. Lee on April 9, 1865, and the anticipated surrender of the Confederate Trans-Mississippi Department on June 2, Judge Baker hoped that legal proceedings would return to normal and a tremendous backlog of cases would finally move toward resolution. Writing to Rowena at the close of business on June 1, James devoted four pages to political news about the probability of a military governor being named in Texas and the prospects for successful emancipation. He warned her that attempts to avoid military occupation by holding state conventions probably would fail: "If they want to effect [emancipation] by law, or by gradual emancipation, it will require time, perhaps years—and hence it must be done by military occupation and will be done so here as in other states." The judge also understood the economic problems facing the state and believed the rates of hire fixed by the Superintendent of Freedmen for Louisiana "make the condition of the negro [*sic*] infinitely worse than that of slavery. . . . But this is a matter between the negro [*sic*] and the yankee [*sic*]." James's tone was philosophical and accepting but practical and skeptical as well; he foresaw the dilemma of an impoverished agrarian economy: farmers whose only assets were in land had no cash to employ freedmen for wages, and landless freedmen trained only to work the land had no other way to earn a living. Despite his doubts, James remained an optimist: "I am cheerful and fully prepared for all I anticipate [in emancipation] . . . we will get along. I feel that as long as the lives of ourselves and children are preserved and our health continued I can begin the world a third time with all the ardor and cheerfulness of youth. . . . So don't be gloomy over the prospect of things but be cheerful."

Judge Baker soon discovered that his political career had ended when he dismissed court on June 1. On June 14, 1865, President Andrew Johnson named Andrew Hamilton provisional governor of Texas and began replacing all officials who had served the Confederacy. On June 19, Maj. Gen. Gordon Granger issued General Order Three emancipating Texas' slaves. The next day Union soldiers occupied the courthouse in Houston and closed its doors until November 27, 1865, when Judge Colbert Caldwell accepted appointment to the 7th District Court bench. Judge Baker's personal experience of elective office, his view that judicial office should not be politicized by electioneering, and his observations of immediate postwar Republican politics, viewed by many former Confederate Democrats as a mixture of repression, excessive government spending, corruption, and demagoguery, left him with a distaste for political solutions—especially at the state and national levels. His son and namesake would later remember that his father had "kept him out of politics."[48]

A POSTWAR CHILDHOOD

Judge Baker, as he was now known until the end of his life, returned to Huntsville, where he was readmitted to the practice of law and continued his career as lawyer, planter, and businessman. At home he found Jimmie, now 8, Minnie, 7, Anna B, 4, and Nettie, 2. Rowena, pregnant for the sixth time, delivered Little Rowena in November 1865. Two more children followed the baby's death a few months later, a son Robert Lee (July 27, 1867–February 2, 1939), and a sixth daughter Little Willie, who lived only a few weeks (1869). The grieving parents buried their infant daughters next to Beverly in the family plot in Huntsville's Oakwood Cemetery. Andrew Baker's wife Julia died in 1865, his business failed, and he spent much of the next decades traveling on business while his mother Jane Baker Cobb raised his son Andrew Morgan, born to Julia after her difficult 1862 pregnancy. Two brothers, Dr. Gabriel (Gill) and Matt Baker, died during the yellow fever epidemic that decimated the town's population in 1867. Although summer trips to tiny Wheelock, a stagecoach stop with "beautiful roads and fine scenery" in the rolling countryside of Robertson County, provided a healthy summer refuge for Rowena and the children, no economic advantage could be found there.

Huntsville did not rebound quickly after the war, and the town's refusal to let the railroad build a depot there presaged steady economic decline. Reduced revenue from cotton production and Baker & Hightower store sales forced the Judge to leave home frequently to rebuild his law practice. While "not making much" during his travels, he trusted he was "casting bread upon the waters which will return after a while." As usual, the family missed him, and in 1868 Jimmie, then 11, sent his "first letter" to his absent Papa. The Judge was overjoyed and immediately responded, "I am proud to have a little son that can write his papa so nice a letter, and I love him the more dearly to know that he thinks about his papa in his absence." He continued, "When from home I am always anxious about your Mama and the dear little children and am delighted often to hear from them. . . . I shall take care of your sweet little letter and keep it as a token of your parental love—and in memory of the opening up of a new source of present and future pleasure and happiness."[49]

Rowena filled her days with domestic activities and usually wrote her long letters by candle or lamp light after the children had gone to sleep. Household management was complex and never-ending: meat had to be salted down, vegetables and fruits pickled or preserved, bread and pies baked weekly, clothing and linens sewn and repaired. Freed slaves meant new labor relations, living arrangements, and wage restructuring. Rowena did not complain about her multiple duties and family responsibilities, in part because she was a talented manager and in part because she employed her former slaves as cooks, laundresses, and cleaning staff. But she did worry constantly about the health of her husband and children. Such fears were not unwarranted since so little could be done for anyone stricken by illness; even broken bones presented serious problems, and yellow fever, malaria, and cholera reappeared almost yearly. Rowena took the children's little fears and troubles seriously and often reported them to their father.[50]

Yellow fever peril and Huntsville's economic slide suggest only part of the story. Martial law fell on Walker County in February 1871, making the town's future even more precarious. Maintaining order and reestablishing legal routes to conflict resolution challenged the abilities of Edmund J. Davis, Republican governor during the postwar Reconstruction era. Thousands of immigrants, jobless freedmen, and impoverished—often bitter—white citizens struggled to rebuild their lives in a sluggish economy, creating a volatile environment. Texas' Twelfth Legislature, dominated by Republicans, approved strong anticrime measures, including formation of a state police and militia, in an attempt to curb lawlessness and strengthen the governor's position. Conflict immediately resulted as local authorities challenged measures viewed as punitive and intrusive by many white Texans. Judge Baker soon found himself embroiled in a sensational trial.

In December 1870 Samuel Jenkins, a seventy-year-old Walker County freedman, dared to testify in court against four white men who had beaten him severely after he complained about a crop-sharing agreement. On December 5 Jenkins was murdered, and his body was left on the roadside near Huntsville. State police arrested four suspects: Fred Parks (whose stingy agreement with Jenkins had started the quarrel), Nat Outlaw, Jo Wright, and twenty-year-old John McKinley Parish.[51] The young hotheads, members of prominent Huntsville families, secured the town's best legal team—Judge Baker, Judge Maxey, and Baker's nephew, Lewis Buckner Hightower—for a three-day trial that roused anger among townspeople, who warned the court that the prisoners would never go to jail if convicted. Despite the arguments of "learned, zealous and over active counsel" who tried "to create the impression that a great judicial wrong was perpetrated" by the arrest of the defendants, only Parks was dismissed. Before taking the convicted men to jail, Police Captain Leander McNelly began a routine prisoner search and asked Nat Outlaw if he was armed; when Outlaw replied "yes," the policeman grabbed his gun and turned it over to the guilty man's counsel, Judge Baker.

Immediately, gunfire broke out. Brandishing previously concealed weapons and abetted by dozens of friends who wounded two policemen, Wright and Parish escaped, "shooting off their pistols and yelling like savages." Thirty or forty shots rang out in the courtroom and several more in the street before the prisoners mounted waiting horses and galloped off. Later that night a former sheriff, who had actively abetted the escape, tried to assassinate trial Judge J. H. Benton. Although evidence pointed to the defendants as the murderers and although the original murder and gunfight clearly had no extenuating circumstances, many in the courtroom accused the judge of favoring the prosecution.

Dozens of Huntsville citizens refused to form a posse to track down the escaped prisoners and were subsequently fined $100 each. The public was further incensed when the governor declared martial law in Walker County on February 20, 1871, and imposed a tax of about $.75 per citizen to reimburse the state for costs incurred while state militia occupied the county. One Huntsville resident angrily blamed "radicals" in the state government who "hatch up some charge against the rebels" when they want money.[52] Even the state police captain voiced his opposition to the governor's move in a press interview that March. The captain blamed the sheriff for not disarming the prisoners and insisted he could have controlled the courtroom if all guns had been collected. Despite the gunfight, the captain declared martial law was unwarranted. Courts martial and additional prosecutions followed, but Parish and Wright were never captured. Political squabbles clouded the legal proceedings. In the end, all defendants in the several cases received pardons by March 11, 1871, when the governor remitted Nat Outlaw's sentence, even though he restated the prisoner's guilt. The governor's dubious logic seemed incomprehensible to contemporary journalists but may have been a plea for peace. Most of Walker County had sided with the murderers in a direct repudiation of Republican rule; Judge Baker even insisted he would not pay any fines allotted to him. The process and results infuriated or disgusted Walker County opinion-makers, and the governor failed to improve his popularity or secure a just result, although he did restore order.[53]

In post-bellum East Texas everyone struggled to wrest prosperity from a sluggish economy and fulfill prewar aspirations for a comfortable life. Yet James and Rowena managed to provide a secure, happy childhood for their rambunctious children, who were free to explore their parents' gardens, fields, and woods. Huntsville's rural environment provided a natural classroom and playground. Cousins and neighbors were daily playmates. Jimmie, Minnie, Anna B, and the babies were sturdy, healthy children—buddies who played imaginative make-believe games under Jimmie's authoritative direction. As he grew older, Jimmie joined a gang of swimming-hole pals who shared adventures and remained friends for life. Their adult reunions in Huntsville continued through the 1930s.[54] When the children grew up they ventured to nearby towns to visit favorite relatives and strengthen family bonds that bound the extensive Baker clan.

It is difficult to trace the course of Jimmie's early education. Rowena notes with humor in the summer of 1866 that "Jimmie is delighted at learning to play cards but he receives no encouragement from me. I told him he should never be able to say his mother taught him to play cards."[55] Although the Presbyterian preceptress disdained card lessons, she did teach her son and his siblings basic reading, writing, and arithmetic and gave them piano lessons. Jimmie also attended Judge A. C. Woodall's Academy in Huntsville with his swimming-hole gang, and he spent at least one year in the Preparatory Department of Austin College before leaving Huntsville for Austin in the fall of 1874 to enroll at the Texas Military Institute.[56]

Jimmie Baker grew up in an extended family household strengthened by strong Presbyterian beliefs. He watched his father manage a multifaceted career that encompassed law, business, banking, and civic responsibility, and he heard his parents debate the importance of education. Even as a young boy, he knew his parents expected him to work hard and do his best. During the years in Huntsville, James and Rowena had found personal happiness and community respect despite war, separations, and the loss of children, relatives, and friends. Their curiosity, ambition, and sense of adventure brought them to Huntsville, where they worked hard to improve the town. Yet Huntsville did not regain its antebellum commercial momentum, although it continued as county seat and home of the state penitentiary. Following the sensational Jenkins murder trial and the political debacle of martial law, Judge Baker turned his ambitions toward Houston with "all the ardor and cheerfulness of youth" to "begin the world a third time." In 1872 at age fifty-one, the Judge accepted an invitation from Peter Gray and Walter Browne Botts to join their partnership in the growing city on Buffalo Bayou. His decision changed forever the Baker family fortunes and recast the destiny of his son and namesake.

CHAPTER TWO

Baker, Botts & Baker

JUDGE BAKER SET OUT ALONE to seek his fortune in Houston, a small market town on a humid coastal bayou that had welcomed ambitious men and women since its founding in 1836. Rowena and the children remained in Huntsville for the next four years while James commuted by stage and railroad between the two towns. She managed their Huntsville properties and prepared the girls for boarding school while James gradually sold his Huntsville holdings and transferred his business and legal interests to Houston. Young Jimmie boarded at Austin College before enrolling at Texas Military Institute in 1874. That year Minnie also left home to study at a female seminary in Baltimore.

OPPORTUNITY IN HOUSTON

When the judge arrived in Houston in 1872, the town's sixteen square miles were home to 9,382 residents, but the third-largest urban area in the sparsely populated agrarian state had few amenities. Storms turned its unpaved streets to gullies of mud, and wooden plank sidewalks built by business owners stretched only a few blocks. Residents relied on rainwater caught in cisterns and walked to work. Publicly supported schools,

Illustrations: Judge Baker, Captain Baker. Private Collection.

Houston, Texas, 1870s. Buffalo Bayou at White Oak Bayou, showing railroad bridge across White Oak Bayou (*upper right*). Mss 0029-0001 (T. W. House Papers), Houston Public Library, Houston Metropolitan Research Center.

electricity, and telephones were not yet available.[1] Two towns outpaced Houston when the decade began. San Antonio, the gateway to southern Texas, the Rio Grande Valley, and Mexico, was second in size with 12,000 inhabitants in 1870 and supported an army garrison and a publicly funded elementary school. Galveston, the reigning American port west of New Orleans, was a beautifully planned resort and mercantile headquarters of 13,898 citizens, who enjoyed garden-lined streets, landscaped public squares, and handsome homes.

Lying forty miles upriver from the island port on the southwest bank of Buffalo Bayou at its juncture with White Oak Bayou, Houston had challenged Galveston and aspired to be the region's entrepot since New York state land speculators Augustus Chapman Allen and John Kirby Allen laid out their town in 1836. The Allens imagined a great commercial and cultural capital rising on their 6,642-acre investment on the flat, seemingly endless grassland prairie. Waterways provided the only practical highway to carry agricultural products and lumber from East Texas to the coast for distribution to state, national, and world markets, and Buffalo Bayou, lined with magnolias, laurels, and rhododendrons, was the only consistently navigable stream emptying into Galveston's bay. The Allen brothers positioned Houston where land, river, and sea transportation met, and they built wharves along the bayou to collect cotton, rice, sugar, and logs from the surrounding region.

Although business in Houston and Galveston had been severely curtailed during the war, these cities suffered less than many parts of the South. As headquarters of the Confederacy's Trans-Mississippi Department and home to refugees from the battle zones, Houston actually gained population during the war and continued to grow afterwards; when the blockade lifted, Galveston's port activity resumed immediately. Investors made wealthy by their willingness to run the blockade began to improve Houston. They organized the city's first street railway and the Board of Trade and Cotton Exchange. In 1866 they chartered the Houston Gas Company, the city's first public utility, built a plant, and laid mains to major public buildings. The same year they established the First National Bank of Houston, the city's first nationally chartered banking institution. The bank's directors numbered merchants, factors, auctioneers, a lawyer, and Unionist Harris County Chief Justice Dr. Ingham S. Roberts; original stockholders included railroad builder Paul Bremond and attorney Peter Gray.[2]

By 1870 Texas investors had made Houston the hub of several railroads that were expanding slowly into the interior. Cotton processing plants and woolen mills sprang up along the bayou in a manufacturing district that also supported saw mills, foundries, brick yards, packing plants, and machine shops. Ninety percent of Texas commerce passed through Galveston where steamers left daily for New Orleans, Indianola, and Corpus Christi, weekly for Havana, and monthly for Liverpool, England. The Galveston, Houston, and Henderson Railroad connected Galveston Island to the mainland, and a ten-mile canal brought Brazos River cotton to the island city. During the post-Civil War decades, a race to become the Gulf Coast transportation center consumed civic leaders of both cities. Houston investors began to deepen and widen Buffalo Bayou to create commercial port facilities near Houston's nascent manufacturing district and to avoid Galveston's wharf fees and the costs of transshipment up the bayou from the island; Galveston shippers built piers and jetties to create a deep-water port that accommodated seagoing vessels and to prolong the city's reign as Texas's premier port. Not until nature intervened in 1900 was the outcome of this contest clear.

Judge Baker's Residence, ca. 1885, 1104 San Jacinto at Lamar (owned 1876–1898). Private Collection.

By September 17, 1876, Rowena had left her tree-shaded garden and plantation fields near Huntsville and settled the family in a clapboard Greek-Revival-style home James had purchased on the corner of San Jacinto and Lamar in bustling downtown Houston.[3] Like other post-war heads of household, the Judge offered shelter and support not only to Rowena and his own children, but also to the two widowed grand-mothers, Jane Baker Croft Cobb and Anna McRobert Crawford, to his nephew Morgan Baker, and to ten former slaves and their eight children. Of these eighteen nonfamily dependents, at least ten, by the ages listed in the census, were either too old or too young to find work beyond the home.[4]

GRAY & BOTTS

Judge Baker was well aware of Houston's postwar resurgence and had been thinking about the city's economic and cultural advantages for some time. In 1865 he confided to Rowena that a home in Houston would promote their interests.[5] He knew Peter Gray and other lawyers well and realized that practicing law in Houston meant great opportunity. Judge

Baker was well-versed in the legal problems confronting Houston's expanding railroad industry. State and federal courts sat in Houston and Galveston, providing a steady stream of trial work, and city lawyers had just organized their practice in a bar association (1870). Most significant, lawyers were active participants in the formation and management of local companies and banks; as investors and directors of these new enterprises, they were shaping the growth of their city and amassing personal fortunes.

The firm that became Baker Botts L.L.P. in the twentieth century was preceded by partnerships that began in May 1837, when Colonel William Fairfax Gray opened a law office on Travis Street in a two-room red house. Colonel Gray's colorful diaries of trips to Texas as an agent for two investor friends from Washington, DC, describe conditions at the moment Anglo-American settlers declared independence from Mexico. Gray brought his family from Virginia to Houston, served as district attorney for southeastern Texas, and helped create the Republic's legal system. In 1840 the colonel's son Peter joined his father and Judge John Scott in the general practice of law at the firm then known as Scott & Gray, both before and after the elder Gray's death in 1841.[6] Associations of lawyers before the Civil War were informal and small; two or three friends supervised occasional clerks or apprentices, who performed mundane tasks and "read" their mentors' law books long enough to qualify as practicing attorneys. While the lawyers might share office space, refer clients to each other, and engage in camaraderie, each lawyer was responsible for his own clients and kept any fees garnered from the business he generated. Personality and reputation defined success.

Peter Gray followed his father as district attorney for Galveston-Houston (1841–1845), served as alderman and member of the board of health in Houston, and was elected first representative of Harris County to the Republic's legislature. He and Judge Royal T. Wheeler spearheaded the Practice Act of 1846, which established the Texas State court system after Annexation and resolved conflicts among legal traditions followed in the United States, Mexico, and the Texas Republic. Peter's law practice flourished, and by 1850, at age thirty-one, he owned Harris County property valued at $10,000—a substantial sum on the undercapitalized frontier.[7] This wealth allowed the younger Gray to help organize the first Episcopal congregation at Christ Church, to found the Houston Lyceum (1848) as a free public reading room and library, and to

Colonel Walter Browne
Botts, 1835–1894.
Courtesy of Baker Botts
L.L.P.

underwrite publication of Henderson Yoakum's *History of Texas*, the first
serious attempt to record the story of the Lone Star State. From 1854 to
1860 Gray sat as judge of the 7th district court, where he saw James Addison Baker in action as a courtroom orator and legal counsel. When war
came, Gray served in the Confederate Congress, joined the Confederate
army as an aide to Gen. John Bankhead Magruder, and became treasury
agent for the Trans-Mississippi Department. During the war years, Gray
asked a young lawyer and cousin, Walter Browne Botts, to handle legal
matters for his major clients.

Walter Browne Botts (1835–1894) spent his early life in Freder-
icksburg, Virginia. Like Gray, Botts came from a distinguished family
of lawyers: a grandfather had defended Aaron Burr against charges of
treason, and his brother was appointed by the court as counsel to John
Brown after the abolitionist's capture at Harper's Ferry. An 1854 graduate of Virginia Military Institute in Lexington, W. B. Botts read law in

Charles Town in western Virginia. He arrived in Houston in 1857, immediately was elected to the legislature, and was admitted to the Texas bar in 1858. When war came, Botts resigned from the legislature and joined the Bayou City Guards as a private. The Guards became part of Hood's Brigade (the Fifth Texas Infantry) and shipped out to Virginia. Botts's fellow soldiers immediately recognized his VMI training and elected him major; his superiors promoted him to lieutenant colonel. Botts saw action in the prolonged Peninsula Campaign and was one of 7,997 Confederate casualties at the Battle of Seven Pines on May 31, 1862. Severely wounded, he succumbed to pneumonia and was forced to abandon his military career. Instead, he returned to Houston and the practice of law.

Early in 1865, as the war drew to a close, Peter Gray asked Colonel Botts to make his wartime agreement permanent and to form a law partnership, Gray & Botts. Former Confederate partisans were required to seek reinstatement in the Texas bar. On November 27, 1865, the first day court resumed after the close of hostilities, Judge Colbert Caldwell (November 1865–June 1866), appointed to replace Judge Baker, admitted Walter Browne Botts and fourteen other lawyers to the practice of law. Former Confederate government officials were required to sign a written oath of amnesty before resuming law practice, so on June 28, 1865, Gray took the oath and awaited an official pardon, which was granted November 1, 1865.[8] Confident that a pardon would be granted, Gray & Botts/Attorneys and Counsellors at Law/Houston placed an advertisement in the *Houston Tri-Weekly Telegraph* that was printed in a front-page column near an announcement by Jas. A. Baker/Attorney & Counsellor at Law/Huntsville, on October 25, 1865.[9]

Gray & Botts prospered in their small office opposite the courthouse; both men were "highly esteemed" for their deep understanding of the law and thorough preparation for trial. Although Botts "shrank from the personal conduct of cases . . . and making of oral arguments," his colleagues valued his wise counsel, sound judgment, and earnest devotion to the law.[10] Like Gray, Botts brought important clients to the firm. His brother, Benjamin Botts, helped organize the Houston Ship Channel Company, created in 1868 to widen Buffalo Bayou and build the city's port facilities. In 1870 Colonel Botts and Benjamin developed City Bank of Houston, capitalized at $500,000, a very large sum for the era. Benjamin served as president while Colonel Botts and Frederick Allyn Rice, William Marsh Rice's brother, sat on the board of directors. In 1875 Colonel Botts and fellow attorney Joseph Chappell Hutcheson organized the Houston Land & Trust Company, capitalized at $6,000, and founded the Houston Bank and Trust. Fellow attorneys elected Gray first president of the Houston Bar Association, organized in 1870 to elevate the profession and build a law library. The same year, Gray & Botts signed a memorandum of agreement with the Houston and Texas Central Railway Company (H&TC), to begin the firm's long formal association with the railroad industry. H&TC board members present at this momentous occasion for the law partners included William Marsh Rice, Paul Bremond, T. H. House, William J. Hutchins, and Cornelius Ennis—the city's most aggressive investors.

As their practice expanded to include Houston's critical industries and sources of capital, Gray and Botts recognized they needed help. They turned to their longtime friend Judge James Addison Baker, whose reputation as an effective advocate, knowledgeable railroad lawyer, and man of integrity enhanced their ability to meet the needs of their clients. The partnership formed in 1872 prospered, and in 1873 Gray, Botts & Baker were named general attorneys for Houston & Texas Central railroad at the comfortable retainer of $8,000 per year. Gray perhaps best understood the urgent need to enlarge the partnership.[11] In the last years of his life he suffered from pulmonary tuberculosis, a common but incurable ailment in the nineteenth century. He resigned from the firm in 1874 to accept a place on the Texas Supreme Court, but after a few months was forced to step down and died October 3, 1874, at age fifty-four. News accounts estimated that three thousand mourners crowded into Christ Church and its surrounding gardens, while seventy-five carriages overflowing with grieving friends and family followed the elaborate procession of Masons and Houston Bar associates to Glenwood Cemetery.[12] Renamed Baker & Botts in 1875, the firm Peter Gray had nurtured for nearly a decade continued to grow.

CADET BAKER

While Judge Baker was establishing his law practice in Houston, his children were traveling to schools far from home for the first time. Their departure opened a new era in family relations, defined by a lively correspondence between the children and their parents and among the siblings. The children quickly discovered that lawyering for the railroad meant their father could request free railroad passes for his family, a benefit that enabled three generations of Bakers to travel extensively for nearly seventy years. Despite free, safe travel, private education for five children was so expensive that both Jimmie and Minnie cut short their formal education by one year when changes in the Houston & Texas Central Railroad management temporarily "decrease[d] very much" their father's income in 1877.[13]

Both parents valued education and chose schools for their children that provided classic college-preparatory and college curricula. While Jimmie studied in Texas, Minnie, Anna B, and Nettie, carefully chaperoned by Rowena or the Judge, took the long railroad journey to Winchester, Tennessee, or Baltimore, Maryland. Shortly after Jimmie matriculated at Texas Military Institute, Minnie enrolled at Notre Dame of Maryland Preparatory School and Collegiate Institute for Young Ladies, founded by German nuns in 1873 to provide higher education for women. During her years in the northeast (1874–1877), Minnie toured the Philadelphia Centennial Exposition in 1876 and visited New York and Boston. Letters home regaled the family with dramatic schoolgirl adventures.[14] Anna B attended prestigious Mary Sharp College, chartered in 1850 by Dr. Z. C. Graves and the Baptist Church in Winchester, Tennessee. Named for abolitionist Mary Sharp, the college modeled its curriculum on offerings at Amherst, Brown, and the University of Virginia.[15] The school's emphasis on religious and moral training and Dr. Graves's belief that women were physically and mentally capable of higher learning undoubtedly appealed to Rowena, although Anna B confided to her younger sister Nettie that she was "miserable" and warned that the "very solemn discourse" at her prayer meetings might produce a "Sister Baptist."[16] Nettie spent two years at Mary Sharp College (September 1878 to June 1880) before transferring to Notre Dame of Maryland (September 1880 to June 1883). Her letters reveal more about fashion than classroom conduct. Always the strict schoolmarm, Rowena insisted Nettie purchase a dictionary to sit on her desk at all times for consultation while composing letters to her family. She confided, "The idea of our spending so much money on your children's education and having them spell incorrectly is more than I can . . . hear."[17] Rowena and Judge Baker must have been relieved when nine-year-old Robert enrolled in Houston's first free publicly funded school in the fall of 1878.[18]

In the fall of 1874, Jimmie became Cadet Baker at the Texas Military

Institute, which had moved from a campus in Bastrop (1858 to the Civil War) to Austin in 1870, after citizens there raised $10,000 in gold to build classrooms and a barracks to house 400 students. Although students wore uniforms and followed a military regimen modeled on West Point, the school also taught foreign languages, literature, and sciences. Tuition and fees reached about $375 a year, but school enrollment did not meet expectations. Early in 1875 there were only about fifty-five students, and Jimmie reported "general dissatisfaction among most of the students" and rumors the school might close.[19] Perhaps tuition could not cover costs, for in 1879 the Institute's president and faculty moved to the state-funded Agricultural and Mechanical College of Texas, which had opened three years earlier in Brazos County at College Station. Tasked with a specific mission to teach male students agriculture and military techniques, the forerunner of Texas A&M University operated like its predecessor Texas Military Institute and built the state's premier cadet corps.[20]

Cadet Baker proved an excellent and highly satisfactory student. His mother's solid preparation and the time at Austin College allowed him to take Intermediate Latin, Junior Greek, and Intermediate Mathematics in his first year. In mathematics he ranked first of thirty students. The second year, with parental approval, Cadet Baker substituted German for Greek and Latin. Because he was such a promising student—"one of our best boys and it is gratifying to know that he is so well pleased"—the Institute superintendent accepted his request to drop the classics curriculum. Jimmie's fine progress continued with mathematics, chemistry, history, literature, and infantry tactics.[21] Cadet Baker recorded youthful intellectual explorations in his "Private Note, Scrap and Letter Book" of 1876. Poems, news clippings, and the Texas Centennial Oration delivered by Governor B. B. Hubbard at the Philadelphia Exposition show his growing awareness of literature and current events. An essay on "Moral Courage" recommended its readers "stand firm" and be true to their duty, and another essay posed the question, "Are the American People a Nation?" The scrapbook also contains summaries of law cases and a copy of the sermon "Sin Will Surely Be Punished."[22] In letters to his parents, Jimmie confessed he thought "of home every day of my life I reckon," but he denied being homesick, described his "comfortable" room with its heating stove, and discussed his courses and examinations.[23]

In Jimmie's last year, 1877, the Institute Superintendent Colonel John

Garland James wrote to Judge Baker, "We have never had any Cadet who enjoyed more fully than he does our entire esteem and confidence; and it will always be a real pleasure to us to advance by all means in our power his true interests."[24] Admired by his teachers, Cadet Baker was popular with his contemporaries, too. Most of his social life took place at church-sponsored socials or benefit parties. In 1874 he wrote Minnie about a supper at the Episcopal church, where he did not know anyone until "the boys introduced me to several pretty young ladies, and I had a very pleasant time at last."[25] In March 1875 he told his father proudly that the Calhoun Debate Society "had conferred on [him] the honor of Record-ing Secretary," which he would "endeavor to fill to the best of my ability." In April he described the ball organized for the benefit of the Debate So-ciety and confessed he "enjoyed myself hugely . . . and took quite a part in the dance, which you doubtless know I am quite fond of."[26]

During his years at TMI Cadet Baker and his parents exchanged affec-tionate, open letters that are surprisingly adult as all three writers begin to share concerns, disappointments, and delights. The Judge's letters were often quite short and businesslike—sending an allowance or de-scribing "a very handsome case of mathematical drawing instruments" he had purchased for his son. Occasionally the press of business light-ened, and the judge indulged in the pleasure of a long narrative, covering several pages to describe unusual customs like the volkfest of Houston's German community, or business affairs that kept him away from home and family. Always these letters stressed Judge Baker's love of family. In one he wrote, "But to labor thus for the benefit of my family—so near and dear to me, is to me, my greatest pleasure next to having them all around the same table and fireside. So you see, my son, as I said before, I can not stop or slacken my efforts."[27]

On October 1, 1874, the Judge penned a four-page letter to his son in which he enclosed $2.50 for his monthly pocket money and relayed news from his sister Minnie that "all are well at home." Most of the letter responded to his son's request that the judge explain the story behind the development of Houston's Ship Channel Company, chartered and incorporated by the state legislature. The Judge outlined the company's primary mission "to dredge out a channel through the bay sufficiently wide and deep to allow vessels that come into Galveston, to come also, to Houston." All goods were reshipped from Galveston to Houston in bay boats, he said, and a deep channel would allow vessels to unload in

Galveston or Houston without the delay and expense of reshipment. The Judge explained the high cost to date ($100,000), the need to find additional capital, and the importance of connecting port facilities to railroad terminals in Houston to "greatly lighten the cost of transportation." The letter also contained an extract from a speech delivered by "eminent lawyer" General Albert Pike to veterans of the Mexican War, which the Judge praised for its "elegance, beauty and poetry."[28]

The Judge's comments about working hard and anxiety about money provoked two responses from his son: concern that his father was overworked and an effort to spend as little as possible. Jimmie told Rowena to take care of his father and wrote worriedly about the Judge's work habits. "I am very much affraid [sic] that he is injuring himself by working so hard," he warned. "I would not be surprised if he shortens his life several years by overworking himself. I noticed . . . at Christmas that his head was 'silvering over' very fast, and I have written him telling him about it." Jimmie understood his father's ambition—"[h]e is so anxious to make something for us all"—but he admonished his mother to make her husband slow down and concluded, "I had a great deal rather he would not leave me a red cent than to injure himself by working as hard."[29] When Jimmie redoubled his efforts to save money, he was so successful his father sent a warning, "You are very thoughtful and good in considering my expenses and in practicing such admirable economy. But you must not practice it to such an extent as to acquire a reputation for penuriousness."[30]

Rowena, ever the moralist and teacher, sent Jimmie lots of advice and news about the family and commented on the books she was reading and her hopes for this beloved older son. In the fall of 1876, when she learned that the Temperance Council of Huntsville, supported by the Bakers, had disbanded, Rowena warned, "I hope my dear Son that you will not feel that you are released from your pledge, the longer I live the more I am opposed to liquor and tobacco particularly liquor. I dont [sic] believe it does any one any good, but always does some harm, the least of which is the cost."[31] Presbyterians of the era proselytized temperance, and generations of young men pledged, often with the inducement of a monetary reward, not to smoke or drink until age twenty-one. Since Captain Baker in later life was frequently photographed with a cigar in his hand and was renowned for his generous hospitality, it seems his mother's wish did not survive into middle age. Rowena's moral counsel was always softened by her unquestioning love. Eight days after his twentieth birthday, Rowena told her son, "you were in my thoughts . . . I wished for you all the happiness that a mother could desire for a dearly loved good and dutiful son." He had "always been a pleasure to your Mother from the hour she first saw your beautiful baby face till the present, when you are almost ready to take upon you the duties and responsibilities of manhood." Rowena confessed that if she could choose his pathway of life, "it should be free from trials and cares." Realizing that the choice would be Jimmie's, she commended her dear son to God's care and wished him "no greater blessing than that you should accept of His proffered love and guidance."[32]

From these loving, subtly demanding parents, three lessons became plain: each Baker child was expected to acquire as much education as the family could afford, every family member was encouraged to strive for excellence in all endeavors, and Jimmie and his siblings assumed they would follow the path of duty and Christian morality taken by their parents. As Cadet Baker and his sisters ventured into the world, they accepted these values even as they took small independent actions or expressed their own wishes and concerns. Finding that she had little free time, Minnie wrote to her brother on a Sunday, although she knew her mother would not approve of activity on the Sabbath and did not think she approved either. The Judge allowed Jimmie and Anna B to substitute German and French for Greek and Latin, but he made clear that education was a serious undertaking and explained his expectations to his son. "Perhaps you feel that you have never applied yourself with very great earnestness," he began, "and in all your studies you will find it a great thing to concentrate your mind on whatever you are studying. That is to give it that close attention which will crowd out from the mind for the time all thought of every thing else."[33] Rowena knew Jimmie felt "the importance of making good use of your advantages,"[34] but she also advised him not to work for prizes and the recognition of others, but "for your present and future good." She emphasized, " if you made an honest effort to do your best in your studies I would be perfectly satisfied no matter what others thought of you, that is no matter whether you stood at the head of your class or not." His desire to do his "utmost to succeed" was "all that can be expected of any one."[35] When the Judge complimented his son on a report card, Jimmie replied that he appreciated his father's praise but continued, "It is not as good as I wanted. It affords me a great deal of pleasure to please my parents in my quarterly reports and I want to try to do better in the final examination."[36]

LEGAL APPRENTICE

Cadet Baker's successful educational career ended earlier than his parents had hoped when they realized that one or two years at a national university was beyond their financial means, but he left TMI at the top of his class. Jimmie was asked to salute his fellow graduates and their families at commencement exercises on June 13, 1877, much to the delight of the family, who gathered in Austin for his debut on the public stage.[37] Minnie hurried home from school, chaperoned on her journey by a Houston friend. Excited telegrams from every stopping point promised her arrival in time to be with her brother on his triumphant day. The cadet, who had been "carefully examined in all the branches of the Arts, Sciences, and Literature," was "declared a Graduate" and spent the summer surrounded by family.[38] He returned to TMI to teach for a term, but the press of business at Baker & Botts following Peter Gray's death in 1874 and Jimmie's expressed wish to help his father brought him back to Houston, where he began his lifelong employment on December 1, 1877. As an apprentice learning the practice of law, Jimmie helped organize documents for trial and performed routine clerical duties while observing in court and reading the volumes in his father's law library. Baker & Botts's two-room office and the city's opera stage occupied the second floor of the three-story Opera House, built by Judge Peter Gray on Court House Square.[39]

Young Baker's legal education was not restricted to long hours reading musty law books or running errands at the courthouse. In September and October 1878, he traveled around Texas on a trip sponsored by his parents. Judge Baker endorsed his visits to friends and family in several towns: "Acquaintances that you make on such tours . . . not infrequently prove of advantage in after life—And always add to one's pleasure. . . . Try to remember the name and individuality of each acquaintance you make . . . endeavor to cultivate a love for talking and making others as well as yourself agreeable by the subjects and manner of your conversation. . . . Having ascertained what a man prefers to talk about you can then always be able to interest him—and the probability is that both you and he will be benefited by the result."[40] Rowena believed the trip would be of permanent advantage. "After the constant confinement to books," she noted, "this trip in the free open air will be the very thing to brace up your system . . . and thus you will be the better prepared to prosecute your law studies with energy and zest on your return." She reminded him to learn the state's geography, meet new people, see old friends, stay away from fever, go to church, and write to his sisters. Enclosing a letter she had received from Nettie, she concluded, "It is a great pleasure to me to see my children loving and affectionate to each other."[41]

After reading law for two years, on December 2, 1879, the fledgling lawyer presented his application to practice in district and inferior state courts to the Clerk of the Harris County District Court, where his father had once presided as judge. The court appointed his father's partner Walter Browne Botts and lawyers W. C. Carrington and M. W. Garnett to examine the aspirant. Not surprisingly, they accepted his application to practice law. The new attorney at law continued as a poorly paid clerk until July 1, 1881, at which time James A. Baker Jr. became the third member of the firm, now renamed Baker, Botts & Baker.[42] On December 19, 1884, James A. Baker Jr. was admitted to practice as an attorney and counselor of the Supreme Court, State of Texas "and furnished satisfactory evidence that he is a practicing attorney in good standing in the District Courts of this State and filed the oath required by law."[43]

Sadly, Jimmie's mother did not live to see her son admitted to the practice of law. Rowena died on September 7, 1879, at age fifty-one, while visiting her sister in Huntsville. The Judge, Jimmie (22), Minnie (21), Anna B (19), and Robert (12) were with her during her surprise illness, but Nettie (16), at boarding school in Tennessee, could not reach Huntsville before the end came. Rowena's mother, eighty-one-year-old Anna Crawford, always a favorite with her son-in-law, followed her daughter on July 14, 1881. She lies in Huntsville's Oakwood Cemetery beside her daughter and her sister Elizabeth, the Rev. Daniel Baker's wife, who had died May 11, 1858, at age sixty-three. Two years after Rowena's death, Jimmie asked his sister Nettie, then at school in Baltimore, to write "cheerful letters" to Pa "for he is frequently lowspirited and despondent." Rowena could not be replaced, but she bequeathed her strong character, her passion for higher education, and her sense of humor to her children and their descendants.[44]

HOUSTON LIGHT GUARD CAPTAIN

Shortly after Cadet Baker moved to Houston, Jonas Shearn Rice, an 1874 Texas Military Institute graduate and nephew of William Marsh Rice, recruited his fellow alumnus for the Houston Light Guard, a prestigious militia unit captained by Rice from January 1876 to January 1879. Organized under state charter by thirty-six men on April 21, 1873 "to defend the city against its enemies," the Houston Light Guard was the most successful of fifteen militia units founded in Houston after 1870, when a United States law allowed former Confederate states to organize volunteer military companies again. Only the Light Guard lasted more than a year or two, probably because its membership included the sons of Houston's leading men. Most guardsmen were emerging business leaders or lawyers who used their Light Guard connections to enhance their social prestige and political power. No fewer than seven guardsmen—including Joe Rice's brother and fellow TMI graduate Horace Baldwin Rice—became mayor of Houston in the forty years before World War I. Older businessmen like Frederick A. Rice and Benjamin A. Botts were honorary members, and in 1900 William Marsh Rice held fifteen first mortgage bonds issued by the Houston Light Guard, four for $100 and eleven for $500, all paying 4 percent interest.[45] Peter Gray's brother Edwin Fairfax Gray, a graduate of the United States Naval Academy and Confederate war hero, took command in 1873 to train the first recruits, who drilled every Monday evening during the long summer. A third Gray brother, Allen Charles, owned the *Houston Telegraph*. He encouraged enlistment as a patriotic duty and gave Guard activities good media coverage. E. F. Gray handed leadership to the younger men after a year of hard work and successful duty escorting Comus Rex during the Mardi Gras Parade in February 1874.

Funded largely by Confederate sympathizers, the Guard first chose a uniform that recalled the gray and black of the Lost Cause. By the 1880s British-style uniforms with long-tailed red coats, blue trousers, white cross belts, gold trim, and helmets with white plumes produced such a splendid effect that young ladies swooned at drill competitions, parades, and other entertainments, although they recovered quickly to attend Thursday evening social events and clamored to raise money for the troop at charity balls. The Light Guard was best known as a superb drill team whose victories so dominated rivals in the 1880s that the team was

James A. Baker,
Captain, Houston Light
Guard, August 1879–
August 1880. Private
Collection.

forced to retire from state and national competition in 1889. The Guard
also performed more serious duties. Several times the Guard maintained
law and order; in 1900 the troop rescued hurricane victims in Galveston,
and in 1903 it reorganized under the Dick Militia Act as part of the National Guard. During World War I, as Company G in the 143rd Infantry, the Houston Light Guard saw action in France, and in World War II
as part of the 36th Texas Division, its members fought in North Africa,
Italy, France, and Germany.

Jimmie Baker's military training at TMI, his association with the Gray,
Rice, and Botts families, and his sociable personality made membership
in this group inevitable. Named 1st Sergeant in May 1878, the slim, athletic recruit with a shock of wavy brown hair and sporty mustache was
quickly promoted and became captain and commander of the unit from
August 1879 to August 1880. During Ulysses S. Grant's visit to Houston
in March 1880, Baker commanded the presidential honor guard, and

he prepared the group for its first interstate drill competition in 1881.[46] Baker retired as an active guardsman shortly after he relinquished his command, but he never surrendered his rank. As time passed only old TMI friends like the Rice brothers addressed their fellow guardsman as Jim; to most colleagues and acquaintances he would always be Captain Baker, although some close friends affectionately called him Captain Jim.[47] The Captain remained loyal to the Guard, attending its dances during the 1890s and enjoying camaraderie at the Houston Light Guard Club organized in July 1893. In 1889 Baker served on the building committee to plan a three-story armory. The committee used $20,000 in drill team prize money and a $30,000 bond issue to cover expenses. When the building was sold in 1925, Baker solicited support for a new $125,000 armory designed by popular local architect Alfred C. Finn on land at Caroline and Truxillo streets. Unfortunately, the guard could not maintain this building during the Depression, despite efforts by Baker and others to arrange financing and secure tax-exempt status. The troop sold its armory to the state to become Texas' first armory in 1938.

ALICE GRAHAM

In the 1880s Judge Baker's children discovered romance. Feisty Minnie, who could defend her interests against her older brother, returned to Huntsville and married John McKinley Parish on April 28, 1880, a decade after his scrape with martial law in Walker County. Some time in 1882 the dashing Light Guard captain met the beautiful young lady who would become his wife on his twenty-sixth birthday, January 10, 1883.[48]

Alice Graham was one of four daughters born to Frank H. Graham and Mary Augusta Wilson on October 18, 1864, and like the Captain claimed Scottish, English, and Virginian ancestors. She had been raised a Baptist but on September 29, 1895, joined Houston's First Presbyterian Church, where her husband and father-in-law had been communicants since 1878. Throughout her life, Alice remained close to her sisters, Frances Malcolm (Frankie), who married Walter P. Stewart and settled in Dallas; Eddie, who married George W. P. Coates and moved to Abilene; and Anna, who married W. D. Herring and remained in Waco. Until after Judge Baker's death in 1897, Captain Baker and his young family formed part of the large household at San Jacinto and Lamar.[49]

Just nine months after her marriage and bridal tour to St. Louis, Alice

(*Above*) Captain Baker and his fiancée Alice Graham, 1882. He balances her parasol, and she holds his hat in her lap, indicating an engagement portrait. Pictured with her are girlhood friends: Mrs. Tankersley, Marian Seward (Mrs. Orren T.) Holt, Mrs. G. C. Street. Private Collection.

(*Opposite, top*) Alice Graham Baker, 1880s. Private Collection.

(*Opposite, bottom*) Frank H. Graham and Mary Augusta Wilson, parents of Alice Graham. Private Collection.

became a mother when Frank Graham Baker arrived on her nineteenth birthday, October 18, 1883. This beloved honeymoon baby was named for Alice's father and sister. He was followed three and one-half years later by Alice Graham Baker on May 13, 1887, and five and one-half years after that by Captain Baker's namesake, James Addison Baker Jr., on November 3, 1892. Not long after young James arrived, Captain Baker gave his daughter Alice a playhouse to reward good behavior. Especially designed as a miniature version of the Judge's Greek Revival home, the small rectangular building had white clapboard siding and a pedimented porch supported by turned wooden posts. Alice arranged her dolls and toys in the sunny room, the headquarters for elaborate tea parties and neighborhood gatherings. Three generations of Baker girls prized the playhouse and moved it from one Baker home to another for sixty years.[50]

After welcoming Alice to his family, the Judge hosted two more weddings. Daughter Anna B married George Washington Thompson, a native of Winchester, Tennessee, and the couple settled in Ft. Worth, where they brought up four children. Houston's First Presbyterian Church was the setting for Jeanette's marriage to Alexander Perry Duncan, from Calvert, Texas, on Wednesday, January 20, 1886. The Duncans raised six children and moved his hardware and banking business to Waco in 1894, when the Houston & Texas Central Railroad opened a depot there. Youngest brother Robert remained a bachelor; he worked briefly for client railroad firms, clerked for his father and brother from 1890 to 1900, and then became a claim agent for the Sunset Central Lines office in Dallas.[51] Poet Thomas Gray's gentle words, carved on his Glenwood Cemetery grave marker, reflect Robert's quiet life: "An affectionate brother and faithful friend, modest, retiring, unassuming, loyal, 'like a beautiful flower born to blush unseen and waste its sweetness in the desert air.'"[52]

Not long after Graham Baker's birth in 1883, Captain Baker suffered a serious illness that caused him to reconsider his family responsibilities. Although never named in later correspondence, this illness made the new father realize the critical importance of life insurance and financial planning. In 1940 Baker wrote thoughtful letters addressed personally to each of his grandchildren, some of whom were only toddlers. In lawyerly fashion, he explained that "had this illness proved fatal your grandmother would have been left alone with my son Graham . . . with practically no means of support." In each letter he enclosed a life insurance policy, payable at age sixty-five, and explained that "Life insurance . . .

Graham Baker, Alice Baker, James A. Baker Jr., ca. 1894. Private Collection.

helps men and women to help themselves in ways that far exceed their fondest hopes" by allowing individuals to create an estate, borrow for education, enjoy an income in their "declining years," or "guarantee comfort for your loved ones."[53] This message to a young child, imagining him as an old man and wishing to teach him prudence and responsibility, exemplifies the foresight that enabled Captain Baker to visualize the great enterprises of his life.

While unnamed, the illness may have had lifelong consequences. Baker suffered from sciatic rheumatism all his life, and after World War I he was diagnosed with diabetes. If the 1880s illness had been severe pancreatitis, it might have weakened the ability of the pancreas to make insulin. Since replacement insulin was not available in quantity until the early 1920s, it is probable Captain Baker managed his blood glucose level through frequent testing, diet modification, and exercise until insulin could be added to his treatment. Aspirin was used to lessen pain by 1899, but there was little that could be done for rheumatism, although Baker consulted specialists in Boston and Baltimore. Baker never dwelt on his health, named his ailments, or complained to his correspondents, but he and Alice frequently boarded the Houston & Texas Central Railway for trips to spas in Marlin, south of Waco, and in Hot Wells, south of San Antonio, where the steamy waters might palliate discomfort. Baker also visited doctors in Boston, where he consulted rheumatism specialists and where Dr. Elliott Joslin, a pioneer in diabetes treatment, ran a path-breaking clinic.[54]

In the 1880s and 1890s Captain Baker and Alice established a traditional late nineteenth-century division of duties that defined their marriage for over forty years. He attended to business outside the home, while she managed the complicated household and cared for aging relatives and her growing family. Remembered by her first grandchild as a woman "who never lost touch with the Lord," Alice's gentle empathy enveloped everyone who crossed her path in warm affection.[55] Family members adored her. On Sundays she gathered family and servants for Bible readings and hymn singing, which she accompanied on her piano. In later years, Alice developed important social service organizations for underserved Houstonians and devoted long hours to leadership in the Ladies' Association of the First Presbyterian Church. She believed that her community efforts to improve Houston's quality of life for everyone as well as her social hospitality to friends and business associates supported her husband's legal, business, and civic career and fulfilled her duties as a practicing Presbyterian. In return, Captain Baker understood how hard Alice worked to make home a welcoming haven; he consulted her about many of his own endeavors, and he actively promoted her service projects with monetary support and legal advice.[56] The Bakers built a partnership predicated on the belief that their example and hard work would promote personal happiness and make Houston a better place for their children and for the generations who would follow them.

Contemporaries described Captain Baker as a man's man who also charmed the ladies. Of medium height with "a twinkle in his eye," the slim young cadet gradually filled out to a fairly stocky middle-aged man whose presence was felt when he entered a room. He enjoyed the outdoors, hunting, shooting, fishing, and hiking with friends and family. Cigar smokers and stag dinners with colleagues filled many evening hours, and he "always had a good story to tell."[57] Maintaining his youthful zest for a good card game, the Captain won the Gentleman Guest's Prize at the Third Ward Euchre Club on May 18, 1894, a newsworthy item in small-town nineteenth-century Houston.[58] The dancing habits noted in letters from Texas Military Institute, a light-hearted tendency to tease, and impeccable manners made him a welcome dinner partner among his wife's friends, too, but beneath this easy, outgoing manner lay a strong, determined, ambitious character. Captain Baker displayed confident integrity and an uncanny ability to analyze situations and seize opportunities in the worlds of business, banking, and law. Some contemporaries found his pursuit of excellence intimidating; most recognized a leader of men whose quiet but persuasive voice settled debate. He often misled his enemies by his affable demeanor, and the twinkling eyes could narrow to a steely glint in the courtroom. The boy who orchestrated playtime for his younger sisters and little brother assumed the responsibilities of civic and professional leadership with ease.[59]

JUNIOR PARTNER

When Captain Baker began practicing law in 1879, Baker & Botts was the best known law firm in the region, with a roster of clients demanding general legal services, but one client and one specialty stood out. William Marsh Rice, with his far-flung business investments, was the partnership's most valued individual client, and Judge Baker had become one of the state's finest exponents of railroad law, attracting a growing list of corporate clients to the firm.[60] Because Colonel Botts disliked courtroom appearances, the partnership took small steps toward specialization: Judge Baker handled litigation, and Colonel Botts provided consultation and research to regional businesses. Pleadings bore the firm's name, the firm collected all fees, and Judge Baker and Colonel Botts divided proceeds by arrangement, which they reviewed annually. In 1880 the three lawyers moved to the recently constructed Fox Building at 27 Main Street. Merchant Henry Fox occupied the first floor of his three-story building, which adjoined the T. W. House Bank building. Baker, Botts & Baker (as the firm was known after July 1881) occupied two rooms on the second floor. Judge Baker's office doubled as the library, at that time a lawyer's personal possession. The other room extended from the front to the rear of the building and was shared by Colonel Botts on the east and Captain Baker on the west end. A stenographer and clerk sat between them. Rent was $40 per month.[61] Down the hall, Orren T. Holt, a young lawyer employed by the Houston & Texas Central Railroad, maintained an office. Captain Baker and Holt were social acquaintances whose wives had grown up together, but they would find themselves locked in a legal struggle by the end of the century.

Years later Captain Baker recalled working with his father and Colonel Botts. No one, he believed, enjoyed greater confidence and respect than Colonel Botts. One day the young attorney sought advice from his father's partner about a difficult case. "What is the ethical thing to do?"

Captain Baker's Office, ca. 1895. Private Collection.

he asked. Colonel Botts answered, "Jimmie . . . why do you ask me?" When the younger man replied, "Colonel, because I have a doubt about it," the older man responded, "You have answered your own question. The fact that you have a doubt about it, my boy, is sufficient answer to your question,—don't do it."[62] Baker also remembered a trial that began shortly after he earned his license and continued until Baker & Botts had become Baker, Botts & Baker. His father took the case of *Henry & Dilley v. Galveston, Harrisburg & San Antonio Railway Company*; Judge E. P. Hill, general counsel for the Southern Pacific lines at the time, represented the railway. Henry & Dilley, which built rail lines around the state, had agreed to excavate lines for G. H. & S. A. but had not been paid. The young Captain watched his father write out the petition by hand, remembered the trial in the old Market House building, and recalled the "very successful litigation." When the case had wound its way through the appeals process and the Supreme Court had affirmed lower-court decisions, Henry & Dilley's $10,000 check brought "comfort and solace" to the winners, Judge Baker and Colonel Botts.[63]

In an era when trials decided most disagreements, the Judge found his son's arrival doubly welcome. Captain Baker handled dozens of cases for his father's railroad clients and quickly earned praise for his court-room skill. Years later District Judge Charles E. Ashe remembered the young litigator as "the most brilliant trial lawyer" who came before him. Skilled at cross examination, the quiet-spoken Captain "never attempted to brow-beat, threaten or confuse a witness, but appealed to his sense of honesty and fairness,—so much so that he completely disarmed even the most hostile witness and drew from him additional testimony and admissions which greatly weakened, and sometimes completely de-stroyed, his adverse testimony."[64]

A confident young man, Captain Baker was quick to introduce himself to the business community, and he received many invitations to partici-pate in civic and social activities. On May 31, 1879, the aspiring attorney offered his services as secretary and treasurer of the Houston Loan and Building Association even though "forced to confess that I have never had any practical experience as Secretary of such an institution." As a member of the association, he explained, he was "desirous of advanc-ing its interests." He felt sure he could perform the duties and, as further inducement, suggested he accept stock instead of salary if named to the post.[65]

As soon as he qualified to practice in 1879, Captain Baker joined Houston's Bar Association, organized in 1870 under the leadership of Peter Gray. Members of the Houston Bar recognized Baker's talent and drive and asked him to represent them at the July 15–17, 1882 meeting held to organize the Texas Bar Association. The youthful attorney was one of forty-six individuals and firms to attend preliminary meetings in Galveston, where the group outlined the association's purpose: "advanc-ing the science of jurisprudence, promoting uniformity of legislation in the administration of justice throughout the state, upholding the honor of the profession of law, and encouraging intercourse among members."[66] Baker returned to the island city six months later when three hundred men held their first convention on December 12. Like most bar associa-tions of the era, the Texas Bar Association appealed to urban attorneys, judges, educators, and appellate specialists who wanted to transform an egalitarian trade with casual court proceedings learned through apprenticeship into a standardized profession requiring specialized education, preferably at accredited law schools.[67] Of the 4,600 men and 17 women who were licensed to practice law in Texas in 1900, only 315 belonged to the state bar association.

JUDGE BAKER AND THE RAILROADS OF TEXAS

In the 1880s Judge Baker expanded his extensive railroad practice, while his son gradually turned his attention to William Marsh Rice's complex business empire. Railroad capitalists created the first national corporations in the United States and introduced new legal challenges as their large businesses expanded through multiple state jurisdictions to build the first national industrial empires. The entrepreneurial activism of these railroad barons initially won enthusiastic popular support because the new transportation technology united a continent and brought unimagined opportunities to isolated towns and farms. Before and after the Civil War, Texas investors, with occasional nonstate or "foreign" partners, began building several local railway lines. William Marsh Rice and his father-in-law Paul Bremond brought the railroad age to Houston when they invested in the Buffalo Bayou, Brazos & Colorado Railway Company and the Houston & Texas Central Railway in the 1850s. These lines connected Galveston and Houston to the East Texas interior and to New Orleans. Seen as cheap, fast transportation that opened local markets to a wider world, the railroads were welcomed as state and local assets, and railroad lawyers became able spokesmen for the economic development and progress that wider markets and new technology promised.

After the Civil War, Texans expected their state government to promote private enterprise, and legislators encouraged railroad rebuilding, passed laws favorable to railroad expansion, and approved dozens of corporate charters for new lines. Railroad promoters were the state's most prominent citizens, most enthusiastic boosters of economic progress, and most cosmopolitan businessmen. Promised land or favorable financial inducements in exchange for investing in Texas, railroad companies inched their way from the Gulf toward Dallas, Austin, and San Antonio in the 1870s when the Galveston, Harrisburg & San Antonio Railway, the Houston & Texas Central Railway Company, and the Missouri, Kansas

& Texas (Katy) lines hired Baker & Botts to do their legal work. Directors for the Houston & Texas Central lived in New York and Houston. William Marsh Rice, who listed New York City as his residence, acted as financial agent and director for the line and frequently assisted the enterprise during financial crises.[68] His friend Alfred S. Richardson served as secretary and his brother Frederick A. Rice as treasurer of the important rail carrier, the first Texas railroad to refurbish and expand its lines in the late 1860s.

As Texas rails moved north, they began to connect with east-west interstate systems being organized after the opening of the first transcontinental railroad in 1869 when the Central Pacific, moving east, joined the Union Pacific, moving west to fulfill a popular dream to connect Atlantic and Pacific coasts by rail. Transcontinental railroads spurred competition as promoters planned northern, central, and southern coast-to-coast systems with interstate north-south connections. After nationwide bank failures in the financial Panic of 1873, investors in intrastate Texas rail lines faced ruin. Into the breach stepped Jason (Jay) Gould (May 27, 1836–December 2, 1892), who controlled 15 percent of the United States tracks by 1882 in his multistate Missouri-Pacific Railway Company. When Gould wanted to consolidate Texas lines into his system in 1879–1881, he traveled to Texas to consult prominent Galveston attorney William Pitt Ballinger, who had helped write the 1876 Texas Constitution, which was hostile to non-Texas investors and would not permit outright takeover of Texas corporations by nonstate entities. Ballinger and Gould devised a leasing system that allowed lines Gould controlled to retain a Texas corporate identity within Gould's larger multistate network.[69] Judge Baker began to offer Gould general advice about coordinating legal business along his affiliated lines when Gould integrated the Missouri, Kansas & Texas, the Texas & Pacific, the Galveston, Houston & Henderson—all Baker & Botts clients—and the International & Great Northern into his Missouri-Pacific system.[70] Until 1892 Judge Baker continued to represent these Texas-based clients as general attorney while he also served as general counsel in Texas for the Missouri-Pacific system.

Railroad companies and the law firms that represented them developed together, each responding to the complex economic, social, legal, and political challenges posed by giant businesses serving national markets. Railroad business crossed state and federal jurisdictions, railways used multiple sources of funding and required huge capital outlays, they employed thousands of workers whose skills varied immensely, they gave life to the towns and landscapes through which their lines passed, and access to their speeding cars spurred commercial agriculture and enabled large-scale manufacturing. Even telegraph companies followed in the rail line's wake, using the same rights of way for their wires. But railroading was risky; entrepreneurs borrowed heavily and staked other people's money to build their empires. If uncertain for the investor, this new industry proved lucrative for the legal profession.

To provide legal services to the Gould System and its successor, Southern Pacific system, Judge Baker and his son constructed a statewide web of lawyers, supervised and controlled from the office in Houston. The tiered system had a profound impact on the profession because it sought the most talented attorneys throughout the state and monitored their performance closely. While attorneys in New York City, site of the system's national headquarters, handled strategic issues and financing for the national system, Baker, Botts & Baker managed tactics for company affairs in Texas, Louisiana, Oklahoma, and much of the trans-Mississippi region. From the 1880s to the century's end, the law firm emphasized its relationship to its railroad clients by using special "Legal Department" letterhead for each railroad it served as general attorney, emblazoning this stationery with the railroad's name across the top and the firm's name as General Attorneys discreetly engraved on the left.[71]

In each county seat through which a client's railroad ran, Baker, Botts & Baker hired and supervised division attorneys who were kept on permanent retainer to handle county tax payments and to try routine court cases involving injuries to passengers and crew, property disputes, and rights of way conflict. Local attorneys assisted the division attorneys in small towns or rural areas. The Houston lawyers paid these small-town attorneys by the case to settle claims, make title searches, or try minor damage suits. While the work paid well, association with powerful city lawyers and their national clients had a price. G. G. Kelley, a lawyer from Wharton who had for twenty years "rendered faithful and efficient service" under Baker, Botts & Baker supervision, complained that being attorney for the railroad entailed risks "you gentlemen in the city may not appreciate. . . . an attorney who is known as a representative of a railroad company is looked upon by many people with more or less disfavor, and often looses [sic] business that would have come to him otherwise."

Of course, appropriate compensation, suggested at the close of Kelley's letter, would alleviate this distress.[72]

By the 1880s the colorful personalities and manipulative tactics—many later pronounced illegal—of nineteenth-century railroad "Robber Barons" generated Populist opposition and journalists' outrage as more and more farmers and residents of towns bypassed by the big national systems began to protest rate hikes and to fear losing control over the lucrative and critical industry. Shoddy construction and lax maintenance caused accidents that maimed or killed workers, passengers, and wandering livestock. Railroad operators themselves found dealing with legislators impossible, as each new session brought amended laws that affected management's ability to structure financial arrangements and predict income with which to maintain lines, pay workers, and reimburse investors.

In 1885 five major rail lines formed the Texas Traffic Association with, in their view, the businesslike goal of establishing fair and uniform rates and procedures. Railroad opponents exploded, raising old hatreds of monopoly power and "foreign" investors as well as general disgust with free-wheeling, political corruption.[73] Answering the unforeseen consequences of railroad expansion and flamboyant behavior, reformist politicians inspired by the oratory and determination of James Stephen Hogg addressed Populist outcries against perceived "monopolization of transportation." As attorney general (1887–1891) and governor (1891–1895), Hogg recognized that Texans needed, and wanted, railroad transportation, but he also advocated competition and demanded that railroad executives obey their charters, consider public interest when establishing routes and rates, and assure safe conditions along the rail routes. Most important, he wanted Texans to retain control over routes traversing their giant state. Nationwide outcries against the arrogance and greed of several railroad speculators and complications arising from financial manipulation and growing interstate business had already prompted Congress to create the Interstate Commerce Commission in 1887 to examine complaints and regulate commerce among the states. The next year Attorney General Hogg challenged the Texas Traffic Association and brought suit against its nine railroads in Travis County District Court.

Hogg charged the association created a monopoly, prevented competition, pooled rates, and disregarded member charters and public interest. Hogg won the first round against Baker, Botts & Baker and Judge

71

J. W. Terry, counselors for the defendants, when Judge John C. Townes granted a permanent injunction restraining the railroads from continuing their association. On advice of counsel, the railroads immediately appealed this decision. Judge Baker and his team pointed out several "errors" and explained the voluntary nature of the association, which was created to adjust differences, facilitate business, and discuss—not mandate—rates. Most important, Baker, Botts & Baker claimed Congress had created the Interstate Commerce Commission to regulate interstate commerce and therefore Texas had no jurisdiction over the Association's far-flung interstate businesses. Although Hogg's argument was reaffirmed by Texas courts, the battle heralded a new era of struggle over appropriate jurisdiction and caused the railroads to create an "international" association headquartered outside Texas.

Attorney General Hogg understood the railroads would seek federal jurisdiction to override Texas supervision, but he still wanted to control business activity within the state. In November 1890 he rallied voters behind a constitutional amendment to declare railroad companies common carriers and railroads public highways, subject to the legislature's authority. In 1891, after a long battle and several proposals, Hogg persuaded legislators to establish a Railroad Commission to "prevent discrimination and extortion in railroad charges." Support was overwhelming; 92-5 in the House, unanimous in the Senate.[74] Although railroad executives and their attorneys viewed the Commission with skepticism at first, as time passed Baker, Botts & Baker began to see the value of dealing with regulators instead of arguing before legislators, whose oversight changed with each election. The commissioners' expertise and data gathering provided consistent approaches to transportation issues. Railroad advocates often served as intermediaries who explained regulatory and political boundaries to their corporate clients and business issues to the commissioners. Although they represented different constituencies, the commissioners, the railroad executives, and the lawyers shaped a new body of law that defined the powers of government and private industry in inter- and intrastate markets during the late nineteenth century.

CAPTAIN BAKER AND THE BUSINESS OF HOUSTON

When Captain Baker joined his father's practice, he undertook some railroad litigation and helped establish the partnership's reputation be-

William Marsh Rice in middle
age. Early Rice Collection,
Woodson Research Center,
Rice University.

yond Texas, but he focused his attention on opportunities offered by
Houston's business expansion and by the partnership's long service as
legal counsel to William Marsh Rice. Judge Baker had invested in several Rice enterprises, and his son also served as director or officer for
businesses in which Rice held an interest.[75] Captain Baker noted many
years later, when his father "advanced into the evening of life I gradually
took on greater responsibilities in the firm and very naturally succeeded
to much of the business which formerly received his personal attention,
thereby bringing me more and more into contact with Mr. Rice, both
personally and professionally."[76]

William Marsh Rice (1816–1900), a native of Springfield, Massachusetts, amassed one of Texas' great fortunes. The short, slim New En-
glander arrived in Houston late in 1838 and by February 1839 had secured
a head right certificate to 320 acres in Harris County, conditional upon
settlement. Rice formed a long-term partnership with Ebenezer B. Nichols — Rice & Nichols, Exporters, Importers and Wholesale Grocers of

Houston—with offices and a storefront on the east side of Main Street between Congress and Franklin and a branch in Galveston. On June 29, 1850, Rice married eighteen-year-old Margaret Bremond, daughter of railroad pioneer Paul Bremond, and further cemented his business and social position in the frontier town. His mercantile, cotton, and railroad partnerships with Nichols and later with his younger brother Frederick Allyn Rice (1830–1901) proved so successful that by 1860 William Marsh Rice was said to be the second wealthiest man in Texas, with real and personal property valued at $750,000. Nearly every major Houston enterprise carried his name on the roster of its officers, directors, or stockholders, and R. G. Dunn & Co. consistently rated his credit as "perfectly solvent" and described his businesses as large or very large.[77]

The Civil War made Rice a millionaire. When his wife Margaret died on August 13, 1863, Rice, who never sympathized with the Southern secessionist position, disbanded his Houston office, refused to accept Confederate notes, and spent the months between December 1863 and August 1865 in Monterrey or Matamoros, Mexico, and in Havana, Cuba. When Northern forces placed Galveston's port under blockade, Houston factors loaded cotton bales on wagons drawn by teams of ten or more oxen and sent them on a dangerous four-to-six-week journey down the barren Texas coast to Matamoros, Mexico. There Rice's ships, often American steamers registered temporarily to friendly Mexican nationals, carried the cargo to Cuba or the Bahamas for transfer to steamers bound for the textile mills of England and New England. In exchange for the cotton, Rice loaded returning ships with arms, medicines, household goods, and clothing needed by Confederates at home and on the battlefield.

After the Civil War, Rice spent most of his time in New Jersey and New York City, where he owned property and maintained a home, but he continued to expand his businesses in Houston and served on the boards of several local companies and banks. Long interested in the transportation problems associated with moving raw materials and manufactured goods to market, Rice promoted railroad building and street paving, and supported dredging Buffalo Bayou so steamships carrying his products could travel more easily to Houston—and avoid extra transshipping charges at Galveston's wharves. As Rice's primary business and legal counselor in Texas, Captain Baker kept him informed about the activities of five railroads, five manufacturing firms, eight banks, ship channel companies, and properties in Texas and Louisiana—all entities in which the aging entrepreneur had invested. Rice was the largest individual shareholder in the Merchants & Planters Oil Company, the South Texas National Bank of Houston, the Houston Brick Works, and the Galveston Wharf Company. He also held major positions in the Houston Ice & Brewing Company, the Houston Gas Light Company, and the Houston Drug Company. Several other companies, whose business had declined, owed Rice large sums of money when he died in September 1900.[78] By 1897 Merchants & Planters Oil Company, which converted cottonseed to a variety of products, was shipping meal and oil to Rotterdam, Hamburg, and Great Britain through Galveston, although the Southern Pacific Railroad was competing for customers who would ship cottonseed to New Orleans by rail, rather than to Galveston by water.

Rice deputized the energetic younger Baker to serve as officer or director of his companies. Baker was vice president of the Merchants & Planters Oil Company, and he represented Rice's interest as a director of Houston Ice & Brewing, Houston Brick Works, and the Houston Gas Light Company. He attended board meetings and sent his client detailed reports about improvements, industry competition, election of officers, and company problems. Rice often replied by jotting his thoughts on the back of Baker's clear, neatly typed letters. Handling legal and business matters for Rice was time-consuming but produced steady income.[79] Despite their age difference, Rice and Baker formed bonds of trust that would prove critical. On occasion the younger man wrote the older about topics of current interest and told Rice he would "be glad to have your views." While always courteous, Baker never hesitated to state his own opinion or explain why some business directorship or other responsibility was "inconvenient" for him to fulfill.[80]

Contemporaries and later law partners believed the Captain's business acumen and banking abilities equaled his skills as a lawyer, and he began to engage in entrepreneurial activity independent of William Marsh Rice's interest. By 1887 he was wearing two hats as partner of Baker, Botts & Baker and vice president of Texas Rolling Mills. In 1892 he put together the Houston Abstract Company and served as president and director for several years. In 1894 he was named one of five directors of the Houston Gas Light Company, founded in 1866 by T. W. House, and in the same year Baker became president of the Citizens Electric Light & Power Company, thereby playing a central role in spreading utilities throughout the city and building a utilities practice for the firm.[81] In 1895 Captain Baker joined fellow business leaders to form the Houston Business League to coordinate business activity and address quality of life issues. League members advocated forcefully for progressive civic reform, paved roads, and a municipal drainage system. The League promoted Houston as a regional leader and reorganized in 1910 as the Chamber of Commerce. In 1886 the Captain helped found Commercial National Bank and in the 1890s served as director of Houston National Bank (organized 1889). He joined the board of Commercial National Bank in 1896 and became vice president the next year. As the nineteenth century drew to a close, Captain Baker had demonstrated exceptional talents as a lawyer, a businessman, and a banker. He had learned from his father's example and success, he had used his association with William Marsh Rice to his advantage, and he had recognized the potential of new industries for Houston's future. Captain Baker was well positioned to advance Houston's business and civic life. By 1900 his firm represented eight of the seventeen railroads that met the sea at the port of Houston and counseled two of the city's four banks.

LAW FIRM CHANGES

In the mid-1890s, the partnership of Baker, Botts & Baker changed dramatically. In 1892 Judge Baker began to shift his business practice to his son and his railroad work to two firm newcomers, Robert Scott Lovett and Edwin Brewington Parker. Lovett spent his adult life in the railroad industry after growing up in rural San Jacinto County; a high school dropout, he started as a day laborer on the tracks. Someone urged him to read law, and soon after he received his license Judge Baker noticed the smart young man and hired him to handle minor matters for the Houston, East & West Texas lines in San Jacinto County. When Gould moved his Missouri-Pacific headquarters to Dallas in 1892, Judge Baker sent Lovett north to oversee legal matters as general attorney for the Texas & Pacific, a client of Baker, Botts & Baker. By October 1, 1892, Lovett was back in Houston, where he joined the firm, renamed Baker, Botts, Baker & Lovett on January 1, 1893. That year Collis P. Huntington won his railroad war against the Gould interests and began to consolidate his transcontinental empire. The next year Baker, Botts, Baker & Lovett became general attorney in Texas for Huntington's Southern Pacific Railroad holding company, chartered in Kentucky and called the Sunset-Central Line in Texas. This lucrative association would last for decades, produce steady income for the firm, and enable Baker, Botts, Baker & Lovett to influence legal practice throughout the region.[82]

By 1894 Judge Baker had relinquished most of his duties to his son, and that year Walter Browne Botts and his beloved wife died within days of each other, leaving guardianship of their youngest son Tom to Captain Baker. To accommodate the firm's increased workload, the Bakers and Lovett hired the firm's first law school graduate, Edwin Brewington Parker, who had finished his studies at the University of Texas in 1889. Parker soon demonstrated his brilliance as a legal expert and organizational genius, and the developing careers of Lovett and Parker vaulted Baker, Botts, Baker & Lovett to the forefront of railroad lawyers nationally. By the mid-1890s Captain Baker and his aggressive young associates were well-placed to handle a new era of lawyering for the railroad that entailed interpreting a new body of regulatory law for their corporate clients. At first Lovett and Parker managed Southern Pacific's trial docket, while Baker negotiated firm compensation with Julius Kruttschnitt, general manager of the Southern Pacific Company in Houston. By 1891 the firm was charging $5,000 annually to represent the railroad before the legislature, as well as fees for business advice and trial work. In 1894 Baker, Botts, Baker & Lovett took on additional trial work when a favorite Southern Pacific litigator retired.[83] In 1896 Lovett negotiated a substantial increase in the firm retainer during lengthy discussions in New York, and on April 1, 1897, Southern Pacific began paying a retainer of $27,800 a year, in place until 1913.

In 1894 the expanding law firm moved again, to the Gibbs Building built by Colonel C. C. Gibbs, land commissioner of the Southern Pacific lines, on the corner of Fannin and Franklin. The three-story office building was distinguished by a round tower on its southeast corner. Considered the finest building of its day, it housed E. A. Peden's Iron and Steel Company and Wells Fargo Express, clients of Baker, Botts, Baker & Lovett. For $75 a month, the firm occupied a suite of five rooms. Captain Baker enjoyed the tower room. Adjoining his office was a large space serving as a general office. Eula Gray, the Captain's indispensable stenographer, sat outside his door, and John H. McClung, the firm's bookkeeper and clerk, sat at a long table beyond her desk. The only firm telephone was attached to the wall at the far end of the room. The library occupied another room, and two other offices originally reserved for Colonel Botts and Judge Baker were soon turned over to Robert Lovett and Edwin Parker.[84] On frequent business trips to other cities and states, Baker, Lovett, and Parker visited correspondents and friends to build collegial relations and court client referrals.[85] From 1894 through March 1, 1900, Captain Baker and Robert Lovett split the firm's proceeds fifty-fifty after paying E. B. Parker a salary that increased from $1,000 in 1894 to $3,000 in 1899. After Parker became a partner in 1900, he continued to earn a salary of $3,000 plus 3/23 of net earnings for the next three years, while Baker and Lovett split the remaining net earnings. In 1899 Jesse Andrews came on board as a young associate paid $900 his first year.[86] In the new century, these younger men, under Captain Baker's guiding hand, would develop Houston's first modern law firm.

HOME AND FAMILY

Captain Baker learned the importance of relaxation at an early age and balanced his intense legal and business career with social engagements and family vacations. He joined Houston's most popular men at the Z. Z. Club, which sponsored debutante balls and other dancing parties. Like his father, Captain Baker belonged to the Benevolent and Protective Order of Elks, and he also joined the Houston Turnverein and the Press Club. Both the Judge and the Captain were founding members of the Houston Club. Chartered on June 20, 1894, the club was organized "for literary purposes: to promote social intercourse among its members, and to provide for them the convenience of a Club House."[87] Immediately the club's headquarters became a gathering place for the city's business, civic, and cultural leaders. Its roster of 110 founders included the Bakers' law partners, clients, and friends, as well as men who would later oppose the firm in court. Every summer during the 1890s found Captain Baker with Alice and the children in Colorado, where he traveled with his sisters Nettie Duncan and Anna B. Thompson and their husbands and children. The families hiked and rode mules through the rocky terrain or fished the rushing mountain streams. Alice and her sisters also remained close and enjoyed yearly reunions. The siblings welcomed family members to their homes for long visits, and the cousins and their children remained good friends.[88]

In November 1896 the Judge wrote his daughter Nettie Duncan in Waco that he had recovered completely from illness but was "lighter than you have seen me for more than two years." He attributed his failure to gain weight to the "period in life" when weight "is disposed to fall off." But by January 4, 1897, Captain Baker told a more serious story. In a lengthy typewritten letter, he wrote Nettie "very plainly about the Judge's condition" and described in detail the indigestion and other ailments that had occurred during their father's two-month sojourn in Somerset, Virginia, and had now left him bedridden. In a handwritten postscript, the worried son concluded, "He is no better this evening— probably worse. Unless his fever abates . . . I fear the worst. How soon I can't possibly tell."[89] On February 23, 1897, the Judge, nearly seventy-six, died peacefully at home with his family at his bedside. Friends remembered the dignified gentleman as "kindly, gracious and genial," a "true Christian in his deportment, and a noble man in all his transactions." In a "Tribute of Reverence and Affection" made before the Supreme Court of Texas on March 18, 1897, Norman Kittrell recalled a life of "arduous toil, honorable ambition and lofty living" and said he knew no Texas lawyer asked "to grapple with legal problems of greater difficulty, or in which larger financial interests were involved, and he unfailingly met every requirement."[90] A special car attached to an International & Great Northern train carried the coffin and mourners to Huntsville, where the Judge was laid to rest beside his "dearest Row" and their four infant children in Oakwood Cemetery.[91] In 1899, two years after James's death, his family and former congregation dedicated a stained glass window picturing the risen Christ to the memory of Judge and Rowena Baker.

Captain Baker, forty in 1897, was the senior man in his father's law firm. With Robert Scott Lovett and Edwin Brewington Parker, he supervised a regional network of district and local attorneys who handled business for the Southern Pacific Railroad system and managed all legal matters relating to William Marsh Rice's investment empire. Houstonians turned to Baker, Botts, Baker & Lovett for advice about civic projects of any importance, and law firms from St. Louis, Kansas City, Chicago, Boston, New Orleans, and New York sought the firm's counsel when their clients had business in the Southwest.[92] As the century drew to a close, the Bakers found themselves enmeshed in a web of relationships that included family members, law partners, and business associates who be-

Baker Family Home, 1416 Main Street (owned 1898–1922). Private Collection.

lieved Houston was a city of opportunity. Through long association and hard work, Captain Baker had proved he could build businesses, provide access to government leaders and sources of capital, and collaborate with others to shape Houston's future.

After the Judge's death, Captain Baker and Alice purchased a house at 1416 Main Street, a few blocks away from the Judge's old home site. Designed by highly regarded architect George E. Dickey and built in 1888–1889 for cotton broker Samuel K. Dick, the large asymmetrical house was embellished with loggias, a pointed tower, bays, gables, arches, finials, and a high-pitched slate roof; it even boasted a greenhouse with sliding glass panels. Newspapers reported its construction as one of the city's most important homes, and frequently photographed the house during the Bakers' residency.[93] Mrs. Baker planted flower borders, shrubbery, and trees on the large city block, and Captain Baker had Alice's beloved playhouse moved to the new site.

On New Year's Day 1899, not long after the Bakers had occupied the house, they welcomed their friends for a day-long reception that included lunch at midday and dancing in the evening. Alice, "a charming hostess . . . seemed everywhere at once, winning the hearts of every one by her gracious sweetness." She adorned the house with garlands, wreaths, and red satin ribbon and stoked a glowing fire opposite the front door. Green holly leaves across the central arch announced 1899. Mrs. Baker draped the dining table "with white satin with ruchings and frill of white mousseline de soie" and covered the cloth with glass, silver, flowers, and refreshments. Assisting her as hostesses were twenty friends and several young ladies.[94] No one attending this soiree could have guessed that events unfolding in the following year would change profoundly the fate of Houston and the Baker family.

CHAPTER THREE
On Trial

CAPTAIN AND MRS. BAKER spent a quiet New Year's Day in 1900, awaiting the birth of their fourth child. On January 23, Walter Browne Baker, named for his father's former partner Walter Browne Botts, joined Graham (16), Alice (12), and Jim (7) at 1416 Main Street. The year that began so happily brought unexpected challenges to the Baker family and to Houston, now the second largest city in Texas and home to 44,633 residents.[1]

TRAGEDY: SEPTEMBER 1900

On Saturday, September 8, mother-of-pearl skies and mild breezes in Galveston gave way to a furious storm: cyclonic winds estimated at 120 miles per hour, torrential rain lasting fifteen hours, and ruinous floods deluged Galveston Island. At least 6,000 of the town's 38,000 residents drowned; over 4,000 buildings collapsed in rubble. Houston suffered minor property loss, temporary electrical failure, and one death. Five days after the storm, Dr. S. O. Young described 100-mile winds that "drove sheets of spray and rain which were blinding. . . . The roar was something awful." He watched as his neighbor's house "rose like a huge

Illustration: Captain Baker, ca. 1900. Early Rice Collection, Woodson Research Center, Rice University.

Alice Baker, ca. 1900. Early Rice
Collection, Woodson Research
Center, Rice University.

steamboat, was swept back and suddenly disappeared," carrying the husband, wife, son, and two daughters to their frightening deaths.[2] Bridges
to the mainland crumpled, ships anchored in Galveston Bay flew inland
ten to twenty miles, nearly every church on the island lay in ruins, water
mains gave way, and no one repaired communication lines for days. Reporters who reached the island by sailboat recorded a shocking saga of
suffering and loss, riveting the attention of Houston newspaper readers
day after day with images of devastation and details of heroism and tragedy as the Houston Light Guard and other rescue teams tried to help
stranded survivors. Galveston never recovered its status as the state's
major port but ceded economic power on the Gulf to Houston, lying
fifty miles inland from the treacherous sea.[3]

Still reeling from the disaster that had befallen their elegant sister city and worried about rising water on the Colorado, Brazos, and Trinity rivers, *Houston Daily Post* readers opened their morning papers on September 25 to learn that "eccentric millionaire" William Marsh Rice had died at his apartment in New York City on Sunday September 23 "due chiefly to old age." The dignified announcement at the top of page 2 noted Rice's commercial interests and better-known Houston relations: his brother and business partner Captain Frederick Allyn Rice and his nephews, former Mayor Horace Baldwin Rice and current superintendent of Texas penitentiaries Captain Jonas Shearn Rice.[4] Only the most astute reader would have felt alarm at the article's mention of "his attorney, Mr. Patrick" or the choice of "chiefly" to describe the cause of death. Two days later, the September 27 page 2 headline—"Developments in the Rice Case"—warned Houston readers of the suspicious circumstances surrounding Rice's death. As Rice's brother, Frederick A. Rice, and his lawyer, James A. Baker, rushed to the scene by train, another lawyer, Albert T. Patrick, had "taken charge" and was talking volubly to the press. Beneficiaries of a will drawn by the late Mrs. William Marsh Rice were "much surprised" to read that Patrick claimed to be Mr. Rice's attorney because they knew full well that Patrick participated on a legal team locked in an acrimonious four-year battle with William Marsh Rice regarding the contents of his late wife's will.

A wire story rushed to the *Houston Post* on Saturday, September 29, explained more developments and confirmed the public's suspicions that Rice had died "under circumstances which have led the coroner and police and the district attorney to make a searching investigation." Captain Baker was the "most prominent figure in the case" and "practically in charge of matters," and the district attorney was "ready to act if necessary." On October 4, 1900, authorities charged lawyer Albert T. Patrick and William Marsh Rice's valet Charlie Jones with forging "a signature to checks and assignments drawn by the late millionaire," an allegation based on the testimony of three handwriting experts who "examined the checks separately" but agreed "that the signatures were forged." The next day Captain Baker, although "reticent" to explain his words, announced "that the most sensational developments were yet to come in connection with the Rice case." In an interview with the *Houston Post*'s New York stringer, Baker stated, "I am investigating things thoroughly and will let The Post know as I become informed myself."[5] So began the public story of Captain James Addison Baker's tenacious fight to defend the trust of his client, William Marsh Rice. The Rice case would make Baker famous and place his law firm securely on the national stage. The Institute created by Rice's fortune would stimulate Houston's development as a major American city. The world press would expend millions of words—many of them fictional speculation—to retell what newsmen quickly called the trial of the century.

THE FINAL TESTAMENT OF LIBBIE RICE

William Marsh Rice's untimely demise was linked directly to events surrounding the fatal illness and death of his second wife, Julia Elizabeth Baldwin Brown Rice, early in the morning of July 24, 1896. After his first wife's death and his sojourn in Mexico during the Civil War, William M. Rice traveled between Houston and New York to reestablish his business interests. While in Houston during the winter of 1866–1867, Rice spent many hours at the home of his brother Frederick, who had married Charlotte Baldwin Randon, a young widow, in 1854. Frederick and Charlotte were the parents of ten children, lively nieces and nephews much beloved by their widowed, childless uncle. Another constant visitor that winter was Julia Elizabeth (Libbie) Baldwin Brown, Charlotte's older sister. The widow of John H. Brown, a failed shopkeeper who had done business with the Rice brothers before the Civil War, Libbie hoped to sell some land Brown had owned in Texas but discovered it was almost worthless. On June 16, 1867, the wealthy fifty-one-year-old widower married his impoverished thirty-nine-year-old sister-in-law. After paying the requisite bridal visits, the couple escaped one of Houston's worst yellow fever epidemics, so virulent that it killed eight doctors and several hundred residents of Houston and spread inland as far as Huntsville, where two of Judge James Baker's brothers succumbed. The newlyweds traveled to New York City, and for the next twenty-nine years William Marsh and Elizabeth Baldwin Rice maintained their primary residence in Manhattan or on an estate in rural Dunellen, New Jersey, although they made frequent trips to Houston during the winter months.

William Marsh Rice's biographers, citing testimony of relatives and friends, conclude that Rice treated his wife "with unfailing, if unyielding, affection and courtesy."[6] Captain Baker, in gallant formal remarks made long after Mrs. Rice's death, remembered her as "a brilliant woman, unusually handsome, tall and as straight as an Indian . . . with wondrous eyes and a handsome suit of hair."[7] On other occasions he recalled, with less enthusiasm, that she was "ambitious," "fond of society," and liked "being in the public eye."[8] Apparently, she disliked country life, followed the latest fashions in clothing and household decoration, and hoped to cut a dash in New York society; her husband preferred a few friends, wanted no notoriety, and liked to make—not spend—money. As William M. Rice aged, his single passion became the proper use of his fortune to "bring greatest good to the greatest number."[9] While there is little evidence to judge the success of this marriage, there is considerable mystery surrounding the final weeks of Libbie Rice's life.

Mrs. Rice was ill in the winter of 1895. In April 1896 the Rices returned to Houston and were ensconced in their apartment at the Capitol Hotel, one of William M. Rice's prime urban properties. A lawyer, Orren Thaddeus Holt, and his wife, Marian Seward Holt, had rented rooms near the Rice suite, and Mrs. Rice and Mrs. Holt soon became intimate friends.[10] Mrs. Rice's niece, Mamie Baldwin Huntington of Cleveland, Ohio, was also in residence at the Capitol Hotel on her annual visit with her aunt. In May 1896 Mrs. Rice suffered a "slight attack of paralysis," and for several weeks Mrs. Huntington and Mrs. Holt never left the stricken woman's side as they helped nurse her through a second stroke.[11]

Libbie Rice had prepared simple, straightforward wills in 1886 and again in 1892, in both cases stating her residence as the City of New York. The one-sheet 1886 will made a few bequests to friends, a sister, and the Diet Kitchen Society of New York; the estate's residue passed to her husband. The four-page will of 1892 named three executors who lived in New York City, stated that any income from Libbie's estate would go to her husband during his lifetime, and bequeathed $5,000 legacies to several charities in Houston; in this will the residue of the estate passed to seven Houston friends. Neither will contemplated an unusually large estate.[12] Despite these two attempts to leave a final testament, Mrs. Rice apparently told Mrs. Holt that she had not prepared a will and wished to do so. Not only did Marian Holt explain that a wife is entitled to half her husband's fortune in Texas, a community property state, but also she suggested that Libbie Rice consult Mr. Holt about making a will.[13]

Orren T. Holt's role in the ensuing drama is ambiguous. On the one hand, he was and remained a "sincerely esteemed" member of the Houston bar whose "integrity was never questioned." A "commanding figure," tall and heavy-set with a gray mustache, he served as mayor of Houston from 1902–1904.[14] Despite a long, acrimonious legal contest to carry out Mrs. Rice's apparent wishes, Holt and Captain Baker maintained cordial relations until Holt's sudden death from a stroke on February 8, 1913. In fact, some years before the will contest began, Baker, Botts, Baker & Lovett, general counsel for the Houston & Texas Central Railroad, one of Rice's major investments, had hired Holt to settle claims with ranchers who complained passing trains had killed their straying cattle. The names of Holt and Baker appear on several business and social rosters. Marian Holt and Alice Baker, who were close girlhood friends in Waco, performed hostess duties together at numerous functions recorded in the social columns of Houston's newspapers.[15]

However, Holt's dealings with Mrs. Rice raise serious questions about his judgment, intelligence, and integrity. Holt knew Libbie Rice was ill; he knew she acted without her husband's knowledge (an unusual circumstance in the nineteenth century); he named himself sole executor with the promise of "10% for receiving and 10% for paying out the funds of the Estate" as compensation; and he had the will witnessed by his wife's mother and sister. Even more startling, the Holt will included a generous bequest to Mamie Huntington, who had not been mentioned in the earlier documents at all. This niece and constant companion during her aunt's final illness was to receive $200,000 outright; $100,000 would pass to Mamie's daughter Lillian; and $50,000 would go to Mamie's father Jonas Baldwin for use during his lifetime and then to Mamie at the older man's death.[16] Perhaps Holt did urge Mrs. Rice to tell her husband she was planning a new will, and she refused to listen; and perhaps Holt did believe the Rices maintained their primary domicile in Houston, although he should have researched this issue. Maybe Holt used handy witnesses in deference to an ailing client, although he should have realized how peculiar and self-serving his choices would appear; and maybe Mamie Huntington exerted no undue influence over her aunt, although her sudden good fortune looked suspicious.

In sum, it is difficult not to see Holt as a careless attorney unable to perceive the consequences of his actions. Certainly, he should have had enough sense to protect himself by naming at least one other executor for what promised to be the most significant will yet probated in Harris County. As written, Mrs. Rice's testament would have dispersed nearly $2 million—or perhaps more—depending on the actual value of Mr. Rice's properties.[17] Surely Holt would have considered that William Marsh Rice might contest this plundering of his fortune—a fortune based largely on investments made before he married his second wife. Surely Holt, like most Houston businessmen, knew that in 1891 Rice, with his wife's support, had chartered an Institute for the Advancement of Literature, Science, and Art, to be built in Houston after the donor's death. Surely Holt remembered that the Rices had already begun endowing this future civic asset since record of the gifts had been published in 1892.[18] Indeed, the will Libbie signed on June 1, 1896, itself makes explicit that Holt knew exactly how matters stood. In Clause 37, Mrs. Rice does "solemnly declare that if I signed any papers at any time, giving away or willing away any of my property, I did so without knowing their purpose, and so declare them void . . . as I did not wish at any time . . . to sign away my rights." She concludes her statement by trusting her husband "will give no trouble to my executor . . . as I have considered this writing of my will for many months."[19]

Unaware that his wife had signed a document, which, if enforced, would severely restrict his ability to fund an institute dedicated to higher learning, William M. Rice took Libbie to Waukesha, Wisconsin, where the Park Hotel promised restorative waters for its convalescent clients. Accompanied by their doctor, a nurse, and Alex Stanberry, a strong young man hired to help lift Mrs. Rice, the couple left Houston about June 4. At first the cool Wisconsin weather seemed to help the invalid, although she dismissed the Houston doctor and nurse as soon as she rallied. After three weeks at the spa, her husband, who had not felt well in Waukesha, went on to New York and the comforts of his own home, a recently rented apartment at 500 Madison Avenue. Rice left his wife in the care of a good local physician, but three weeks after her husband's departure, she suffered a third stroke and died at 9:00 a.m. on July 24, 1896. Rice rushed back to his wife's side, oversaw her burial in Milwaukee, and told Stanberry to send all her belongings to Houston before joining him in New York as valet and secretary.

WILLIAM M. RICE V. O. T. HOLT, EXECUTOR

At first, Rice assumed his wife had died intestate, but in September 1896 Captain Baker wired him shocking news. Elizabeth Baldwin Rice, with the help of Orren T. Holt, had signed a will that left half the couple's estate to a long list of relatives, friends, and charities in Houston, New York City, and Baldwinsville, New York. Moreover, Holt was planning to file this will for probate. Baker urged Rice to return immediately to Houston and suggested that Mrs. Rice must not have been competent to endorse a will on June 1, 1896. In subsequent depositions her maid, a close friend, and the doctor in Wisconsin all described the dying woman as feeble, unable to understand what was said to her or to make her wishes understood, paralyzed on the right side, and confused.[20] On September 15, 1896, Rice sent Baker explicit instructions to write a will for him and "outlined in great detail how he wanted it prepared . . . in his own handwriting."[21] A few days later, Baker submitted a document to his client that provided modest bequests totaling $100,000 for his brother Frederick A. Rice and his sisters Minerva Olds and Charlotte McKee and their children but left the residue of Rice's estate to his Institute for the Advancement of Literature, Science, and Art. Rice named his nephew William Marsh Rice II, his friend Judge John D. Bartine, and his trusted attorney James A. Baker as executors.[22]

Despite Rice's insistence that his wife was not of sound mind, had no claim to his property, and could not have executed a proper testament, Holt filed Mrs. Rice's will for probate before the Harris County clerk on March 22, 1897; Jones & Garnett represented Holt as executor while Baker, Botts, Baker & Lovett spoke for Mr. Rice. Testimony concluded on March 27. Newspapers hailed Mrs. Rice's generosity and raised "a very great public sentiment in favor of the probate of the will." Impressed by bequests to many Houston institutions and the promise of a large city park, the judge admitted the will to probate and issued letters testamentary to Holt as executor. Three men were appointed to appraise the estate, and Baker filed notice of an appeal.[23] Holt next filed suit in Harris, Jones, and Washington counties against William Marsh Rice, the Institute, and other parties to claim the late Mrs. Rice's alleged community interest in land located there. Holt also filed suit in Waller County to recover $500,000, his estimate of half the community rents, income, and other cash or securities owned by the couple.

While awaiting the outcome of the probate contest in March 1897, Rice met Charles Freeman Jones, a clerk at the Capitol Hotel and an acquaintance of Alex Stanberry. Charlie, the uneducated son of a tenant farmer, was an agreeable young man who had worked on a schooner that carried freight from Galveston Island to the mainland. Through mismanagement of Libbie Rice's belongings after her death, Stanberry had incurred his employer's distrust; in April 1897, Rice hired Charlie Jones to replace Stanberry as his valet/secretary, and on May 7 the two men left Houston for New York City, arriving at 500 Madison Avenue three days later.

Baker's appeal of the probate decision was dismissed, but Baker and his client changed tactics and in the fall of 1897 filed a countersuit on the equity docket in the U.S. Circuit Court for the Eastern District of Texas in Galveston. In this suit against Orren T. Holt as executor, Baker now argued that the executor of Mrs. Rice's estate had no interest in Mr. Rice's estate under her will "because neither Mr. Rice nor his wife were ever residents of Texas after their marriage," and the community laws of Texas had no application to them.[24] Baker further stated that Holt's claim against these properties "was a cloud upon the title" of Mr. Rice's land, and he asked the court to remove the claim. Baker succeeded in consolidating the cases relating to Mrs. Rice's estate and moving them to Federal Court.[25] "Bitter and unrelenting," Rice vehemently insisted that he and Libbie has always made New York or New Jersey their permanent domicile, that he would not entertain any compromise or settlement, and that Mr. and Mrs. Holt conspired with others to write an improper document. Rice despised Holt and "regarded every lawyer engaged in any litigation against him as a personal enemy."[26] Ironically, Holt hired Hutcheson & Campbell to handle the trial before the federal bench. Former Congressman Captain Joseph Chappell Hutcheson (1842–1924) was a successful litigator and a friend of the slightly younger Baker; his partner Ben Campbell later served as a popular, progressive mayor (1913–1917) who espoused city planning and strengthened Houston's park system.[27] In the end, the Hutcheson/Baker friendship probably enabled a reasonably amicable conclusion to the battle, but at the time of William Marsh Rice's death in September 1900, both sides were preparing for a trial to begin that October.[28]

The fight over Mrs. Rice's will turned on one issue: where did William Marsh and Elizabeth Baldwin Rice maintain their primary residence? Many of Mrs. Rice's friends and relatives recalled her affection for Houston but acknowledged that Mr. Rice had always insisted the couple spend more than six months every year in the northeast.[29] The widower's obstinate refusal to consider compromise made an open trial inevitable, but the situation was awkward. Holt and Baker enjoyed good professional reputations. William Marsh Rice continued to play a critical role in Houston's development, in part because of his access to New York City's financial markets. Elizabeth Baldwin Rice was related to members of Houston's founding family, the Allens, and her will promised great benefits to the city. After Rice decamped to New York City, only his legal advisers, James A. Baker, Robert S. Lovett, and Edwin B. Parker (who visited him regularly at his Madison Avenue apartment), and a small coterie of friends heard his fulminations.

Baker, Botts, Baker & Lovett and their opponents, Holt and Hutcheson, spent the next three years trawling for witnesses who could confirm the Rices' preferred domicile since there seemed to be no incontestable legal documents to settle the issue. William M. Rice suggested individuals who might help his case, and Baker conducted "protracted" interviews with dozens of friends, furniture movers, ticket agents, business associates, and servants who would swear that Rice spoke of New Jersey or New York "as [his] home" or that "Mrs. Rice did not want to live in Texas, but always preferred New York."[30] Holt, too, pursued witnesses Baker suspected would be used to show that Rice had "made [contradictory] statements at different times as to [his] domicile." Baker dismissed this evidence as "maliciously false" but noted it would necessitate placing Rice on the witness stand.[31]

From July 1898 through the spring of 1900 Baker traveled between New York and Houston to depose witnesses, often taking his family with him.[32] Whenever Lovett or Parker came to New York on business of any kind, they, too, called on Rice to discuss his commercial activities and pending lawsuits. Parker had "spent several hours" consulting with Rice about business matters and the Holt litigation on the afternoon of August 29, 1900, and felt "the old gentleman had never been so cordial . . . before."[33] Lovett saw Rice several times on business during the week before his client died. Baker noted repeatedly in later trial testimony that Baker, Botts, Baker & Lovett "received if not one letter a week, one a fortnight" from Rice during 1900.[34] There is no evidence from the 1850s forward that Rice consulted any other lawyer for business or personal legal advice except Judge John D. Bartine, a friend, former neighbor, and counselor who lived in Dunellen, New Jersey, and who helped Rice purchase property in New Jersey and write wills prior to the 1896 testament.[35]

While taking depositions from witnesses in Houston, Baker became suspicious of Holt's trial preparations. On August 29, 1899, he wrote Rice that Holt seemed to have information he could have received only from a close Rice associate. Baker believed that information about Rice's personal correspondence had "in some way . . . leaked out from New York" and warned Rice to "be very careful and be certain that all those with whom you have dealings of a private nature are entirely faithful and loyal to you." Baker entrusted his letter to Houston investor and social arbiter Spencer Hutchins, a friend of Mr. Rice and a former Light Guard officer who was going to New York, and he warned his "Friend Hutch" to "be certain that no one is within hearing distance" while he talked with Rice. Baker could "hardly believe" Charlie Jones would be the source of the leak, but he was sufficiently concerned to ask Rice to return the letter to Hutchins "so that I will be certain it falls into the hands of no one else."[36] As events unfolded, Baker's trust in Jones's obsequious good manners proved misplaced.

In the fall of 1899 Baker and Holt spent nearly two months in New York, and Baker later recalled his interviews of crucial witnesses:

> Prior to his coming to New York Mr. Holt engaged the services of A. T. Patrick, a New York attorney, to assist in taking this testimony. While the testimony was being taken Patrick was always working to secure a settlement of the litigation. He importuned me constantly on the subject. Feeling the greatest confidence in the ultimate result of the litigation, I always refused to advise a settlement except by the payment of practically a nominal amount. Patrick asked me to pay as much as $750,000, then $500,000, gradually coming down until he finally told me the case could be settled for $250,000. I declined to consider the proposition, but told him that I would recommend the payment of $50,000, because I thought it would cost Mr. Rice this amount and more to defeat the litigation.[37]

Baker also noted that Patrick's "conduct was scandalous" and his methods of taking testimony and bullying female witnesses were "very objectionable, not to say unprofessional." Baker "was forced to employ" a man to keep track of Patrick's activities. During the whole time he was in New York, Baker never saw Rice with Patrick or Holt.

Rice and Baker "knew Patrick by reputation, a reputation established in Texas and a very unsavory one."[38] Once again, Holt had shown bad judgment when he used a weak tool to dig for evidence. The son of a "trustworthy" man who had been employed as a freight agent for the

Houston & Texas Central Railroad, Patrick was unable to establish a successful law practice in Houston. He left Texas under a cloud after accepting payment from both parties to a divorce suit and bringing nuisance charges against Judge Aleck Boarman and Captain Joseph C. Hutcheson. In 1891 Patrick petitioned Congress to impeach Republican Judge Boarman of the Western District of Louisiana, alleging he had taken "moneys paid into the registry of his court." In 1893 Patrick tried to secure the disbarment of Captain Joseph C. Hutcheson, whom he accused of violating legal ethics and conspiring to defraud the estate of Paul Bremond, one of Hutcheson's clients.[39] Hutcheson had just been elected to the US House of Representatives (served 1893–1897), was a former state legislator who had drafted the bill to create the University of Texas, and enjoyed an unblemished professional reputation and considerable personal popularity. Judge Boarman, who presided over the disbarment proceeding against Captain Hutcheson, "had been wondering whether [Patrick] was crazy or a villain and had made up his mind that he was both."[40] Boarman dismissed Patrick's complaint against Hutcheson as "wholly unfounded" and told the Harris County district attorney to find evidence for Patrick's disbarment because Boarman discovered Patrick had been paid to press unfounded charges against Hutcheson.[41] Patrick then left Texas and pursued his vendetta against Hutcheson by trying to make Congress censure a colleague. The federal lawmakers ignored Patrick's complaints against Judge Boarman and Representative Hutcheson.[42] Given the history that lay between Patrick and Captain Hutcheson, it is particularly surprising that Holt sought Patrick's services in New York.

DEATH OVERTAKES WILLIAM MARSH RICE

The seeds of a plot to relieve Rice of his millions began to grow by late August 1899 when someone provided information about Rice's private correspondence to Orren T. Holt.[43] Sometime that summer Patrick formed a friendship with Rice's valet/secretary Charlie Jones. By the fall of 1899, the two men were communicating regularly and, as was later revealed, were conspiring to profit from Jones's association with William Marsh Rice.[44] In late September 1900, the lawsuits resulting from Mrs. Rice's death and the disasters following the hurricane converged unexpectedly to trigger another tragedy—the murder of a gruff but generous old man for his money.

WILLIAM MARSH RICE, MILLIONAIRE.

This is the latest photograph Mr. Rice had taken.

William Marsh Rice at the time of his death, newspaper clipping. Early Rice Collection, Woodson Research Center, Rice University.

The September 8 hurricane and a fire at noon on September 16 destroyed one of William M. Rice's most important industrial assets, the cotton processing works of the Merchants & Planters Oil Company on Buffalo Bayou. Henry Oliver Jr., manager of the mill, described the hurricane damage to Rice, prompting the investor to reply on September 15 that he would "furnish you One Hundred and Fifty Thousand Dollars . . . now, and if you need more will see what I can do." The next day when Rice received telegrams about the fire from his manager Henry Oliver, his Houston banker T. H. House, and his attorney James A. Baker, he had already decided to use cash on hand in New York to rebuild the factory and had written Oliver to wire when he needed money, "so I shall have time to notify" the bankers.[45] Rice and Lovett discussed the situation further during Lovett's visit with Rice on Tuesday, September 18, at which time Rice appeared perfectly healthy.[46] On September 19, Rice wrote cogent instructions to Baker and to House to explain his thinking further: during the rebuilding he did not want to carry the cost of mill employees or incur further operating debt. Still planning for the future, Rice did not sound like an ailing man who was about to die.[47]

On Thursday, September 20, Jones informed Patrick that Rice had decided to rebuild the mill. On Friday, September 21, the valet intercepted a messenger bringing a $25,000 check for Rice's signature and told the man to return the following Monday, September 24, 1900, because Rice was not feeling well.[48] When Jones shared these developments with Patrick, the plotting attorney realized he and Jones must act. On Monday morning, September 24, checks worth $185,000 signed by William Marsh Rice and drawn to the order of Albert T. Patrick "were presented for certification to a trust company bank and a firm of private bankers. . . . Two of them calling for $160,000, were certified by the trust company, after which the company was notified that Mr. Rice had died the day before. . . . The firm of private bankers refused to certify a check for $25,000 . . . and, learning that Mr. Rice was dead, thought the transaction peculiar enough to call their lawyers, who notified the police."[49]

About three o'clock on the afternoon of September 24, James A. Baker received a telegram from Jones announcing that "Mr. Rice died 8 o'clock last night under care physician death certificate old age weak heart diarrahue [sic] left instruction to be interred at Milwaukee with wife. Funeral ten A.M. to-morrow at 500 Madison Ave. when will you come." Startled by the news of his client's death, Baker immediately notified Frederick A. Rice and telegraphed Jones that his message had been received. He told Jones to "place all papers and the appartment [sic] in charge of N. S. Meldrum . . . Please co-operate with Mr. Meldrum in preserving everything intact until I can reach New York I leave tonight." Baker rushed another telegram to Norman Meldrum at the Waldorf Astoria explaining the sudden turn of events and asking him to see Jones "at once" to secure all papers. Meldrum, a longtime resident of Houston who had recently become president of the Securities Companies, a financial firm located at 45 Wall Street, had known Baker and the Rice family in the 1890s during his tenure as general manager of the Houston & East Texas Railway, headquartered in Houston. He was familiar with the millionaire's business and signature.[50] Baker knew he must leave for New York immediately to oversee Rice's affairs and begin proceedings to probate the will he had written for Rice after Libbie's death in 1896.

Baker and Frederick A. Rice were preparing to catch the night train when a telegram arrived about 5:40 Monday evening from Rice's banker, S. M. Swenson & Sons: a lawyer had appeared that morning at the bank with a "draft for large amount and assignment to himself of all securities and moneys in our hands." Suspicious because the large check was made out to Abert Patrick but signed by Albert Patrick, Eric Swenson called Rice's apartment, discovered that Mr. Rice had died, consulted his lawyers Bowers & Sands, and in his telegram to Baker sought "authority from some relative about the disposition of body," which was scheduled for cremation at nine o'clock Tuesday morning. Fearing the worst, Baker and Rice acted promptly: both wired Bowers & Sands with instructions to consult Norman S. Meldrum about preserving papers and holding the body until William M. Rice's "brother and nearest relative" could reach New York Thursday morning. Another wire to Bowers & Sands stated explicitly that Patrick "did not have Mr. Rice's confidence."[51] To Judge John D. Bartine, Baker telegraphed: "I believe William M. Rice, who died last night, left a will naming you and myself executors. Telegram from Swenson indicates probable tampering with his papers. Suggest you go immediately to Rice's apartments . . . and confer with N. S. Meldrum . . . and Bowers & Sands . . . , to whom we have wired to look after preservation of papers." With no other information but considerable foreboding, Frederick A. Rice and Captain Baker boarded the Southern Pacific at 7:25 p.m. and headed east for New Orleans and north to New York City.[52]

As the train carrying the dead man's brother and lawyer sped through the night, suspicious associates of Rice and authorities in New York took action. Thirty-three-year-old James W. Gerard, a patrician lawyer with Bowers & Sands, knew something was wrong and paid a visit to his friend, District Attorney Asa Bird Gardner, who agreed with the younger man's analysis, alerted the city's Detective Bureau, and secured a warrant for the coroner to perform an autopsy. Meantime, Norman Meldrum, who had been leaving for the theater with a party of friends when the telegram from Baker arrived about 8:15 p.m., decided to check on matters after the theater and went to Rice's apartment about midnight. There he found Jones and learned that Patrick had already ordered funeral arrangements and cremation proceedings and had secured all papers "on written authority of Mr. Rice."[53] Before retiring for the evening, Meldrum telegraphed Baker, Botts, Baker & Lovett to warn that A. T. Patrick had taken charge; he promised to visit Patrick the next morning.[54] Early

Tuesday morning, detectives disguised as lawyers also called on Patrick and Jones, whom they questioned until after 2:00 a.m.

Tuesday morning when Baker and Frederick A. Rice arrived in Mobile, Alabama, they found a telegram from Robert S. Lovett relaying Meldrum's warning about Patrick's involvement. Their return wire stated their firm belief that Patrick did not have Mr. Rice's confidence, and a second wire asked Lovett or Parker to visit Harris County Judge E. H. Vasmer to explain the situation and warn him to oppose any action Patrick might try to take in County Court. In Montgomery, Alabama, another wire from Baker's office mentioned that "Patrick holds assignments to everything" but promised that nothing would happen until Baker arrived.

Meanwhile, at 10:00 a.m. a funeral service attended by some twenty mourners, including a nephew from Massachusetts and detectives disguised as guests, proceeded on schedule in Rice's New York apartment. Following the service, the detectives stepped forward to direct the corpse to the morgue for an autopsy and to ask Patrick and Jones to go with them to police headquarters. There the suspects waited until early afternoon, when Assistant District Attorney James Osborne arrived to question them about the case. At the morgue a one-hour autopsy proved inconclusive, in part because the body had been saturated with embalming fluid that Monday on Patrick's orders—to prevent deterioration in the hot weather, the wily conspirator claimed.[55] Professor Rudolph Witthaus, a distinguished chemist and professor of toxicology at the Cornell Medical School, removed organs for closer chemical analysis. The corpse was returned to Madison Avenue and later dispatched to the crematory.

On Tuesday afternoon, Meldrum sent a handwritten summary to Robert Lovett outlining his activities that day: he had learned that Mr. Rice had been ill on Sunday; that Swenson's had refused to cash a $25,000 check on Monday morning when Eric Swenson learned Rice had died Sunday night; that James Gerard had seen Patrick Monday afternoon; that cremation was planned for Tuesday but stopped by the police who were investigating the death; that Patrick had called on the New York Safe Deposit Company on Monday but was unable to examine Rice's papers without Baker's presence; and that nothing would be done until Baker arrived. Meldrum also revealed for the first time that probably "Patrick will produce another will naming himself and Baker as Executors and that all property has been delivered over to him in trust."[56]

Since long-distance telephone service was not yet commercially viable and since letters took up to four days to travel from New York City to Houston, brief telegrams served as critical communication tools for immediate information, their contents to be explained more fully in subsequent letters.[57]

On Wednesday September 26, Lovett sent a wire to the travelers in Danville, Virginia, forwarding news from New York: an autopsy would be performed, and Jones was "weakening"; he might be willing to talk. No word of a 1900 will had yet penetrated the morning press or reached Houston, but by late afternoon, Lovett had seen Galveston papers that reported the Patrick will, and he immediately wired Baker to express the "obvious" conclusion that Patrick and Jones had conspired against Rice.[58] From information telegraphed to them as they traveled north, Baker and Frederick A. Rice surmised what had happened. Although they did not know the details and could not yet foresee the path to proving Patrick's guilt, they were sure that the conniving lawyer and his willing flunky, Charlie Jones, lay behind a plot to dispatch William M. Rice and seize the old man's fortune. Baker explained a few days later that he "could not believe it possible that Mr. Rice knowingly executed . . . instruments or willingly entered into any negotiations with Patrick, looking to the settlement of his suit or the preparation of his will. When I last saw Mr. Rice he heartily detested Patrick."[59] At 6:00 a.m. on Thursday, September 27, Baker and Frederick A. Rice stepped off the train at Jersey City to board a ferry for Manhattan. Rice checked in at the Hotel Normandie, and Baker hurried to a 7:00 a.m. breakfast with James Gerard, Eric Swenson, and Norman Meldrum at the Waldorf Astoria, where he learned the latest details.[60]

Once Baker had arrived in New York, the mystery surrounding Rice's death began to unravel quickly, even as the myriad issues and a road to resolution grew more complex. After breakfast on Thursday, Baker, Meldrum, and Frederick A. Rice repaired to Rice's apartment where they talked briefly with Jones and discovered Patrick, who requested a private conversation with Baker. The two antagonists retreated to a back parlor, where Baker assumed a cordiality that masked his true feelings, but fooled Patrick; occasionally the Captain asked a leading, brief question. Emboldened by Baker's friendly demeanor, Patrick proceeded to embroider a tissue of improbable details explaining how "he and Rice got chummy." Patrick claimed Rice had lost faith in Baker's legal counsel, while insinuating, paradoxically, that Baker would benefit financially by the 1900 will Patrick had drawn at the dead man's request.[61] Patrick's inconsistent story confirmed Baker's suspicions and would eventually enable the canny lawyer to build a case against his duplicitous adversary, who, as Baker quickly realized, "threw out abundant baits for me to swallow with the hope that I would be satisfied."[62]

Following his lengthy interview with Patrick, Baker challenged Jones to explain why he had waited nineteen hours to telegraph news of Rice's death when Baker himself had told Jones only weeks before to notify Baker, Botts, Baker & Lovett immediately if anything should happen to his client and friend. Jones whined that he did not have enough time but eventually confessed he had followed Patrick's orders.[63] Later that day Baker and Meldrum accompanied Patrick to his boarding house, where the conspirator claimed to have sequestered the 1896 and 1900 wills and papers he had taken from the apartment. Baker could obtain only a copy of the 1900 will, but he pried the original 1896 will from Patrick by giving him a copy. "When that man handed me that will," Baker later told friends, "I knew I had him in Sing-Sing."[64] Patrick watched while Baker and Meldrum broke the seal on a package marked in William M. Rice's handwriting, "Valuable papers to be delivered to James A. Baker and E. Raphael in case of my death." Inside were deeds from Rice and his wife conveying property in Texas and Louisiana to the Institute. Baker proudly wired Lovett about his success and his efforts "to get possession of all property which I think I can do."[65] During their discussions, Patrick feigned cooperation, agreed that Baker should receive all Rice's papers, and pressed Baker to contest the wills in Texas. He also suggested that he and Baker could easily "settle up this whole business between themselves."[66] When Meldrum and Baker compared the 1900 will to other Rice correspondence that evening, they drew the same conclusion: it was a fraud.

The next morning, Friday, September 28, New York readers awoke to sensational news stories about the "strange developments" surrounding Rice's death, developments embellished by the garrulous but evasive Patrick who "received the newspaper men with the greatest cordiality."[67] That day Baker and Patrick made lists of the documents each man held; Patrick gave the disputed checks to Baker; and all papers were placed in the New York Safe Deposit Company vault under Baker's control. Patrick also handed Baker gold watches and a few dollars he had removed from Rice's apartment on Sunday night—although trial testimony showed Patrick had actually pocketed $400 in cash.[68]

The telegraph kept communications open between Baker and Lovett all day Friday. Baker and Frederick A. Rice asked Lovett to "apply at once to Judge E. H. Vasmer to appoint [Baker] temporary administrator with power to collect and preserve the [William M. Rice] estate, sue and defend all suits" in Texas. Lovett and Parker were working on a "considerably broader" order when a surprising telegram arrived from Patrick endorsing the appointment.[69] A further telegram announced Harris County Judge E. H. Vasmer's order appointing Baker temporary administrator of the estate in Texas and asking him to execute a bond of $50,000 and send his oath so that necessary papers could be filed. At the end of the busy day, Lovett composed a letter to Baker repeating the telegraph exchange and expressing his opinion of the case. "Every one here seems to be amazed at Mr. Patrick's performance, and I have yet found no one who did not entertain the opinion that any will or other papers in Patrick's favor were either forgeries or otherwise fraudulent." Convinced that Rice had been murdered, Lovett told his partner the statements of Patrick and Jones were not supported by "other facts, and I am glad to see that they are talking so much." Lovett concluded by mentioning a letter he had received from Rice dated the previous Sunday as being a "very strong circumstance against the claim that [Rice] had been ill for several days."[70]

Baker quickly realized he would be in New York for a long time and by September 27 was arranging Southern Pacific courtesy passes so his secretary Eula Gray and his wife Alice could join him.[71] Eula Gray left Houston on the night train October 6. In New York, as in Houston, she handled correspondence, organized boxes of evidence, and managed her boss's daily schedule. She traveled between Houston and New York several times in the next three years and also developed a "complete description" of all the property in Rice's estate, an enormous and difficult mystery in itself.[72] Alice followed with Jimmy, not quite 8, Browne, just 9 months, and a nurse on October 15, traveling via St. Louis. Daughter Alice, 13, remained in Houston at school, while Graham celebrated his seventeenth birthday at the Hill School in Pottstown, Pennsylvania, on the day his mother and brothers arrived in New York City.

HOW MR. RICE
MET HIS DEATH

The Plot to Murder William Marsh Rice, as dramatized in the New York press, newspaper clipping. Early Rice Collection, Woodson Research Center, Rice University.

THE PLOT

Forged documents, perjured witnesses, transparent lies, and glaring inconsistencies did not discourage Baker and his associates. Working with the district attorney's office and police detectives, they unraveled a plot to dispatch Rice and plunder his fortune, estimated by one Texas banker to be $10 million.[73] Sometime in the summer of 1899, Albert T. Patrick decided to insinuate himself into Rice's confidence so he could persuade the old man to rewrite his will—in Patrick's favor. Unable to gain access to Rice but obsessed by the millionaire's putative fortune, Patrick formed a darker scheme—to seize the money by fraudulent means. He found a pliant subordinate in Rice's valet and secretary Charlie Jones. Over several months beginning late in 1899, Patrick developed an elaborate stratagem, using Jones as his frontman.[74] Although Patrick never met Rice, he called on Jones several times and so was known to the elevator man and other building regulars as a friendly visitor. Patrick introduced Jones to two accomplices, David Short, a commissioner of deeds for Texas, and Morris Meyers, a notary public, who would witness documents for Rice at his home, since the older man rarely left his Madison Avenue apartment in the last months of his life.[75] By March 1898 Jones was typing all Rice's letters from his employer's handwritten drafts, and he was preparing bank drafts for his employer's signature, so it seemed perfectly natural when Jones asked the accomplices to assist him as witnesses on several occasions in 1900. Rice suspected no ulterior motives in their agreeable, efficient behavior, although trial evidence implicated them and Patrick's third co-conspirator, John R. Potts, in several shady business schemes. Short and Meyers were indicted on charges of forgery and perjury but were never brought to trial after the district attorney had nabbed his prime suspect on a murder charge.[76]

In December 1899 Patrick showed Jones a will draft that left half Rice's property to Patrick. Jones gave Patrick a copy of Rice's 1896 will, and the lawyer then adapted many of its elements in his final fraudulent document, including retention of Baker and William Marsh Rice II as executors.[77] While preparing papers for Rice to sign, Jones, from time to time, slipped in blank sheets or bank drafts for signature, a devious ploy Rice failed to notice. These signed blanks provided good samples of Rice's signature for Patrick to study and were later used to create fake correspondence between plotter and victim. Patrick also instructed Jones to mail him about twenty to twenty-five envelopes filled with blank paper but provided with Rice's return address, so the date stamps could "prove" a relationship of several months.[78] According to his confession, Jones "slipped the last page" of what he thought was the final copy of Patrick's will "under other letters" being signed by Rice and witnessed by Patrick's agents on May 26, 1900. Patrick used this page to create the so-called June 30 will and assignments, which "are all forgeries."[79] Jones saw the June 30 will lying on Patrick's desk in early September and noticed the signature "W. M. Rice" on each page. The foolhardy valet failed to question Patrick about his assurances that Rice had remembered Jones in the will.[80]

Sometime early in 1900 Patrick grew too impatient to wait for Rice, then eighty-four, to die of natural causes, and he decided to weaken the elderly man by administering poison in small doses. When Jones contracted catarrhal fever in March 1900, Patrick directed him to call Dr. Walker Curry, an amiable older physician who was unaware of Patrick's unsavory professional reputation but had been treating him for several years. Curry obligingly prescribed protoiodide of mercury as a tonic for Jones to help the young man recover. On April 16 Rice also began to consult Curry about minor digestive issues. According to Jones, Patrick urged his co-conspirator to give Rice the mercury-based tonic and other potions Patrick supplied to "soothe" these little ailments. Patrick eased Jones's conscience by suggesting that "Mr. Rice had poisoned his wife" so it "would be no sin to put him out of his way."[81] In July and August Jones's brother William Lafayette Jones shipped small quantities of chloroform and laudanum from Galveston to Charlie at Rice's New York address so a "friend could make tooth-ache medicine."[82] Patrick was considering options. In August he composed a letter requesting cremation and affixed Rice's signature to it, and he told Jones to fill out four $25,000 checks for later withdrawal from Rice's banks.[83]

The September 8, 1900, hurricane accelerated Patrick's plot. Unsure of Rice's exact fortune, Patrick did not want it spent to rebuild the Merchants & Planters Oil Company mill. When Jones intercepted the agent who, at Rice's request, was bringing a bank draft for signature, both connivers knew they had only a short time to execute their plot. At last, after months of scheming, after drawing a will that considered carefully a number of legal issues, after securing accomplices, and after convincing his landlady and fellow boarders that he was a humble, hymn-singing, helpful friend, Patrick gave the order to dispatch his unsuspecting victim. On September 23, 1900, Patrick told Jones, who had already given Rice a strong dose of medicine for his upset stomach, to smother his frail employer while he slept by placing a cloth saturated with 1½ to 1¾ ounces of chloroform over his face. Described by friends as no taller than 5 feet 4 inches, Rice weighed only 90 pounds at his death, no match for the strong, youthful Jones.[84]

Errors in execution and his own greed proved Patrick's undoing. A check presented to the teller at Swenson and Sons on Monday morning was written to Abert, not Albert, Patrick. This simple act of carelessness led directly to police intervention when Eric Swenson insisted on speaking to William Marsh Rice to verify the check but instead discovered his client was dead. Although Patrick's phony will provided generous legacies or fees to relatives, friends, even adversaries like James A. Baker, the name of Charles Jones could not be found. This self-serving omission would turn Jones against his co-conspirator, despite Patrick's glib assurances he would take care of Jones and had only omitted the young man's name to avert suspicion. Four signatures on the will "were exact copies one with another," suggesting they had been traced from one signature.[85] Patrick could not resist playing a starring role in the unfolding drama; surrounded by press eager for a story, he talked and talked, weaving a web of half-truths and lies that eventually entrapped him. Comments he made in private interviews with Norman S. Meldrum on September 25 and with Frederick A. Rice on September 29 "betrayed his knowledge of the provisions of the 1896 will" when he mentioned raising the amounts being given relatives and forgiving a debt to one of Frederick A. Rice's sons.[86] Baker immediately challenged Patrick's assertion that Rice no longer trusted Baker: why, "if Rice had lost faith in me," had he appointed Baker executor? Because "I asked Rice to do it," came the brazen reply.[87]

Finally, as soon as Baker studied the 1900 will, he noticed three obvious gaffes: First, the Patrick will promised unspecified funds to Rice's institute that, when added to donations already made, would total $250,000. Baker knew well that "donations of Mr. Rice to the Institute before his death largely exceeded $250,000" already.[88] Parker also stressed the importance of Patrick's misstep: "Anyone who knew Mr. Rice knows that he knew almost to a cent just what he had given to this institute up to June 30th, 1900; that he knew better than anyone else that his gifts . . . exceeded in value . . . $250,000."[89] Second, Patrick's will promised each member of the institute board $5,000; Baker, who had worked on the charter for Mr. Rice, knew the trustees "could not take a solitary cent for their services."[90] Third, the 1896 will listed Rice's living siblings by name; Patrick's will mentioned "brothers" and sisters, but only one brother, Frederick A. Rice, was known to be alive in 1900.[91]

The march of events seemed clear to the district attorney and to Baker, but proving the plot and securing conviction would take months of hard work and persistence because Patrick finally learned the virtue of silence and adhered to one story line; he had been at his boarding house accompanying his lady friends on the piano when the events occurred; he was innocent of all charges. Baker confided to Lovett, "The situation is very puzling [sic]. We are up against a masked battery, not knowing what Patrick has in reserve. Everything points to a conspiracy . . . and I confess I do not see how they can explain away the embarrassing situation. . . . While such are my feelings, yet I am always more or less apprehensive and will be until the end comes." Knowing Baker's propensity to see the gloomy side of legal problems, Lovett reassured him a few days later that no one could imagine Patrick had a case.[92]

WILLIAM MARSH RICE, HIS SIGNATURE AND THE APARTMENT HOUSE IN WHICH HE LIVED.

Compiling Evidence, newspaper clipping. Early Rice Collection, Woodson Research Center, Rice University.

COMPILING EVIDENCE

With Rice's papers and the suspicious checks secure in the vault of the New York Safe Deposit Company, Baker considered his legal team. Four issues were already evident: preliminary autopsy reports of suspicious lung congestion suggested Rice had not died of natural causes; there appeared to be a carefully plotted but carelessly executed conspiracy to do away with Rice and seize his money; conspirators had forged the so-called will signed in June 1900 and the checks signed in September; and several of Rice's relatives were poised to dispute both the 1896 and the 1900 wills. In New York Baker turned to James Byrne at Hornblower, Byrne, Miller & Potter, a ten-man law firm that represented Baker, Botts,

Baker & Lovett in New York and was generally considered one of the city's finest. Byrne, a graduate of Harvard Law School and, like Baker, forty-three years old, agreed to take the case and provided office space for his Houston colleague. William B. Hornblower, who was graduated in 1871 from Princeton College and in 1875 from Columbia College Law School, became famous as a bankruptcy lawyer and was unsuccessfully nominated to be justice on the United States Supreme Court. The Hornblower firm hired extra lawyers and kept everyone, "sometimes Hornblower, himself, engaged pretty much all of their time" until the case was settled. James W. Gerard and other lawyers at Bowers & Sands, as principal counsel for Swenson and Sons, were anxious to pursue the men who had tried to swindle their client; the firm maintained friendly relations with the district attorney and the New York surrogate and worked behind the scenes to resolve the issues before them.[93] The arsenal of attorneys held meetings at night and on weekends and worked closely with Baker to prepare his crucial testimony with great care. The New York lawyers agreed that "the advice and judgment of Mr. Hornblower's firm should be controlling and final." "No one," said Baker, "could have done more or better work" than his New York legal team.[94]

In his October 2 summary of events to date, Baker told Lovett, "I am well, and hopeful of success, but the situation is yet quite complicated."[95] He asked his partner to call Institute trustees together "at once" so they could pass a "resolution authorizing me to exercise my judgment and discretion in employing counsel and incurring reasonable expense necessary for the defeat of the Patrick will and the probate of the will of '96." Secretary Emanuel Raphael and Trustee James Everett McAshan quickly responded for the full board and empowered Baker "to take all such action and incur all such expenses as in your judgment may be necessary to secure the probate of the will . . . of 1896."[96] On October 16, Raphael, McAshan, Frederick A. Rice, and Will Rice II formally asked Institute President James A. Baker to take all actions necessary to protect the interests of the Institute and probate the 1896 will.[97] With the assured confidence of Institute trustees, Baker felt comfortable hiring his large legal team without negotiating specific fees. The lawyers shared an unrecorded gentleman's agreement, and all sides understood they would discuss fees at some later date when the scope of the legal battle could be better understood. As Baker explained to the Institute Board in a lengthy report on January 5, 1901, it was "practically impossible . . . to foresee the full nature, scope and character of the employment and volume of work to be performed."[98] That October Baker also asked Lovett to keep an eye on Harris County Court filings in case Patrick tried to file the 1900 will in Texas.

Lovett and Parker proved stalwart allies back in Houston, carrying on the firm's other business, managing "the matters which [Baker] had immediately in hand," and proffering sage strategic counsel to their senior partner. Lovett and Parker immediately understood that "[y]ou have a big fight on your hands and must command us all freely if we can serve you from this end of the line."[99] "The Rice case," they noted, "is the most important that we have ever had or are likely to have and it must have all the attention that its importance demands. It is involved in so many difficulties and complications," that Baker and the other lawyers will have "to devote practically all [their] time to it."[100] Lovett and Parker also realized that "the fight you are making is in the interest of Houston" and pressured the *Post* to make Houstonians understand the value an institute of higher learning would bring to the city.[101] For the next four years, when in New York, Baker wrote long letters every few days to his partners and to fellow executor and friend Will Rice II in which he summarized developments and outlined strategy. His correspondents kept him apprised of Houston news, applauded his decisions, and celebrated his triumphs. From the minute Baker secured Rice's papers, Lovett and Parker "never . . . entertained the slightest doubt . . . that the whole scheme would collapse."[102]

The early days of October 1900 were busy and productive as Baker and Assistant District Attorney James Osborne accumulated evidence to show that Patrick had either committed or planned the murder of William Marsh Rice by administering poison or by suffocating him with chloroform and that he had forged documents to seize the victim's fortune. Baker and Osborne had different goals, but each recognized that the other's success ensured his own. Osborne, a politically ambitious man already famous for prosecuting high-profile Manhattan murderers, wanted another conviction on his résumé. If Baker could prove forgery of the will or of the checks, Osborne had his motive for murder. Baker believed Patrick's actions were "a great outrage," and he was "trying with all the energy which I am able to put forth to probe the matter to the bottom."[103] Baker wanted to prove the 1900 document a fraud so the 1896 will—leaving 90 percent of Rice's estate to the Institute for the Advancement of Literature, Science, and Art—would be accepted for probate. If Osborne could prove Patrick had conspired to kill a helpless old man and plunder his estate, the forgery case gained traction. Osborne kept in close contact with Baker and Byrne, who sent him copies of the forged checks and assignments, the cremation directive, reports from private detectives, and other information essential to proving the criminal cases.[104]

In Houston, Lovett searched unsuccessfully for the combination to Rice's safe deposit box and collected letters signed by Rice, especially those sent to his trusted agent Arthur B. Cohn, who had handled Rice's Houston business for several years. Cohn received dozens of documents from Rice each year, and after close examination of letters sent in the last few months, Cohn concluded that signatures on some letters purporting to be from Rice and written on a typewriter were unlike letters written by Rice in his own hand and were "well worth a close examination." Parker warned Baker that a man plotting forgery might well commingle genuine and false documents to cloud detection.[105]

In New York, Baker and Byrne hired the nation's most respected handwriting, paper, and ink experts—every expert in the country, according to the *New York World*—to study in laborious and minute detail the checks and assignments presented to Swenson's Bank and to the Fifth Avenue Trust Company.[106] Working "under cover"—keeping as much information as possible from the press—Baker and Byrne gathered stacks of letters that described Rice's desire to found an institute or emphasized Rice's disdain for Holt, Patrick, and anyone associated with his late wife's will.[107] Several writers insisted "Mr. Rice always spoke in the kindest terms of and expressed the greatest confidence in [Baker, Botts, Baker & Lovett] and in [Baker] especially." One correspondent claimed Mrs. Rice "seemed to be very enthusiastic about . . . [the Institute] 'their pet,' trying to convey the idea that at last they . . . had realized an object upon which to bestow their care, affection and money."[108]

In both cities, Baker and his partners called on potential witnesses and deposed members of the Institute's Board, friends of the dead man, and upstanding Houstonians to support the validity of the 1896 will. They took affidavits from reporters who had interviewed Patrick, and they hired Robert A. Pinkerton of Pinkerton's Detective Agency to track suspects in New York and to hunt down an important young witness who had fled to relatives in Germany.[109] Baker maneuvered the probate process so his 1896 will and the 1900 Patrick instrument would be handled together; he surmised that by disqualifying the 1900 document, he would easily secure probate for the 1896 will. Moreover, Patrick and Jones convicted themselves by making contradictory statements; soon it was clear that "every circumstance surrounding the execution of the papers and the death of Mr. Rice condemns the proceeding in unmeasured terms."[110]

On Thursday, October 4, at 4:30 p.m., Patrick, Swenson, and Baker watched technicians drill Rice's safety deposit box open to reveal over $2 million in corporate securities. The lawyers carefully examined and recorded each security, a process that took several hours.[111] After viewing the contents of the safe and talking to the waiting press, police officers took Patrick to headquarters, where he found Jones, who had been in custody since late afternoon. The next day, the magistrate formally charged Patrick and Jones with forging several documents, including the checks, the June 1900 will, and the so-called cremation letter. Unable to make $10,000 bail each but consistently protesting their innocence, the suspects returned to their cells in the Tombs, New York City's damp, stone-walled municipal prison. Evening newspaper headlines on October 5 screamed "Baker Hints at Murder in the Rice Case," using the word "murder" for the first time. Reporters had pursued Baker relentlessly since his arrival the previous Thursday, but only on October 5 did the lawyer make his first "direct statement." "I am convinced," he announced, "that a bold attempt was made to criminally get possession of Mr. Rice's vast estate. Other disclosures are coming equally as startling as those already made." He had "evidence of the forgery" but wanted to get "every bit of Mr. Rice's property" in his hands before commenting further. He declined to speculate about the cause of Mr. Rice's death, insisting his "business here is as executor of Mr. Rice's will. . . . I am not managing the criminal aspects of this case."[112] On October 5, to Baker's great relief, William Marsh Rice II arrived in New York, and the executors and their counsel discussed how best to proceed toward probate.

On October 12 Hornblower, Byrne, Miller & Potter, attorneys for the executors, James Baker, Judge Bartine, and Will Rice II, filed the 1896 will for probate and secured a preliminary order against Patrick "to show cause why he should not be required to surrender the original [1900] will for examination."[113] Later that night the police gave copies of the so-called Patrick will to the press. All parties who would benefit if Rice left no will were notified of the filing and told they had until December 6,

1900, to enter a protest. Immediately, numerous relatives from Massachusetts and Missouri came forward to claim some part of William M. Rice's estate, although Houstonian Frederick A. Rice consistently supported Baker and the 1896 will. Baker and Byrne pressed for quick action by the probate court, agreeing with Parker that the estate was "bound to suffer unless there is some party in charge, clothed with [the] wide discretion" of an executor.[114] Developments in the criminal cases delayed probate proceedings, but Baker and Byrne were well prepared for the contest whenever the case might be called.

CRIMINAL TRIALS

Even with Patrick and Jones secluded in the Tombs, the press continued to bombard readers, repeating stories, tracking down relatives, and interviewing interested parties who might let slip new information. Each New York paper seemed to have favorite characters: the *Tribune* and *World* talked to Jones and then Patrick; the *Times* favored Dr. Curry, who had treated Rice in New York, then turned to Patrick and finally to Jones; the *World* and *Sun* pursued Dr. Curry.[115] When there was no hard news, reporters recounted the details of the Holt/Baker litigation over Mrs. Rice's will or ran essays on poison and hypnotism.[116] Columbus, Ohio, media favored particularly lurid details: The *Dispatch* on November 1 placed Jones in a SWEAT-BOX; on November 2, the *Press Post* pronounced Patrick a FIEND INCARNATE.[117]

As police detectives pursued their investigation and Assistant District Attorney Osborne deposed witnesses in early October, Jones and his lawyers Frederick B. House and Moses Grossman prepared a seventy-two-page statement relating the young man's Christian youth and his humble duties for Rice; perhaps to assert male bravado, Jones also listed his many female conquests, some of whom were then called as witnesses. Jones's description of the will signing and of Rice's last illness and natural death contained occasional details that turned out to be true and a fog of misleading fantasy, but the prisoner insisted no criminal acts had been committed.[118] On October 15 the magistrate opened a preliminary hearing on forgery charges in the Criminal Courts Building. The district attorney called witnesses for four days to illustrate why the judge should remand Patrick and Jones for trial. On October 24 the defense requested dismissal. On Saturday, October 27, the magistrate announced

District Attorney Charles W. Osborne, newspaper clipping. Early Rice Collection, Woodson Research Center, Rice University.

the defendants would be held for a grand jury hearing. More interesting, that day Professor Witthaus revealed his discovery of arsenic "in notable quantity" in the stomach and a "relatively large amount" of mercury in the intestines.[119] Although inconclusive, Witthaus believed the quantities of poison found in Rice's system could have caused his death. Doctors immediately rushed into print with differing opinions, but the judge ordered a coroner's inquest for Tuesday, October 30.

On October 29, Osborne, Baker, Byrne, Miller, and a friend Jones had used as an intermediary to Baker heard what would prove to be Charlie Jones's first written confession.[120] Fearing for his life and furious that he had been excluded from Patrick's will, Jones turned on his co-conspirator and began a series of statements and confessions that confused the public but finally enabled him to turn state's evidence and ultimately to escape trial altogether. Jones realized "his only salvation lay in his plea (for mercy) through a voluntary confession." Now "morose and thoughtful" after reading Witthaus's report of mercury and arsenic in Rice's body, Jones lost confidence in his case and revealed that Patrick had murdered Rice by placing a chloroform-saturated towel over the sleeping man's face.[121] As if these revelations were not sufficient drama for Jones, he took center stage November 1 by attempting suicide with a small knife given

James A. Baker in court, newspaper clipping. Early Rice Collection, Woodson Research Center, Rice University.

him by Patrick, who was probably hoping an induced suicide would eliminate his now unnecessary pawn. Jones was immediately committed to Bellevue Hospital's psychiatric ward under police surveillance. Baker confided to Lovett that the confession had "many statements in it and it is impossible for me to distinguish between the true and the apparent false statements. While he apparently puts the blame on Patrick, yet he fully implicates himself, not only in the forgery, but in the murder."[122] Although Jones was clearly an unreliable witness, Osborne and Baker realized they could break the case wide open with his testimony. But they also knew they would have to corroborate every one of Jones's claims with other evidence if his confession were to hold up in court.

All communication between Patrick and Jones ceased. Baker consulted with the Hornblower, Byrne team and with the district attorney and police chief about lawyers for Jones. Everyone agreed Baker should help Jones procure his own counsel, so Baker visited Jones in the hospital. He recommended the patient hire George Gordon Battle, an excellent defense attorney from South Carolina who had studied law at Columbia University and served in New York City's district attorney's office before entering private practice. Jones was released to the city's House of Detention on November 12 and began negotiating for some kind of immunity, which Baker was confident he would receive. Probably Baker defrayed Battle's legal fees as an expense needed to prove Patrick's guilt and save the Institute's trust, but the method of payment was never committed to paper because Baker did not want his name or the name of his firm associated with Jones's attorney.[123] Patrick now found persistent supporters in his sister May Patrick Milliken and her millionaire husband John T. Milliken, a drug manufacturer from St. Louis, who promised to pay his brother-in-law's legal fees for as long as it took to clear Patrick's name.[124]

Early in February 1901 Baker again talked to Jones about his role in Rice's death and about his story's many inconsistencies. On February 7, the day the probate contest was set to begin, Jones said he wanted to speak to Osborne again. Jones now told the district attorney that Rice had never met Patrick. More amazing, Jones confessed that he, not Patrick, had committed the actual act of murder, but under Patrick's strict instructions and guidance.[125] Feeling Jones was at last beginning to unveil what had actually happened and wanting to keep this sensational news for the witness stand, Osborne did not make the second confession public. When Millikin and a new team of defense lawyers tried to pay Patrick's bail and secure his release on February 26, Osborne acted quickly. The assistant district attorney rearrested Patrick for the murder of Rice by "mercury and divers other deadly poisons" on February 27, 1901.[126] The suspect was held without bail pending a preliminary hearing on the new charges.

On March 26, 1901, the preliminary hearing to ascertain whether Patrick should be remanded to the grand jury for trial on a charge of murder in the first degree opened in the crowded library of Justice William Travers Jerome. Lawyers, the accused, and witnesses for each side crowded around a wooden table to hear the well-connected justice, a "Jeffersonian-Cleveland democrat" of "unswervable" anti-Tammany views, call the first witness.[127] Robert M. Moore, a former blacksmith and rough-hewn defense attorney from upstate New York who at thirty-three had gained some notoriety in recent murder trials, represented Patrick, who was described in newspaper accounts as "a tall, stoutly built man about forty . . . , bald-headed and with a closely cropped red beard." On April 1 Mrs. Addie Francis, an attractive, well-dressed widow of unspecified age, avoided several questions for fear of self-incrimination. Although she refused to say what room she occupied in the boardinghouse she managed, she swore that Patrick had been with her all day on September 23, 1900, playing the piano and singing hymns.[128]

On April 3 and 4, Jones "created a sensation" by assuming a "Mask of Piety" during his interrogation. He stated Patrick and Rice had never met; he revealed Patrick as the mastermind behind Rice's murder; he claimed Patrick had forced the frightened valet to administer chloroform; and he confessed that both conspirators had agreed to a suicide pact.[129] Pale but not nervous, Jones spun a "thrilling and revolting story" that mixed fact and fantasy. For four hours Jones sat within three feet of the accused man who "listened like a schoolmaster hearing a recitation . . . without interest." As Jones was talking, Captain Baker entered the courtroom, having just arrived from Houston earlier that day. He was carrying "a bundle of papers and some typewritten evidence, and said he might be called as a witness."[130] In cross examination, Jones cowered before Moore, but the attorney's relentless pounding failed to shake Jones's story. On April 5 the hearing was continued until the following week. Patrick responded to Jones's revelations by retorting, behind "this prosecution are men who are seeking to deprive me of my life and liberty to gain the fortune."[131]

On April 10 Captain Baker was the first witness called, and he testified for most of the day. Described as "big of frame, gray of hair, square of jaw and sharp of eye," he talked "with a half drawl, which becomes snappy and combative when his good nature is disturbed. A scrubby iron-gray mustache partly covers a small, but very determined mouth. He dresses well, but modestly, in the fashion of the Southwest, with a low, wide white collar and string tie. He is good to look at . . . and invites confidence, but palpably he is not a proposition to be lightly regarded if physical prowess and courage is to be considered." Speaking "in a clear voice, without evidence of any embarrassment," Baker faced the judge "and seemed not to know that Patrick was in the room" as he explained his relationship to Rice, denied Patrick had ever been the dead man's legal adviser, and stated that the signatures on the will and assignments were not made by Rice.[132] He carefully recounted his conversations with Patrick, including the prisoner's rather odd statement that he did not care which will was filed for probate and could not endorse the 1900 will because he had not been present when it was signed. Always in control of his exchange with opposing counsel, Baker ignored interruptions and questions designed to annoy him. The hearing closed with testimony from Professor Witthaus about the poison in Rice's stomach and intestines. Within days, Justice Jerome sent the case to the grand jury, which met on April 22 to consider the murder charge and decide whether there was enough evidence to merit a trial by jury. The panel called several witnesses and dismissed a few motions before setting the trial of *People v. Albert T. Patrick* for January 22, 1902. When William Travers Jerome became district attorney in October 1901, he asked Osborne to continue pursuing the criminal cases against Patrick.

Baker disclaimed credit for managing the criminal trial and praised Osborne and the detectives for unraveling the "story of crime and ingratitude," but his imposing personality and quiet, measured testimony made him a pivotal witness for the prosecution in each step of the process.[133] The evidence he, Byrne, and their colleagues amassed to prove the 1900 will a fraud provided a motive for murder and a clear outline of events. Relentless reams of repetitive testimony about Rice's handwriting style, letter by letter, revealed exactly how Patrick and Jones forged the documents. Experts compared the contested signatures to Rice's authenticated signature over and over again, and examined papers for pinprick signs of tracing. George W. Wood came from Pittsburgh, Pennsylvania, to study signatures for one- and one-half hours using two plates of glass to examine examples through transmitted light, a technique thought to detect tracing.

> He produced two plates of glass, from ⅛ to ¼ of an inch in thickness. . . . He then proceeded to examine the four signatures of the will with the aid of a microscope, shifting and changing the lenses of the instrument variously. He apparently examined each letter of each signature very carefully and made notes in a book concerning the same. He also used a pair of compasses in taking the measurements of the signatures and various letters.[134]

In court, handwriting experts put on a slide show with glass-plate negatives so jury and spectators could see just how closely the forged signatures resembled each other.[135] Baker's detailed analysis of inconsistent statements made by defense witnesses and Jones's confessions further destroyed arguments made on Patrick's behalf.

THE CIVIL CASES

As Assistant District Attorney Osborne developed his criminal case, Baker and Byrne proceeded with the civil cases. When Hornblower, Byrne, Miller & Potter filed the 1896 will for probate on October 12, 1900, they pressed for quick action so executors could take control of estate assets and relieve court-appointed administrators in Texas and New York of their duties. Baker's colleagues even hoped Patrick might abandon the 1900 will as his legal troubles mounted, and some laid bets the prisoner would never file. Patrick did delay to the last possible moment and hired a new legal team, Logan, Demond & Harby, to handle his probate cases, but he finally told his lawyers to file the 1900 will for probate on November 30, 1900. Baker described the scene in a letter to Lovett that evening: as soon as Patrick's lawyers filed the 1900 document, expert Kingsley examined the signatures of Mr. Rice and unhesitatingly pronounced them tracings similar to those found on the forged checks. The examination was rather hasty, "as council for Patrick was protesting all the time." Baker concluded the protest action "is making evidence against them" by suggesting Patrick had something to hide.[136]

On December 6, Patrick's lawyers joined seventeen Rice family members to challenge the 1896 will on the "purely technical" grounds that Rice had not declared "the instrument to be his last will and testament in the presence of witnesses."[137] Since two clerks in Swenson's office had attested to Rice's signature, Baker was not worried.[138] Baker immediately petitioned Surrogate Frank T. Fitzgerald to combine the cases and decide which will was valid. On December 21, Fitzgerald agreed to Baker's request, and the trial was called for February 7, 1901. Developments in the criminal trial interfered with the probate suits, which were "granted about twenty adjournments at the urgent request" of Patrick's lawyers, who stalled to avoid trial.[139] On June 19, 1901, the probate trial was permanently postponed until a decision could be reached in the criminal proceedings. Not surprisingly, Patrick and his defense counsel did not want to risk a judgment that the 1900 will was a fraud while they were fighting a murder charge. Although disappointed that the probate contest had been sidetracked, the legal team maintained grueling schedules through 1901 as they continued to interview witnesses, amass evidence, and evaluate Rice's properties.

ANOTHER DEATH

Rice's murder and the ensuing trials brought national attention to Baker, Botts, Baker & Lovett, but they disrupted the Bakers' family life. Captain Baker's practice had demanded some travel to Washington, Chicago, New York, and Boston and regular attendance at court in Galveston or New Orleans, but the pace of work in nineteenth-century Houston was leisurely, the nature of his civil practice collegial, the corporate and financial work focused on issues that promised prosperity for himself and his city. Suddenly this lawyer and businessman was thrown into an unsavory criminal underworld. He was spending long hours at police headquarters interrogating devious, self-serving witnesses. Fending off greedy heirs who would dispute Rice's final wishes and deprive Houston of its institute for higher learning proved equally dispiriting, especially when Baker reflected that he had spent seven months in New York City from September 1900 through December 1901 and 170 days there between January 15 and July 19, 1902.[140]

Forty-three when the battle to save Rice's trust began, Baker took great comfort in family life. Alice and his two younger sons made the stressful pace of work in October and November 1900 bearable, but Alice began to miss Little Alice, who continued her schooling at home, and baby Browne "suffered from a bronchial affection" his doctor blamed on the climate. Reluctantly, Baker said good-bye to his wife and sons when they boarded a train for Houston on November 22. Four days later he wrote his friend Norman Meldrum about a trial matter and closed the short letter mournfully, "I have long since grown tired of New York and wish heartily for the day to come when I can leave for home. It was all very pleasant as long as my family was here, but the monotony now grows more irksome every day. I get along pretty well in the day time, but at night I grow lonesome."[141]

Through 1904 Baker made regular trips to and from Houston and always stayed several weeks in each city before boarding the Southern Pacific once again. He rented an office at 32 Broad Street with Hornblower, Byrne, Miller & Potter and put a nameplate on the door. There he conducted business for his partners, administered the Rice estate, prepared for the numerous court cases resulting from the will contest, and began to research educational institutions in preparation for the day when he and the Institute trustees could at last fulfill Rice's legacy. Robert Lovett frequently visited Alice and the children while the Captain was in New York City and reported their minor ailments and other domestic news to his partner.[142]

The strain of her husband's long absences and the distress she felt about his involvement in a sensational, highly publicized murder trial began to depress Alice. In January 1902 Captain Baker confided to his friend Will Rice that Alice "has not been well and is needing the benefit of a change." Leaving the children at home, Captain Baker and his wife boarded the Southern Pacific for New York on January 15 so he could testify in Patrick's first-degree murder trial, which began Monday morning, January 20, before Recorder John William Goff in the Criminal Court Building. Ironically, on the same Monday, Colonel Orren T. Holt announced he was running for mayor of Houston at the behest of Houston petitioners, who asked him to step forward, and a delegation of all labor unions in the city.[143]

Newspapers across the country carried detailed accounts of Patrick's trial, illustrated stories of Baker's lengthy testimony, and speculation that the prosecution might fail to prove its case. For nearly two days during the second week of the trial, on January 28 and 29, Baker withstood grueling interrogation with "quiet dignity."[144] Asked several times to "kindly keep your voice up," Baker explained once again his long relationship to Rice, the litigation regarding Mrs. Rice's will, and his reasons for doubting the signatures on several documents. "Mr. Rice's genuine signature, as I know it, shades the downward strokes, and was light on the upward strokes; and to my mind the signature before me is a studied cramped signature which i [sic] do not find in the full, expressive signature of Mr. Rice."[145] Defense council Robert M. Moore interrupted Baker's narrative frequently to raise objections that were usually overruled by a judge who grew exasperated during the lengthy and repetitive questioning and testily rebuked Moore's acrimonious attitude and attempts to suggest Baker influenced other witnesses. After the prosecution's recross examination, Baker stepped down but remained in the courtroom, which was crowded with witnesses from Houston ready to vouch for Baker and explain Rice's intentions regarding his estate. On February 1 Baker wrote a friend that he had finally fallen into bed for thirteen hours of sleep after several sleepless nights.[146] The Bakers had endured three weeks of exhausting, repetitive testimony and tense strategy sessions among the lawyers when a frightening telegram arrived from the Hill School, where their oldest child Graham was in his final year—their spirited son had pneumonia.

The Hill, a well-respected college preparatory school founded by Presbyterian minister Matthew Meigs in 1851, stood on a commanding hillside, "affording an extensive and beautiful prospect of the surrounding country" in Pottstown, Pennsylvania, forty miles northwest of Philadelphia.[147] In 1901 the school enrolled 228 boys from 23 states and provided a classical curriculum enriched by a full music program, extensive athletics, and military drill (until 1905).[148] Why Baker chose the Hill for his sons is not clear, but the military training and Presbyterian influence may have appealed to him. Certainly the Bakers agreed with the ideals stressed by Headmaster John Meigs, son of the founder. The younger Meigs believed the model school should provide "an atmosphere and influence" of "a home at its best," and he possessed a "passionate zest for life" similar to Captain Baker's own energetic drive. Years later Baker wrote, "I have always regarded [Hill] very highly, not only in the efficiency of its teaching, but in its discipline, and particularly the wonderful moral influence thrown about the student body," which was given "little liberty" in neighboring Pottstown.[149] Baker believed he had selected one of the nation's finest college preparatory schools for his sons, and

Graham Baker, during his last year at the Hill School, 1902. Private Collection.

his choice influenced fellow Institute Board member Cesar Lombardi and his law partner Robert S. Lovett, whose sons were graduated from the Hill in 1907 and 1914. Robert S. Lovett later donated money for the school's theatre and served on the Hill's first board of trustees.[150]

In 1902 Headmaster Meigs and his wife Marion "suffered the deepest anguish of their lives" when two boys died of pneumonia during the winter term and five more of typhoid fever just after commencement.[151] A pneumonia epidemic had struck several boarding schools that winter. Since February 7, readers of the *Houston Chronicle* had been following the story of Teddy Roosevelt Jr. The president's son was stricken with pneumonia after "running bareheaded," and Mrs. Roosevelt, "attended only by her maid" had rushed to his bedside at Groton School in Massachusetts. By February 12 the young man was coughing with double pneumonia as the illness approached its crisis point; the president canceled all engagements and joined his wife and son.[152] At the Hill, twenty-four boys fell ill. As readers across the country followed young Roosevelt's progress, John Meigs, who had lost daughters in 1890 and 1900 to similar epidemics, telegraphed terrible news to the families of George Lawrence Laflin in Chicago and Graham Baker, whose parents "chanced to be in New York."

It is impossible to imagine the Bakers' fearful train ride through the gray, wintry countryside of New Jersey and Pennsylvania before they reached their son on Sunday evening, February 9. Although Graham seemed to improve on Monday, by Wednesday morning, February 12, "his condition became so hopeless that, in order to avert from the fellows the shock of a second death [Meigs] decided to close the school for a fortnight."[153] That afternoon, his parents at his bedside, Graham slipped away. News of his illness had been printed on the *Houston Chronicle*'s front page on Tuesday, relayed to the paper by distressed relatives and law partners who had received messages from Captain Baker. On February 13, *Chronicle* readers learned "Young Teddy" had won his fight and was "now pronounced out of danger." The same paper also described the "Bright Young Houstonian" who "passed away at Pottstown, Pa." Sorrowful telegrams "from day to day" had described the last illness of "the idolized treasure of a happy household" who was "just entering upon the rich heritage of young manhood."[154]

As reporters wired the happy news that "Little Teddy" was "Doing Well" across the country, Captain and Mrs. Baker began the sad railroad journey home with the body of their first-born child. Reverend William Hayne Leavell of the First Presbyterian Church conducted the funeral service in Graham's home, 1416 Main Street, at 10:00 a.m. on February 17. A choir from the church "rendered some beautiful music, notably 'Nearer, My God, to Thee.'" Eight schoolmates carried the coffin from the house, and "an unusual number of friends and acquaintances" followed the funeral procession to Glenwood cemetery, where floral tributes covered Graham's grave.[155] Frank Graham Baker was eighteen years, four months old and had been scheduled to enter Princeton College in the fall of 1902. A plaque at his school commemorates Graham's years at the Hill, September 1899–February 12, 1902, and his classmates "most affectionately dedicated" the *Dial*, their yearbook, to his memory.[156]

Graham's parents were heartbroken. Captain Baker knew he was needed in New York, even though James Byrne assured him on February 21 that the Patrick trial "has gone on wonderfully well" and "there is no reason why you should be worried about the case."[157] Writing the same day to Byrne, Baker explained the situation at home: "There are reasons outside of business why I should prefer to remain here as long as possible. Mrs. Baker, while not confined to her bed, is far from well, and I want to be with her as long as I can. She, however, realizes that it may be necessary for me to return to New York, and in that event she will be perfectly willing for me to do so."[158] Expressing confidence in the prosecution, Byrne advised, "You ought to be back before the people close their case" about the middle of March.[159] On March 19 Captain and Mrs. Baker, with Alice, Jimmy, and Browne, returned to New York. The tragic death of their promising oldest son was "life changing," according to one grandson; another believes that his grandfather's quest to save the Rice trust and build a great institute in Houston became not just a duty to his deceased client, but a mission to assuage the loss of his child.[160] Mrs. Baker never fully overcame the loss, but as time passed she not only gave birth to two more children, Ruth Graham (1904) and Malcolm Graham (1906), but also introduced Houston to the settlement house movement and devoted her life outside the home to social service and church projects in the community.

THE VERDICT

On Friday, March 21, 1902, the eight-week murder trial of Albert T. Patrick came to a close at 11:15 a.m. The defense rested its case without calling Patrick to testify. Captain Baker, who believed an innocent man would face his jurors openly, thought this omission confirmed Patrick's guilt.[161] The Baker family arrived in New York on Saturday, and on Monday morning Captain Baker and the prosecution team entered a crowded courtroom eager to hear summary statements. Sitting just behind the lawyers' enclosure, Baker impassively tapped a silver-headed cane as he listened to Robert Moore close the case for the defense.[162] After reminding the jury that "a human life is in your keeping," Moore proceeded, step by step, through the evidence. At every turn, Moore accused Baker of plotting with a "coterie of people in Houston, Texas" to seize control of Rice's money. To exculpate his client, Moore claimed that Baker "isn't an entirely disinterested gentleman," and he insinuated that "little things were said by Captain Baker here that would tend to give a different color and to convey a different meaning from what he intended." Moore called the Institute "this thing of air," and, warming to his theme, he asserted that Baker, "recreant and cowardly as he was," would do anything to get the Rice fortune "into his possession." Moore accused Baker of holding "private and secret confabs" with Jones, of bribing witnesses, and of using Jones as a "pliant and willing tool" to build a murder case against Patrick. Although Moore never named the "Texas contingent," he asserted its members had "private arrangements with Baker" to "get more under the 1896 will" than under Patrick's 1900 instrument. After defaming Baker for almost two hours without offering any proof for his accusations, Moore then tried to unsettle the minds of the jurors by alleging "in all candor and in all fairness, that the prosecution have not proven, beyond a reasonable doubt, that old man Rice met his death by criminal means." Press reaction ranged from shock to glee, as might be expected, but several reporters noted that Baker, still mourning the death of his son, remained unmoved by Moore's diatribe.

James W. Osborne sprang to Baker's defense the next morning when court resumed on Tuesday, March 25, at 11:00 a.m.[163] Pacing before the jury, his clever, spirited rebuttal of Moore's closing remarks captured the attention of all attendees for nearly six hours. The prosecutor congratulated the jury because the trial was nearly over, and then he attacked his opponent. "I heard yesterday an assault made on the character of a man here in open Court that I do not think is possible in any jurisdiction or in any courts, except in the courts of New York," he declared. "If any of you gentlemen can find in this record one solitary thing against Baker, I want it known now." Expressing evident horror, Osborne exclaimed, "I have never in my life had my intelligence so insulted, and neither has any jury ever been treated with the contempt that Mr. Moore treated you gentlemen; because not one solitary sentence is there in that record against the character or conduct of Baker." After vehemently defending Captain Baker, Osborne dismissed Moore's arguments: "I think Mr. Moore did the best he possibly could do for a desperate case . . . and like other people in desperate situations, the only thing that suggested itself to him was abuse."

Next Osborne turned to the evidence. Moore had told the jury that Jones's testimony was worthless unless corroborated by others because Jones was a confessed conspirator and murderer. Osborne immediately agreed "to disregard the testimony of Jones. . . . Out the door goes

Jones! . . . I base this [summary] entirely upon evidence outside of Jones." Osborne then reviewed the evidence pertaining to Rice's character—a man who "had but one design, and that was to build an institution for the benefit of mankind." He recalled the many unbiased witnesses who had seen Jones "going time and time again to Patrick's office." Most damning, he used testimony from the defense's own witnesses to condemn the accused and verify the plot. Osborne cast doubt on the reliability of critical witnesses, reminding the jury that Dr. Curry was a gullible old man, who "was the family physician of Patrick," and noting that Mrs. Addie F. Francis, Patrick's landlady, was "the woman who slept in the front parlor while Patrick slept in the back with the folding doors between them." He hammered on the many inconsistencies as so many nails in the coffin of Patrick's flawed will and chastised the defendant for choosing feckless accomplices.

Truth, he told the jury, "is a wonderful thing, and truth is a thing you dare not trifle with." A criminal cannot have universal knowledge; he will be caught by his own ignorance. Like all criminals, Patrick "is caught in his own back alley" plan for escape—the cremation letter, which "convinces every honest man that he is guilty of the crime of murder." Patrick's own actions after the murder, Osborne stated, incriminated and condemned him: taking Rice's papers, sending misleading telegrams to the family, embroiling others in his plot, trying to cash checks. But it was the forged cremation letter that led "irrevocably" to Patrick's arrest; if Rice had died a natural death, Patrick would not have used the letter in a failed attempt to destroy evidence of murder. In short, Osborne told the jury, "You may go all around this case, and you find absolutely that every line of force points in the one direction and to a given centre, and that direction is towards this defendant, and that centre is this defendant, Albert T. Patrick." Baker "had nothing to do with [Patrick's plot] at all," Osborne insisted in closing.

On March 26, 1902, Recorder John Goff began his charge to the jury at 11:00 a.m.[164] He complimented the jury for listening to the "testimony of witnesses and to all the other tedious matters" connected with a long trial, noting "your attention has never flagged and you have never ceased to manifest your sense of the great responsibility which rested upon you." As mandated by law, the judge reminded the twelve men that "the burden of proving [the defendant's guilt] rests upon the prosecution," that the jury "are exclusive judges of all questions of fact," and that in first degree murder cases, "there must be a deliberate and premeditated design to kill." Judge Goff told the jurors that the "basic question to determine and the one upon which the whole case rests is, Did the application of chloroform to the face of Mr. Rice cause his death?" Goff also reviewed the facts of the case, briefly, and defined several terms. He agreed to additional charges provided by the defense and at 1:50 p.m. closed discussion. The jury retired to eat lunch and consider the case.

At 5:58 p.m. on March 26, 1902, the jury reentered the courtroom. Patrick was brought back from the Tombs, and Moore returned to the defense table. With all parties present, the foreman announced the jury's verdict: guilty of murder in the first degree. Patrick, his supporters, and his counsel were shocked and surprised; they immediately took their case to the press. Baker, reserved as always, celebrated with his team at Byrne's home but made no public statement. Patrick's lawyers requested time to demand a new trial, and the judge set sentencing for April 7. On Sunday, March 30, Patrick, now thirty-six, and Addie Francis, his forty-three-year-old landlady, signed a marriage contract in the Tombs in the presence of his father, sister, and youngest daughter.[165] On Monday morning, April 7, the judge sentenced the groom and convicted murderer to death; that afternoon Patrick left for Sing Sing Prison in Ossining, New York.

Patrick's bride never doubted her husband's innocence. Working with the Millikins and an expanded legal team, she began a ten-year battle to appeal the verdict and secure Patrick's release. Although the courts rejected every appeal, on December 20, 1906, Governor Frank Higgins commuted the death sentence to life in prison; on November 27, Thanksgiving Eve 1912, Governor John A. Dix granted Patrick full pardon. Many believed the Millikins had used their millions effectively to secure Patrick's release; Captain Baker suggested Governor Dix pardoned Patrick because he had been convicted "in great measure by the testimony of an accomplice who went free."[166] In June 1902 Charlie Jones left the Tombs. He returned to Texas and disappeared from public scrutiny. A year later, neither Osborne nor Baker knew exactly where he had gone.

Telegrams and letters of congratulation streamed into Baker's office after the March 1902 verdict. His brother-in-law, Walter P. Stewart, sent "heartfelt congratulations for the hard fight and great victory that you, together with your able counsel, have won over that rascal Patrick in his malicious endeavors to secure control of the princely estate of Mr.

Rice, after so foully having murdered the poor old man. . . . the verdict was even better than I had cause to hope for after so much conflicting testimony."[167] Edward Andrew Peden, while not wanting to "rejoice in anyone's misfortune," spoke for Baker's Houston friends: "The verdict rendered by the Jury in the Patrick Case yesterday is considered just and proper by everyone in Houston, who . . . extend to you our heartiest congratulations upon your complete victory, for the Jury in convicting Patrick, clearly acknowledged their belief that the 1900 will was a forgery."

Baker, himself, was "gratified at the verdict" and confided to Lovett, "The defense, so far as its merits are concerned, was a disappointment to every one who heard it. Not a single man was put on the stand to testify that the signatures to the disputed checks, assignments or will were genuine signatures of Mr. Rice." He told his partner that "Moore's concluding argument is conceded by all to have been a great disappointment; at least one-half of it, or one-third, was devoted to a criticism of me, without any evidence to justify such criticism." Apparently, two jurors had told Assistant District Attorney Garvan that "Moore's speech in this respect had operated very much against the defense and emphasized the weakness of the defense. Osborne's summing up was an able effort, and absolutely convincing and unanswerable. . . . The manner of the Recorder indicates that he was satisfied of Patrick's guilt."[168]

With the villainous Patrick behind bars, Baker turned his focus to the will cases and pushed them forward "without any more delay than is necessary."[169] Eight years would pass before Baker could declare the case closed. As he fought to settle all claims and pay all legitimate heirs, he also turned his attention to the great task that lay ahead—to preserve Rice's trust and build his Institute for the Advancement of Literature, Science, and Art. If the Patrick case receded in importance, its implications were never far from Captain Baker's mind. Years after the trial, correspondents still inquired about the case, although in 1915 Baker told one writer he had heard nothing from Patrick in a long time. After Patrick was released, Mrs. Baker experienced nervous worries that he or Jones would seek revenge, and she often fretted about keeping the doors of their house in Houston locked.

Jones stayed in Texas for a few years but disappeared after 1905. He surfaced in Missouri in the 1920s and returned to the Baytown area in the 1930s. In 1954 he shot himself, leaving a small estate of $9,000. Patrick continued to fulminate and even wrote his attorney in December 1912 about beginning legal proceedings "to vindicate myself as to all of my relations with William Marsh Rice," but he never reopened his dubious case.[170] Millikin helped him find work in Oklahoma, where he dabbled in the oil business and was part owner of an auto supply company. The state bar in Oklahoma denied him admission, and in November 1930 he was barred from practicing in federal courts. Patrick married a third time and died in 1940; his last known employer was an Oklahoma Oldsmobile dealership. Although he escaped death and achieved a political pardon, Patrick never transcended the notoriety of his sordid plot to murder a feeble old man and defraud his estate.

CHAPTER FOUR

Fulfilling the Trust

CRIMINAL PROCEEDINGS AGAINST Albert T. Patrick and his accomplices made eye-catching headlines, but Captain James A. Baker focused on the tangle of civil cases filed by claimants hungry for the easy money a rich man's estate promised. In his fight to fulfill William Marsh Rice's last will and testament of September 1896, Captain Baker overcame opponents who contested the wills, appealed the rulings, sued to prevent payouts, and generally caused trouble for a responsible lawyer trying to salvage every penny of his dead client's estate. On April 16, 1902, only days after the gates of Sing Sing prison clanged shut behind Albert Patrick, Frank T. Fitzgerald, surrogate for the County of New York, reopened probate hearings in the Rice will case. Eighteen months had passed since Captain Baker had filed Rice's 1896 will with Fitzgerald's

Illustration: Board of Trustees, Rice Institute, 1911. (*Seated, left to right*: James Everett McAshan, vice chairman; Cesar Maurice Lombardi; Captain James Addison Baker, chairman; *Standing, left to right*: Benjamin Botts Rice, treasurer; President Edgar Odell Lovett; Emanuel Raphael, secretary; William Marsh Rice II). Early Rice Collection, Woodson Research Center, Rice University.

court, and during that time, the fate of Rice's fortune awaited the verdict of his murderer.

ESTATE ADMINISTRATION

Administration of Rice's extensive investments proved the most pressing problem in September 1900. In Houston, Baker's law partners acted promptly to have him named temporary administrator in Texas, effective October 2, 1900, with authority to conduct business and take legal action concerning Rice's property in that state until the 1896 will could be probated or a permanent administrator could be appointed. A broad range of issues demanded immediate attention: debt collection, reconstruction of the Merchants & Planters Oil Company mill, settling the Holt claims against the estate in Texas, managing 5,000 head of cattle and large stretches of rural land, and elevator installation at the Capitol Hotel (renamed the Rice Hotel on October 16, 1900). The complexity of the criminal and civil trials in New York and Baker's prolonged absences from Houston made the job of daily oversight in Houston difficult.[1] After persuasive jawboning by Hornblower and Byrne, Baker reluctantly agreed to cede his duties as temporary administrator. For the "onerous" services he and his law partners had rendered during his six-month term, Baker, Botts, Baker & Lovett received $10,250, a substantial sum.[2] On March 27, 1901, Baker submitted a final report of his administration and conveyed Texas assets to Frederick A. Rice, newly appointed permanent administrator in Texas.

Eleven days later on Friday, April 6, Frederick A. Rice was talking and laughing with friends on the train from Galveston to Houston when suddenly his head fell back against the seat; traveling companions pronounced him dead moments later. Within a week, H. Baldwin Rice had agreed to take his father's place as administrator of William M. Rice's property in Texas. Frederick A. Rice's children reassured Baker and Lovett they would "place themselves entirely in your hands" regarding all legal matters.[3] Relatives in Springfield, Massachusetts, appealed this appointment, but all complaints were dismissed, and on December 12, 1901, H. Baldwin Rice qualified as Permanent Administrator of William M. Rice's estate in Texas.[4] During his administration (December 12, 1901 to April 4, 1905), Baldwin Rice worked out a settlement with the heirs listed in Mrs. Rice's will and liquidated much of his uncle's far-flung rural property by selling sixty parcels of land in twenty-eight counties, Waco, and Houston for $244,199.56. As the agent for these transactions he earned a comfortable income.[5]

Meanwhile in New York, when it became clear that criminal proceedings and the existence of Patrick's spurious 1900 will would make quick probate proceedings impossible, talk turned to naming a temporary administrator there as well. Baker suggested himself as the best candidate to handle Rice's assets because of his familiarity with Rice's property and because he was named as an executor in both contested wills. Mark Potter discouraged his partners at Hornblower, Byrne, Miller & Potter from urging Baker's appointment because he feared New York politicians and Patrick's lawyers would oppose it.[6] Estate administration was lucrative and a prime reward for political loyalists. Rice estate administrators earned up to 5 percent for receiving or disbursing funds, and since Rice's complex business affairs included many transactions, the administrator stood to reap a tidy income.[7] Surrogate Fitzgerald awarded Tammany politician John P. O'Brien the post of temporary administrator for Rice's assets in New York on January 31, 1901.

Baker monitored the Texas and New York administrators and mediated differences between them, while Hornblower's firm took charge of all litigation arising from Patrick's claims to the estate in New York. The Texan found dealing with O'Brien a test of his patience and diplomatic skill because, Baker explained, O'Brien, "in common with the natives of this country [New York], desires all he can get," and his demands for information and access to all New York assets, while anticipated by Baker's legal team, were tinged with hostility.[8] Three issues proved particularly tricky: rebuilding the Merchants & Planters Oil Company mill, selling estate securities, and jurisdiction over debt collection and interest payments. Baker asked trustees of the Institute, now the largest shareholder of Merchants & Planters Oil Company, to support a loan from New York assets to cover rebuilding costs, and O'Brien agreed to lend money to the mill managers to fulfill promises made by William M. Rice just before his unexpected death.[9] Baker and Baldwin Rice suspected O'Brien's attempt to sell securities found in Rice's New York safe deposit box was a wasteful scheme to collect fees. When the Surrogate denied the administrator's efforts to trade estate funds, he essentially sided with Baker and the family against O'Brien.[10] Baker negotiated jurisdiction issues over the collection of debts and payment of dividend interest on a case-by-case basis, citing two central arguments: first, "promissory notes shall be assets in the hands of the administrator where they are found," and second, "stock in a corporation is [an asset] where the corporation is, not where the certificates of stock are."[11] Baker retained ultimate control over Rice's estate because he selected the banks that transacted all estate business and held the reins of Rice Institute, the primary beneficiary under the 1896 testament.

HOLT V. RICE CONCLUDED

The battle over Mrs. Rice's will also demanded immediate attention in the fall of 1900. Rice died a few weeks before trial was set to begin, and Orren T. Holt immediately requested a continuance of court proceedings in Galveston. He assured Robert S. Lovett on October 14, 1900, that he was "wholly ignorant of any negotiations between Patrick and Rice" and "he didn't believe Rice ever had anything to do with Patrick."[12] Baker knew Rice's nephews were eager to end the legal squabble, and by November 9, 1900, Holt was also anxious to settle. Captain Joseph C. Hutcheson, who had been handling litigation for Holt, anticipated a long contest over Mr. Rice's will and told Lovett that he and Holt did not want settlement of the Elizabeth B. Rice estate delayed by probate proceedings relating to William M. Rice's will. Hutcheson suggested the two sides work toward settlement immediately. Baker thought "Hutcheson's position . . . entirely reasonable," and Parker confided to his partner, "Holt is getting restless and impatient and is anxious to be doing something, although Captain Hutcheson intimated that Holt is not sure just what he ought to do."[13] It is not surprising Holt was unsure what action to take; the implication that he might be complicit in forgery and murder through his association with Patrick horrified the attorney.[14]

In early November 1900, Baker, Lovett, and Parker discussed "considerations of conscience" that Baker faced in the complex will controversies. Of primary concern was whether Baker could use estate funds to settle with claimants not named by Rice himself. As executor of William M. Rice's estate, Baker was duty-bound to carry out Rice's "cherished plans" to "do for him what he would have done under like circumstances" by probating the will of 1896 and obeying its terms. As president of the Institute, a trust and principle legatee of Rice's 1896 will, Baker was also bound to adhere to Rice's wishes to disburse the estate only to individuals and in amounts specifically approved by Rice. Yet the will was challenged by numerous claims against it, and the success of its probate was threatened by Patrick's spurious will. Lovett believed Rice's "will is either valid or it isn't . . . if it is valid [the heirs] are only entitled to what he gave them," and as executor Baker "ought to carry out to the last resort the intentions of the testator."[15] Parker, on the other hand, took a more pragmatic approach, suggesting "if the will itself is threatened, it must be protected and defended," even if the executors must "use a portion of the residuary estate for that purpose."[16] Baker responded to evolving events by incorporating the advice of both partners: while he tried "to carry out to the last resort" the wishes of his deceased client, he recognized that the expenses of extended litigation required compromise with the more than one hundred claimants to Rice's fortune under the Holt, Patrick, and Baker instruments. Baker adapted Parker's eloquent argument that even obstinate William M. Rice, rather than see his "cherished plans shattered," would have made "some comparatively trivial voluntary concessions" to preserve his primary goal.[17]

During the next few months, Baker and the Rice brothers continued discussions with their friend Captain Hutcheson, who essentially mediated the dispute between Holt and his adversaries. On May 15, 1901, Hutcheson wrote Holt a long, cogent letter outlining reasons why he believed their side would ultimately fail in court and should instead compromise. Adopting Baker's long-held arguments, Hutcheson told Holt that their side would lose the suit relating to claims on lands in Texas because there was no evidence the Rices lived in Texas at the time of purchase. Likewise, Hutcheson felt there was little hope that Holt's claim to half of $500,000 in community property rents and income Holt believed had been collected by Rice during his marriage would succeed. Everyone knew, Hutcheson asserted, that Rice considered New York his domicile after his marriage and never discussed his income with anyone during his lifetime. Hutcheson urged Holt to settle for $200,000, inclusive of legal fees; he also reminded his colleague that Hutcheson, Campbell & Hutcheson had not been paid, although he personally had litigated all the suits pending against the Rice estate. Hutcheson concluded by demanding $10,000 for past services and announcing that he would not continue to litigate unless another $10,000 were guaranteed.[18] In the face of Hutcheson's discouraging analysis and his ultimatum about pay, Holt had little reason to reject settlement terms.

Released from William M. Rice's implacable refusal to compromise, Baker and Rice's nephews decided to resolve one set of problems. By December 2, 1901, all parties had "practically agreed" on settlement terms "very favorable to the estate." On December 11, while in Houston, Baker presented settlement plans to the Institute Board for ratification. Just before leaving Houston for New York to testify at Patrick's criminal trial in late January 1902, Baker summarized progress to date for Hutcheson. He explained that Robert Lovett and the firm's chief clerk John H. Mc-Clung had Baker's proposed draft agreement, based on earlier discussions between Baker and Hutcheson; pending acquiescence from the Hutcheson-Holt team, his colleagues would complete the document and distribute it to the heirs. By January 20, 1902, almost all the heirs and legatees under Mrs. Rice's will had accepted the terms; three notices of settlement had been returned as undeliverable, and six legatees had not been heard from.[19]

Harris County Judge E. H. Vasmer approved the final settlement of Mrs. Rice's will on April 2, 1902, after Baldwin Rice testified that the agreement was in the best interests of the estate. Holt accepted $200,000, of which $53,000 would be paid to him as executor and to the other lawyers involved in his suit; $147,000 would be distributed to Mrs. Rice's heirs in amounts proportional to the gifts stipulated in her June 1896 testament. In addition, Holt agreed to accept and support the will written by Captain Baker for William M. Rice in September 1896. By September 11, 1902, all but fifteen heirs had been paid and had signed releases saying they accepted the settlement and would make no claim on William M. Rice's estate. Most of the remaining legatees were planning to execute releases but had encountered legal hurdles. Only niece Adele Baldwin and six other women refused to cooperate.[20] When the settlement was upheld in Texas, these disaffected claimants brought several suits against the administrators and executors of Mr. Rice's estate in New York. At issue once again was Mrs. Rice's putative right to a community interest in her husband's fortune. Adele Baldwin's lawyers now claimed an agreement made in Texas was not binding on New York assets and demanded $200,000 ($50,000 to each disaffected party). Hornblower, Byrne, Miller & Potter immediately prepared to defend against Adele Baldwin's demands.

Captain Baker asked Lovett "not to say anything to Hutcheson or Holt or anyone else except [Administrator] Baldwin Rice, about the

Adele Baldwin suit, and in the meantime have Baldwin Rice settle with as many of the heirs as possible before they have knowledge of the filing" by Adele Baldwin's attorneys. Baker's stratagem of silence was successful because no one else raised objections. Litigation of the Adele Baldwin suits dragged on for years as Hornblower et al. allowed the matter to languish while amassing opinion from lawyers in Texas and New York that the claimants had no title to William M. Rice's assets in New York. Adele Baldwin died on March 5, 1907, and her niece and executrix Mary E. Turnure and five remaining legatees under Mrs. Rice's will finally agreed on May 8, 1907, to settle their claims on the estate of William M. Rice and his Institute for $40,000, essentially their share of the original agreement. The final legatee, the Drawing Room Society of New York, waived its rights to any claims against Rice's estate and consented to the original settlement decree on September 13, 1907, eleven years after Holt first attempted to gain $2 million for the long list of hopeful heirs in Mrs. Rice's June 1896 final testament. Baker's legal acumen and unshakeable persistence had cost the estate and Rice's beloved institute a mere 10 percent of Holt's original demand.[21]

THE HEIRS OF WILLIAM MARSH RICE

Disgruntled relatives of William Marsh Rice, who hoped to benefit from the will controversy, proved most dangerous to the Institute's interests. The will Baker prepared for Rice in September 1896 mentioned four beneficiaries: his brother Frederick Allyn Rice of Texas, his sisters Minerva Olds and Charlotte McKee of Massachusetts, and the Institute for the Advancement of Literature, Science, and Art in Houston. The small bequests to his siblings would eventually benefit their offspring. After the executors paid debts, bequests, and fees, the Institute would receive 90 percent of its benefactor's wealth. Patrick's document of June 1900 named a longer list of individual beneficiaries and provided more generous funds to them all. The Institute stood to gain no more than $250,000, and Patrick received most of the estate. In February 1901 Frederick A. Rice confided to Lovett that "dozens of people," including some of his children, advised him to challenge the 1896 will, but he "knew his brother's wishes and had no right to the estate, and intended to make every effort in his power" to carry out the 1896 will. "Jim [Baker] certainly knows how I stand about this matter, and I am the only Texas heir, since . . . my children could not inherit except through me." He reassured Baker, Lovett, and Parker on several occasions that he and his children fully supported the intent of the 1896 will.[22]

Massachusetts heirs were not so sure they wanted to endorse Baker's 1896 will, and Frank H. McKee traveled to New York to discuss their options at length with Baker and Byrne. Baker surmised to his fellow executor, Will Rice, that Rice's family in Massachusetts, "while repudiating Patrick and his methods, [were] anxious to receive under the will of 1896 as much as they are given under the Patrick will" and were being "importuned by lawyers to contest the will of 1896 and otherwise give trouble."[23] Baker tried to enlist McKee's support: he explained that in New York heirs had one year to protest a will after it had been probated, and he urged the Massachusetts relatives "to take up the matter again with the William M. Rice Institute" after probate proceedings had eliminated the 1900 will from consideration.[24] Frederick A. Rice traveled several times to Massachusetts to counsel his sisters and their children to stand by the 1896 will. He and Baker described the evidence of forgery and fraud being collected to disprove Patrick's document, and by November 1900, most Massachusetts heirs sided with their Houston relatives. They agreed to "assist in defeating the Patrick conspiracy as far as [they] could" and to seek satisfaction from the executors after the court granted letters testamentary.[25] By January 30, 1901, only Joseph Blinn and Charles W. Rice refused to conform and hired lawyers to challenge the 1896 will.[26]

Just when it seemed Baker had convinced the Rice family to cooperate—or at least to postpone their protests until after the 1896 will was secure—a new claimant announced himself. On November 28, 1900, Benjamin Franklin Rice wrote on behalf of his family from Radical, Missouri, where he had learned of Rice's murder through newspaper stories. Benjamin F. Rice's father, David Rice, one of William M. Rice's brothers, had left Massachusetts in the 1840s and settled in Missouri after the Civil War.[27] Naturally the Massachusetts and Texas heirs, who had not heard from these relations in decades, were suspicious, and Frederick A. Rice began making plans to travel to rural Missouri in January 1901 to meet these unknown family members at a railroad siding near Radical. Fortunately for the older man, Baker hired a young lawyer, Norman Gibbs, to search for the lost heirs. Gibbs carried documents for Benjamin F. Rice and his relations to sign, which stated they agreed not to contest the 1896 will or to claim property already deeded to the Institute. Gibbs's recitation of his adventures during the Christmas season lays bare the rigors of doing business in 1901. "Our heirs," Gibbs wrote, "lived from 55 to 65 miles over the mountains from the R. R. Station and it would take more than . . . 4 weeks" to find them. "There are no bridges . . . and there are 2 rivers to be crossed and when below zero, these rivers are dangerous to cross and sometimes impassable." Gibbs was writing "in the midst of a blizzard with the thermometers below zero" and would send the required papers as soon as a messenger returned with them from "a peculiar section of this great country."[28]

After Frederick A. Rice died in April 1901, his children ignored their father's vigorous defense of his brother's wishes as written in 1896 and explored their rights to contest the will. In October and November 1901, Jonas Shearn Rice (Joe) and Will Rice II visited Baker in New York and told him they were "anxious to settle the Rice litigation." They proposed payouts totaling $1,333,333.00, a sum that shocked Baker, who did not think a compromise "upon these terms is to be considered for a moment . . . it would be better for the Trustees to fight out the litigation to the end and lose the whole estate." Bowers and Byrne agreed "that a settlement at a million dollars would be inadvisable."[29] As time passed and legal troubles mounted, Baker, Bowers, and Byrne realized some compromise with the Houston heirs was unavoidable. With approval from the Institute Board, the legal team offered the children of Frederick A. Rice $75,000 as their share of the settlement and another $200,000, plus $20,306.50 interest for services they and their father had rendered to the estate during the long litigation period, if they would support the 1896 will.[30]

In 1901 Baker spent as much time negotiating with lawyers who represented disputatious claimants as he did arming for battle against Patrick's pernicious schemes. Baker needed support from the heirs in his probate contest, and he wanted their help to prove the purpose of William M. Rice's institute. Patrick and those who supported the 1900 will tried to show that the Institute was a "paper" corporation with no mission or assets. Rice and his wife deeded significant properties in Texas and Louisiana to the Institute during their lifetimes, the transfers to take effect after Mr. Rice's death. To safeguard these assets and the real property listed in Rice's last testament and to underline the Institute's corporeal reality, Hornblower, Byrne, Miller & Potter drafted certificates to be signed by all heirs and next of kin conveying to Rice Institute any interest they might have claimed in any property previously owned by William M. Rice. Because Rice had owned property in Texas, Louisiana, and New Jersey and because heirs resided in Texas, New York, Massachusetts, and Missouri, Hornblower and Baker scrutinized statutes to make the certificates conform as much as possible to the laws of six states.

PROBATE COURT

When Surrogate Court resumed in April 1902, Baker and James Byrne grumbled at the sluggish pace. Baker was particularly anxious to proceed; Alice Baker, still grieving over the death of her son, had developed a nagging cough that would not abate, and the children wanted to go home. Patrick's new legal team under the aggressive leadership of prominent litigator John C. Tomlinson stalled on every point but failed to sustain the validity of Patrick's document. Baker, Byrne, and their witnesses repeated the story of Rice's murder and the plot to secure his fortune by forged documents in monotonous detail. Finally, on June 19, 1902, Surrogate Fitzgerald accepted the 1896 will and dismissed Patrick's claims under the 1900 instrument, which the judge declared a blatant forgery. On June 27 Fitzgerald signed the decree formally admitting the 1896 will to probate in New York State, and the executors applied for possession of Rice's property in the state. Captain Baker expressed his relief to a friend: "I have had a long, tedious and irritating litigation in a cold and callous community where I was a stranger to everyone and everyone a stranger to me, and in looking back to the work of the last few months I must confess that I am particularly gratified that so far I and my counsel have been successful at every point."[31]

His patience "almost exhausted" by the lengthy litigation, the weary but victorious lawyer boarded a train for the journey home to Houston on Saturday, July 19, 1902. Two days later, while still en route, Baker sent a confidential, handwritten letter to Lovett suggesting the executors also consider settling with Patrick to avoid the inevitable delays of appeal and threats to the Institute should Patrick be able to overturn his murder conviction. Discouraged by the lengthy process, Baker saw "nothing in the past history of this litigation to justify the belief that Patrick, or those representing him, will be discouraged by successive defeats from bringing new suits."[32] He was right: year after year, Addie Francis Patrick, backed by "money without stint," sought a full pardon for her husband.

As late as 1910, Patrick still claimed he could "show that he was rail-roaded" and "would sue to recover the [Rice] estate."[33] But Baker's suggestion on that hot July train ride home met strong opposition. Lovett and Parker telegraphed back a vehement "no" to compromise of any kind and counseled patience, as complete victory over Patrick and vindication for their side were now inevitable. Will Rice wrote Baker on July 21, "I cannot consent to entertain any proposition from Patrick." On July 23, Judge Bartine exclaimed, "Under no circumstances will I ever consent that a single dollar of the estate of William M. Rice shall ever go directly or indirectly to that damn [crossed out] scoundrel who robbed him and murdered him."[34]

Continued delays, including Surrogate Fitzgerald's prolonged summer vacation, plagued final resolution of the probate case, but on October 22, 1902, Captain James A. Baker, Judge John D. Bartine, and William Marsh Rice II, executors of Rice's estate in New York, received letters testamentary, which they secured with a $7 million bond the surrogate demanded.[35] Almost a month later, on November 21, temporary administration of New York assets ended, and on December 15, the executors took control of Rice's properties, then valued at $3,481,030.72.[36]

Neither prison bars nor Surrogate Fitzgerald's strong condemnation of the 1900 document as entirely fraudulent deterred Patrick and his supporters, who immediately filed an appeal. On March 30, 1903, the Appellate Division was unanimous in sustaining the Surrogate and declaring the 1900 instrument a "transparent forgery," a decisive decision "satisfactory on every point" to Baker, Hornblower, and Byrne.[37] Patrick next took his case to the Court of Appeals in Albany, where William B. Hornblower personally argued the case for the 1896 will. On October 27, 1903, the Albany panel affirmed the Appellate decision without making further comment. On April 29, 1904, when New York County's Surrogate Court approved the executors' final report that listed assets of $3,415,809.08, Baker and his team could begin to distribute legacies to the heirs.[38]

Baker now consolidated assets and most legal work in Houston. After learning that the New York Surrogate's decision had been twice upheld, Baker filed the 1896 will for probate in Harris County on December 16, 1903, but not until May 11, 1904 — two weeks after administration in New York had terminated — were letters testamentary granted Captain Baker, Judge Bartine, and Will Rice as executors of the estate in Texas. For the next several months, Baker's assistants labored to make a full inventory of all Rice's property while outside auditors completed an "appraise-ment" of estate assets in Texas. On December 1, 1905, the executors filed their final inventory and appraisal in Harris County Court.

Although the path to distribution of Rice's estate was now cleared of most obstacles, the executors spent nearly five more years settling claims, arguing about tax matters, and making final disbursements to the heirs. The death of Frederick A. Rice's widow, Charlotte Baldwin Rice, in De-cember 1906 enabled the executors to distribute the $80,000 trust estab-lished for Frederick A. Rice and his wife during their lifetimes. In 1907 Baker and the other executors were back in New York debating technical accounting details pursued by the "Tin Barnacles in the Surrogate's of-fice" because Baker wanted the Institute to take possession of the Rice estate assets still in New York "as speedily as possible."[39] Baker distrib-uted the trusts established for Rice's sisters Minerva Olds and Charlotte McKee to their children in 1910, the same year Judge Bartine died, and the estate of William Marsh Rice was finally closed.

The fight to preserve William Marsh Rice's fortune for his institute had been tedious, stressful, and expensive. Several lawyers succumbed to the pressure of "enormous and . . . practically continuous" work in a "gi-gantic undertaking" marked by dozens of lawsuits, motions, and appeals in two states. Charles Boston and William M. Wherry left wrenching ac-counts of their breakdowns, and Wherry had "to go away for the better part of a year." In November 1904 he wrote to Captain Baker requesting help as he tried to rebuild his legal practice.[40] Over one hundred claim-ants to three wills battled each other for a share of the spoils. Lawyers, de-tectives, accountants, appraisers, stenographers, expert witnesses, press clippers, messengers, and telegraphers all reaped handsome rewards. Ac-counts of assets varied slightly as the years passed, but when the fight was almost over, Rice Institute business manager John McCants outlined the Institute endowment on April 29, 1904: Cash of $1,082,408.62 and secu-rities in stocks, bonds, notes, checks, and jewelry valued at $2,333,406.46 totaled $3,415,809.08. Land deeded to the Institute in 1892 was worth $972,050.00 in 1904, while notes and interest added another $243,400.00 and brought the endowment fund to $4,631,259.08.[41]

What did Baker's fight to fulfill Rice's trust cost? Hornblower, Byrne, Miller & Potter received $280,000; Bowers & Sands, $120,000; Baker, Botts, Baker & Lovett, $100,000; Byrne & Cutcheon, $16,053.84 to close the estate.[42] The seventy-seven heirs and their lawyers under Mrs. Rice's will gained $200,000. Under the 1896 will of William M. Rice, fourteen claimants and their lawyers acquired $463,983.90, most in payments of $75,000 plus interest to Olds and McKee relatives in Massachusetts and a lesser lump sum to the Rice descendants in Missouri. The descendants of Frederick A. Rice secured $295,306.50, and the three executors, James A. Baker, John D. Bartine, and William Marsh Rice II, paid themselves $79,511.34 each (the total, $238,534.02, being 5 percent as specified in paragraph ten of the will). The State of New York claimed $119,387.58 as inheritance taxes and the federal government, $2,750.00 in death duties. Patrick's greed and chicanery and Orren T. Holt's meddling cost the estate over $1.8 million instead of the $100,000 in fraternal trusts and $238,534 in executors' pay that William Marsh Rice contemplated in the September 1896 document.[43] Nearly one-third of a fortune that had taken over sixty years to build was spent on the terrible struggle.

Were payments never imagined by Rice justified to save his great educational enterprise? Contemporaries certainly thought so. Rice had been generous to his siblings during his lifetime, building successful businesses with his brother Frederick, educating his nephew and namesake at Princeton, and sending frequent gifts to his sisters and their children in Massachusetts. Perhaps he felt he had done enough for his family, but Baker and his partners agreed the original bequests ($80,000 in trust to Frederick A. Rice and his family, $10,000 to each sister and her children) could have been larger, given the size of the fortune. The $75,000 shares granted to each group who cooperated in defending the 1896 will seemed a reasonable recompense. Given the persistent assault mounted by Patrick and the disaffected heirs, the lawyers' fees were not surprising. Holt filed Mrs. Rice's will in 1897; Baker closed the William M. Rice estate in 1910. From 1897 through 1905, one law firm in Houston and two in New York focused full attention on legal problems arising from William M. Rice's death. Dozens of attorneys in Texas, New York, Massachusetts, and Missouri assisted various claimants to the millionaire's fortune. By 1905, Baker, Botts, Baker & Lovett had hired three lawyers, expanded its support staff, and transformed the firm; Hornblower, Byrne, Miller & Potter added at least two associates to prepare for litigation against the many complainants.

As buildings rose on the Institute's campus, Houstonians recognized with gratitude the work of those who had prevented Rice's estate from being dissipated by greedy scoundrels. Rice had chosen his Board members with care. These veteran bankers and businessmen, with their dedicated lawyer to lead them, husbanded the lands Rice entrusted to them and invested his cash and securities in his adopted city. By 1912, when the Institute welcomed its first class, the school's endowment had grown to $9,817,115.01. More significant, the Board's vision extended well beyond the dreams of its benefactor. Baker and his colleagues understood the great opportunity that custody of Rice's fortune provided; while building their institute's endowment and constructing campus buildings, they used Rice's millions to fuel Houston's development. They watched with pride as city and Institute flourished together.

RICE'S BEQUEST

For five years, periods of intensive preparation, stressful trials, and sleepless nights preceded days of waiting when little could be accomplished. The relentless pace of evidence gathering, depositions, and strategic planning gradually relaxed, and Captain Baker began to complain he had little to do. Always before him was Rice's dream — to build an Institute for the Advancement of Literature, Science, and Art. Claimants to Rice's fortune who contested the 1896 will tried to prove the Institute existed only on paper, was not a properly chartered corporation as Baker asserted, and provided no educational services. To prove the Institute's validity, Baker presented the charter of 1891, several deeds to property held by the Institute, and other documents. He called upon Board members and employees of the Institute to write letters and to testify in court describing Rice's intentions. During this process, he began to discuss the Institute with his New York colleagues, with Judge John Bartine, and with Rice's friends. What, indeed, were Rice's intentions? How did he come to devise his charter of 1891? William Marsh Rice began to consider ways to distribute his fortune for the greater good of his community at least by 1880, at a time when wealthy national figures like John D. Rockefeller and Andrew Carnegie were redefining philanthropy. These industrial giants came to believe charity to needy individuals only palliated distress and perpetuated dependency. They sought proactive responses to social and economic problems created by industrial expansion, population migration, urban growth, and inadequate education. Andrew Carnegie's well-publicized 1889 essays on systematic wealth management showed others how to channel surplus personal funds to address communal problems and educate citizens in a democracy. Rice also wanted to use his fortune to urge others "along the ladder of life" he had climbed so successfully. His father had been a trustee of schools in Massachusetts, and before the Civil War, Rice had supported a schoolhouse run by the rector of Christ Church, helped to incorporate the Houston Academy in 1856, served on the board of the Houston Educational Society, and been trustee of the Texas Medical College and of the Second Ward Free School, a precursor of the city's postwar publicly funded school system.[44] Despite his own lack of formal education, the successful entrepreneur recalled his early struggles and wanted his fortune to benefit American "boys and girls who might need it as badly as he did."[45]

Rice frequently mentioned two men who informed his early thinking: Stephen Girard (1750–1831), a Philadelphia sea captain and financier, and Peter Cooper (1791–1883), a New York inventor and industrialist. Like Rice and Carnegie, these men came from modest homes and enjoyed little or no formal education; like them, these earlier philanthropists had benefited from investments in transformative nineteenth-century technology and believed poor children must be educated to develop their latent talents and lead their communities. Stephen Girard, thought to be the richest man in America at the time of his death in 1831, left his entire fortune, about $7 million, to support civic projects in Philadelphia and Pennsylvania and to build Girard College, whose mission when it opened in 1848 was to teach practical knowledge to poor, white, orphan boys through the high school level in an atmosphere that encouraged freedom of thought and religious expression. Rice visited Girard College and was particularly interested in its origin as an asylum for fatherless boys.[46] In 1859 Peter Cooper founded the Cooper Union for the Advancement of Science and Art upon the radical premise that education should be "as free as air and water" and available to all who could meet stringent entrance requirements. The Cooper Union's first classes for men, held at night, offered applied sciences and architectural drawing. The college's daytime Female School of Design taught photography, telegraphy, and typewriting—all advanced technological skills in that era. On several occasions in the 1880s and 1890s, Rice walked from his Wall Street office to explore the campus of this unusual but well-endowed school at Astor Place in lower Manhattan.

While living in New Jersey during the 1870s and 1880s, Rice discussed his estate plan with his neighbor Judge John Bartine. After studying Girard's will, curriculum, and principles, Rice asked Bartine to outline his own wishes in a testament the Judge prepared in 1882. Bartine adapted the concepts and language of Girard's 1831 bequest to define Rice's major points.[47] Naming his brother Frederick A. Rice and the New York bankers S. M. and E. P. Swenson executors, Rice provided several annuities to his wife and various relatives but left the bulk of his estate to the governor of the state of New Jersey to provide for the maintenance and education of "as many poor, male orphan children of American birth as possible." He instructed his executors to build a campus of "durable materials . . . avoiding needless ornament" on seventy-nine acres in New Jersey. In paragraph after paragraph, Rice laid out in minute detail exactly how he wanted his money to be spent and by whom. He also stipulated that only the income was to be used and that "no part of the principal fund shall ever be used for any purpose whatever."[48]

No sooner had Rice completed this will than his wife persuaded him to leave his country home and move to the more exciting and elegant avenues of New York City. After 1883 Rice spent no time in Dunellen, sold the property, and abandoned his New Jersey orphan home project. At the same time he began to spend more time in Houston, to reinterest himself in that city's development, and to work closely with young James A. Baker, then launching his legal and business career. Houstonians had long relied on small private schools, often held in the teacher's front parlor, to provide rudimentary skills to their children. Not until 1871 did Harris County open its first free public school; in 1876 the state constitution mandated segregation of all public schools, and in 1877 the city took over county schools within city limits. By the 1880s, when Rice again turned his attention to Houston's educational needs, the city school system comprised one free high school, six free white elementary schools, and five free black elementary schools, one in each ward. Houstonians, then numbering about 20,000, could also pay for courses in four schools of music and art, a business college, two German schools, two ladies boarding schools, a Young Ladies Institute where Miss Kate Botts taught French, three Catholic parish schools, several small private elementary schools, and four private schools for the "colored" population.[49] Because these educational offerings seemed insufficient to educate citizens in an industrializing nation, civic leaders were exploring ways to improve the system.

On his annual trips to Houston, Rice discussed the city's educational needs with Baker and with two business friends who wanted to expand Houston's public schools, Cesar Lombardi and Emanuel Raphael. Baker remembered that Rice had remarked: "Texas received me when I was penniless, without friends or even acquaintances, and now in the evening of my life I recognize my obligation to her and to her children. I wish now to leave to the boys and girls, struggling for a place in the sun, the fortune that I have been able to accumulate."[50] One day in 1886 or 1887, Lombardi invited Rice to his office, locked the door so they would not be disturbed, and "talked for about an hour." Lombardi, an accountant and man of wide business experience, was president of the Houston School Board and was trying to persuade the City Council to fund an up-to-date high school building, but he had been told by a leading politician that "a high school was highfaluting nonsense." As Lombardi well understood, high school was "the only chance offered to the people to obtain a higher education."[51] Lombardi reminded Rice "he had made his fortune in Houston and . . . it was poetic justice that Houston should become the beneficiary of his surplus wealth." Lombardi asked Rice to finance construction of a building to be called William M. Rice High School; he was sufficiently encouraged by Rice's reaction to send plans to Rice in New York, but Rice never responded.[52]

A few years later in early spring 1891, Rice invited Baker to his suite at the Capitol Hotel to talk about his estate and a plan he was forming to build an institution of higher learning for the young people of Houston and Texas. One evening in March or April Captain Baker called on Cesar Lombardi to tell him Rice wanted to talk to his old friend about an educational institute. The next evening Lombardi visited Rice at his suite in the Capitol Hotel, where he learned Rice "had decided not to build a High School building" but to found in Houston an institution "modeled somewhat after the Cooper's Institute in New York," which he had investigated thoroughly the previous winter. Rice described the library, night school, commercial classes, and "lectures upon the arts and sciences and their application to the practical affairs of life" and told Lombardi he hoped to incorporate these ideas in his Institute.[53]

Coincidentally, Emanuel Raphael, then a trustee of the Houston Public Schools and an officer of the First National Bank, approached Rice and asked him to build "a new and commodious High School to cost about $100,000." Rice turned down the proposal and told Raphael that city authorities should provide public school buildings. Much to Raphael's surprise, Rice "then and there" unfolded a plan "he had long been entertaining" to endow "a large college or Institute of learning" in Houston. Rice asked Raphael to serve as a trustee for the project that would include a public library, be free for "the youth of Houston, of either sex," and would prepare enrollees for trades or practical occupations. He also described plans for an endowment and seven-member board.[54] Within a few days Rice had enlisted his brother Captain Frederick A. Rice, his lawyer Captain James A. Baker, Emanuel Raphael, Cesar Lombardi, and banker James Everett McAshan as trustees. Three or four weeks later he completed the list with railroad attorney Alfred Stephen Richardson.

Like Rice himself, the original Board members who served with Captain Baker had not experienced traditional college life and therefore approached the project with few preconceptions. William M. Rice's brother, Frederick Allyn Rice (1830–1901) had come to Texas in 1850 and prospered as Rice family businesses grew. He invested in lumber, insurance, banks, manufacturing, and railroads and served as director or officer of several important Houston corporations, including the Houston Savings Bank (president), the City Bank of Houston (vice president), the Houston Cotton Exchange, the Houston & Texas Central Railway (treasurer), and the Houston Brick Works (secretary). Alfred Stephen Richardson (1830–1899) had spent a year at Harvard Law School before coming to Houston, where transportation issues shaped his career with the Buffalo Bayou Ship Channel Company, as secretary of the Houston & Texas Central Railway, and as receiver for the Houston East & West Texas Railway (1885). A former member of the Texas legislature, he was secretary of the City of Houston (1890–1896) when Rice wrote his charter. Although both men discussed the founder's plan with him, neither lived to see Rice's dream fulfilled.

Cesar Maurice Lombardi (1845–1919), a Swiss émigré, studied at Jesuit College in New Orleans before joining William D. Cleveland & Company, cotton brokers. Lombardi married Caroline Ennis (1877), whose father Cornelius was a close friend of Rice and an early director of the Houston & Texas Central Railway. After 1898 Lombardi lived in Portland, Oregon, where he managed a wholesale grain business, and in Dallas, where he ran his brother-in-law's publishing empire, A. H. Belo & Company. As president of Houston's School Board (1886–1898), he and Emanuel Raphael (1847–1913), also a School Board member, were best suited to explain Houston's educational needs.

The son of an English rabbi and a cultured man, Raphael, like the others, had not completed a college baccalaureate course, although he had read law and qualified for the bar in Texas.[55] As a teenager he helped build the telegraph line along the right of way of the Texas & New Orleans Railroad (1863), and he served as clerk for the Houston & Texas Central Railway (1868), was head cashier (mid-1870s) and president (1880) of Houston Savings Bank, manager of the Clearing House of Houston (1890), and founder of Raphael Brothers fire insurance company. An ambitious and talented businessman, Raphael had been named president of Houston Electric Light & Power Company at age thirty-six in 1884 and was considered one of Rice's closest personal and business friends. In 1877 he married Louise Cohn, whose younger brother Arthur managed Rice's business for many years.[56] Raphael's leadership role, at a time when most prominent universities discriminated against Jews, reinforced William Marsh Rice's broad-minded values and visionary mission to build a nonpartisan, nonsectarian, tuition-free institution.

James Everett McAshan (1857–1916), founder and chief operating officer of the South Texas National Bank of Houston, was the son and father of bankers and also served on the boards of several local companies. Well-connected and well-traveled, he was willing to explore alternatives but, like the other men, lacked personal knowledge of higher education issues. Rice had known McAshan as a boy, spoke to him often about plans for an institute, and was a major stockholder and director of the younger man's bank.

THE CHARTER

With his Board in place in early April 1891, Rice met almost daily with Baker and Raphael to prepare documents that would establish his trust and incorporate his institute under Texas law.[57] On May 13, 1891, William M. Rice signed an indenture with his six chosen trustees to establish a trust whose purposes were twofold: to accept and administer a $200,000 endowment conveyed to the trustees by a deed of gift signed by Mr. and Mrs. Rice and to incorporate under the laws of Texas. On May 16, Rice and the other trustees signed the proposed charter and sent it immediately to Austin for filing with Secretary of State George W. Smith. On May 19, 1891, Smith endorsed the document, and Rice Institute for the Advancement of Literature, Science, and Art was in business. Before returning to New York, Rice signed a note for $200,000 to establish the endowment and promised to make additional gifts each year and to provide handsomely for the Institute in his will. On June 24, 1891, the trustees held their first Board meeting in the office of Raphael Brothers. The signed charter had arrived from Austin and was deposited with the $200,000 note and other papers of the Institute in the safety deposit vaults of South Texas National Bank of Houston, opened in 1890 by James Everett McAshan. At this organizational meeting attended by all but William M. and Frederick A. Rice, Baker was elected president, Lombardi vice president, and Raphael secretary, as Rice had requested. Rice also told his fellow trustees he wished to maintain control of the funds during his lifetime and to serve as treasurer.

The charter drawn with such care established the Institute for the Advancement of Literature, Science, and Art under the 1874 Texas statute defining private corporations. In force for fifty years, the charter allowed the Institute to "receive, hold, and enjoy property, real, personal and mixed"—a critical point during the contest over William M. Rice's last testament because it enabled the Institute to accept his bequest. The charter outlined the intents and purposes to be:

> [T]he establishment and maintenance, in the City of Houston, Texas, of a public library, and the maintenance of an institute for the advancement of literature, science, art, philosophy and letters; the establishment and maintenance of a Polytechnic school; for procuring and maintaining scientific collection; collections of chemical and philosophical apparatus, mechanical and artistic models, drawings, pictures and statues; and for cultivating other means of instruction for the white inhabitants of the City of Houston, and State of Texas.[58]

The charter established a seven-member Board who "shall hold their offices . . . for life," and it stated clearly that the trustees, who could not receive compensation for their services, were "expressly forbidden ever to permit any lien, encumbrance, debt or mortgage to be placed upon any of the property, or funds, belonging now, or that may hereafter belong to the Institute . . . [so] the Institute shall always be kept free from debt."[59]

Provisions of the charter relating to Rice's academic goals as well as the Institute's formal name resemble closely the charter that established Cooper Union in New York City in 1859.

True to his word, Rice and his wife began making additional gifts in 1892. On June 20 they executed four deeds transferring property to the Institute in the watchful presence of Institute President Baker and Secretary Raphael.[60] The Rices conveyed 9,345 acres of land in Jones County, more than six acres of land in the Obedience Smith Survey on Louisiana Street in Houston, the Capitol Hotel in Houston, and 47,155 acres of pine land in Calcasieu Parish, Louisiana. Because he disliked publicity, Rice told Raphael to publish and put on record only the deed for the Obedience Smith Survey land, since it was to be used for the Institute campus. As instructed, Baker and Raphael placed the other deeds in the South Texas National Bank vault for safekeeping, to be recorded and published after Rice's death. By 1900 this property bore an approximate value of $270,000.[61] In June 1893 Rice donated a contract he had made with his nephew H. Baldwin Rice so that his share of profits (whether in cash, land, or livestock) realized from the operation of the Rice Ranch in Harris County (now Bellaire, Texas) could be paid to the Institute.[62] Rice also turned over several loans to the Institute, allowing the Board to collect interest income, and he gave the Institute eighteen oil paintings, which were hanging temporarily in the Capitol Hotel, to begin a college art collection. During their lifetimes, the Rices "showed the liveliest interest" in "beautifying and laying out" the downtown plot with four hundred oaks and elms.[63]

Rice reinforced his support for the Institute when planning a new will he signed in 1893. His friend John Bartine prepared the document, which named James Baker, William M. Rice II of Hyatt, Texas, and John Bartine as executors and trustees. Written while his lively, younger wife enjoyed excellent health, the will divided Rice's assets in two equal parts. One half of his estate Rice bequeathed to the William Marsh Rice Institute in Houston; the other half, he subdivided into fifty shares to be distributed to his wife, his brother, his sisters, and various nieces and nephews. Not surprisingly, as soon as his wife died, Rice wanted to supersede this will, with its division of the estate into two equal parts. The will Baker prepared in 1896, Rice's final attempt to manage his wealth for future generations, was far less generous to any surviving relatives and instead bequeathed nearly 90 percent of Rice's assets to his institute.

INTERPRETING THE CHARTER

Rice continued to cite Girard College and Cooper Union as models for his institute, and he turned to Peter Cooper's charter as the basis for his plan, but the goals he outlined in the Institute charter proved both specific and vague. Was the Institute to be a high school (like Girard), or a trade and design school (like Cooper Union), a polytechnic school (as specified in the charter), or a liberal arts college (as suggested by the Institute's name)? What sort of higher learning did Rice have in mind? He intended the Institute to be free, nonsectarian, nonpartisan, and practical. He did not envision a haven for scholars or a training ground for the ministry or law, the concepts underlying most of the nation's oldest colleges. Instead, Rice wanted Institute leaders to address problems created by new technologies, urban living, and the practical application of research, but during his lifetime there was little discussion about how this should be done.

While Rice had been drawn to the experiments at Girard College and Cooper Union, the men on his Board knew that late nineteenth-century reformers were founding new institutions and transforming traditional colleges and universities into engines of discovery and partners of urban culture. As early as October 21, 1900, an unnamed trustee told a *Houston Post* reporter that Rice's legacy of several million might be "somewhat short of the Leland Stanford university" but "ahead of the Vanderbilt university in Nashville, the Chicago (Rockefeller) university, and the Peter Cooper Union of New York City."[64] Clearly this trustee was aware of several new institutions rising across the country that promoted pure research to acquire new knowledge as well as practical applications to train a dynamic, sophisticated workforce. Johns Hopkins University, incorporated by bachelor merchant and financier Hopkins in 1867 (opened 1876), introduced the German model of seminar discussions and laboratory experiments. Merchant Paul Tulane's gift of $1 million (1884) enabled New Orleans' academics to restructure private higher education in the South's largest city and introduce the first coordinate college system in the nation, a model widely emulated to accommodate male and female students. Railroad magnate Leland Stanford and his wife (1884) reinforced contemporary beliefs that the doors of academe should be opened to a broad public and that private funds should be used to uplift citizens of a democracy through education. Investor Marshall Field and oil king John D. Rockefeller were determined that their University of Chicago (incorporated 1890) would attract renowned researchers to a Midwestern university that combined general studies with concentration in a major field and balanced theoretical research with practical application. Charles W. Eliot at Harvard (1869–1909) and Woodrow Wilson at Princeton (1902–1910) introduced path-breaking curricular and organizational reforms that allowed the older private foundations to maintain their long-standing reputations as national leaders in higher education.

Contemporaries praised James Baker as a "great educator" who "studied educational problems and guided their application to Rice Institute." Sometime early in 1901 he decided that he wanted to learn more about the institutions of higher learning that already existed in the United States.[65] He needed information to defend Rice Institute and its charter in court, and he discovered the data used to explain Rice's goals was also invaluable to the trustees as they began planning the institution that would embody Rice's legacy. In March 1901 Baker and his team at Hornblower, Byrne, Miller & Potter sent a questionnaire to presidents, treasurers, and Board members of seventy-one private and public colleges and universities "to obtain some information in regard to the character of the property of your institution." The letter assured recipients that any information they were willing to share would "in no way . . . affect the interests of the University to its disadvantage," and asked how each school had been organized, who were its benefactors, how it received and managed its property, and what sort of charter had been granted to it. Question eleven inquired about "any suits in regard to property."

From the responses, Baker learned that Mrs. Stanford considered the trust "holy" and that the design of the founders was "to make specialists . . . so that every graduate will feel himself master of some one thing, and be enabled to battle with life with that feeling of confidence in himself." The California School of Mechanical Arts included brochures and a detailed budget for the cost and maintenance of its buildings. Baker discovered "there are very few institutions organized on the same plan as the W. M. Rice Institute, and nearly all of these have large endowments and no limitations." A summary of the findings described several trade schools at length, including Cooper Union, the "absolutely free" Jacob Tome Institute in Maryland, and Pratt Institute of Brooklyn, endowed with $4 million by Charles Pratt in 1887 "to teach such branches of useful and practical knowledge as are not generally taught in public and private schools." This summary also listed universities in nineteen states, showing endowments (divided between property and productive funds) ranging from $770,000 (Colgate) to $13 million (Columbia). Several institutions sent charters that explained the mission of their founders, although the thrust of the questions concerned organization and financial support.

Despite efforts to give full consideration to the technical schools their benefactor praised, Baker and other Board members began to pursue a different path to advance literature, science, and art. In June 1902, Edwin B. Parker called Baker's attention to an article about Johns Hopkins, noting "I had not known before that Mr. Rice so closely followed the plan adopted by Johns Hopkins in founding the University which bears his name."[66] Hopkins had invited twelve prominent citizens of Baltimore to join him in incorporating an institution, he had left $7 million to endow a university and a medical school/hospital, and he had requested that nothing be done until after his death. The selection of Daniel Coit Gilman, a Yale graduate and professor of physical geography, was widely acclaimed as brilliant when Johns Hopkins quickly took the lead in academic innovation.

Baker also sought outside opinion and in August 1905 asked Joseph J. Pastoriza to consider "ways and means regarding the Rice Institute." In a well-argued four-page response that October, the innovative tax expert and future mayor said he had corresponded with several university presidents, who confirmed his ideas. First, Pastoriza recommended the campus be placed on a large tract of land along Buffalo Bayou that was owned by the Rice Estate but was at the time developed as a golf course. Pastoriza then devoted much of his letter to buildings, which he recommended be "simple, but in the very best architectural taste": an academic building, an engineering and shop building, laboratories for physics, chemistry, and biology, a dormitory, a dining hall, and a president's house. Any preparatory department should be placed in a separate structure, he advised. Finally, Pastoriza declared, "the most important work of the Trustees will be to select a President who shall give his whole thought and time to the Institute before a brick is laid."[67] As events unfolded, Pastoriza's advice proved prescient.

Board members often visited academic institutions, and Board Treasurer Emanuel Raphael told fellow trustees in December 1905 that in addition to his fiduciary duties, he had also tried to define the Institute's mission. He had written to two libraries, three institutes, and the universities of Chicago and Stanford and had studied their charters and bylaws while working with Baker and William M. Rice on similar instruments for Rice Institute. He had made personal visits to Vanderbilt, Peter Cooper Union, the Museum of Natural History in New York City, and six libraries, including the Library of Congress, "for the purpose of observing and familiarizing [himself] with the workings of these Institutions of Learning, of Art and Public Libraries."[68]

Baker's personal experience reinforced his interest in the university model. His friend Will Rice II, during his years at Princeton, had experienced an environment where pure research was translated to practical purposes in a traditional academic setting. William Hornblower and James Byrne, Baker's associates in New York, were graduates of Princeton and Harvard; his own son Graham had been admitted to Princeton at the time of his death; and his father Judge Baker had served on the board of Huntsville's Austin College, founded by a Princeton graduate. Baker's railroad clients, his travels to Boston, New York, and Washington, DC, and his interaction with a strong, well-educated legal team during the Patrick murder trials had shown him the advantages of association with men who had received the nation's best academic training.

Baker's ambitious parents had been unable to afford the most sophisticated education for their son; now Baker had access to a great fortune. Should he not seize that opportunity to address the educational problems of the South and create a great university there; could he not fulfill Rice's wishes to provide practical knowledge to the children of Houston and Texas free of charge while also building an outstanding foundation for the advancement of literature, science, and art? A new institution of national importance could propel Houston and Texas into the sophisticated, specialized, professional world of the twentieth century's industrial economy by producing the region's best-trained minds. From childhood, Baker had been urged to do his best and praised for succeeding; surely he could do no less for his client than build the best educational institution possible. In the years ahead, Baker expanded William Marsh Rice's dream to train young men and women for technical careers and conceived a much grander scheme—to build a transformative center of learning where scholars would create new knowledge and drive forward the city, region, and nation. The most charming, persuasive man on Rice's

Board and the donor's chosen leader, Baker played a critical hand in broadening the Institute's mission.

SEARCH FOR A LEADER

Rice had made clear that he did not want to start building during his lifetime, so regular Board meetings in the 1890s focused on managing the land Rice had donated, considering investment opportunities for income generated by the properties, and authorizing landscaping on the original campus site. From May 1891 forward, the Institute, like any operating corporation, published an annual account of its receipts and expenditures, maintained an office in Houston, and dealt with occasional legal problems. In October 1892, for example, Baker used his influence at city hall to prevent the mayor and aldermen from authorizing road construction through the downtown Institute property planned for the campus. Promising a park "suggestive of rest, pure air and sylvan beauty," Baker successfully persuaded the council to protect the acreage as a "place of proper recreation and resort." By municipal authority, the site was officially reserved for college or public library purposes.[69]

In the decade after Rice's death, the Board gradually tackled numerous business problems arising from their benefactor's wide-ranging investments and slowly developed its own vision of how best to fulfill Rice's mandate to advance knowledge and educate young people. Board members faced two immediate questions: converting unproductive properties into income-producing investments and building a business management team to administer Institute assets. Although Baker had not at first been enthusiastic about young accountant Arthur B. Cohn (1871–1938), Rice's dedicated business manager since June 1, 1893, he came to trust the young man's veracity during the fight over Libbie Rice's will, and after William M. Rice's death, Baker asked Cohn to manage day-to-day business problems as general agent for the Institute and assistant secretary to the Board. As the executors distributed more and more assets, Cohn gained direct oversight of timberlands, hotels, real estate, industrial mills, and ranch properties as chief operating officer.

Following Alfred S. Richardson's death in 1899, lumberman William Marsh Rice II of Hyatt, Texas, joined his uncle's Board. Given a traditional baccalaureate education by his uncle, Will Rice II completed four years in engineering at Princeton in 1879, the same year a Virginian

Edgar Odell Lovett,
ca. 1909, Rice Institute
president 1908–1946.
Early Rice Collection,
Woodson Research
Center, Rice University.

named Woodrow Wilson was graduated from the school he would later transform. On March 30, 1901, Board members Baker, Frederick A. Rice, McAshan, and Raphael elected Benjamin Botts Rice to fill his uncle's place and begin a term that lasted forty-five years. A University of the South alumnus, Ben B. Rice managed one of his uncle's most important investments, the Merchants & Planters Oil Company. Despite this activity, Houstonians felt the Board was not moving quickly enough; in December 1904, the mayor sent a three-man delegation to call on the trustees and express the city's deep interest in the Institute's progress "towards carrying out the purposes of their trust."[70] Still struggling to settle lawsuits and determine the direction they wanted to take, the deliberate directors explained they were not yet ready to hire an academic leader or build any buildings.

The Board did take an important step that gave formal authority to their actions by adopting its first set of by-laws on August 9, 1905. Baker paid serious attention to by-laws, and several nonprofit organizations established in Houston during the early years of the twentieth century benefited from his interest and legal expertise. In June 1905 he appointed McAshan, Will Rice, and Raphael to a drafting committee. Dry and straightforward, the by-laws established several rules followed for years. The president centralized power in his hands: he nominated all committees, signed all bonds, deeds, and contracts, and held "general supervisory power" over the entire institution. As described, the president ran the Institute and hired all faculty and staff. Articles 11–13 described the library, polytechnic school, night classes, and other elements of Rice's plan that would be introduced "as soon as the income will admit of such expenditure." Baker immediately appointed four committees: Finance, headed by James E. McAshan; Library, with Emanuel Raphael as chairman; Building, under Benjamin B. Rice's direction; and Visiting, led by Will Rice II.[71] When the Board rented an office on Franklin Avenue in 1907, hired Arthur B. Cohn and H. H. Lummis as full-time employees, and adopted a new bookkeeping system at Cohn's recommendation, the Institute could finally begin its transformation from idea to reality.[72]

On January 9, 1907, Baker asked Raphael and McAshan to begin the Board's search for an academic director. Next day, the two men sent twenty-five letters to presidents, regents, and educators at major colleges, universities, and polytechnic schools, asking each recipient to list qualities necessary for leadership of an academic institution and to recommend possible candidates. They also wrote to several "prominent gentlemen who take interest in educational matters of large scope," including President Theodore Roosevelt and William Jennings Bryan.[73] Former President Grover Cleveland suggested Howard McClenahan, professor of electrical engineering in the Scientific Department at Princeton. The presidents of Stanford and Cornell recommended Albert Ross Hill, Dean of Teachers College at Missouri State. By the February 20 Board meeting, Raphael had received forty-five names to pursue, including the presidents of Vanderbilt and the University of Virginia. He had also visited Dr. Hill on a trip to St. Louis. He described the thirty-eight-year-old father of two children as "tall of stature" with fine address and "a large amount of reserve power" who had considerable experience since he began teaching at age sixteen. Apparently one contender's deafness knocked him off the list, and Professor McClenahan wanted to know about compensation before considering the position. Baker and Benjamin B. Rice, who listened to Raphael's February 20 report, agreed to compensation of $6,000 plus a house. They asked McAshan and Raphael to invite Albert Ross Hill to Houston and to pursue Prof. McClenahan of Princeton and Prof. Richards of Columbia.

In March the Board entertained Ross Hill. Although he impressed McAshan and Raphael as "the right man for the headship," he proved a hard man to catch as "several other institutions [were] after him," including his own university and Columbia Teachers College; ultimately, he withdrew from the chase. On March 11 Woodrow Wilson finally responded to the letter of inquiry sent in January with a letter strongly recommending Professor Edgar Odell Lovett, a fast-rising scholar from Princeton's astronomy and mathematics department. At the March 20 Board meeting, McAshan, Raphael, and the two Rice brothers decided to invite Professors McClenahan and Lovett from Princeton and Professor Richards of Columbia to Houston to interview. McClenahan visited Houston April 8, Lovett appeared on April 10 and 11, and Richards arrived on April 24.

Lovett reached Houston on the midnight train and checked into a room at the Rice Hotel. The next morning he strolled down Main Street past the Carnegie Library, opened in 1904. Raphael and McAshan drove Lovett around the city to show him the Rice Ranch, the original city lot donated by Rice in 1892, and other expanses of land that might be appropriate for a campus, including land along Buffalo Bayou formerly leased to the Houston Golf Club. That night Lovett met with the Board—an evening he remembered afterwards as a "most trying ordeal." Everyone asked questions that surprised him. He managed to handle the queries and made several telling suggestions that showed he had read the charter carefully but had clear ideas of his own. Lovett recommended a larger campus site and a comprehensive architectural plan, he agreed that the institution should live on its income from the endowment, and he stressed that pure science and new research should not take second place to applied science and utilitarian learning. He disliked the term "Institute" because it implied a narrow focus on technology or an institution for people with special needs. The exchange of views provoked much thought on both sides, but Lovett boarded the Southern Pacific without an offer. Lovett confided to his wife that he was anxious to hear the Board's decision and strongly hoped it would be positive. He recognized the great opportunity and opined that he stood a good chance of being chosen.[74]

On the day Lovett arrived for his interview, Baker wrote to Principal Henry Carr Pritchett of Sam Houston Normal School in Huntsville to seek his advice about steps needed to establish the Institute. Baker explained that the Board was looking for someone like the renowned University of Chicago founding President William Rainey Harper or Harvard reformer Charles W. Eliot, who, during a forty-year presidency modernized the ancient school. On May 1 Pritchett conferred with the entire Board. He spent the night with Baker and gave the Board chairman "an opportunity to discover his liberal views, broad culture, quiet, modest, but dignified demeanor, and his evident force of character." But Baker must have decided he was looking for someone with national, even international, connections, deep scholarship, and a charismatic presence. He tactfully explained to a Huntsville friend who had written on Pritchett's behalf that the Board thought Pritchett might provide ideas for the Institute but not that he would leave his present post.[75]

It is not certain what happened next. Pritchett, McClenahan, and Richards clearly did not answer the Board's needs, but what of Lovett? Was there disagreement among Board members? Did Lovett's insistence that he did not want to create a technical school for utilitarian training or that he did want a much larger campus worry those who interpreted Rice's wishes modestly? Had Lovett demanded more money? For some reason, Baker wanted to look at more candidates. Raphael was eager to make a decision, but Baker was more deliberate. He wrote to Dr. D. F. Houston, president of the University of Texas, to see if he would consider the post of educational head or president of the Institute but was turned down.

In May and June several members of the Board talked to President Robert Stewart Hyer (1860–1929) of Southwestern University in Georgetown (1898–1911). Hyer made such a favorable impression on McAshan, Raphael, and Ben Rice that Ben Rice assumed Hyer was the choice when he left town with his brother for a lengthy vacation in Europe. But Baker was not convinced. A confidential source whose opinion he trusted described Hyer as a "modest, scholarly gentleman . . . a scholar rather than an administrator" with "narrowing tendencies" often found in sectarian institutions. The first lay president of the Methodist school, Hyer preferred teaching and research to administration but built six new buildings on Southwestern's campus and significantly increased the school's endowment during his tenure. In 1911 Hyer left Southwestern to serve as founding president of Southern Methodist University in Dallas (1911–1920).[76]

Dissatisfied with Hyer's seeming predilection for study and his devout Methodism, Baker contacted Dr. Sidney E. Mezes, dean of the University of Texas faculty, and interviewed him at length. On July 5 Mezes and Baker spoke "over the phone," and the dean assured Baker he would "favorably consider a call to the Presidency" if one were offered.[77] Baker then took his family to The Willows, a vacation house in Easton, Maryland, for the summer. On July 7 Raphael visited with Mezes for two hours while in Austin and wrote Baker that Mezes, thirty-eight, would make an excellent academic head because he had strong administrative experience. He realized Baker's impressions "were not so strong" as his own, but he warned Baker, "The time has come for us to act."[78] Despite his wish to move forward, Raphael found that reaching a consensus by wire and cable while all other Board members were on vacation was impossible. Confusion and misunderstanding caused a split that could only be healed when everyone returned in cooler weather. McAshan did not like Mezes at all; Ben Rice was "very much surprised" to learn that Mezes was being seriously considered while Hyer had been abandoned, and he refused to commit to Mezes, whom he did not know personally. The group agreed to drop Hyer and write again to A. Ross Hill to see if he would be interested, at a higher salary.

Meanwhile, two candidates proposed themselves. Arthur Lefevre, Superintendent of Victoria Public Schools, wrote Baker October 26, 1907, but the Board president politely deflected his request. William Hayne Leavell, Baker's pastor at First Presbyterian Church, proved more difficult. A vain man, Leavell may have misinterpreted Baker's cordiality, but Baker, when importuned, explained that "the sentiment of a majority of the Board . . . is in favor of someone . . . who combines educational experience with administrative ability."[79] Leavell recalled in his memoirs that Baker "believed he could secure the appointment" for Leavell, who was disappointed "not to be given the opportunity to organize the Institute . . . along lines intended by Mr. Rice."[80] By November 1908 Albert Ross Hill had been named president of the University of Missouri and Sidney Edward Mezes president of the University of Texas. By 1911 Arthur Lefevre was secretary for research at Will Hogg's organization to improve higher education in Texas, which former Governor James Stephen Hogg's oldest son created as an alumni support group at his alma mater that year.[81]

When Institute Board members returned to town in the fall of 1907 and could meet face to face, they swiftly resolved the issue. The Board had written to prominent educators all over the country, had examined many academic charters, and had interviewed men from Texas and from outside the state. By November 20, 1907, when Baker, McAshan, Raphael, and the Rice brothers met for the regularly scheduled Board meeting, they held one final "full discussion." Armed with a proxy vote from Cesar Lombardi, Will Rice nominated Edgar Odell Lovett to take charge as educational head of the Institute. Raphael seconded the motion, and Lovett was declared the unanimous choice. Will Rice agreed "to proceed to Princeton" to call upon Lovett; he was told to offer no more than $7,500 per year, a house, and a five-year contract. On December 3, Rice wrote a handwritten letter to Lovett saying he would be in New York City on December 14 and would like to visit him that day. Four days later, now back in Houston, Rice reported to the Board that he had spent the evening with Lovett and made the offer. Lovett seemed to hesitate, saying he had just taken on new research projects and the $6,000 offered by Rice was insufficient. Rice then proposed $7,000 and a home, but Lovett continued to waver, although Rice told the Board he did not think compensation was the only issue. Finally, Rice suggested that Lovett take thirty days to consider the unique opportunity.

Baker and Raphael were pleased that negotiations had gone well but saw they must press the Institute's case. The next day, December 19, Baker began the assault. Expressing disappointment that Lovett "had not been able so far to give the Trustees a definite answer," he was now writing "to urge upon you to cast your lot with us." He reassured Lovett the Trustees had proceeded deliberately and had "talked to a great many persons in and out of Texas . . . but I want you to know that the position has been offered to no one except to you." Baker went on to say the trustees liked his manner, his frankness and candor, his qualifications, and his youth. He also understood Lovett's reluctance to leave Princeton but assured him "that in coming to Houston you and your family will find a warm welcome among generous and hospitable people, who will strive in every way to make you feel at home among them." Choosing his words carefully, Baker then mentioned the endowment, the largest in the South. He confided that the trustees were "without experience in educational matters and . . . disposed to give you a very free hand." "As a rule," Baker continued, "they are broad minded and liberal and desire in establishing the new institution to lay its foundations broad and deep, and to employ at all times the best talent that can be had anywhere." The opportunity to found a new institution of the first rank was "unusual," and Lovett should "be slow in declining. Such an opportunity rarely comes to one so young in life." A few days later Emanuel Raphael was even more insistent. He told Lovett the Board wanted him to accept, that its members were young and harmonious, and that the opportunity, as he had previously noted, was national in scope. This encouragement proved successful. At a special meeting of the Board on December 28, Will Rice read Lovett's response: the candidate had accepted the call provided the trustees would agree to a salary of $8,000 and a house. If Lovett could be released from his duties at Princeton, he planned to begin on March 1, 1908. That afternoon Raphael wired affirmation of Lovett's terms.[82]

On January 22, 1908, the trustees placed Lovett's formal letter of acceptance, addressed to Secretary Emanuel Raphael and dated January 18, 1908, in the minute book. Lovett's eloquence matched his "deep sense of the obligation to service imposed by the donor's philanthropy and a firm faith in the determination of his Trustees." He pledged "whatever of strength or training I may have to the great task in which we hereby join hands and hearts, believing that in common counsel we are going to find the wisdom which shall issue in constructive ability to plan and execute, courage to achieve the manifold possibilities of the splendid foundation on which we have the good fortune to build." Expressing his "abiding confidence" in Texan characteristics of independence, courage, and loyalty, Lovett promised to call on friends of education in the city and state and to accept the privilege of leadership accorded him. With "largeness of mind, strength of character, determined purpose, fire of genius, [and] devoted loyalty," he vowed to train a "continuous column" of men and women "trained in the highest degree, equipped in the largest way for positions of trust in the public service, for commanding careers in the affairs of the world." As Baker, McAshan, Raphael, and Ben Rice listened to these words, they realized their newly chosen academic leader aspired to the same lofty goals they had decided to pursue.[83]

With the choice of Edgar Odell Lovett, the evolution of the trustees' thinking was complete. The William Marsh Rice Institute for the Advancement of Literature, Science, and Art would be a great national, even international, university; its leaders would strive for the best in academic performance; it would develop in the tradition of Princeton, Harvard, and Yale, influenced by the innovative ambitions of Johns Hopkins University, the University of Chicago, and the Massachusetts Institute of Technology. While striving for greatness on a large stage, the trustees also would remember Rice's wishes: they would live within their income; students would pay no tuition; the university would benefit all Texans and maintain good relations with its home city; and pure research and practical application would be harmoniously blended in the work of its students and faculty. While the Institute would provide a liberal education and "make a distinct contribution to the architecture of the country," it would "begin [the] university program at the science end" and introduce engineering courses early "to meet local demands" for practical application of research findings.[84] The trustees quickly learned they had chosen wisely. Baker remarked that Lovett was blessed with "youth, vigor, experience, and ambition." As Lovett's biographer notes, Lovett's credentials were superior: he held two doctorates; he listed teaching experience at Princeton, the University of Virginia, Johns Hopkins, and the University of Chicago, where he had absorbed lessons in leadership, reform, innovation, and progressive thought; his understanding of science, literature, and classical and modern languages was broad; and he knew well many scholars at home and in Europe.[85]

PREPARATION

Lovett, now education head of the Institute, arrived in Houston for an introductory visit on February 29, 1908, and Baker welcomed him to the regular Board meeting on March 11. The new leader spoke briefly about his ideas to organize the Institute and suggested he make a tour of observation to accomplish three goals: study the best universities and technical colleges in the United States, Europe, and Japan; introduce Rice Institute to academicians around the globe; and interview potential faculty members. Houston's government officials and business leaders also greeted Lovett warmly. Mayor H. Baldwin Rice, in his second term, took Lovett and the Institute trustees for a trip down Buffalo Bayou on his yacht, and the Houston Business League invited him to a Smoker so "representative men of the city" might become acquainted with the Institute's new academic chief immediately.[86]

In the spring, Baker became chairman of the Board, and Lovett assumed the title of president to affirm his lofty mission. He submitted a list of fifty-eight institutions in seventeen countries he wished to visit (later pared to thirty-three locations). He proposed a budget of $1,625 (based on $5 or $6 per diem) for travel and other expenses and hired F. Carrington Weems, a Houstonian and recent Princeton graduate, as his secretary. In April Baker accepted Lovett's plans and outlined quarterly payments of his salary. Anticipating the cordial relations he hoped to nurture, Baker closed with a personal note. He and Mrs. Baker were leaving Houston the following week for a ten-day visit in New York City: "If you happen to be in New York while we are there, we hope to have the pleasure of seeing you." While not couched as a command performance, there can be no doubt Lovett made every effort to visit since the two men had much to discuss about immediate decisions regarding property acquisitions for the campus and long-term planning for the task that lay ahead when the academic pioneer returned from his trip abroad.[87]

On July 24, 1908, E. O. Lovett, his wife Mary Hale, and secretary Weems sailed from Montreal on the *Empress of Ireland* for a trip that would take them to Europe, across Russia on the Trans-Siberian Express from Moscow to Vladivostok, to Japan and Hawaii, and finally to Houston via Stanford and Berkeley. Lovett and Weems recorded this magical voyage of academic discovery in two large volumes. Raphael published Lovett's descriptive letters in Houston's newspapers so readers could follow the journey, "gather food for thought," and anticipate what to expect when their city's center of higher learning finally took shape.[88]

While Lovett was circling the globe, announcing the new institute planned for faraway Texas, and meeting scholars from every field of intellectual endeavor, James McAshan made his own trip to Europe. Before returning home, he visited Paris's Polytechnique, considered the greatest technological school in Europe; Heidelberg and Oxford, where colleges had less land than the Institute's Louisiana Street property; and Princeton and Johns Hopkins, the nation's most innovative campuses. In each case he reported the acreage of the campus and the distance students had to walk from class to class and from academic buildings to athletic fields. He also described facilities and student body composition. "My interviews with educators," McAshan told the Board, "lead me to believe that the only way we can command patronage is to have men and apparatus that will challenge the appreciation of the earnest students of the world, who desire to achieve success, and not cater too much to those students who only go to college as a matter of good form."[89]

CREATING A CAMPUS

With an academic leader in place, Baker turned his attention to acquiring land suitable for a campus. During Board discussions about the Institute's future academic head, trustees had also reconsidered campus size. By the spring of 1907, they realized the city block set aside for a campus by William Marsh Rice might not meet their aspirations for a world-class institution. On the day Edgar Odell Lovett was due to arrive for his interview, the Board requested a legal opinion regarding its ability to purchase undeveloped land outside city limits to accommodate a much larger campus.[90] During the interview process, Lovett confirmed the trustees' conclusion that the downtown acreage held since 1892 would not satisfy the far more ambitious institution now envisioned. Using Princeton's extensive real estate holdings as his model, Lovett told the trustees the Rice Ranch (present-day Bellaire, Texas) was too far from the city, but expressed interest in the flat farmland lying south of downtown outside city limits along dusty Main Street Road. Early in 1908 Baker began talking quietly to knowledgeable friends about available land at a reasonable price. As with any major real estate purchase, discretion was paramount to keep prices down and land available before his interest became widely known.

On February 4, 1908, Baker received a letter from land developer, friend, and civic leader Henry F. MacGregor describing a recent discussion with rancher George Hermann. MacGregor explained Hermann's "present inclinations," but he warned "you can not always depend on any statement he has made for any length of time, and before you offer to buy any other property you should have him tied up in writing." MacGregor strongly believed Hermann was willing to sell frontage property along Main at a good price if Baker would take "the bulk of the land" behind it, and he suggested a complicated land swap among several landholders in the area to provide about 120 acres on the west side of Main for the Institute campus.[91] George H. Hermann (August 6, 1843–October 21, 1914) was a bachelor Houstonian who owned thousands of acres in Harris County, including a 370-acre cattle ranch straddling Main Street Road and over 2,500 acres in North Harris County where prospectors discovered oil in 1904. Now an aging millionaire with no heirs, Hermann was thinking about the best way to distribute his estate. Shortly before his death, Hermann gave the land along Main Street Road opposite the Rice campus to the city of Houston for its first large nature preserve and recreational space.[92]

Armed with MacGregor's information, Baker began plotting a strategy with Will Rice and that spring named him a committee of one to acquire land for the campus. After the June 10, 1908, Board meeting, Baker wrote Lovett that the Board expected to select a site during the summer, and he asked Lovett to send his opinion on number of acres, location, and advisability of purchase if he could not return to Houston before his trip abroad. Lovett hurried to Houston to attend the June 24 Board meeting and discuss at length the critical issues of campus size and location. Baker, Raphael, the Rice brothers, and Lovett determined that as much as three hundred acres would be required to meet their goals, and the group authorized Will Rice to negotiate an option on Hermann's property at not more than $1,000 an acre, good until fall. Lovett then departed for his tour, while Baker took his family to Asheville, North Carolina, for a summer vacation.

Working through realtor David Hannah, Will Rice could report by July 1 that he had talked to George Hermann about a series of purchases and sales that would enable Hermann to acquire more land east of Main Street Road, and would allow the Institute to amass a site to the west of Main. When the Board gathered again on September 30, Will described options on 175 acres at an average price of $660 per acre. The Board authorized him to close those deals and acquire at least 25 more acres. Will bought the first two parcels (nearly 47 acres) on October 24 and November 10, and on February 18, 1909, he completed the purchase of another 95.149 acres from Hermann. At the April 7, 1909, Board meeting, Will outlined his action and announced he had options on 135.949 additional acres. Authorized to proceed, Will acted swiftly and by May 4 had acquired 277.851 acres. Charles Weber held out until March 1910, ceding his eight-acre pig farm for a very expensive $50,800.[93]

One small property remained—a ten-acre sliver owned by Du Pont Powder Company. Turned down flat by the local manager in March 1909, Baker wrote a long letter to Texas Senator Joseph W. Bailey pleading the Institute's case and asking the senator to speak with his fellow Senator H. A. du Pont on the Institute's behalf. Assuring Bailey that the Board would pay full market value and hesitating to trouble him, Baker concluded, "The Trustees of the Institute, and I as well, will be greatly obliged if you will simply call this matter to the attention of the Senator from Delaware." Although Bailey obliged and Senator du Pont wrote to his cousin, T. C. du Pont, president of the corporation, the effort was in vain; not until 1921 were five of the ten acres added to complete the Rice campus.[94]

Will Rice had acquired a campus of 290.340 acres for $249,020.71, including fill dirt and realty and legal expenses ($1,359.68). This flat, barren patchwork expanse three miles from the central business district comprised a group of farms surrounded by prairie with only a few small structures and one clump of trees. Harris Gulley traversed one corner, and water covered most of the acreage after a heavy rain. Edgar Odell Lovett and the architects he hired faced a challenging task to transform this unprepossessing expanse into an academic park connected to Houston's center of commerce by a boulevard extension of the city's principal street. Baker took Lovett to inspect the site as soon as he returned from his travels. The next day, May 8, 1909, Lovett prepared a formal announcement for the press to let Houstonians know that, at last, Institute trustees had selected a campus location sufficiently spacious to accommodate the halls of a great university.[95]

A WORTHY MONUMENT

Lovett completed his global journey in time to attend the May 12, 1909, Board meeting. From that meeting forward, the relationship between the Institute's president and its chairman was clear. Baker and the Board assumed fiduciary responsibility and control of the budget; Lovett shaped the Institute's physical space and academic destiny. As the years passed Baker and Lovett built a close friendship based on mutual respect and the bond forged as founders of Rice Institute. Their difference in age and the inescapable fact that Baker was ultimately responsible for the Institute's well-being probably made true intimacy impossible, but the Board chairman knew he could rely on his president, who in turn knew Baker would do all in his considerable power to promote the Institute's success.

In May 1909 Lovett gave an informal report of his tour around the globe to the full Board. He described the educational establishments he had visited and the notable scholars he had met. All agreed that the first-class, innovative institution they were planning deserved buildings that would "make a distinct contribution to the architecture of the country," be "conspicuous alike for their beauty and for their utility," and stand "as a worthy monument" to the founder's philanthropy.[96] Several architects had already written to Baker or Lovett about building the campus, and on May 12 the Board authorized Lovett to set out once again on a tour to interview firms able to conceive a long-range master plan for the campus and design its first structures. By encouraging Lovett to hire architects of national or international acclaim, the "trustees . . . boldly avowed their belief in the potency of a noble and impressive architecture as an inspiration to the youth who live and study within its shadow."[97]

On July 14 Lovett reported a productive trip: he had visited a dozen architectural firms and would interview further three "eminent architects." He had also formed an advisory committee to help plan the buildings' interiors and furnish the laboratories with equipment of the highest standard. The advisors, each of whom would receive a $500 honorarium for his service, were impressive. Joseph Sweetman Ames directed the physical laboratory at Johns Hopkins and had recently designed a new facility for the university's cutting-edge research curriculum. Edwin Grant Conklin had just become director of a "magnificently equipped" biological laboratory at Princeton, constructed to his own design on a campus then undergoing transformation in its curriculum and physical plant. Theodore William Richards of Harvard's chemistry department had recently been teaching at the University of Berlin, considered a model research environment. Samuel Wesley Stratton, who had designed the School of Engineering at the University of Chicago, now headed the National Bureau of Standards, rapidly becoming one of the most prominent scientific establishments in the world.[98] On July 16, at Lovett's request, Raphael outlined the president's progress in a long letter to Baker, who was spending the summer with his family at Loon Lake in the Adirondacks. To assure full understanding, he sent all Board members who had been unable to attend the meeting a similar report and asked for their approval.

Lovett made clear he wanted the most imaginative architects of the day. Lovett knew "Houstonians . . . were in a hurry" with fortunes being made every day and buildings rising quickly around the city. Residents "could not understand why plans for a university built for a thousand years could not proceed at the same pace," but he had to make his selection with deliberate care.[99] In August Lovett announced Cram, Goodhue, and Ferguson of Boston would design the Institute campus, and, with Board approval, he signed a letter of understanding with the firm on September 2, 1909. Although reluctant to choose Ralph Adams Cram (1863–1942) and Bertram Grosvenor Goodhue (1869–1924) because they were at the time redefining Princeton's appearance to dramatize the old college's new academic program, Lovett made an "intuitive" choice after repeated interviews, concluding the firm had "the liveliest construction imagination available."[100] He would establish his independence of Princeton influence in other ways. Clearly Lovett was much attached to Wilson's reforms: an enhanced student honor system, a curriculum of seminars and research, a mission of service to the nation, and performance at the highest level. But Lovett also hoped, in a new institution untrammeled by long traditions, to put in place two goals Wilson could not achieve: residential colleges where students and faculty lived, ate, and worked together and integration of graduate and undergraduate programs—when the Institute had matured enough to offer advanced degrees.

In the summer of 1909 Cram and Goodhue and a young associate, William Ward Watkin, began work on a design proposal and campus plan. Cram and Goodhue traveled to Houston for their first visit with the Board November 30 and December 1. Cram later described the site as "level and stupid"—flat, barren, muddy, and treeless—but he was inspired by the challenge of a "new situation" with "no historical or stylistic precedent" where he could produce "something that was beautiful . . . Southern in spirit, and with some quality of continuity with the historic and cultural past." Cram recognized that the "transmuted Gothic" he had fashioned at West Point (1902–1908) and Princeton (1906–1929) was "manifestly out of place" on the hot southwestern prairie. Seeking to retain the "religious and energizing force" of Gothic enthusiasm, Cram reassembled architectural elements indigenous to the Mediterranean basin and created "a measurably new style that, while built on a classical basis, should have the Gothic romanticism, pictorial quality, and structural integrity" of well-established universities.[101]

He and Goodhue discussed plans at length with Baker, McAshan, Raphael, Lovett, and the two Rice brothers during their short visit. Peppered with questions and charged to reduce costs where possible, the architects left the November 30 meeting to revisit the site and return to their drawing board. The next day, again after protracted discussion, Cram and Goodhue made a proposal satisfactory to the Board; they would design five buildings—a central structure for administration and classrooms, a dormitory and dining hall, a mechanical engineering laboratory attached to a power house, and physical and chemical laboratories—for an estimated cost of $880,000. On December 1 the Board authorized Cram and Goodhue to proceed, and the architects promised to put a "special force of draftsmen" on the project and to complete plans and specifications as fast as possible.[102]

Baker drafted a contract that specified a 5 percent commission to the architects, payable over the course of the job. His tough negotiating nearly derailed the project. Cram told Lovett that had the architects known the "Trustees would be so demanding, they should have been compelled to decline to go ahead with the work until a satisfactory contract had been signed." Describing the trustees' payment scheme as "unique" and "intolerable," Cram noted even the "shrewdest and richest bankers, lawyers and business men" of New York City and bureaucrats in the United States government, "notoriously the hardest taskmaster architects have to contend with," had not been so difficult.[103] Only Lovett's talents as a peacemaker could have produced a quick resolution, allowing all parties to sign a contract a few days after this outburst. Lovett noted later that "teamwork was not always easy with trustees sitting tight on the money bags and an architect's imagination soaring to the stars, but after a little we got the wonderful thing under way."[104] Once the Board approved general plans, accepted the proposed budget, and signed the contract, its members expected Lovett to handle details and only stepped in occasionally to facilitate completion of the project on schedule.

If Houstonians felt the complex project proceeded too slowly, in fact the team moved quite quickly at first. On May 25, 1910, bids went out to contractors and by June 27 the Board had accepted a proposal for the

Administration building. But on August 17 when William Ward Watkin arrived in Houston to oversee operations for Cram, Goodhue & Ferguson, construction had stopped. Undaunted by the steamy weather, the youthful associate traveled to the Ozarks to discover why marble quarries were not delivering as promised. Watkin accomplished his mission, the first of many in a long, distinguished career as head of Rice's architecture school and prominent designer of many houses, churches, and public buildings in his adoptive city. In November 1910 when shipments of crushed stone needed for Institute roadways and sidewalks had been held up for weeks, Lovett asked Baker to request "more favorable treatment" from Houston & Texas Central Railway and the Southern Pacific. Within days Baker's legal team had researched the issue and written railroad officials to point out the great local interest felt by "people at large in Houston," who wanted the Institute project completed quickly; would officials please deliver the stone promptly?[105] Although the Board had hoped to welcome its first class in 1911, that schedule proved impossible. Heavy rains slowed progress; the architects, who had accepted several huge academic projects, had not begun plans for the laboratories or the dormitory by May 1910; and the Board did not receive construction bids for the eating commons until October 1911.

On March 2, 1911, the seventy-fifth anniversary of Texas independence from Mexico, the Institute's seven trustees laid the cornerstone of the Administration Building in a simple ceremony unattended by guests or the press. At high noon Captain Baker used a silver trowel, manufactured in Houston and inscribed with the trustees' names and the date, to set the 6,500-pound stone of pale Ozark marble. Carved with shields of the Institute and Texas, it was placed at eye-level on the right side of the Sallyport. Secretary Raphael deposited in the stone's recess carefully selected records sealed in a copper box engraved with a list of its contents: a copy of the Bible in King James translation, the Institute's charter on parchment, a biography of William Marsh Rice, short sketches of founding trustees Frederick A. Rice and Alfred S. Richardson, an architect's rendering of the site plan mounted on linen, and copies of the *Houston Chronicle* and *Houston Daily Post*, printed on linen paper. The trustees chose an inscription for the stone panel that expressed the "devotion both to science and to humanism, which the founder desired when he dedicated the new institution to the advancement of literature, science and art"; the words of philosopher Democritus, in Greek lettering—

Captain Baker laying the cornerstone for the Administration Building, March 2, 1911. Early Rice Collection, Woodson Research Center, Rice University.

"Rather would I discover the cause of one fact than become king of the Persians"—would inspire future Rice scholars.[106] Despite another season of heavy floods in the spring of 1912, plans proceeded for a fall opening and for the Academic Festival that introduced Rice to the world in October 1912. The slower pace allowed Lovett to spend the fall of 1911 traveling in the Northeast and Europe. He invited scholars to be honored guests and lecturers at the 1912 opening, and he interviewed prospective candidates for his faculty, which he advertised as "a group of scientists and scholars through whose productive work, the new university may come into a place of competence among the established institutions of the country."[107]

FINANCING CONSTRUCTION

While Lovett reviewed architectural plans and academic credentials, Baker, McAshan, and Raphael maintained close supervision of all construction costs. For some time Baker had been considering ways to finance the project without touching endowment or using current income. By the time Lovett's architects and contracting team were ready to break ground, Baker had found a solution. He would pay for the project by producing new income from the Louisiana lands. Within a few months of William M. Rice's death, lumbermen had tried to purchase the 47,000 acres of timberland in Calcasieu Parish, Louisiana. For several years, while trials prevented settlement of Rice's estate, Baker could easily deny their requests, and the Board stood firm in refusing to sell the land. But the lands and their management were constantly under discussion as the Board found itself running a major lumber company. Will Rice made many trips to the timberlands, especially to examine damage following seasonal hurricanes, and Baker frequently stopped in New Orleans to confer with lawyers there about problems relating to title and timber leases; rights-of-way for railways, oil pipelines, and telegraph wires; and injuries suffered on the property. Lumbermen continued to offer Baker deals, but the Board remained firm that the land was not for sale.

As Baker and the trustees looked for ways to finance campus construction, they decided, after considerable deliberation among themselves and at two Board meetings devoted to the topic in June 1909, to sell the timber but keep the land. In this way, the Institute retained control of the land, which could be developed in other ways as economic conditions permitted, but were spared the trouble of day-to-day oversight of the logging operations. In June the Board advertised for bids and by August 2 had received five serious proposals: from the Sabine Tram Company, an old William Marsh Rice investment whose rail line ran through the property; from Houston builder Jesse H. Jones; from lumberman James M. (Silver Dollar) West; from Thompson-Ford consortium; and from Central Coal & Coke Co. of Kansas City, whose June appearance before the Board had not impressed Baker. Not much was done all summer because four trustees were out of town, but Raphael, McAshan, and Ben Rice favored West's bid. Baker told Parker he, too, "would be very glad to see West acquire" the contract. Baker's idea, he further explained, had "always been that we should sell the timber at a fixed price per thousand feet, to be paid for partly in cash and the balance on time at 5% interest, the deferred payments to extend over a period of twenty years [so] the institute would have its money invested at a fair rate of interest."[108]

Negotiations continued into January 1910; both Jim West and C. S. Keith, president of Central Coal & Coke, made additional presentations to the Board, but still the Board took no action, perhaps because of legal problems that arose. On April 11, 1910, Baker called a special meeting with Raphael, McAshan, and Lombardi at his law office in the Commercial National Bank Building. The Rice brothers were not present because they were "adversely interested in the matters presented." Three challenges threatened to scuttle the timber deal. First, like a recurring nightmare, new claims had been laid against the estate of William M. Rice, this time by the heirs of Charlotte M. Rice, deceased, widow of Frederick A. Rice and mother of Will and Ben, the absent trustees. These heirs, Charlotte's several children and grandchildren, now asked for a one-sixth interest in all property in Louisiana and Texas that might have belonged to the community estate of William Marsh Rice and Elizabeth Baldwin Rice. Second, when the Rices executed their 1892 deed of gift for the Louisiana land, no doubt "by inadvertence," 2,168.31 acres of land had been omitted from the property description. Third, Louisiana lawyer E. H. Farrar informed his Texas neighbors that the Institute was holding its lands "contrary to the laws" of Louisiana, whose statutes of incorporation did not permit ownership by charitable trusts (whose beneficiaries were the general public) or enable entities that issued no stock.

Baker and Parker reviewed these questions "pretty fully" with Farrar, a seasoned attorney from New Orleans. In Farrar's view, they could fix the deed problem and the heirs had no claim to any Institute lands, but litigation "would excite comment" and might "draw the attention" of Louisiana's attorney general to the Institute's position as landowner. In a letter to Baker, Farrar commented, "I was taught by my father, who was a distinguished lawyer of large practice, that a bad compromise is always better than a good law suit." For thirty-eight years Farrar had subscribed to this wisdom, and he advised the Institute to settle with the heirs and transfer the Louisiana lands to a lumber company incorporated in his state. Of course, Baker would not have read this long letter to his colleagues if he did not applaud its sentiments himself. The four trustees present authorized Institute officers to pay the heirs at law of Charlotte M. Rice, deceased, the sum of $100,000, and they asked their lawyers at Baker, Botts, Parker & Garwood to consider how best to create the suggested lumber corporation.

At a special meeting on December 23, 1910, Baker laid before the Board his plans for incorporating the Rice-Land Lumber Company under the laws of Louisiana, its purpose being to take over and hold the timberlands William M. Rice and his wife had deeded to the Institute.

Baker, Botts, Parker & Garwood, working with Farrar, Jones, Goldsborough, & Goldberg of New Orleans, outlined a proposal: the seven incorporators and seven directors of the Rice-Land Lumber Company would be the seven Institute trustees; the company's headquarters would be in Lake Charles; its capital stock would be $1 million; the trustee/directors would purchase thirty shares, each valued at $100; the Institute would transfer its Louisiana land to the Rice-Land Lumber Company and receive the remaining shares of stock in exchange.[109] After some refinements, the Board adopted the proposal, and on February 27, 1911, Raphael and McAshan, the new company's officers, held the organizing meeting of the Rice-Land Lumber Company in Lake Charles.

On April 13, 1911, trustees of the Institute, the Rice-Land Lumber Company's primary shareholder, accepted a $4 million deal with Jim West and his partner Sam Parks of Beaumont, who would purchase timber from the company over a fifteen-year period for cash and payments every six months at 5 percent interest. Baker and the Board were careful to publicize all transactions surrounding the formation of Rice-Land Lumber Company, the transfer of Institute lands to the company, and the sale of its timber to West and his associates, organized as the American Lumber Company. Baker had successfully steered the Board through a difficult business negotiation to a resolution that provided immediate income and preserved long-term investment potential. The cash he generated paid for the Institute's buildings without touching operating funds or capital endowment.

MAKING CONNECTIONS

As buildings took shape on campus, Captain Baker continued to expand the Institute's community presence and deepen his friendship with the Lovett family. The Captain and his wife Alice included Lovett and his wife Mary at social events, introduced them to Houston's civic leaders, and encouraged their children to be playmates. In January 1910 the Bakers held a grand reception in the Lovetts' honor. Mary sent her sister Annie Hale a newspaper clipping and described the "big affair, so beautifully planned and handsomely carried out," in a long letter. Artistic flower arrangements filled the reception room, and the dining room done in "orchid shades in candies cakes candle ribbons was a perfect dream. The prettiest I think I ever saw." Wishing her sister could have seen the trium-

Administration Building under construction, 1912. Early Rice Collection, Woodson Research Center, Rice University.

phant event, Mary exclaimed at the "large crowd, one continuous 'living chain' of three & one half hours duration greeted us most cordially." Mary hoped these welcoming men and women would "be perhaps our life long friends & associates." Best of all, Captain and Mrs. Baker "are themselves charming people, so democratic, and certainly know how to do things of the grand scale. With such supporters we can not fail—we must succeed in this great work."[110]

While Lovett was busy with architects, contractors, and faculty correspondence, Baker and the Board worked with municipal officials and business associates to connect the campus to Houston's central business district. Through Baker's railroad affiliations, the Board ordered a rail spur built to the site of the Power House to bring in materials and fuel (coal and later oil). In April 1910 Baker and Edwin B. Parker, whose relations with County Judge Earl Amerman were "very pleasant" because Parker had rendered him assistance with a bond election, worked out a compromise between the Judge and the Institute's neighbors along Main Street to widen the road to 120 feet and run a trolley toward the campus on a parallel strip that became Fannin Street. Landowners along Main Street promised to donate enough land to develop the wide gravel roadway. As soon as investors discovered where the Institute had decided to build, they began buying undeveloped property and farmland surrounding the site and along the route from downtown to the campus because they realized the Institute would be a catalyst for commercial and residential expansion in the area. In 1908 Baker himself purchased a large block of raw land, north of the campus and west of Main Street, which he and his son would develop in the 1920s.

Board members were so pleased by Lovett's handling of the construction project, they decided he should join their ranks. With his usual deliberation, Baker had already been considering the relationship between the president and the Board for some time. In August 1908 Baker asked Lovett to gather statistics about thirty-three major educational institutions. He learned that thirteen universities, including the University of Virginia, Vanderbilt, and Columbia, placed the president on the Board; twelve, including Princeton, Yale, and Harvard, named their academic president the Board's presiding officer; and only eight, including Stanford, Tulane, and the University of Texas, excluded the president from the Board.[111] In May 1909 Cesar Lombardi told Baker he felt Lovett should be elected to fill the seat long left vacant by Frederick A. Rice's death because "we will want his views and his counsel at almost every meeting as soon as we embark in the practical building of our institution." Lombardi believed all successful enterprises include their executive head as a director, and he noted that Lovett would receive compensation as president, not as a trustee, just as Baker was receiving fees as a lawyer and Raphael was paid to be treasurer while each served as trustee. Baker replied that he concurred completely with Lombardi's views but could not take action for several months. Baker wanted to establish precedent for the fledgling institution and thought it appropriate to make important changes at annual meetings. On February 2, 1910, the Board invited Lovett to attend all future Board meetings. On June 1, 1910, at its Annual Meeting, the Board formally elected Lovett to fill the seat of Frederick A. Rice. On June 16 Baker appointed a Committee on Grounds and Buildings with Lovett as chairman and McAshan and the Rice brothers as members. The Board promptly empowered the committee to make decisions about construction problems whenever it was "impracticable" to convene the full Board. Clearly, Baker wanted the committee to handle all problems not pertaining to financing the project.

Combining his talents as an advocate, an organizer, and a conciliator, Captain Baker adopted the dream of William Marsh Rice as his own cause. He fought those who would destroy Rice's legacy; he brought together men of exceptional talent to advance literature, science, and art;

and he challenged his colleagues and fellow Houstonians to build an academic institution that aspired to excellence at the national level. Contemporaries believed "the hand and heart and brain of Captain Baker
was the hand and heart and brain that set and kept the Institute on its
feet, steadied it through its difficulties, brought it out of its defeats, gave
it the vital power that made possible its success."[112] Having overseen its
conception and birth, Baker monitored the Institute's growth with care
and pride. As the years passed, he deferred almost all scholastic matters
to President Lovett, continued to expand the endowment and monitor
expenditures, and took pleasure in watching the fledgling institution
mature.

CHAPTER FIVE

Building Institutions

CAPTAIN BAKER APPLIED the full force of his considerable emotional energy, intellectual ingenuity, and professional pride to a single, monumental quest from the moment a messenger handed him Charlie Jones's telegram on Monday afternoon, September 23, 1900, until the hour he climbed to the speakers' platform at the Rice Institute Academic Festival on Saturday morning, October 12, 1912. Before him for more than twelve years loomed his task: to protect the legacy of his client William Marsh Rice and to create an institution for the advancement of science, literature, and art. Although he was forced to focus on this overarching challenge, Captain Baker's world did not stand still.

URBAN POWERHOUSE

Houston, a pleasant market town of 45,000 in 1900, became Texas' largest city by 1910, with 79,000 residents; by the close of World War I, Houston was a major American manufacturing and commercial center of 138,000, "growing a thousand acres of skyscrapers, building schools and factories

Illustrations: Portraits of Alice Baker and Captain Baker painted by Elizabeth Gowdy Baker, New York City, 1910. Courtesy of Baker College Library.

and churches and homes."[1] One Institute professor described the energy that thrilled newcomers: "When I began my work at Rice, stonecutters from Italy were still chiseling on the ornamental figures outside my office windows: great dredges were biting deep into the inland soil of Texas, slowly but surely bringing the waters of the world's 'seven seas' to the doorsteps of Houston . . . it <u>was</u> an inspiring moment."[2] At the hub of this activity stood James A, Baker, senior partner of Houston's oldest and most forward-looking law firm, chairman of an educational institution whose endowment comprised the largest single financial resource in the region, president of the city's second-largest bank, and officer or director of several important regional companies.

Change was the by-word of the young century, and Captain Baker saw opportunity in the city's transformation. The 1900 hurricane changed Galveston's relationship to Houston, which supplanted the island city as Texas' flagship port. Legal battles following William M. Rice's death changed Baker's law practice and propelled him to modernize and enlarge his firm. Rice's legacy changed the city's appearance as Baker expanded the Institute's endowment by lending funds to Houston builders who were developing commercial and domestic real estate projects for the hundreds arriving daily to live and work in the Bayou City. While Baker was pursuing Rice's murderer in New York, an event occurred near Beaumont, Texas, eighty-five miles to the east, that introduced a new source of wealth to Texans. At 10:30 a.m. on January 10, 1901, Captain Anthony F. Lucas's gusher erupted at a salt dome called Spindletop. For nine days the well spewed oil two hundred feet into the air; within weeks, nearly 50,000 fortune seekers rushed to the area and erected hundreds of wobbly wooden derricks to pump for black gold.[3] The petrochemical industry soon dominated Houston business as oilmen made investments that changed the region's economy.

Newcomers like oil entrepreneur Joseph S. Cullinan, civic visionary William C. Hogg, and drill-bit inventor Walter Benona Sharp not only brought fresh ideas and modern industries to the city, but also they understood the farsighted idealism of William Marsh Rice and his hand-picked trustees, who believed a great educational institution would make Houston a great city. Like Baker and the other Institute directors, they identified personal and family success and good fortune with the achievement of their community and the well-being of their neighbors. In the years after Spindletop, they joined the men and women who had

Houston, ca. 1911. Early Houston Collection, Woodson Research Center, Rice University.

already prospered in Houston to build commercial, cultural, and social service institutions they believed would attract talented citizens and allow Houston to compete on a national and world stage. While Captain Baker focused his attention on securing the Rice legacy, he and his wife Alice took major steps to change Houston's economic and civic life. The Captain wielded power through his access to legal and financial resources in New York, Boston, Chicago, Kansas City, and Houston. To Alice every Houstonian was a neighbor. She used her social position to empower families and improve urban life.

MODERNIZING THE LAW FIRM

Baker, Botts, Baker & Lovett had begun to specialize in legal problems facing large corporations during the last years of the nineteenth century as Robert Scott Lovett and the slightly younger Edwin Brewington Parker concentrated on interstate railroad clients, while Captain Baker

Robert Scott Lovett
(with the firm 1892–1904).
Courtesy of Baker Botts
L.L.P.

focused on William Marsh Rice's complex corporate empire. But it was Baker's direct and prolonged experience with Hornblower, Byrne, Miller & Potter, considered large at ten lawyers, that demonstrated the value of a centralized practice organized to meet the demands of large, hierarchical corporations, whose multiple legal requirements varied widely from strategic negotiation to settling small claims. The law firm structure that dominated twentieth-century corporate practice in New York, Chicago, San Francisco, and Houston stressed loyalty to the firm and office organization. Able partners, who shared in the firm's financial success, attracted the most talented graduates of acclaimed law schools; the young, salaried associates endured tough apprenticeships, competing to join partner ranks. Ability trumped connections in the hiring process—at least that was the theory articulated by legal giants like James A. Baker, recognized as a man of sound judgment, and Edwin B. Parker, acclaimed as an organizational genius.[4]

Captain Baker's parents had encouraged him to strive for the best result in every endeavor, and as senior partner for nearly half a century,

Edwin Brewington Parker
(with the firm 1894–1926).
Courtesy of Baker Botts
L.L.P.

he built Houston's leading law firm with one goal in mind—to deliver professional excellence. As the firm evolved and expanded in response to its clients' needs, Baker gathered about him a group of lawyers—all men in his day—who took pride in the profession, were loyal to each other and to the firm, and emphasized personal integrity. Baker placed those values at the heart of his practice.[5] He identified the firm's success and his own with the growth and prosperity of his adopted city and drew his colleagues into community life. He enjoyed working with the younger men, closely supervising them, and gradually giving them more responsibility. He taught his subordinates by questioning and by challenging them to discover solutions to legal problems. He saw firm meetings as critical hours of learning—about the firm's business, about new legislation or Supreme Court decisions, about the way law worked in everyday life. His partners were his friends, but he reached out to the younger men, taking them to his home for lunch, treating them to Rice football games, and talking over their concerns.[6]

Captain Baker understood the importance of a structured, specialized practice, but it was Parker who initiated the firm's plan of action. Always nattily attired with spats, cane, and a well-groomed Vandyke, Parker was viewed by his respectful but often long-suffering colleagues as "a manager at heart, an autocrat by nature."[7] Soon after joining Baker and Lovett as a partner in 1900, Parker began his quest to centralize the practice. As a de facto managing partner, Parker started to assign matters brought to the firm and kept a close eye on the trial docket.[8] Fees, letters to clients, expenses, all flowed across his desk; stenographers now worked for the firm, not for specific lawyers; and meetings of the lawyers to review firm progress became standard. Parker also collected statistics about clients, fees, hours spent on each case, numbers of employees, and other issues pertaining to the quotidian practice of law. Even more important was his hunt for additional legal talent and support staff.

By 1902 the firm's letterhead listed partners Baker, Lovett, and Parker and attorneys Jesse Andrews, W. H. Kimbrough, Clarence Ray Wharton, and Thomas Hutchinson Botts. Office management fell to John H. McClung, chief clerk, with Craig Belk as his youthful assistant; McClung implemented Parker's commands, while Belk would move on to become a successful insurance man and real estate developer. Andrews and Wharton, who were admitted to the partnership in 1906, became two of the firm's leading lawyers. Andrews, a tall, slim starting guard on the University of Texas's first football team, accepted employment at $75 a month on December 1, 1899; he was general counsel of Long-Bell Lumber Company and ran a satellite office in Kansas City for many years. Wharton, a fiery orator and aggressive trial attorney who "gave no quarter" to his opponents, trained many young litigators.[9] Kimbrough, the former head of Houston's public schools, departed before World War I, and Botts, son of the firm's founder Walter Browne Botts and a great favorite of Captain Baker, joined the partnership in 1915 but died at age forty-three in 1922. Captain Baker had been a surrogate father to the young Botts and had mentored his progress as a scholarly lawyer who often researched projects for the senior man. In a tribute before the Harris County Bar Association, Baker described himself as overcome by his young partner's death, which when it came "tears our hearts and wrings our souls": Tom Botts, the Captain said, possessed "those qualities that go to make up a lawyer and a man—strong in his friendship, loyal in his friendship, true to his duty, loyal to his duty, true to his family, loyal to his family . . . an example worthy of emulation" by all members of the profession.[10]

The year 1904 was critical for Captain Baker's growing firm. Although still devoting long weeks to settling William Marsh Rice's will, Baker also turned his attention to changes in his law office. Robert S. Lovett, who had overseen legislative matters in Austin for the firm's railroad clients for a decade, was spending most of his time in New York City on business for the Southern Pacific Railroad, now part of Edward Henry Harriman's transportation empire that included Southern Pacific and Union Pacific systems. Impressed by Lovett's brilliant ability to interpret federal and state law, articulate the powers of state authority, and negotiate proper jurisdiction over interstate conflicts, Harriman invited Lovett to take over as attorney at corporate headquarters, and the Lovett family moved to New York City in 1904. Lovett's subsequent career as Harriman's chosen heir, who served as president and finally chairman after the older man's death in 1909, continued to benefit his Houston law firm and its city for the next three decades.[11] "No one," said a Baker Botts colleague, "could more clearly apprehend or more forcefully present the determining issue in a case or more safely guide a great enterprise to a successful end."[12] Parker, who had shared Lovett's railroad docket, took charge of Southern Pacific legal services in the region until he was called to Washington during World War I.

Lovett's departure left a serious gap in the firm's senior ranks, one Baker and Parker filled by inviting Hiram Morgan Garwood (1904–1930), an eloquent orator and successful trial attorney with strong ties to state government, to join them. Judge Garwood had served as a Texas representative and senator and a county judge. He had helped draft the act that established the Texas Railroad Commission, and he knew exactly how to fight for the Southern Pacific before the Texas legislature and the railroad commissioners. The Judge moved to Austin for months at a time when the Legislature was in session so he could mold and monitor legislation that affected his client. He worked with the Baker Botts network of district and local lawyers to generate goodwill for railroads in small towns and rural counties, whose residents had long feared the giant corporations but were desperate for the transportation services railroads provided. A spellbinding storyteller, Garwood was a serious scholar whose deeply disciplined mind grasped the critical points of

Hiram Morgan Garwood
(with the firm 1904–1930).
Courtesy of Baker Botts
L.L.P.

every legal issue.[13] In 1904 the firm changed its name to Baker, Botts, Parker & Garwood and moved from the Gibbs Building, where it had been since 1892, to larger quarters in the elegant Commercial National Bank Building, where it remained until 1927. A catwalk connected the firm's sixth floor offices to the Southern Pacific legal department in the railroad's office building next door.

Five future partners began their careers with Baker, Botts, Parker & Garwood before World War I. Clarence Leon Carter (1907–1936) practiced law in Livingston, Texas (1891–1902) and was associated with the firm from 1902 to 1906 as division attorney for the Southern Pacific Railway. He found railroad work so time-consuming and tedious that he engaged in solo general practice for a year until Clarence Wharton persuaded him to join the firm and share Wharton's more varied trial practice. After Carter's death in 1936, Wharton recalled his friend's "force of character" and a devotion to the firm so great that overwork shortened his life.[14] Jules H. Tallichet (1909–1937) tried cases for the Southern

Jesse Andrews
(with the firm 1899–1961).
Courtesy of Baker Botts
L.L.P.

Pacific in Austin and West Texas before joining Baker, Botts, Parker & Garwood as Southern Pacific general counsel. A tall, fearless, strong-tempered advocate for his client, Tallichet was reputed to have faced striking railroad workers with pistols strapped to his waist.[15] Captain Baker's nephew Walter Alvis Parish (1910–1953), Minnie Baker Parish's son, left his native Huntsville to practice in Houston and became one of the state's best known utilities lawyers. Walter Hillman Walne (1912–1947), a "pugnacious and tenacious" trial attorney, framed the firm's hiring procedures and strengthened Houston's symphony orchestra after World War I.[16] Ralph Bayard Feagin (1914–1946) came to work in 1914 but spent 1917–1919 with the Red Cross and War Industries Board in New York and Washington, DC.

Baker maintained his strong position as senior partner during the pre-World War I years. Even though Garwood came on board as a name partner in 1904, he received a straight salary his first year, while Baker and Parker divided net earnings on a 7:3 basis. From 1905–1911 Garwood began to share in the firm's proceeds but continued to receive a guaranteed salary; not until 1909 did Baker and Parker share net income equally, and only in 1912 did the partners sign a formal agreement. Between 1895 and 1915, firm income grew from $32,000 to $256,000. In 1913, ten lawyers, six of whom were partners, served 293 clients, only twelve of whom paid fees or retainers of more than $1,000. These twelve, however, accounted for $94,000 in business. By the end of World War I the firm kept an average daily bank balance of $50,000 in three banks, all closely associated with Captain Baker and his partners; in 1918 sixteen lawyers, twelve stenographers, and seven clerks or messengers served the firm's growing clientele.[17] Assignment and collection of fees and retainers occupied many hours' discussion at firm meetings and lengthy negotiations with clients. Robert Lovett noted in 1900 that the fees for the "strictly legal service" Baker rendered to resolve the Patrick case "belong to your firm and not to you individually, and . . . such legal business as you control is necessarily controlled for and by the firm."[18] Nearly three decades later young associates were told to consult their elders about fees "to be certain we are receiving adequate compensation for our services, and at the same time leaving our clients and correspondents satisfied with the charges."[19] Except as practiced by Judge Garwood on behalf of the Sunset-Central Lines, as Southern Pacific affiliates were called in Texas, lobbying made the partners uncomfortable, and the firm charged additional fees for work done before the legislature or hired specialists to represent their clients in Austin.[20]

Working conditions in high-rise buildings before the days of centrally cooled air challenged the good nature of partners and their employees, and long summer vacations became standard practice. Everyone kept paperweights to control stacks of briefs in rooms cooled only by open windows or whirring ceiling fans. Winter or summer, official hours were long, from 8:30 a.m. until 5:30 or 6:00 p.m. during the week and from 8:30 a.m. to 4:00 p.m. on Saturdays, with half-day Saturdays from June through September.[21] Regardless of stated hours, it was tacitly understood that lawyers devoted as much time as was needed to resolve each client's problem even if it meant working at night or on Sundays. The telephone was a technology still regarded with suspicion by many, and the chief clerk oversaw use of the firm's three instruments, each attached to the wall. Lawyers long remembered Jules Tallichet, who regularly became enraged while trying to make connections. More than once he was overheard yelling into the receiver before yanking the phone from the wall and throwing it out the window, left open to catch any breeze that might be stirring from the Gulf, fifty miles away. Memoranda from Parker commanded in ponderous tones, "It is imperative that there should be someone at the telephone board at all times during business hours" to connect the client's call to an appropriate phone. "Seconds count in telephone service," laggard clerks learned, and the reception office was not a "lounging room." To better serve clients, Parker requested everyone to provide a memorandum at the end of each day listing "the number of times during the day where a call from our office had to wait on account of our lines being busy."[22] Until World War I spurred nationwide connections, there was no national long-distance service, and lawyers continued to rely on the telegraph. Clients provided code books so lawyers and executives could carry on correspondence in cipher, thereby protecting business decisions requiring quick attention.[23] Lawyers who needed to meet with out-of-city clients personally had to plan ahead since free railroad passes were dispensed by the pass bureaus of client rail lines and took several days to arrange.

With Baker's approval, Parker pushed the Baker, Botts, Parker & Garwood lawyers, whether experienced or neophyte, toward businesslike practices. Both men recognized that their growing clientele and employee roster demanded careful management. On May 20, 1907, Parker revealed his first Plan of Organization, in which he laid out the duties of each lawyer and staff member. Central to his plan was the Creed he repeated each year: "Professional preeminence, excellence of professional services, living fully up to the traditions of the Firm and to the standards set by those who have gone before us, and so conducting ourselves and our work in the minutest details as to reflect credit upon them—this must be our first care—our dominating purpose."[24] By 1911 when Parker's Plan for the coming year reached sixteen pages, he hoped "everyone in the office, from Capt. Baker to the office boy, [would] feel entirely free to offer any suggestions." Parker set forth annual goals that fostered efficiency and ensured no client's business lay neglected. "Our first care," he explained, "must continue to be, as it ever has been for more than forty years past, to maintain the good name of the firm for integrity, fair dealing and legal ability. . . . Whatever is worth doing at all is worth doing well." Reminding his colleagues that "the individual must be subordinated to the firm," he explained, "It is through consolidation of effort and ability and concentration of energy that the best results are obtained."[25]

Not everyone appreciated Parker's zealous quest for centralized order. A memorandum of July 21, 1916, informed its readers that Houstonians were "enjoying delightful summer weather," and that everyone "remaining on duty" at the office must be particularly careful to organize work, systematize time, and "re-double our efforts" because five partners were on vacation. Clarence Wharton was not amused and scribbled an exasperated note to Jesse Andrews (one of those who was absent), opining that "in addition to his other manifold duties," Parker had now become a weatherman.[26] Baker mitigated Parker's earnest and unrelenting management exhortations by good-humoredly placating his junior partners' protests while remaining Parker's close friend and advocate. Together the diplomat and the autocrat steadily molded their ambitious, articulate, argumentative colleagues into a loyal, well-organized legal powerhouse.

A BANKING CAREER

Contemporaries applauded Captain Baker's business acumen as often as they praised his legal expertise. His father's example, his association with William Marsh Rice, and his early business success led him inexorably to a second career as a banker. Not only did he actively participate as an officer and director of major Houston financial institutions, but also he used Institute funds to bankroll Houston's growth. Baker had observed "banking" activity from early childhood. For twenty years Judge Baker, through Baker & Hightower mercantile, had provided limited banking services to Huntsville customers by extending short-term credit and reinvesting interest earned. When the Judge arrived in Houston, he discovered his two partners were invested in the city's infant banking industry. T. W. House, who used his Civil War fortune to build Houston's most esteemed private bank, was a firm client, and William Marsh Rice frequently made loans to entrepreneurs who were building Houston businesses.

Shortage of capital had plagued European explorers who introduced North America's untapped bounty to the world's insatiable market, and traders pushing inland or settlers seeking fertile soil relied on financial backers in London, Rotterdam, or Paris. The Anglo-American adventurers who came to Texas in the nineteenth century were no different, and they counted on capital amassed in Boston, New York, or Philadelphia to fund their enterprises. Dependence on these distant financial masters bred a popular suspicion of money power that hobbled the development of a banking system in Texas and slowed the industrializing process.[27] By 1872 the First National Bank, the City Bank of Houston, and three or four private banks—which operated without charters—provided banking services to the city's businessmen. Several Confederate sympathizers, including railroad builder Paul Bremond, banker T. W. House, and Judge Baker's future partner Peter Gray, established First National Bank in 1866, the first investors in Houston to take advantage of new federal banking laws.[28] They asked fellow director and Union sympathizer Ingham S. Roberts, MD, to negotiate the bank's charter with the United States Comptroller of the Currency and made an initial capital investment of $100,000, twice the amount demanded by federal law. Situated in a two-story building at Main and Franklin, the bank attracted reliable depositors and talented personnel throughout Captain Baker's lifetime.[29] City Bank of Houston, formed in 1870 by Benjamin Botts and B. F. Weems, took advantage of Reconstruction laws allowing state charters. Benjamin's brother Walter Browne Botts served as legal counsel and director of the small bank. A few other Reconstruction-era state banks struggled for a while, but most had disappeared by the late 1880s. To handle trust business and real estate investment loans, Colonel Botts, Captain Joseph C. Hutcheson, and four other stockholders chartered the Houston Land and Trust Company in 1875. Capitalized at $6,000, Houston Land and Trust developed an important relationship with Baker, Botts & Baker that lasted beyond Captain Baker's lifetime and relied heavily on Rice family investments in the company.[30]

Captain Baker made a major business decision on June 10, 1886, when he joined cotton broker William B. Chew, several railroad executives, and investors from New Orleans to charter Commercial National Bank, with capital of $200,000. Only Baker's death fifty-five years later would sever the connection. Chew was a director of the bank from 1886 until it merged to form a larger enterprise in 1912 and was named president in 1891. From 1897 to 1912 Baker served on the board, and from 1897 to 1903 he was one of three vice presidents. Southern Pacific and Union Pacific officials were directors, and on December 20, 1901, Baker recommended that the Texas Administrator for the William M. Rice estate place funds in an account at the Commercial National Bank "because Mr. [Robert S.] Lovett and I are stockholders and directors of it, and know that it is one of the best and most solvent monied institutions in the State."[31] In 1902 Baker used his association and friendship with Chew to secure a favorable line of credit for the Institute to pay the Missouri heirs $34,500 and reimburse Hornblower's firm for expenses.[32] By 1910 Commercial National recorded over $4 million in deposits, its success largely due to Rice Institute patronage.

Within a few years, investors had opened three more national banks to expand investment opportunities in Houston. In 1889 developer Henry S. Fox formed Houston National Bank, which he managed until 1909. In 1890 lumberman John Kirby founded Planters & Mechanics National Bank (1890–1907), capitalized at $200,000. Aggressive and innovative, Kirby served as the bank's president (1901–1905) and relied on local financing and small depositors. Although popular with lumbermen and local businessmen, Kirby's concept did not survive the Panic of 1907 even though Baldwin Rice, administrator of William M. Rice's estate in Texas, asked that substantial funds from Rice's estate be placed in Planters & Mechanics National.[33] South Texas National Bank took a different approach. Capitalized at $500,000 — an enormous sum for the era — South Texas National founders attracted Kansas City investors, and major local stockholders included Captain Baker, Will Rice, developer Henry MacGregor, rancher Sam Allen, retailers Abe and Ike Levy, T. W. House, and James Everett McAshan, who was named chief operating officer from 1890 to 1912. McAshan, a brilliant intellectual who wrote scholarly articles for banking industry publications, would soon join Baker on William M. Rice's original Institute Board. For over a decade Institute Board meetings met at McAshan's office in the South Texas National Bank building, and on August 4, 1905, the trustees named South Texas National Bank its third major depository for Institute funds.[34]

In 1905 Texas legislators heeded the demands of commercial planters, Austin's most vocal lobbyists, and passed laws to authorize state banks under conditions they hoped would favor local bank ownership and make credit accessible to small borrowers.[35] The new laws forbade branch banking and required low start-up capitalization; allowed savings departments, which paid interest on small deposits; permitted borrowing with real estate as collateral; did not limit the amount of loans dependent on warehoused cotton as collateral; and permitted banks to

Commercial National
Bank Building under
construction. Early
Rice Collection,
Woodson Research
Center, Rice
University.

Commercial National Bank Building (firm offices 1904–
1927). Early Rice Collection, Woodson Research Center,
Rice University.

open trust departments—all benefits denied nationally chartered institutions. Taking advantage of the new laws, Captain Baker joined Frank Andrews, Thomas Henry Ball, Will and Jonas S. Rice, Captain Joseph C. Hutcheson, W. T. Carter, and Jesse Jones to charter the Union Bank & Trust Co. in 1905, and the group named Joe Rice president. Two years later Union Bank & Trust absorbed Kirby's Planters & Mechanics National, a victim of the Panic of 1907. With large blocks of stock owned by the Rice and Carter families and large deposits from the William M. Rice Estate, Union Bank & Trust grew quickly to rival First National Bank, amass $10 million in deposits by 1910, and become the largest state-chartered bank in Texas.

The Panic of 1907 brought in its wake demands for reform and regulation. Particularly worrisome to the Union Bank & Trust directors was the Texas Guaranty Fund Law of 1909, which required each state bank to place as much as 2 percent of its average daily balance in a state fund to protect otherwise unsecured deposits in member banks. President Jonas S. Rice and the directors feared their fast-growing bank would be forced to support weaker state banks, and in 1910, before the new provisions could take effect, Union Bank & Trust reorganized as Union National Bank, absorbing Union Bank & Trust and Merchants' National Bank in the process. Merchants' National, founded in 1901, was almost wholly owned by Jesse Jones, who had also organized National City Bank in 1906 to begin his banking career. Samuel Fain Carter saw the 1907 panic as an opportunity. He sold his substantial lumber interests and chartered the eponymous Lumberman's National Bank that year. In 1909 he bought Jesse Jones's National City Bank, and the next year he absorbed Central Bank & Trust and American National Bank, chartered in August 1908 by several land developers. In 1923 Lumberman's National, no longer linked exclusively to the lumber industry, changed its name to Second National Bank.[36]

Nineteenth-century banking proved an uncertain business with little regulation, frequent fluctuations, and many failures that led to serious panics in 1893 and 1907. To strengthen public faith in banking practices, Texas bankers founded the Texas Bankers' Association in 1884. Through annual meetings and publications, members tried to stabilize the industry by discussing modern banking practices, sharing common problems, and defining industry standards. In September 1890 two banks associated with Captain Baker—Commercial National and South Texas National—and First National, Houston National, and Planters & Mechanics National formed the Houston Clearing House under the direction of Emanuel Raphael. The clearing house expedited debit and credit transactions and provided a forum for cooperation, especially in economic hard times. Houston's economy suffered severely during the financial Panic of 1907 that threatened nationwide economic collapse until a consortium led by J. P. Morgan guaranteed $35 million and the federal treasury promised an additional $25 million to stabilize New York banks, replenish the money supply, and encourage new investment. Houstonians were shocked when the venerable T. W. House & Company, now managed by the founder's sons, filed for bankruptcy during the panic. Tied closely to the cotton trade and dependent on London credit to finance its loans to Texas planters, T. W. House & Company could not withstand a shrinking money supply, tighter credit from London lenders, and a bank run in the fall of 1907.[37] Clearing House banks had traditionally followed conservative lending policies, and during the Panic they cooperated to steady the local market. In September 1907 Commercial National Bank President William B. Chew illuminated Clearing House caution when he called in loans his bank had made to Jesse Jones because "this bank does not care to loan money to any borrowing concern who keeps one or more other borrowing accounts locally."[38]

Clearing House banks made a crucial contribution to the city of Houston and the surrounding region by supporting Houston Ship Channel improvements. In 1896 United States Representative Captain Joseph C. Hutcheson, who had long advocated deepening Houston's bayou system to create a major port, introduced legislation in Congress to resurvey Buffalo Bayou and begin the development process. He then invited the Rivers and Harbors Committee to Houston, where he and his second wife Bettie Palmer Milby Hutcheson hosted a huge reception at their spacious home on McKinney Avenue so Houston's business leaders and their wives could meet and persuade the politicians. The next year, Hutcheson summoned a Texas delegation, including Charles Dillingham, president of South Texas National Bank, and William B. Chew, president of Commercial National Bank, to Washington to lobby for federal support of ship channel improvements.

Huntsville native Thomas Henry (Tom) Ball, one of Captain Baker's school chums, succeeded Hutcheson in the US House (1897–1903), where he also served on the Rivers and Harbors Committee. Often called

"Father of the Port," Ball spent the next two decades lobbying in Austin and Washington to improve the ship channel and build a deepwater port in Houston, achieving success with a grand opening in 1914.[39]

SOUTH TEXAS COMMERCIAL NATIONAL BANK

Captain Baker found himself at the center of two critical institutional projects in 1912: the opening of Rice Institute and the creation of a new bank. Late in 1911 Baker began discussions that led to the first merger of two strong, well-financed Houston-based banks: South Texas National Bank, in which Rice Institute owned 640 shares, and Commercial National Bank, of which Baker was a director and shareholder. Both were stable institutions with a limited number of important accounts; both were members of the Clearing House; both catered to prominent cotton brokers, lumber barons, railroad entrepreneurs, and merchant wholesalers; both maintained unimpeachable reputations for integrity and safety; both worked to build Houston institutions. By 1911 each was feeling serious competition from First National, which had recovered well after the Panic of 1907, and from Union National, whose 1910 merger had been successful. Union National had deposits of $8.577 million; First National of $8.4 million; South Texas National of $5.5 million; and Commercial National of $4.7 million.[40] To compete, Baker realized South Texas National and Commercial National needed to grow, and merger seemed the best way to increase size and competitive edge without sacrificing institutional principles.

On January 20, 1912, Baker called a special meeting of the Rice Board in his office: attending were James E. McAshan, chief operating officer of South Texas National; Benjamin Botts Rice, brother of Union National Bank's Joe and Will Rice; and Emanuel Raphael, organizer of the Houston Clearing House. In their roles as trustees of Rice Institute, they had come together to adopt a resolution authorizing formation of a new bank. The National Bank Act required that two-thirds of the shareholders agree to terms; with its large block of stock, Rice Institute cast a critical vote. The trustees accepted the plan drawn by Baker, McAshan, and the directors of the two banks. All parties agreed to liquidate both banks and secure a new charter. The former owners of both banks would become the stockholders of the new South Texas Commercial National

Bank, capitalized at $1 million. Charles Dillingham of South Texas National would become chairman while William B. Chew, former president of Commercial National, would serve as president of the new institution. Vice presidents would include Baker, McAshan, and three other officers of the liquidated banks. Those present at the Institute Board meeting authorized Baker to represent the Institute's 640 shares in the final merger negotiations. Six weeks later on March 2, 1912, Commercial National employees moved into the handsome headquarters only recently built by South Texas National. In 1914 Captain Baker became president of the bank that would be associated with him for the rest of his life. He held the post until 1922, at which point he became chairman of the board, a position he relinquished only at death.

Other banking developments also intrigued Houston's business world in 1912. Jesse Jones had been dabbling in banking for several years and was a major stockholder of Union National Bank, but he often disagreed with W. T. Carter, Baker, and the Rice brothers. On July 3, 1912, a group of investors, including Jones and former mayor Orren T. Holt, met in the offices of *Houston Chronicle* editor Arch MacDonald to create a new bank. Holt was chosen president of the National Bank of Commerce; Jones assumed the mantel of major stockholder; the owners named directors with interests in lumber, cotton, railroads, and oil; and offices opened in the old Commercial National Bank Building. The first years were difficult: Holt died in February 1913, operations moved to the Mason Building later that year, and the second president was not a success. Finally Roy Montgomery Farrar agreed to take the presidency, which he held from 1915 until 1921, when he resigned because of a public dispute with Jesse Jones over development of the ship channel turning basin. Jones became a director of National Bank of Commerce in 1914, president from 1922–1934, and was associated with the bank's success for the rest of his life. In 1917 Jones's quarrel with W. T. Carter erupted again because Union National directors and officers disputed Jones's business methods and found it very difficult to cooperate with him during economic crises. Jones sold his Union National stock to Carter and withdrew from all association with that bank to develop National Bank of Commerce.[41]

Just as Captain Baker understood the need to enlarge his law firm and to streamline its practice, he recognized that Houston banks had to accumulate more capital if they were to serve businesses reaching out to national and even international markets. Baker positioned South Texas Commercial National Bank as a depository for small Texas banks and as a liaison to the nation's sources of capital in Boston, New York, Kansas City, and Chicago. In 1914 South Texas Commercial National listed deposits of $7,277,105; First National, of $8,490,256; and Union National, of $6,257,823, all of them far ahead of Second National with deposits of $3,949,692 and of Jesse Jones's National Bank of Commerce with $1,295,291.[42]

Because South Texas Commercial National's charter did not offer trust services and could not make loans using real estate as collateral, Captain Baker asked Clarence M. Malone (1885–1960), a young friend who was secretary of Bankers Trust, and other investors to organize Guardian Trust Company, capitalized at $200,000. Baker, Botts, Parker & Garwood prepared the charter in 1917, Baker acted as president in the early years, and Guardian Trust opened an office for Malone and one stenographer on the fourth floor of the Commercial National Bank Building. A year later Guardian Trust occupied half the ground floor of the building. By May 1920 the entire first floor did not provide enough space, and Baker Botts had helped the successful business recapitalize at $300,000. Malone had taken over as president, and Captain Baker had assumed the chairmanship, which he held for life.[43]

THE TRUSTEE

For fifty years Captain Baker believed his greatest civic and business duty lay in his ability to conserve, protect, and enhance the bequest of William Marsh Rice. As custodian of his deceased client's property, Baker attached great importance to his role as trustee and to the meaning of the word "trust" in its legal and lay interpretations, explaining to one correspondent: "In my capacity as Trustee . . . I am a representative of the public and a servant of the people, and always glad to receive suggestions and advice from those who . . . have at heart the true interests of the Wm. M. Rice Institute."[44] Squandering wealth or misinterpreting Rice's wishes were anathema to him. Time and again he asked legal scholars to research and define the duties of a trustee. Baker's contemporaries praised his loyal tenacity: "Without Captain Baker there could scarcely have been a Rice Institute," explained English Professor Stockton Axson.

His admirers believed Baker rescued William M. Rice's bequest by re-sourceful legal action, augmented the endowment by wise but cautious reinvestment, and studied educational problems and "guided their application" to the Institute.[45]

While Baker saw the benefits of placing Institute assets in banks over which he exercised authority and of seeking legal advice from his own partners, he also recognized the dangers of close association and knew that critics might question his resolve to remain disinterested. It is a mark of his success that contemporaries did not doubt his ability to act fairly and to interpret faithfully his client's last will; men and women who knew him spoke often of his integrity, strength, and deter-mination—of the confidence he inspired in others. Usually Baker relied on his best judgment when making decisions and left few letters and no diaries to clarify his thinking; when on Institute business, however, his approach was especially careful and circumspect. A clear paper trail fol-lows him down the years because he reinforced his decisions with ex-pert opinions and referred Institute issues to appropriate legal counsel, financial advisor, or academic authority before taking action. Indeed, he told one supplicant, "I would be much flattered if I had the influence on the Board you imagine. The truth is . . . that each Trustee is a man of affairs with a successful business career behind him and they all have their own independent views in respect to every business proposition."[46] While ample evidence shows his influence was as great as the flattering petitioner suggested, colleagues claimed Captain Baker never pressured them and was careful to separate his roles as attorney, bank officer, and Institute chairman.

As soon as William M. Rice began to pay interest on his $200,000 note, the trustees developed an investment policy to reinvest this in-come. Almost at once they agreed on a two-pronged approach that was essentially conservative but allowed for growth. Viewing stocks with caution, they placed their cash in highest rated corporate bonds or treasury notes. Once they had accumulated some capital, they began to lend money to the men and women who were building Houston, secur-ing each loan with assets worth twice the loan amount and charging interest at market rates. During Baker's tenure as Board chairman, the trustees paid close attention to land management issues and filled most pages of their minute books with financial deliberations and investment decisions.[47]

THE COUNSELOR

In the years before World War I, Baker, Botts, Parker & Garwood continued to diversify. The firm expanded its lucrative railroad practice, which included an extensive court docket. Building on its experience representing William M. Rice's interests in the Houston Gas Light Company, of which Captain Baker was a director and stockholder, the firm also developed an important utilities clientele that included Houston Gas & Fuel and Houston Lighting & Power companies. Lumber baron W. T. Carter placed the firm on retainer at $125 a month from 1912 to 1920, and Parker traveled widely on behalf of Long-Bell Lumber Company, which paid substantial annual fees, reaching $2,500 a month by 1918. When Clarence Wharton helped the Texas Company reorganize as a Delaware corporation and move its headquarters to New York, he brought a lucrative oil industry client to the firm; for years Baker Botts represented Texas Company interests in the region. Considered the finest firm in the Southwest—by some the best west of the Mississippi— Baker, Botts, Parker & Garwood was often asked by national companies to prepare the contracts necessary for them to do business in Texas and then to represent their company's interest in the region.[48]

With the Patrick case drama behind him, Baker handled personally all matters associated with Rice Institute and his banking business and counseled a few important clients who had been associated with the firm for many years. Clients valued his ability to provide access to Institute and South Texas Commercial National Bank funds as well as his legal expertise and pragmatic approach to solving corporate problems. Partners sought his advice about decisions affecting the firm as a whole, and he stepped in to address difficult legal puzzles or client conflicts. He also devoted much of his time to maintaining the firm's national reputation by affirming good relations with business, government, and legal leaders in Boston, New York, Washington, DC, Chicago, and New Orleans. When traveling he called on clients, attorneys, and civic leaders who might refer business to the partnership. When in Houston, he continued long-term relationships with friends like Edward Andrew Peden, president of Peden Iron & Steel. Peden once recalled delivering messages to Judge Baker and Colonel Botts while a boy in the 1880s; by 1903 he had placed the manufacturing company on retainer with Captain Baker's firm.[49] To protect Institute interests, Baker continued as director of William Marsh Rice's former businesses, now the property of Rice Institute, and he oversaw the corporate reorganizations or sales of several assets. During the decade after Rice's death, Baker helped define the laws covering exemption from taxation for educational institutions by arguing that the Institute should not pay Houston property taxes since it provided only educational services and by paying lobbyists in Austin to fight for legislation exempting the endowment funds of educational institutions from taxation.[50]

Friends and clients of Institute trustees found an attentive audience when they appeared before the Board in person or sent letters explaining projects they were hoping to finance with Institute funds. Baker, like most Houstonians, believed that doing business with people whose reputations were well-known to him made good sense. Baker retained fond memories of his time at Austin College and answered a plea for help in 1908 by persuading Institute trustees to purchase a $30,000 bond at 8 percent so the college could build a new dormitory, provided the Institute's attorneys (Baker, Botts, Parker & Garwood) approved the title and vetted all documents. Austin College trustees expressed appreciation by awarding Baker an honorary Doctor of Laws (LLD) on May 31, 1910. Two years later, the Institute advanced another $30,000 to the college to remodel its Main Building—a poor investment, as it turned out, because a student arsonist burned the newly renovated structure to the ground in January 1913. Baker worked with the board of his old school to rebuild the facility, and the Institute received full repayment a few years later.[51]

Through his railroad contacts, Baker closed a deal with Iowan William Wright Baldwin to sell the 9,449-acre Rice Ranch to Baldwin's newly chartered South End Land Company in 1908, payable over eight years. Baldwin, vice president of the Burlington Railroad, laid out the city of Bellaire on part of the property and set aside the rest for truck farms and nurseries in a subdivision he called Westmoreland Farms. His lavish advertisements urged farmers from the Middle West to relocate in Texas. The area south of the Institute campus grew slowly at first, although Baldwin did succeed in luring horticulturalist and nurseryman Edward Teas to his development in 1910. Teas would go on to create Houston's premier landscaping business, would plant most of the trees on the Rice campus, and would create some of the city's best-known gardens.

In 1909 the Institute trustees decided to support "Carter's Folly," a project that characterized Houston's progress. Samuel Fain Carter, well-known to Board members as a millionaire lumberman, banker, and friend, sent a long letter to the trustees' meeting on March 10, 1909, in which he described his plans for a sixteen-story steel-frame and brick building on Main at Rusk—the highest in Texas at that time. He proposed to finance the $650,000 estimated cost by issuing stock in his building corporation and first mortgage 6 percent "gold bonds" not to exceed $400,000. Carter explained he would be purchasing most of the stock and half of the bonds but "cannot afford to begin the construction of this building" unless he could persuade the Institute to take the remaining bonds, which would be issued only as needed for construction and would not exceed an outlay of $200,000. After considerable discussion, the trustees agreed to participate in Houston's most ambitious commercial endeavor—but only after Institute attorneys (Baker, Botts, Parker & Garwood) examined all titles and approved all bonds. When Carter requested an additional $100,000 on June 13 so he could add four or five more stories, the Board replied that its original investment was "sufficient," and Carter's Folly did not exceed the original sixteen stories, although by 1913 it sported a multistory radio tower on its roof.[52] Within three years Carter had completed the building and settled accounts with the Institute.

Two major hotel projects owed their success to Institute investment. E. L. and F. V. Bender borrowed $100,000 in 1911 so they could complete their modern Bender Hotel, considered the city's finest when Captain Baker and Edgar Odell Lovett began planning events for the Institute's opening celebration. The Board also undertook complex negotiations with Jesse Jones, who wanted to construct a new Rice Hotel on the site of the older building. Jones's interest in hotel construction ultimately solved certain problems for the Institute Board, but he proved to be one of the Institute's most challenging customers. Considered a ruthless businessman by many contemporaries, Jones was a tough, self-assured negotiator used to accomplishing goals on his own terms. He was also well-known to change elements of the deal just when the other side thought negotiation was over.

The fate of William M. Rice's hotel had been in question for several years, and the old hostelry had proven a management headache for the Institute trustees. While dealing with trial and probate matters, Baker was frequently asked to address lease problems, repair issues, and flagging customer satisfaction in a building that needed to be updated, or even replaced. In 1906 five investors, including William B. Chew and

Jesse Jones, decided to form the Houston Hotel Company to secure "a modern and up-to-date hotel second to none in the South and surpassed by few elsewhere" at Main, Rusk, and Travis near the Institute's hotel. The Carter brothers, lumberman John Kirby, and Jim "Million Dollar" West joined the consortium of subscribers who purchased shares at $100 each, conditioned upon further support of $375,000 from "the citizens of Houston." Additional funding was not forthcoming, and the Panic of 1907 halted further discussion.[53]

In 1909 Jones approached Baker about restarting his hotel project at Main, Rusk, and Travis. Baker asked him to drop the project because the Institute trustees planned to build a modern hotel on the site of their Rice Hotel and annex at Main, Travis, and Texas. A few months later, while Baker was vacationing with his family at Loon Lake House in New York State, Jones began promoting his hotel company to Baker's partner, Edwin B. Parker. As Parker explained to Baker in detailed correspondence, Jones asked the lawyer to draw up papers outlining Jones's ideas. Jones told Parker he "has concluded to go forward . . . unless he has some definite assurance that the Trustees of the Institute will, at an early day, carry into effect their plans" because the city needed a modern hotel. Jones insisted he could begin building immediately and already had a few underwriters lined up. Parker also conferred with Raphael, who said the Trustees had informal plans to build at some point but that the old hotel was making money again; he wanted Parker to do "everything that could be consistently done . . . to discourage Jones from going ahead with his hotel promotion plans." Parker must have found Jones convincing since he wrote Baker that he did not think "we can ask Jones to abandon his plans and get out of the way . . . unless the Institute can give him some assurance."[54]

When Baker returned in the fall of 1909, he and Jones began to bargain. While Baker refused to break the management lease for the old building, he was willing to let it lapse, and plans to build a world-class hotel moved forward. On June 18, 1910, Jones and the Institute signed a ninety-nine-year lease for use of the Rice Hotel land that included provision for a loan of $500,000 toward construction expenses contingent on Institute approval of plans by Mauran, Russell & Crowell, the architects from St. Louis hired by Jones to design the new hotel building. A year later, Will Rice and James E. McAshan, appointed to oversee the Rice Hotel project for the trustees, reported on Jones's request for a new contract and an additional $250,000. On June 22, 1911, the new contract, signed by Captain Baker and witnessed by Raphael, was read into the minutes—a fairly unusual occurrence, but the amount in question was unusually large and the client sufficiently unpredictable to warrant care. In October the Institute trustees hired Sanguinet & Staats, architects, to represent their interests during the hotel's construction, to examine all plans for the hotel, and to ensure that contractors followed specifications exactly and adhered to Institute agreements. By mutual consent, all sub-contracts, work orders, and changes would require the signatures of Jesse Jones and James A. Baker.[55]

Will Rice submitted a three-page report to the Board on June 5, 1912, and explained that he and Baker had been conferring regularly with Jones, who now wanted to sign yet another contract with the Institute. Under the new contract the Institute would advance $850,000 while Jones, through his newly chartered Houston Hotel Association (June 20, 1912), would absorb $700,000 in building costs; later Jones would take over operation of the building. Jones provided $191,500 personally; J. L. West-lake, the general contractor, and forty-six other participants, including all of the subcontractors, provided the rest of the funds. On November 6, 1912, the Board accepted the final contract, which had been examined carefully by Baker, Botts, Parker & Garwood and included a provision for the Institute to name two individuals to the Houston Hotel Associa-tion's five-member board.[56] Although the process had been difficult, the result pleased both sides when the new Rice Hotel became the center of Houston's social, commercial, and entertainment life. In 1918 Jesse Jones offered the Institute Board $500,000 over forty years at 6 percent interest to purchase the ground beneath the hotel but was turned down because neither the price nor the terms were "sufficiently attractive."[57]

Among the steadiest customers for Institute funds were US Repre-sentative Captain Joseph C. Hutcheson (1842–1924), his son, the former mayor of Houston and federal Judge Joseph C. Hutcheson Jr. (1879–1973), and his second wife Harriet Elizabeth (Bettie) Palmer Milby Hutcheson (1851–ca. 1930). The men borrowed regularly to finance vari-ous unspecified projects, all their loans secured by rural land.

Native Houstonian Bettie Palmer inherited six hundred acres along Oyster Creek (Palmer Plantation) from her father, Judge Edward Albert Palmer, and additional property in Houston from her first husband Ed-ward Milby. In 1886 she married Captain Joseph C. Hutcheson, a widower with a large family of young children, and the middle-aged couple added a son and a daughter to the family. Bettie's descendants remembered her as a strong-willed, independent business woman who trotted about Houston in her buggy collecting rents in person. As Houston's industrial district expanded along the Ship Channel, Bettie began developing her property, but she did not approach the Institute in person. In 1914 Captain Hutcheson wrote letters on her behalf to request a small loan at 7 percent interest that was secured by land on the Harrisburg Road near the Turning Basin. Two years later the Hutchesons increased the size of her loan and began to subdivide the property. When Bettie's son Palmer Hutcheson joined Baker, Botts, Parker & Garwood in 1919, he became his mother's spokesman before the Institute and continued to secure cash to develop Palmer land, using the real estate itself as collateral. After Bettie's death, Palmer administered her estate and, like many of the Institute's cash-poor borrowers in the 1930s, he occasionally renegotiated the loans or asked for extensions.[58]

As a young lawyer, Captain Baker had worked with rancher and entrepreneur Samuel W. Allen (1826–1888). For the rest of his life, Baker counseled members of Allen's family, whose carefully preserved records demonstrate how Baker combined his legal, banking, and Institute ties to benefit his clients, the institutions he led, and the city he loved. In the years following Spindletop, commercial and residential developers moving north, southeast, and south of Buffalo Bayou began to covet the ranch land lying along Buffalo Bayou between downtown and Galveston Bay. Samuel W. Allen, a Kentucky native who had settled in Harris County in the 1840s, amassed large swaths of land in Harris, Galveston, Brazoria, and Fort Bend counties. He built a vast cattle ranch in the area and formed the state's largest cattle shipping business, Allen & Poole, before his death in 1888. For legal advice regarding his Galveston shipping business, which maintained offices on the Strand, Allen consulted William Pitt Ballinger, the city's most prominent attorney; in Houston, he placed his business affairs in the hands of Baker & Botts. When his son Samuel Ezekiel Allen (1848–1913) inherited his father's estate, he asked Captain Baker and Colonel Botts to do his legal work and in 1888 had Baker prepare a will, which Botts witnessed. In 1913, when his friend and client died, Captain Baker personally handled the probate of Samuel E. Allen's simple one-page document, which left "all of the estate" to his "beloved" wife Rosa Christie Lum Allen.

An elegant woman remembered by her contemporaries as a gracious hostess who was always beautifully dressed, Rosa, like most women of her generation, had focused her attention on family, home, and friends. Her husband's death placed her in charge of a complex business empire that included over twelve thousand acres of ranch land in Harris County, eighteen thousand acres in Brazoria County, and the Oriental Textile Mills, the world's largest manufacturer of press cloth for the cotton industry, with offices in New York, London, and elsewhere. An intelligent, well-traveled woman, Rosa turned to Captain Baker as her principal adviser, supported by her trustees—attorney Frank Andrews, banker John T. Scott at First National Bank, real estate investor Frank Michaux—and the F. G. Masquelette accounting firm that kept her extensive records in order. Shortly after Samuel E. Allen's death, Baker helped Rosa purchase former Mayor H. Baldwin Rice's house that was situated at 1916 Main Street, not far from the Baker and Frank Andrews homesteads. Rosa financed this purchase with a $75,000 loan from the Institute, payable over six years at 7 percent and secured by 6,400 acres of rural land.[59] Between 1917 and 1931 Baker worked with Rosa to dissolve the Allen Ranch in a way that benefited her estate and the city of Houston.

Following the opening of the Ship Channel in 1914, Houston's political and business leaders began to consider how best to protect the city's interests and control commerce on the Ship Channel; by 1916 Captain S. Taliaferro and his brother Thomas had suggested the City of Houston purchase the Tod ranch at the juncture of Green's and Buffalo bayous and a portion of the Allen ranch at the juncture of Sims' and Buffalo bayous. Rosa Allen consulted with Baker about this proposal; and she and Judge Tod allowed the Taliaferros to place options on their properties. Not surprisingly, the municipal authorities could not reach an agreement to commit nearly $900,000 to the project. Meanwhile Captain Baker asked Rosa to consider a different proposal. Working with John T. Scott, president of First City National Bank, and Walter C. Hardcastle, who represented Sinclair Gulf Refining Company, a Baker, Botts, Parker & Garwood client, Baker helped Rosa Allen and her family complete a complex transfer of property to Sinclair, who subsequently constructed the first refinery complex and pipeline on Houston's Ship Channel. Rosa's beautiful ranch home, a replica of her parents' antebellum plantation house in Fort Bend County, was taken apart piece by piece and reconstructed as a large vacation house at Sylvan Beach near La Porte on Galveston Bay. In 1921 Rosa allowed the Young People's Service League of the Episcopal Diocese of Texas to use the house and surrounding property for girls' and boys' summer camps. By 1928 the original Camp Allen facilities no longer met the needs of the popular summer program, and Rosa provided funds so the Diocese could purchase property and build a campsite on Trinity Bay near Baytown for the second Camp Allen.[60]

In the 1920s, when W. T. Carter Jr. and his family began amassing land that became Houston's first commercial airport, Baker saw another opportunity for Rosa Allen. In 1887 Baker had helped Samuel E. Allen purchase part of the Peter Mahen League for his ranching operation, and he recognized that the flat rural land not far from Houston's commercial center would suit Carter's goals. Baker, Botts, Parker & Garwood helped Carter organize the Houston Airport Corporation to build and operate Carter Field, renamed Hobby Field in 1967. Captain Baker worked with Rosa Allen and her trustees to transfer acreage to Carter, who then used 600 acres for the airport and the remainder to develop the Garden Villas residential subdivision. Rosa's son-in-law Robert C. Stuart, a real estate investor, worked with Carter and Baker to complete the real estate transfer and in 1927, when the airport was ready for business, accepted an invitation to ride on the first airplane to take off from the air field.[61]

Baker's long-standing representation of railroad clients brought him to the attention of Judge Walter T. Burns in 1914 when the International & Great Northern was facing bankruptcy and its fourth receivership. The I&GN had for nearly three decades been part of the Gould/Missouri-Pacific interests, and Captain Baker was well aware of the company's history. In 1914 an $11 million bond issue was coming due, and the company had no way to repay the bondholders; requests for an extension failed. On August 10, 1914, Judge Burns appointed Captain James A, Baker and Colonel Cecil A. Lyon of Sherman receivers and Thomas H. Ball, master in chancery, for the railroad. Efforts to reorganize in 1916 and again in 1917 proved fruitless for the same reasons the I&GN had defaulted: the war in Europe tightened financial credit worldwide; due to problems in Mexico, traffic with that country had been suspended; and Texas crops were bad. Once the United States entered the war and nationalized the railroads, reorganization became impossible. Not until 1922 could Baker, by then sole receiver due to Colonel Lyon's death, settle the issue.

FAMILY AND FRIENDS

Early twentieth-century Houstonians, eager to attract the "most desirable people" to their growing city, extolled the "culture, good taste, handsome women and loyal men" who extended "cordiality, hospitality and kindly charm" to newcomers. Boasting of the city's long roster of athletic, patriotic, artistic, and social clubs, one writer noted in 1907 that the "charming home receptions and elaborate public functions" as well as the beautiful homes, spacious boulevards, and "picturesque parks all reflect . . . a standard of society . . . unsurpassed by any in the United States."[62] Such hyperbole at a time when most roads were unpaved and most cultural institutions were only dreams of their founders, expressed the aspirations if not the reality of life for most Houstonians. Yet the city's well-known willingness to draw talented newcomers into its leadership ranks had made Houston thrive; the men and women who raised office towers, dredged for deep water, energized industry, and built civic institutions also valued recreation.

Captain Baker and his beautiful wife Alice often found their names on newspaper social pages, and the entertainments at 1416 Main Street, their showplace home and gardens, set a standard emulated by others. Both delighted in the company of friends and family, and both understood the value of cordial relations, which made civic projects and business dealings run smoothly. Both also genuinely loved young people. Generations of lawyers remembered Captain Baker as a caring mentor. "He neither criticized nor complained," wrote the firm historian and business manager, J. H. Freeman, "but asked so many questions: he was teaching me by his favorite method—cross examination."[63] As Institute chairman Baker rarely intervened on a student's or parent's behalf, but he invited Rice undergraduates to dine with his family and gathered parties of young people for Institute athletic events until the last summer of his life. Alice often asked younger women to share hostess duties with her at Institute events and at private receptions.

The town's many clubs provided places where Houston leaders and their families could meet to build personal, business, and civic networks and to debate municipal problems in a relaxed, friendly atmosphere. The Z. Z. Club (Houston's oldest social group, which Baker had joined when he moved to Houston) was succeeded by the Thalian Club, founded by young business leaders on October 24, 1901, at industrialist John F.

Dickson's elaborate Victorian villa on Main Street. Social aspirants acclaimed both clubs for their dancing assemblies and debutante balls, and the Thalians built a handsome four-story clubhouse not far from their members' homes. The Thalians' library and meeting rooms fulfilled the club's mission to support a literary club and promote "painting, music and other fine arts."[64] When E. B. Parker and other friends chartered the Houston Club in 1894 as a place to gather downtown, Judge Baker, Captain Baker, and Robert S. Lovett signed on as original members. Ten years later, as the sport of golf was becoming fashionable, Baker met with the Rice brothers, Tom Ball, William Chew, and other enthusiasts to form the Houston Golf Club. Remembered as an indifferent but enthusiastic golfer by his more athletic grandsons, the Captain paid $.50 an hour for private lessons.[65]

Baker's enthusiasm for golf reflected a national trend fostered by the growth of suburbia, rail transit, and a new social institution that was uniquely American—the country club, which combined club facilities, family entertainment, and sports in a relaxing natural setting removed from the bustle of downtown commercial activity.[66] Throughout his life, Baker balanced work and play, and he realized access to popular sports, like access to financial markets, legal advice, and educational excellence, would attract the "most desirable people" to Houston. Scot John Peebles, captain in the Black Watch, had introduced golf to the colonies while stationed on Long Island during the Revolutionary War.[67] Americans played sporadically until the late nineteenth century, when interest in the sport blossomed. On November 14, 1888, another Scot, John Reid, created the first golf club in the United States, a six-hole course in a pasture near Yonkers, New York; he called it St. Andrews Golf Club. In 1891 golfers incorporated Shinnecock Hills on Long Island and built a twelve-hole course for men and a nine-hole course for women. By 1900 there were one thousand golf clubs in the United States, five of them in Texas.[68]

For a few years Houston duffers cleared pathway "greens" near the Houston Gun Club (property later developed as Courtlandt Place) and putted into tomato cans. Then on March 22, 1904, Baker and his friends met at the Houston Club to establish a club devoted to golf. Baker and the Rice brothers offered to lease Institute property along Buffalo Bayou for a six-hole course.[69] The founders elected cotton broker Austin W. Pollard president and Will Rice II vice president; Baker and ten others agreed to serve as directors. At the next meeting on May 23, the group adopted bylaws, approved a pennant design displaying a red star on a white rectangle bordered in red, and decided to build a club house. Their stated budget was $5,000. On February 22, 1905, the club sponsored its first tournament, the Jesse Jones Cup. Sixteen qualifiers, from thirty entries, competed for the trophy, won by E. J. McCullough, whose 79 beat second-place Baker and another contender by two points.[70]

International players noted Houston's enthusiasm, and promoter Alex H. Findley, representing Boston sporting goods company Wright & Ditson, added Houston to his second World Tour, which took place February 2 through 4, 1906. British and American master players provided an "excellent tonic" for amateur fans from Austin, Beaumont, Dallas, Ft. Worth, Galveston, Houston, San Antonio, and Waco. More than one thousand spectators watched the top three winners collect $75, $50, and $25, and the Houston people presented commemorative pins to each visitor.[71] Such was the enthusiasm that Houston Golf Club membership swelled to 175, and attendees decided to form a Texas Golf Association. Representatives from the eight cities that had participated in the Houston tournament met for a forty-six-man tournament at the Dallas Golf and Country Club, April 19–21, 1906. Harry Lee Edwards, founder of the Dallas club, was crowned the state's first amateur champion and named first president of the association. Founders elected Captain Baker vice president and C. C. Kinney of Dallas secretary.[72]

In 1908 Houston Golf Club sponsors met again to reorganize its 102 members as the Houston Country Club, the first full service country club in the city. Founders chartered their club on August 4 "for the promotion and encouragement of outdoor life, innocent sports and amusements, and for social intercourse and the cultivation of the higher ideals of life."[73] Dues were a modest $1.50 a month, and Golf Club members received a $25 discount when they subscribed to the new club. Capitalized at $50,000, the club sold shares at $100 par value, each share providing one club membership. Early members included Baker's circle of friends and corporate connections: business associates Edward A. Peden, John T. Scott, and Henry MacGregor; Rice colleagues James E. McAshan, Emanuel Raphael, and Arthur B. Cohn; law partners Edwin B. Parker, Hiram M. Garwood, and Clarence Wharton; *Houston Chronicle* publisher Marcellus E. Foster; philanthropists Abe and Haskell Levy and William C. Hogg; and the ubiquitous Orren T. Holt. Captain Baker signed up August 4 as member number 30; by the end of August, 266 sponsors had subscribed, and by November 15, 1909, the club roster listed 507 members.

Set on 150 acres along Brays Bayou, the "remote" club was twenty minutes by streetcar from downtown offices and fashionable residential areas. Will Rice, the club's first president, hired architects Sanguinet & Staats of Ft. Worth to design a spacious clubhouse with a large reception room, wide veranda, special ladies "apartment," men's locker room, and kitchen. He financed construction by issuing $50,000 in bonds, secured by the club's property.[74] Like country clubs throughout suburban America, the Houston Country Club stimulated residential development and offered new career opportunities in club management, sports training, and support staff positions.[75] The clubhouse with its dining facilities provided a restful environment that separated leisure time from quotidian duties; the spacious grounds shaded by huge trees laden with Spanish moss offered all members of the family country quiet and opportunities to relax or compete in golf, tennis, and swimming activities with their friends. When William Howard Taft, a formidable golfer, visited the club in October 1909, some thought his delightful experience made him more inclined to sign into law the $1.25 million appropriation recently secured by club member Tom Ball to complete construction of Houston's ship channel and deepwater port.[76]

Alice, too, engaged in club activities, although her choices were more cerebral than social. In October 1909 twenty women met at the First Presbyterian Church to form a Chautauqua Study Club for "the diligent study of the Chautauqua course and to promote intellectual and social entertainment resulting in good fellowship."[77] Limited to thirty members, the women met monthly for a decade at the Carnegie Library and later at the home of Louise (Mrs. Harris) Masterson, a "brilliant" and strong-minded suffragist who presided over the Young Women's Christian Association for many years. Houston's most interesting women engaged in a serious course of study provided by the Chautauqua Literary and Scientific Circle (organized 1878), which provided programs for member clubs and developed a national speakers' bureau. The Chautauqua movement itself had been founded in 1874 by Methodists who retreated to a Lake Chautauqua, New York, campsite in the summer to discuss the Bible and train Sunday school teachers. Attendees loved the meetings, and soon lecturers were speaking on topics ranging from the Old Testament to history and literature to scientific discoveries. Several presidents of the United States orated to enthusiastic audiences at a pavilion built for the purpose. At the Houston Chautauqua meetings Alice soon found herself in earnest discussion with young Ima Hogg and other progressive women who were attacking problems that affected the quality of life in Houston.[78]

Alice introduced Mary Lovett, wife of the Institute's president, to the Chautauqua group. Mary moved to Houston just as the Chautauqua was forming. She also loved music and art and joined the Public School Art League and the Current Literature Club. As wife of the Institute president, Mary felt it her duty to engage in civic activities, and she encouraged faculty wives to become active in the city's civic and social life. During her early years in Houston, Mary entertained at receptions and other special events and, with her friend Alice Baker, arranged lunches and teas for the women students, who had no living accommodations on campus but instead commuted to their classes.[79] Alice and Mary became good friends, and Walter Browne (Buster to his siblings and friends) discovered two perfect playmates in Adelaide (b. Oct. 27, 1898) and Malcolm (b. Jan. 8, 1902) Lovett. Buster vacationed with the Lovett family in cool Asheville, North Carolina, one happy summer and began corresponding with Adelaide when he was a young teenager.

Since the first years of their marriage the Bakers had taken long vacations to escape Houston's punishing summer heat. In the 1890s they often joined Captain Baker's sisters Anna B Thompson and Nettie Duncan and their families in the Colorado Rockies. After 1900 the family tried different locations in the east, first on Maryland's Eastern Shore and then on Loon Lake in the Adirondacks of Northern New York. Every few years, summer plans included extensive trips to Europe. In 1910 the Bakers boarded a private railcar—the "Dallas"—with their children Alice (23), Jim (20), Walter B (Buster, 10), Ruth (6), and Malcolm (4) and a nanny for the long trip from Houston to Chicago. After a few days there, they continued on to Montreal, where the group, which included family friends, boarded a steamship for England. Alice and Jim occasionally abandoned the family group to visit friends, but for much of the journey Alice trained her camera on the scenery or on her fellow travelers to record an adventure through England and Scotland, across the channel and on to Versailles, the Swiss Alps, Potsdam, Berlin, and

On vacation in 1910: Captain and Mrs. Baker with Walter B, Ruth, and Malcolm boarding the family's private railroad car in Chicago. Private Collection.

Captain and Mrs. Baker in England with Malcolm, Ruth, and their nanny. Private Collection.

Venice. Flat tires provided work for the chauffeur and amusement for the photographer. In one picture, passengers, swathed in long dusters, scarves, and hats to protect their clothing stand about, impatiently waiting to resume the day's excursion in open touring cars.[80] At some point that year Captain and Mrs. Baker and Alice also sat for large pastel portraits by Elizabeth Gowdy Baker at her studio in New York City.[81]

About 1911, the Bakers purchased Rockhaven, a spacious six-bedroom home built in 1906 on a spit of land spearing the Atlantic Ocean at Bass Rocks, Gloucester, Massachusetts. For the next two decades, Captain and Mrs. Baker entertained family members and friends at the resort during the summer and early fall. Bostonians began to develop the near North Shore at Nahant as early as 1817. By the 1850s railroads brought summer visitors to the fishing village of Gloucester and beyond to Cape Ann. By 1900 Bass Rocks was attracting artists and visitors from the Midwest and faraway Texas. Commodious shingle cottages clung to the rocky shoreline, providing bracing sea air and snow-white foam as waves crashed against the jagged outcroppings. Every summer the Bakers would board their private rail car in Houston with family and servants and travel from Houston to Boston and along the shore to Gloucester. While in Massachusetts, Baker hired a stenographer and made frequent trips to Boston to see clients and visit medical specialists. He maintained steady contact with his law, banking, and Institute colleagues while entertaining visitors, hiking along the rocky shore, and enjoying frequent golf games.

The family joined the Bass Rocks Golf Club, founded in 1896 on a large farm property being developed by a local family. Summer residents laid out the links, built a clubhouse, and developed a cottage community for club members. During the season from July through Labor Day, members enjoyed tennis, golf, and the clubhouse. By the time the Bakers purchased their home, the club roster listed 248 golf and 11 tennis memberships. Several Texas families found their way to the North Shore in the early twentieth century. Waco businessman George H. Rotan summered there for nearly forty years. His son George V. Rotan, an early Texas amateur golf champion, began his competitive career at the Bass Rocks Golf Club as 1902 champion. In the 1920s and 1930s the younger Rotan handled investments for Rice Institute.[82] Stockton Axson, later a popular professor of English at the Institute, entertained his brother-in-law Woodrow Wilson at Bass Rocks in 1903.

GROWING UP

While Captain Baker modernized his law firm, watched buildings rise on the Institute campus, and strengthened the South Texas Commercial National Bank, his children were beginning to explore larger worlds. In 1907 Alice, now a young lady of twenty, had completed her education at Spence School in New York City and traveled with Robert S. Lovett and his wife in Europe during the summer. Back in Houston, she was crowned queen of the No-Tsu-Oh ball in November. Her brother Jim, fifteen, had enrolled at the Hill School that September, and seven-year-old Walter Browne (Buster) was big brother to little Ruth, age three, and baby Malcolm, just a year old. Juggling the schedules for this range of ages and activities would test any mother's abilities, but glowing newspaper accounts of Alice's debutante season suggest that Mrs. Baker, with the help of several loyal household employees, handled her duties with grace and charm. With young Alice's debut, the Bakers were about to embark on several seasons of commitment to the No-Tsu-Oh Festival, the city's premier social, commercial, and community event that drew thousands of participants from the surrounding region. For days each November, newspapers heralded coming events.

Businessmen conceived No-Tsu-Oh (Houston spelled backwards) in 1899 to advertise Houston's industry and commerce to the world. An updated version of earlier harvest festivals and agricultural parades, No-Tsu-Oh lasted for one week and celebrated the brief reign of King Nottoc (Cotton) and his youthful Queen. Parades with floats and bands, balls for the leading members of society, demonstrations, exhibitions, a football match, and a carnival of wild animals thrilled the crowds. Each day had a theme: in 1909, when fifty-two-year-old Captain Baker was crowned King Nottoc, Monday was college day; farmers were honored on Tuesday; the press on Wednesday; German day, with speeches and a jousting tournament, filled Thursday; Friday promised a Tek-Ram (Market) pageant of market goods; and Traveling Men's Day, devoted to salesmen, lumbermen, and an illuminated spectacle, filled Saturday's program. The names of King Nottoc and his queen were not revealed until their coronation on Wednesday night at the grand ball held in the city's largest auditorium. On Monday, masked to hide their identities, the king and queen opened the festival with a triumphant entrance.

Alice, Queen of No-Tsu-Oh, November 1907. Private Collection.

They sailed up Buffalo Bayou to Allen's landing at Main Street where His Honor the Mayor presented keys to the city. Each year one of the city's prominent business or civic leaders was named king, while his queen was always the year's favorite debutante. In 1907 Hiram Garwood, Captain Baker's law partner, was King Nottoc IX, while Alice, the Captain's daughter, was queen. In 1909, the Captain himself reigned as Nottoc XI, and his queen was Lillie Neuhaus, who subsequently married W. T. Car-

Captain Baker and Jim in Galveston, ca. 1910. Private Collections.

ter's son. In 1911 Edgar Odell Lovett ruled as King Nottoc XIII, his queen being S. F. Carter's daughter, Annie Vieve.

All was not frivolity and fun at the No-Tsu-Oh Festival. In 1909 King Nottoc XI and his court were able to demonstrate improvements on Buffalo Bayou and officially open the enlarged turning basin. Because of successful dredging operations, the two-hundred-foot, ocean-going *Disa*, a slim Swedish steamship (but the largest vessel to visit Houston in years), was able to sail as far as the Great Northern Railroad wharves

Allen's Landing at the foot of Main Street, ca. 1909. Mss 0157-0058 (Houston Photographic Collection), Houston Public Library, Houston Metropolitan Research Center.

at the northeast corner of Magnolia Park. There Captain Baker disembarked and transferred to "his majesty's royal yacht" to continue on up the channel to the wharf at the end of Main Street. Special streetcars, charging low festival fares, took customers to view the "splendid naval parade" of "beautifully decorated water craft."[83] The foreign vessel negotiated the new turning basin and marked the first phase of ship channel expansion that would make Houston a deepwater port five years later. In November 1914, the No-Tsu-Oh Festival celebrated the reign of King Retaw (Water) I, and Woodrow Wilson pressed a button in the White House that set off a cannon in Houston to announce the Ship Channel project was complete.

In 1907, to honor their daughter, the Bakers produced two splendid parties at their home, each described in elaborate detail by awed reporters. The culmination of No-Tsu-Oh, according to one journalist, was the supper given by the Queen's parents for the King and his royal party. Fifty-two guests enjoyed a five-course repast, "its every detail reflecting to the fullest sense the splendor of the scene." Tables in the reception hall, dining room, and library were resplendent with golden or white chrysanthemums, silver candlesticks, tapers, place cards lettered in gold and tied with ribbon, ferns, Renaissance lace, and fall flowers. "The entire hospitality," said the reporter, "was marked by a tone of dignity and elegant simplicity reflecting the taste of host and hostess to the fullest."[84]

Even more marvelous to readers was the Bakers' "Elegant Reception" for their daughter on December 1, 1907. Japanese, Indian, and Moorish "effects" defined three main entertainment spaces at the Baker home. "Tete-a-tete nooks" were "never vacant throughout the reception hours" from 8:00 to 11:00 p.m., while "the farthest angle of the veranda was given over entirely to the arrangement of college pennants and banners." Japanese umbrellas shone with incandescent lights, and an "immense floral basket, several feet in height, overflowed with red chrysanthemums and asparagus fern." Mrs. Baker wore a gown of lace net embroidered with a delicate gold chrysanthemum design over yellow chiffon and silk, and her daughter was clad in white chiffon sprinkled with seed pearls and golden sequins. Mrs. Baker carried a bouquet of golden chrysanthemums while young Alice held long-stemmed American Beauty roses as they greeted their guests.[85]

About the time of these No-Tsu-Oh festivities and debutante balls, probably sometime around 1911, Captain Baker, Edgar Odell Lovett, and a few other friends decided they needed to hone their dancing skills; "a pretty good group," recalled the Lovetts' son Malcolm, who would sit on the staircase with his friend Buster Baker to watch the activities below. The dancers asked a Miss Settle and her accompanist to teach the group on Friday nights during the winter. Everyone ate dinner, then the dancing began. But the men would dance only with their wives, so Miss Settle invented the Paul Jones: men stood in one line, women in another, and all practiced a step; when Miss Settle blew her whistle, gentlemen had to dance with the nearest lady. So began a tradition carried on to this day by a group who meets twice a year at Houston Country Club.[86]

In the spring of 1911 young Jim Baker Jr. completed his college preparation at the Hill School and that fall matriculated at Princeton College. In November he returned home to celebrate his sister Alice's marriage to Murray Brashear Jones, scion of an old Houston family who was graduated from the University of Texas in 1907, earned a Bachelor of Letters from Princeton the following year, and in 1910 completed a law degree at his Texas alma mater. Alice chose a week crowded with social events to celebrate her wedding on Wednesday, November 21. Her parents wel-

Three generations: Mother Alice Baker Jones, holding baby Alice Baker Jones, with grandmother Alice Graham Baker, late 1915. Private Collection.

comed their sisters, nephews, and nieces from Waco, Ft. Worth, and Huntsville, and a "series of handsome hospitalities" to honor the popular bride filled the *Houston Chronicle*'s "In Society" pages.

Marian Seward (Mrs. Orren T.) Holt was hostess at an elegant Oriental luncheon for the wedding party on Monday. Described as "perfection," the decorations "suggested a visit to Aladdin's Cave" and provided nine courses to the twelve guests. That evening the Bakers hosted an

Malcolm and Ruth
Baker, ca. 1910. Private
Collection.

elegant eight-course dinner for twenty-four, which "formed the culmination of the joys of the day." A table for twelve in the dining room
was adorned with linens hand-embroidered with lavender orchids, the
same flower found in abundance on the table and sideboard; satin ribbons lettered in silver indicated where each guest should sit, and silver
"heart-shaped receptacles" filled with almonds adorned each place setting. Twelve more guests sat at a circular table in the library "overspread
with a Cluny lace cover showing glimpses of lavender satin beneath."
Gold almond containers and place cards lettered in gold completed the
décor. On the evening preceding the wedding, the groom's sister Miss
Irma Jones entertained forty guests at a seven-course meal. The bridal
party sat at a table arranged in the shape of a heart, covered with white
chiffon over a pink satin underskirt. Roses in profusion and large crystal
compotes filled with pink mints and bonbons adorned the table while
Thayer's Orchestra played all evening.

The wedding itself was "marked by a brilliance and elegance never excelled and rarely if ever equaled." Dr. William States Jacobs and Rev. William Hayne Leavell performed the 8:30 evening ceremony at the First Presbyterian Church. Baskets of white flowers, tied with fluffy white tulle, decorated the church; violinist Marie Briscoe and pianist Katharine Parker performed a Schubert serenade. Jim Baker served as best man, eleven-year-old Buster and three friends unrolled satin ribbons to mark the aisle, and seven groomsmen preceded seven bridesmaids to the altar. Then came Ruth, now seven, with three other flower girls, followed by Alice's cousin Mrs. Bert Honea of Ft. Worth as matron of honor and Murray's sister Irma as maid of honor. Little Malcolm, only five, carried the ring on a satin pillow and started down the aisle just before his father and older sister, who was veiled in tulle and orange blossoms and clad in white satin with seed pearl embroidery and rose point lace. Once the bride and groom exchanged vows, everyone recessed to the Baker home, which was "never so superbly adorned" with a "veritable garden of American Beauty roses." After a champagne supper of pressed chicken, parfait, coffee, and cake, the new Mrs. Jones changed into a blue gown trimmed with fur and pink roses, and the couple departed for a tour of California. When they returned, the Joneses resided "temporarily" with Captain and Mrs. Baker.[87]

The few years left before World War I brought more change to the Baker family. Alice and Murray Jones became the parents of a vivacious daughter Alice on September 30, 1915, the Baker's only grandchild for more than a decade. Jim Baker enjoyed his Princeton years (1911–1915) as a vigorous athlete and manager of the Glee Club, and in January 1913 Buster followed his older brothers to the Hill, where he began prepping for college (January 1913–Spring 1917). About the time Jim entered Princeton, he met Bonner Means, who "fell in love [with him] at first sight." She was attending Sweetbriar Academy to prepare for college while Jim was at Princeton, and Captain and Mrs. Baker quickly realized she would someday be part of their family. After a happy visit to Bass Rocks in the summer of 1915, Alice told Bonner how much they all loved her and thanked her for staying with them so long; "you have endeared yourself" to everyone, she assured her guest.[88] By 1913 Captain and Mrs. Baker were left with only Ruth and Malcolm at home.

CHAPTER SIX

Citizen and Patriot

HOUSTON'S THRIVING COMMERCIAL and industrial activity, fueled by oil exploration in the years before World War I, coincided with a vibrant civic life. Entrepreneurs who built new industries also created cultural and social service organizations to improve the quality of life for a growing populace. Houston's early twentieth-century leaders praised individual effort and private enterprise, but many held progressive beliefs that linked the well-being of individual, family, community, and nation, and they began to imagine the elements needed to build a great city. The Bakers and their circle of friends believed that healthy communities must build strong economic foundations based on best business practice; they understood that certain issues like public health and safe roads required well-managed local government; they thought a great city should be home to excellent educational institutions, parklands and open spaces, fine music, and art; and they recognized the need for social services to mitigate suffering, poverty, and poor living conditions. Optimistic problem solvers, these humanitarian leaders knew that commer-

Illustration: Captain James A. Baker. Private Collection.

cial success alone would not define a great city. They worked together to make Houston a center of commerce, community, and culture.[1]

CIVIC LEADERS

The Bakers, like other practicing Presbyterians, pursued their civic and social duties with serious purpose and encouraged others to follow their lead. Judge Baker and his son joined the First Presbyterian Church in 1878. The Judge's annual gift of $60 was the congregation's largest in 1893, when the church called a new pastor, William Hayne Leavell, to serve its expanding flock (1893–1903). The energetic two-hundred-pound, six-foot, three-inch Leavell befriended Judge Baker and his son and welcomed Alice to the fold in 1895, when she left her Baptist congregation to join First Presbyterian by examination and profession of faith. Leavell had not long been in Houston when he explained the need for a new church building to his parishioners. He proved a clever fund-raiser. When an anonymous friend gave him $5,000 to use as he wished, Leavell placed this gift on a subscription list under his own name; he then secured a pledge from the Ladies' Association to raise $10,000 and began to call on likely supporters. Soon Judge Baker had pledged $1,500, and within three weeks other subscribers, loath not to equal the generosity of their own pastor, their most honored communicant, and their ardent female members, met the $50,000 goal.

When Leavell had secured an appropriate site and was ready to build, he asked his friend and parishioner Captain Baker to prepare a construction contract so cleverly "it could not be broken if anything went wrong."[2] After much "anxious solicitude," Leavell preached his first sermon from the new pulpit on May 26, 1895. When costs exceeded expectations, Captain Baker helped Leavell arrange a loan from William Marsh Rice for $20,000. Baker then formed a committee with Norman Meldrum and E. W. Sewell to raise funds and pay off the loan, but Rice was murdered before the church could cancel its debt. As administrator of Rice's estate in Texas, Baker helped Leavell settle the matter on terms favorable to First Presbyterian and fair to the Rice estate. Although later generations remember that Captain Baker served as a church elder, church records do not show him in any leadership role. However, he continued to support Leavell's successor, the charming, highly educated sportsman, baritone, and poet William States Jacobs (1906–1931), who became a close personal friend and important civic leader. Baker asked Institute trustees to approve a $20,000 loan in September 1915 so the church could pay off its indebtedness for a new manse, and he arranged other financing for church projects during his lifetime.[3]

Captain Baker chose colleagues who also enjoyed community activities. With his usual ardent insistence, Edwin B. Parker urged Baker, Botts, Parker & Garwood lawyers to "steer clear of political entanglements" but to "take an active interest in all affairs of State," because the firm's success depended on participation "in the outside business, civic and social life of our community and our Country at large."[4] Captain Baker, Robert S. Lovett, E. B. Parker, and Judge Garwood devoted much of their spare time to organizations related to their law practice. They took active roles in national, state, and local bar associations as officers and panel participants at annual meetings. Always quick to support private initiatives that improved business opportunity, each partner made individual contributions to the ship channel's deepwater fund in 1900, advocated improvements on Buffalo Bayou, and facilitated sale of navigation bonds in 1911. Baker, Parker, and Garwood were members of the Escort Committee, formed in November 1914 to celebrate the grand opening of Houston's Ship Channel and deepwater port—the realization of a long-held dream to bring the world's commerce to the Bayou City's docks.

Baker was a member of the Houston Business League from its founding in 1895 until its reorganization as the Houston Chamber of Commerce in 1910. He served as president of the Houston Industrial Club in 1907 and was an advocate for the Citizens Alliance, a national organization active in Houston from 1903 until 1915. Many viewed the Alliance as an anti-union clique of employers who exploited every man's "right to sell his time or his talents in the highest market to the highest bidder." Baker, "one of Houston's most prominent and noted attorneys," explained a different viewpoint. The Alliance, he told a large, enthusiastic audience at Turner Hall early in the century, "was not organized in opposition to any other organization or union of citizens. . . . This association stands for . . . the rigid enforcement of all laws, in every particular, and [we] hereby pledge ourselves to assist . . . in maintaining and defending the . . . rights of every citizen." Baker further proclaimed the inalienable rights of all citizens to life, liberty, and pursuit of happiness and promised "to help resist any encroachment upon constitutional rights and to promote and encourage harmonious relations between employer and employee upon a basis of equal justice for both." Believing that "both capital and labor have reciprocal rights," he declared, "labor in whatever sphere shall be bountifully rewarded and fully protected in the enjoyment of every right . . . and in the enjoyment of his property."[5] Like many of his peers, Baker did not view counseling corporate clients as antithetical to protecting the rights of individual citizens.

Captain Baker also turned his attention to struggling enterprises that performed broad civic purposes. The Glenwood Cemetery Association, a group long associated with Baker's law firm, sought legal advice from Judge Baker and his son. On July 6, 1871, several investors met with Colonel Walter Browne Botts at the offices of Gray & Botts to form the for-profit Houston Cemetery Company and elect officers, with the goal of creating Houston's first garden cemetery along the wooded northern banks of Buffalo Bayou just west of downtown. Adapting a late-eighteenth-century tradition established in France and Great Britain, Harvard professor Jacob Bigelow introduced the rural cemetery concept to Americans at Cambridge's Mount Auburn Cemetery in 1825. Conceived as "a place that would be peaceful for the living as well as for the dead," the garden cemetery quickly gained admirers. By 1847 the great landscape architect A. J. Downing could write that the "good taste" of the innovation "has been copied almost universally in choosing . . . some diversified wooded surface, some distance from town, affording scenery where *nature* rather than art, should always retain most command over the feelings."[6] When Houston began to experience industrial expansion and population growth, investors who were aware of the garden cemetery movement in other cities decided to place a burial grounds outside city limits, away from residential centers where they could provide a peaceful oasis for contemplative strolling.

By 1872 Glenwood investors had purchased more than fifty-four acres and had begun to offer cemetery plots to subscribers. Walter B. Botts and Frederick A. Rice served on the Cemetery Company's first board while Judge Baker was trustee of the original mortgage (1874). Colonel Botts continued on the board until 1886, when friend and attorney Captain Joseph Chappell Hutcheson became president. Hutcheson monitored several prosperous years, but when he resigned in 1892 to run for Congress, the company succumbed to bad management in the mid-1890s and nearly collapsed when stockholders pillaged the profits, neglected the graves, and faced bankruptcy. In 1896 Captain William Christian, an elder of the First Presbyterian Church, was named receiver and began to revive Glenwood's fortunes. In 1901 he worked with T. W. House Jr. and former president Hutcheson to find a new group of investors who would underwrite long-deferred maintenance and repairs. The troubles of the 1890s made plain the problems inherent in a for-profit corporate structure, laxly monitored by shareholders.

In 1903 Captain Baker reminded investors of a garden cemetery's civic value—as a public park and a nonsectarian resting place for departed loved ones—and suggested they form a nonprofit corporation. House, Hutcheson, Christian, and other friends asked him to create the Glenwood Cemetery Association and named him legal counsel. Remaining calm in the face of chaotic records and continued indebtedness, Baker steered the association toward good financial health. By July 24, 1904, he had shown the group how to incorporate as a nonprofit and had written to fifteen "white knights"—as grateful cemetery plot owners called them— for contributions to "put in proper condition this beautiful home of the dead." At a meeting on July 25, Baker presented by-laws for adoption and named the fifteen contributors as trustees of the new volunteer board. Baker remained a director and member of the executive committee from 1904 until 1916; from 1916 until 1941 he served as the association's volunteer president. Glenwood was dear to his heart as the burial place of his son Graham, and he tackled the association's problems as a matter of personal concern as well as civic responsibility. The angel guarding his family's tree-shaded plot embodied the haven for quiet reflection Glenwood's trustees hoped to establish by encouraging best horticultural and preservation practices. His contemporaries believed Baker was the true white knight who saved a beloved but neglected institution from ruin. Once he had ensured stable management, he fulfilled his presidential duties by calling annual meetings and providing occasional legal advice.[7]

Baker's sense of civic responsibility lifted the hopes of another struggling institution, Houston's branch of the Young Men's Christian Association (YMCA). Founded at an organizational meeting in 1885, the association worked hard to build membership and find rented quarters for a community center. Fire in September 1894 consumed early records and equipment, and the group moved its location frequently until it purchased land and a cottage at Fannin and McKinney streets in March 1902. Low membership, inability to reach fund-raising goals, and debt plagued the institution during its first two decades, but board officers, like colleagues at other YMCA branches around the country, realized membership would continue to stall without a first-rate facility. In 1903 the directors received the promise of $100,000 for a grand building—if the organization could pay off a $10,000 debt. Three years later nothing had happened.

In 1906 YMCA Board President William A. Wilson asked his friend and business associate Captain James A. Baker for help. Baker was a member of the YMCA but had never taken a leadership role. However, he invited several influential Houstonians to meet at his home. The YMCA's paid secretary resigned, and Bruno Hobbs, a secretary of the International Committee, explained to the guests that the International Committee would help the Houston Association if the local group would follow his detailed fund-raising plan, which relied on several committees, each responsible for soliciting a list of prospects. Baker told his friends he stood behind the proposal for a grand building worthy of the city Houston was becoming. He and seven of his dinner guests pledged $5,000 each to a capital campaign and agreed to serve as a Committee on Building to oversee completion of the project.

Within three and one-half weeks (May 12 to June 5, 1906), the committee, following Hobbs's plan, raised almost $190,000 in pledged subscriptions. The Board then suspended its programs until a new five-story building designed by Sanguinet, Staats, and Seutter of Ft. Worth could be completed. In May 1907 Captain Baker, Vice President William D. Cleveland Jr., and General Secretary W. A. Scott placed the cornerstone at a formal ceremony. Inscribed "Jesus Christ Himself Being the Chief Corner Stone," the monument enclosed a box containing the Bible, the plans, a list of YMCA members, *Daily Press* copies, a souvenir program and history of Houston's YMCA, and a list of contributors to the Building Fund.[8]

Constructing the much-expanded YMCA facility—66,000 square feet that included a swimming pool, ninety-one dormitory rooms, and meeting and exercise rooms—took longer than expected, and the pledges proved hard to collect. Early in 1908 William A. Wilson approached Captain Baker again and asked if Rice Institute could arrange a large loan to facilitate payment of construction expenses. On January 27 the YMCA loan committee chairman told his board that Rice Institute, at Baker's request, would lend the YMCA $50,000 to complete construction. "After some discussion" the board passed a motion asking the loan committee to "endeavor to increase the amount of the loan to $75,000." Negotiations followed, and the Rice trustees agreed to a loan of $65,000; finally, on February 19, the Board voted to loan the desired $75,000.[9] On June 10, 1908, the YMCA directors took two important steps: they voted to place Association funds in Lumbermen's National Bank, under the care of Baker's friend S. F. Carter, and they resolved to borrow $75,000 from the Rice Institute. The YMCA had secured one of the Institute's first large loans, and its terms established Baker's standard policy: the loan would be payable in five equal installments, represented by notes of $15,000, each bearing interest of 7 percent, all secured by a deed of trust on the real estate between Fannin and San Jacinto at McKinney and by a chattel mortgage on the building's contents.[10] There would have been no YMCA building in 1908 if Captain Baker had not stepped in to assure other donors the project was worthwhile, to pledge his own support, and to place the wealth of the Institute behind an endeavor that contemporaries believed would improve the quality of life for Houstonians.

MUNICIPAL HOUSEKEEPING

Parker's admonitions to his partners to engage in civic work were also heard by their wives, each of whom took a sphere of city life as her special province. The women married to Houston's business leaders and to the Institute's faculty were among the first to see the negative consequences of industrial boom times and population explosion. Even before Emanuel Raphael and Cesar Lombardi joined William M. Rice's inaugural Board of Trustees in 1891, their wives had founded reading groups and study clubs. Clubwomen quickly broadened their missions of self-education to include civic improvement. In 1893 they formed an umbrella Women's Club.[11] Like other turn-of-the-century women throughout the United States, Houston "women by natural instinct as well as by long training" had become "housekeepers of the world, so it [was] only natural that they should in time become municipal housekeepers as well." Municipal housekeeping, according to renowned contemporary analyst Mary Ritter Beard, included holding kindergarten classes, teaching household arts, building libraries, securing public health benefits, defending child welfare, providing recreational outlets, preventing delinquency, educating mothers, beautifying the environment, and bringing music and art to everyone.[12]

Lavinia Abercrombie (Mrs. Robert S.) Lovett spent only a decade in Houston, but her legacy thrives today. At 4:00 p.m. on March 17, 1900, she and artist Emma Richardson Cherry welcomed four public school teachers, several ladies, and two gentlemen—one of them Robert S. Lovett—to the Lovett home to hear Jean Sherwood of Chicago discuss the benefits of a civic art association. Declaring that they wanted to create an organization to encourage "art and culture in the public schools," the group asked Robert Lovett, Mary B. Hill, and Adele B. Looscan to write a constitution for the Houston Public School Art League. Lavinia agreed to serve as president; Rabbi Henry Barnstein and P. W. Horn, superintendent of public schools, accepted posts as first and second vice president, respectively. So was born the organization that twenty-four years later opened the first municipal museum building in Texas, the Museum of Fine Arts of Houston.

With constitution in hand, the Art League organizers called a membership meeting for March 24. Forty-two men and women joined after that meeting and pledged to enrich children's lives by placing reproductions of great works of art in the city's elementary schools. Lavinia's first large purchase, made in 1901, was a replica of Venus de Milo, originally intended for the high school but placed instead in the public library to avoid shocking teenage sensibilities. Alice Baker made a small donation to her friend's inaugural project, and the League paid all expenses, not to exceed $125, to bring the statue from Paris to Houston. Among the League's seventy-seven charter members were Captain and Mrs. Baker and the E. B. Parkers. When Lavinia left for New York, her sister Corinne Abercrombie Waldo took over as president of the organization. An ardent advocate, she built the membership to six hundred by 1908, offered $1 family memberships, and developed programs and fund-raisers to bring guest speakers to town. Most important, she began to pressure Houston leaders to build a municipal art museum.

Vivacious Katharine Blunt (Mrs. Edwin B.) Parker could probably have been a professional musician had she not placed her domestic life ahead of personal ambition. From 1900 until the 1920s, when the Parkers moved permanently to Washington, Katharine worked to elevate the public's musical taste through education and concert performance. From 1901 to 1909 she served as musical director of the Woman's Choral Club, founded by cultural critic Wille Hutcheson and musician Ione Allen Peden in 1901 to nurture local talent and bring professional singers to Houston.[13] Katharine was the group's third president and for years entertained visiting artists at her home, The Oaks. In 1908 she helped establish the Thursday Morning Musical Club, a serious study and performance group for the city's leading professional and best amateur musicians. Parker was chairwoman of the board of examiners and was rigorous in her demands that aspiring members demonstrate musical excellence before being admitted to the group. The club struggled to find a director and did not survive World War I. Adhering to its premise "that a generous rivalry stimulates to greater achievement," the founders hoped to promote "a higher standard of musical taste and culture" in the city.[14] Eight programs in the first year covered the evolution of music, and members provided two organ recitals and two public concerts. The charter membership listed nine pianists, three violinists, ten vocalists, and two organists, and included several men.

On Wednesday morning, January 25, 1911, possibly at Katharine Parker's urging, Alice Baker convened the first meeting of the Girls Musical Club at her home. Alice and cosponsor Corinne Abercrombie Waldo formed the group "for the purpose of study and self-improvement along musical lines" to encourage younger women to study and perform. For many years the officers were unmarried young ladies; members held meetings in their homes; and three times a year Katharine Parker entertained guests at The Oaks for an open meeting and recital. The founders chose young Alice Baker, now twenty-four, to be the first president in 1911–1912. Twenty-nine-year-old Ima Hogg, who had trained as a concert pianist in New York and Berlin, succeeded Alice as president for two terms from 1912–1914.[15]

For four seasons between 1908 and 1911, several men who wished to promote Houston as a seat of culture and a delightful place to live sponsored the Houston Music Festival Association, the local branch of a national movement to advance the nation's appreciation of classical music. The Association, one of Edwin B. Parker's enthusiasms, brought symphony orchestras from Chicago and New York to towns and cities around the country. In 1911 Captain Baker served on the association's board with Edgar Odell Lovett, Jonas S. Rice, newspaper editor Marcellus E. Foster, Rabbi Henry Barnstein, critic Wille Hutcheson, school superintendent P. W. Horn, Jesse Jones, and Rev. William States Jacobs. Music Festival concerts drew huge crowds and were major social occasions for Houston's leading families. Their success and the excitement generated by Houston's numerous musical clubs made some music lovers believe Houston could support its own symphony orchestra.

Katharine Parker made her most enduring contribution to Houston's musical culture when she invited Ima Hogg, cellist Julien Blitz, music critic Wille Hutcheson, and other musical women to her home in the spring of 1913 to organize a Houston Symphony Association, whose purpose would be the formation of a professional municipal symphony orchestra based in Houston. The group decided to offer a trial concert to the public on June 21, 1913. Blitz promised to find the musicians and conduct the concert. Ima Hogg secured the Majestic Theatre for free—in between matinee and evening performances. All the women agreed to canvass their musical groups to find 125 guarantors. The evening, although warm, was a complete success, and enthusiasm for a Houston-based professional symphony orchestra gained new converts. In the fall, the group met again and decided to form an association to present a season of orchestra concerts. Ima Hogg persuaded Katharine Parker to serve as president although Katharine was not entirely convinced the city could support a resident orchestra. But Ima knew her friend was Houston's leading female advocate of fine music and was, through her husband, well connected to men of wealth who could finance the expense of forming an orchestra. At the first season concert on Thanksgiving afternoon 1913 in the Majestic Theatre, the Parkers and Bakers held subscription boxes, as did their friends oil man Joseph Cullinan, industrialist E. A. Peden, millionaire banker S. F. Carter, and pianist Ima Hogg. Katharine Parker served as president for two years and was succeeded by Ima Hogg, who until her death in 1976 was Houston Symphony's most ardent benefactor.[16]

ALICE BAKER, SOCIAL SERVICE PIONEER

If Lavinia Lovett's love was art and Katharine Parker's was music, Alice Baker's lasting contribution to Houston's quality of life came through her devotion to the social service needs of the city's less privileged residents. At the turn of the century, Houstonians were awakening to the social problems caused by industrial development, immigration, and overcrowded neighborhoods, and they supported a growing roster of service groups. Church ladies' associations, the Bayland Orphans Home (1867), Kezia de Pelchin's Faith Home, the Florence Crittenden Rescue Home for poor unwed mothers, Sheltering Arms for the indigent and the aged, a charity hospital, and several benevolent societies all dispensed relief, but many believed charity would not foster civic pride or urban progress. When Alice decided to attack the causes of social problems through education and example, Houston and much of the nation were engaged in two important debates. One asked whether urban crises should be addressed by palliative charity to provide relief or by proactive efforts to prevent social evils from degrading communities. The other pondered whether individual, private initiatives should be paramount or whether municipal government should play a leading role in resolving social issues. Alice and her friends demonstrated the necessity of private and public participation. In Alice's view, all Houstonians were her neighbors, and poverty, illness, or lack of services in one area affected the well-being of more privileged neighborhoods. As private groups addressed specific issues, their ability to call attention to urban social problems pushed the city itself to pass an ordinance in 1915 to establish the Department of Charity, Benevolence, and Public Welfare. Voters empowered this new municipal department to gather statistics, oversee institutions claiming to serve charitable purposes, and help fund public health and social welfare projects.[17]

The plight of orphaned children awakened Alice's community conscience when she attended a meeting of over one hundred women at the Shearn Methodist Church in 1893 to decide the fate of Kezia de Pelchin's Faith Home for abandoned infants and toddlers. DePelchin, revered for her care of neglected children, had discovered three babies on her doorstep one January night in 1892 and had prevailed on friends to help her provide a safe home for these castaways. After DePelchin died in January 1893, her friend Ruth (Mrs. T. W.) House stepped in and asked Houston's leading women to create the DePelchin Faith Home Association. Captain Baker, at Mrs. House's request, secured a charter incorporating the nonprofit organization on March 23, 1893, and by August 1893 the one hundred supporters had begun a fund-raising effort to build a permanent home. Workmen donated labor and materials, and by 1898 a solid brick building was ready for occupancy. Several committees purchased food and clothing, oversaw programming, and maintained the building project. Captain Baker and five other men formed a male auxiliary to offer financial and legal advice.[18]

The nonsectarian center's founders sheltered orphans and provided young dependent children temporary housing if their parents could not care for them due to family troubles or if the mother had to work outside the home and could not provide childcare. By 1912 the 1898 structure was too small, and Mrs. House and her association began another building campaign. Harriet Levy and her brothers Abe and Haskell provided property; the Reverend Peter Gray Sears, rector of Christ Church, led a drive to find $55,000; and John L. Mauran and Ernest J. Russell, nationally recognized architects practicing in St. Louis, designed a handsome three-story Italianate building of steel, concrete, and brick. Builders broke ground September 1, 1912, and by March 1913 seventy-two children moved into the home. Two years later, Faith Home served 150 youngsters.[19]

Soon after Alice joined the First Presbyterian Church, she became a member of the Ladies' Association, which had been formed by twenty women in 1883 to strengthen friendship and fellowship. As president of the renamed Westminster Guild in 1910, Alice suggested the women settle part of the debt still outstanding on the manse. Her group pledged $300 a year for five years and spurred the congregation's Board of Deacons to raise the remainder. Banker Roy M. Farrar, lawyer Joseph C. Hutcheson Jr., industrialists John F. Dickson and Edward A. Peden, and the other deacons made multiyear pledges of $200 each to follow Mrs. Baker's lead and pay off the mortgage held by the South Texas Commercial National Bank. Captain Baker pledged $100 a year for five years, and Alice made a separate donation of $115 to defray the Guild pledge. Under her leadership, the Guild supported nine service circles and a Bible study class.[20]

Alice, like her friends Lavinia Lovett and Katharine Parker, was an imaginative leader who advocated untried ways to improve Houston's civic life. Turning her attention to the needs of hard-working poor families, she introduced the city to the settlement house movement, made famous by Jane Addams's Hull House in Chicago in the late nineteenth century. Building on a British prototype, Addams and her colleagues were well-educated women and some men who "settled" in houses or buildings in urban areas often dismissed as "slums," although they were typically neighborhoods of hard-working, undereducated, immigrant families struggling to assimilate to United States culture with little understanding of English. Living among their clients, the settlement house sponsors provided classes and activities to improve the quality of life in areas all but ignored by city government and business leaders. Although

Houston settlements were not residential, they followed the English and Chicago prototypes closely in their approach to community programming.

Woman's Club members began working in underserved immigrant neighborhoods when they established the city's first free kindergarten on October 1, 1902, "in a little old store building"; the following year a second kindergarten catering to Houston's growing immigrant population opened in an abandoned church building near downtown. Viewed as "one of Houston's greatest advancements," the schools were staffed by club volunteers, who in 1903 offered a training class to prepare teachers. For several years club activists lobbied the school board, without success, to have kindergartens made a standard part of public school curriculum. Teacher Sybil Campbell demonstrated the importance of industrial training for girls in 1903–1904 when she organized popular sewing classes for immigrant girls and young women living in the Second Ward. Alice Baker committed the Ladies Association of the First Presbyterian Church to fund Campbell's project, while the Woman's Club provided volunteer teachers.

On a cold day early in 1907 Sybil Campbell discovered a sleeping child on the steps of Rusk Elementary School, located on a rise above Buffalo Bayou north of Congress Avenue and east of Main Street near the city's Second Ward cotton mills, docks, and rail yards in the heart of an overcrowded neighborhood populated by Jewish and Mexican immigrants. Campbell realized at once that something had to be done to help neighborhood families who had nowhere to leave small children during the workday. She and Annie Orem, the school's kindergarten teacher, approached Alice Baker, who responded warmly, believing "residents of every section of the city should have a fair chance at proper living conditions and moral surroundings."[21] Alice invited twelve friends, the wives of Houston's leading businessmen and lawyers, to her home on February 19, 1907, to organize a volunteer association.[22] By February 28 Captain Baker had helped his wife write a constitution defining the Houston Settlement Association's purpose to extend "educational, industrial, social, and friendly aid to all those within our reach."[23] When thirty-two charter members held a second meeting, Alice was elected president of a fifteen-member board, and she remained the guiding spirit and president until 1918. Mrs. H. R. Akin, president of the Woman's Club from 1905–1906, was named first vice president, when the club gave its Rusk

Elementary kindergarten building to the newly formed Association to manage. Other early Settlement Association directors included the Bakers' neighbor Roxalee Smith (Mrs. Frank) Andrews, Alice's childhood friend Marian Holt, and Estelle Boughton Sharp, who shaped the organization's policy for over fifty years.[24] Once the group was organized officially, Alice suggested that members spend time educating themselves about the settlement house movement and discovering the particular needs of Houston's underserved. Finally, the association began to outline a plan of action.

Alice's small governing board worked fast to attract volunteers who recognized that many working families lacked training for the modern industrialized workforce and could not afford child care, medical treatment, or basic education. The committee enlisted the support of the Woman's Club, and Alice received permission to place her first settlement at the Rusk Elementary School. When the Federation of Women's Clubs published its *Key to the City of Houston* in 1908, their glowing list of Settlement Association accomplishments revealed that in one year Alice had recruited two hundred members, including twenty men; was limiting Association expenses to "the legitimate income from dues"; and had already provided neighborhood residents with a broad program that included free kindergarten for fifty children, sewing and cooking classes, a weekly story hour, a circulating library, and clubs for women, men, and young men. The *Key to the City* writer estimated that at least two hundred people used the building each week, and the Houston School Board had asked the Association to equip classrooms at Rusk School for domestic science and manual training departments. The report concluded by noting that Rusk Settlement "is not a charity, but rather a social center, and an educational institution, by which we hope to teach people, not only children, but men and women, to help themselves to rise above heredity, environment and whatever would tend to discourage, and make the best of themselves and derive the greatest good and happiness from life."[25]

Alice's early success continued unabated for the next decade. Contemporaries admired her "charm and sweetness . . . strengthened by intelligence, vision, and tenacity of purpose" that overcame obstacles.[26] Volunteers applauded her approach, which provided tools, not handouts, to help families find paths to prosperity. Alice maintained the ambitious pace in 1909. On March 15 the Association rented a large headquarters house adjacent to the school and surrounded by trees and shrubs; Alice

(*Top*) Rusk Settlement, ca. 1910; (*bottom*) children of immigrants to Houston pose with their Easter baskets on the steps of Rusk Settlement House, 1910s. Courtesy of Neighborhood Centers Inc.

furnished the parlor and kitchen and called on friends to refurbish the remaining rooms. The Association hired a visiting nurse and expanded the number of clubs for boys, girls, men, and women. The old house and its grounds became a welcoming playground and social center, where Alice provided a decorated tree at Christmas to establish a tradition carried on each year well beyond her lifetime. Alice invited a representative from New York's Russell Sage Foundation to Houston to discuss ways the city and county could address problems of delinquent boys.[27] In the fall, members decided the Association's programs had already outgrown volunteer management, and they hired James P. Kranz as "head worker" to manage the large pool of enthusiastic volunteers. Kranz had completed study at the New York School of Philanthropy and had worked for settlement projects in Minneapolis, New York, and Philadelphia.[28] With Kranz on board, the Association announced it would develop its athletic program and add a day nursery, a free dispensary, a savings program, Sunday lectures, and legal aid services in 1910.

Most innovative was Alice's thirty-two-page annual report, which she produced because the Settlement Association "feels that all social agencies relying on public contributions for support should make an annual statement." The report showed that money raised in Houston had been spent there, that the public could rely on the agency's management, and that "the money was expended for the purpose for which it is subscribed."[29] The report went on to explain its mission. "Social work is practical economy," the analysis began. It continued with statements that were by no means universally accepted in 1909: social economy, the report asserted, asked "what rights has the individual resident in any community to expect from that community?" Answering the question, Alice and her board concluded "everyone will concede that a person has a right" to be "born physically fit," to a "protected childhood" and "efficient education," to steady work under sanitary conditions, to a decent standard of living, to protection from "preventable disease," to protection from crime, and to comfort in old age.[30] Like a corporate annual report, the Settlement Association compendium listed its officers and directors, its eleven current and past paid workers, and its fourteen volunteer leaders. Several pages explained the Association's understanding of the field of social work, outlined the history of the settlement movement, described the work of Houston's Settlement Association, and provided a financial statement. The authors described programs in detail, included several photographs, and named every subscriber. This model report not only demonstrated Alice's organizational skills and analytical abilities but proclaimed forcefully her vision of the elements necessary to make Houston a great city where every citizen would have a voice and be treated with dignity and where every neighborhood would have proper utilities and be a safe haven for residents.

In 1910 when the old Rusk Elementary School burned to the ground, Alice persuaded the school board to try another experiment that would link the school to the community and keep its doors open when classes were not in session. Alice asked permission to place the Rusk Settlement headquarters in the school itself. Rusk Elementary became the first school in Houston to serve as a community center; the Settlement Association continued to help with kindergarten, athletic, after-school, industrial training, and English language classes. On November 27, 1910, representatives from seven Texas cities arrived in Houston, where the Association and its staff hosted the first State Conference of Charities and Corrections. Twenty-two cities sent representatives to the second conference in Austin the following year. With input from sociologists at the University of Texas, the social service providers inaugurated a permanent state organization.[31] The Houston Settlement Association expanded programming at Rusk Elementary every year and in 1916 opened Brackenridge Settlement on the north side of town where volunteers built a kindergarten, playground, library, and garden.[32] Jennie Belle Murphy Covington studied the Association's success and founded Bethlehem Settlement for African American citizens in 1917. Supported by the Association and administered by an interracial committee, Covington's experiment ran a day nursery, sponsored clubs for adults and children, and organized several singing groups. Volunteers did not live in these settlements; rather, teams of volunteers from women's clubs, church groups, or the Association itself met each day at the community headquarters to organize and oversee projects.[33]

In 1916 Alice visited Corinne Fonde, a trained social worker who toiled in the cotton mills of New Orleans, and persuaded her to manage the Association's work program. In a *Houston Daily Post* article on Sunday, August 6, 1916, Fonde explained how the "social service workers of our center are handling the problems of relief in this ward, and in co-operation with the clinic are working on the principle that 'preventive and cure must go hand in hand.'" The Association members who are "busy women... some grandmothers, some mothers with large families—still find time to meet at the settlement once a week to lend a helping hand in any good cause that is presented." Fonde outlined numerous activities: the Olympic club for young men and boys, the Camp Fire Girls and Boy Scouts, the playground, the library and story hour, the day nursery and clinic, even the watermelon parties for children and the milk delivered each day during the summer. For two happy weeks each summer, children from the neighborhood enjoyed camp in the country at the Association's expense.[34]

Alice Baker's lovely face mirrored a beautiful soul. A true pioneer, she inspired her friends to share her concern for the hard-working families she nurtured through her settlement work. She rewarded her volunteers with Crusader pins adorned with daisies she had picked from her own garden. She encouraged residents who attended settlement programs to form clubs and rally behind neighborhood projects. Every year she invited members of the Second Ward Women's Club, Rusk Settlement's most popular club, to her home for a day together. These women also earned Crusader pins and within a few years had raised $100 to purchase a piano for the settlement.[35] Alice awarded prizes for the best home garden and the best vacant-lot community garden to encourage neighborhood beautification and pride. With her volunteers, Alice "stressed flexibility, professionalism, careful planning, and Christian love." One young woman told a social worker in the 1920s about meeting the Bakers at Rusk Settlement House, "We couldn't speak a word of English.... Captain and Mrs. Baker smiled at us and we knew we had found friends in a new country."[36]

After the city established its department to oversee charity, benevolence, and public welfare in 1915, officials were slow to implement the ordinance directives. In 1917 they created the Houston Foundation to "investigate charities dependent upon public appeal or general solicitation for support," to encourage formation of new private nonprofit groups, and to "foster all worthy enterprises of a philanthropic nature."[37] Implementing these goals through the Social Service Bureau—as the community foundation's operating unit was called—proved challenging. Mayor Ben Campbell asked William C. Hogg, the visionary oldest child of former Governor James Stephen Hogg, to head the foundation. To support the municipal initiative, Judge E. P. Hill, a founder of Houston Land & Trust Company, promised to bequeath $200,000 to the city for charitable purposes and encouraged others to give generously to the new foundation, which also received modest municipal support.

Will Hogg asked the Bakers and Estelle Sharp to help him bring major charitable organizations under the Bureau's supervisory umbrella. Mrs. Sharp had founded United Charities to consolidate charitable fund-raising and had incorporated the Texas School of Civics and Philanthropy to train social workers for public service; she remained a leader in Houston's philanthropic community until her death at age ninety-two in 1965. Will's diary entries through much of 1917 show he consulted frequently with Captain Baker and with Alice about ways to bridge the chasm between the city's independent charities and the foundation's oversight mandate. In June, after a meeting with Captain Baker and Abe Levy about the Bureau's funding needs, Will resigned from the foundation to focus his attention on the Bureau. In September he met with Alice about the Settlement Association's role, and by the end of the year the Houston Settlement Association, the Anti-Tuberculosis League, the Harris County Humane Society, the Kindergarten Association, and the Playgrounds Association had all agreed to coordinate as the Houston Social Service Bureau.[38] In 1918 Alice became volunteer chairwoman of the Bureau's Settlement and Social Service Department, with Corinne Fonde as professional supervisor.

Alice Baker's settlement house activism led her to embrace the playground movement then sweeping the country, and she began lobbying her husband and his friends to develop playgrounds throughout the city, especially in crowded neighborhoods where families did not have private gardens. Captain Baker served as a member of the board of directors of the Houston Play Ground Association, whose chairman in its early years (ca. 1915) was Baker's close business associate, the developer William A. Wilson. Baker heard Alice's plea to find "open air breathing space" for children living in densely populated urban areas, but he drove a hard bargain when Wilson asked the Institute Board to donate Rice land on Louisiana Street for a playground—and pay for its equipment and landscaping. As an Institute trustee, Baker told his friend, he could not give away Institute property or expend Institute funds for noneducational purposes, but he could allow the nonprofit association to use the property, provided the land was exempt from taxation while being used as a city playground.[39] In the fall of 1918 Alice hosted a meeting at her home to hear about plans for the Houston Recreation Department, established by the city that year. Alice's protégé Corinne Fonde became the department's first director.

In her effort to build cordial town-gown relations, Alice encouraged the wives of Rice Institute faculty members to participate in civic organizations. Corinne Stephenson Tsanoff, wife of distinguished Institute Philosophy Professor Radoslav Tsanoff, became a willing convert and took up Alice's leadership mantel to serve as chairman of Rusk Settlement (1932–1933), president of the Houston Settlement Foundation (1935–1942), and Houston representative on the national settlement board (1953–1961).[40] For three generations, Baker family members and their spouses have expanded Alice's legacy through a tradition of support and volunteer leadership with Neighborhood Centers, the Houston Settlement Association's successor organization.

CAPTAIN BAKER AND PRESIDENT LOVETT

During his tenure as chairman of the Rice Institute trustees, Captain Baker defined the lines of authority for the Board chairman and the Institute president. Baker understood that each decision he made set a precedent, and he deliberated carefully before taking action. Baker and the trustees set general policy and oversaw the financial well-being of the institution; no major decision was made without the chairman's approval. President Edgar Odell Lovett, as chief operating officer, was responsible for all aspects of university life, including student activities, academic programs, and hiring of personnel. Parents, graduates, prospective faculty members, friends, and critics wrote to Baker. Unless their letters concerned the Institute's endowment, he graciously explained that Dr. Lovett would handle their concerns and forwarded their requests to the president. Since Lovett was a full member of the Board, he engaged in all financial and investment discussions; he also reported to his colleagues about college life. Baker and Lovett prepared the budget each year with the help of the Institute business office; the Board then reviewed budget needs and gave final approval. In the years before World War I, Institute income exceeded operating expenses by a comfortable surplus as Lovett built the faculty slowly and added programs only when appropriate personnel could be found to implement them. Luring scholars to an academic start-up on a barren stretch of land in a hot climate proved challenging despite Lovett's smooth oratory and beautiful vision. Even though he offered unusually high salaries in the early years, Lovett made trip after trip to the Northeast and to Europe looking for talent. Because his standards were high, the process was slow but produced a firm foundation for future growth.

The friendship between Baker and Lovett continued to deepen, and both men enjoyed their intellectual collaboration. Lovett knew he could rely on his chairman for well-reasoned advice and enthusiastic support. Baker knew his president wholeheartedly endorsed the trustees' wishes to build a first-class institution. When Lovett was planning the Institute's first commencement, the courtly president composed one of his brief, elegantly inscribed letters to the vacationing chairman: "As usual I hesitate to trouble you with details," he explained politely, "but I need your judgment in the matter" of choosing speakers.[41] Baker almost always ratified the president's decisions, although he did not initiate salary or spending increases. While he rarely objected to budget requests that made the academic program grow, Baker expected Lovett to justify requests for a raise. On one occasion, he asked Lovett to study presidential salaries of other institutions and sent him an essay on the subject published in the *Princeton Alumni Weekly* (January 1917). Not surprisingly, Lovett's salary, travel allowance, and housing expenses increased slowly; faculty salaries that had seemed generous in the first decade gradually fell behind national norms by the early 1930s.[42]

Baker may have seemed stingy about salaries, but he wanted the campus to rank among the country's most beautiful. In 1916 he asked his own gardener, Salvatore "Tony" Martino, to maintain Institute landscaping and a large vegetable garden. Tony had migrated from Italy in 1908 to work for Captain and Mrs. Baker, but he tended Rice's trees and shrubbery through the 1950s and became a campus favorite when he cheered the Owls to victory during football season. For many years, Tony used mules to pull the mowing equipment and oversaw their stable on campus. Cram, Goodhue & Ferguson incorporated landscaping in the master plan, and Bellaire nurseryman Edward Teas planted oaks and azaleas to transform flat muddy prairie into stately vistas and shaded pathways.[43]

As spokesmen for the Institute, Baker and the trustees strengthened ties between town and gown. Both Baker and Lovett encouraged Rice professors to participate in civic activities, and the Institute began offering public lectures on campus in 1913. When Louise Cohn (Mrs.

Emanuel) Raphael joined a committee to organize free lecture courses in Houston, she appealed to the Board for financial support. At a meeting held in his office, Baker explained the project, appointed McAshan to represent the Institute on Mrs. Raphael's committee, and authorized a $500 subscription. Baker frequently discussed the Institute's progress with Marcellus Foster, editor of the *Houston Chronicle* and an enthusiastic promoter of the fledgling institution. Baker encouraged Foster to endorse Institute activities in his editorials and reported to Lovett any criticism that had reached Foster's ears.[44] Baker and his wife entertained faculty couples in their home and extended many "kindnesses and courtesies" the recipients never forgot.[45]

Institution building proceeded slowly. Lovett and the trustees heard constant demands to expand the Institute's physical plant, but construction took more time than anticipated. Trustees questioned plans and costs, architects failed to meet deadlines, shipments sat idle, and products could not be found. Yet every year before World War I buildings continued to rise on the campus. While the trustees left most design decisions to their president, they did keep a close watch on costs and completion schedules. Cram, Goodhue & Ferguson, challenged to create a general campus plan and drawings for specific buildings as quickly as possible, struggled to stay on schedule. Lovett, the middle man, shuttled between Boston and Houston. He placated architects but adhered to trustee budget demands, often changing the design or choice of materials. William Ward Watkin, Cram and Goodhue's clerk of the works who supervised construction, believed Baker and the trustees appreciated his efforts to stay on schedule and his frequent progress reports. Early photographs show the tall, pencil-thin Watkin leading his troop of portly middle-aged men in business attire and bowler hats around the evolving construction site. By September 1912, when the beautiful administration building, the practical mechanical laboratory and power house, the first men's dormitory, and the dining commons were finished enough for classes to begin, plans were under way for two more laboratories, additional dormitories, and homes for President Lovett and the faculty.

By April 1913 the trustees had approved a design for the Physics Building, temporarily partitioned to provide space for physics, chemistry, and biology departments until more structures could be completed. Although Baker had officially handed responsibility for campus construction to Lovett and his committee, he could not resist an indepen-

Physics Building under construction, 1913–1914. Early Rice Collection, Woodson Research Center, Rice University.

dent investigation in May. He spoke with S. B. Houx of the American Construction Company, whom he regarded "very highly both person-ally and professionally." Although Houx was not bidding for the project, Baker asked the contractor to comment on the architect's drawings for the physics building from a "purely practical" viewpoint. He sent Houx's comments to Lovett to consider. "I know," he told Lovett, "you will ac-quit me of any desire to erect a cheap building or one that will be out of harmony with those already constructed. At the same time I know you fully appreciate the importance of saving as much as we can in new con-struction."[46] Stewart & Company, a Scottish firm with an international clientele, made the low bid, and construction began in August 1913. By September 1914, the $288,903 Physics Laboratory was ready for use, but laboratory equipment did not arrive until that December. Whether Stewart & Company followed Houx's suggestions was not recorded.

Trustees next approved plans for East Hall, the second dormitory of the residence quadrangle, and signed the construction contract in De-cember 1913. Students occupied the new hall in September 1915. By late that year, trustees had approved plans for West Hall, and on January 11, 1916, they accepted the lowest of seven bids to begin building. When the hall opened in September 1916, it completed the men's residence complex of three-story, fire-proof, well-ventilated structures opening to gardens and courtyards. The living-learning environment comprised student rooms, lodgings for several faculty preceptors, two large halls for literary and debating societies, and modern lavatories and shower baths, and all spaces received power for light and heat from the Institute's central plant.[47] Construction progress then ground to a halt, and no additional buildings appeared until the 1920s, despite the continually expanding student body and the desperate need for more laboratory space. Whether concerns about expansion during wartime or arguments about a president's house underlay the building hiatus is not clear.

The trustees had promised Lovett a president's house as part of his compensation package, and discussion about this important building began in 1910. "Anguished" correspondence and a flurry of sketches produced stalemate. Lovett conceived the house as a home for his family and, more important, as a social center where he and his wife Mary could entertain dignitaries, faculty, students, and friends of the Institute. Cram and Ferguson rendered his concept in sketches in 1911 and suggested a budget of $80,000. Even Lovett blanched at this figure, and, after much discussion, the architects produced drawings that could be executed for $60,000. Until Lovett and his wife enlarged the size of the rooms, there seemed hope for agreement between the president and the architects. Then the trustees sent everyone back to their drawing boards when they made their opinions clear; in July 1913 they authorized an expenditure of $35,000, a handsome sum in that era, but not one that would pay for the presidential palace Lovett imagined. Although the trustees grudgingly raised the sum to $45,000 in August, Lovett realized his dream was not shared by his cost-conscious colleagues. Discussion about the president's house continued, but no agreement was reached before building stopped during the war. In fact, Lovett never did realize his hope for a presidential mansion commensurate with his concept of the presidency's importance.[48] The promised faculty housing did not materialize, either. Instead, the trustees made several construction loans from Institute funds on easy terms to well-established professors after the war.

CAMPUS CONTROVERSIES

Although Baker and the Board rarely interfered in campus business, they did step in occasionally to resolve crises regarding parents, faculty, students, and the public. The Institute's first years were difficult. Public expectations were high, and everyone was impatient to realize the promises envisioned in oratory. From the outset, the Institute held the world's finest institutions as its model and demanded high academic standards. When Lovett notified parents in December 1912 that some members of the first class would not be invited to return because of "deficiencies of scholarship," J. M. Wilkerson objected and explained his concerns to the Board. Worried that his son would be dealt "incalculable injury" if deemed "deficient," he begged Lovett to give those dismissed "another trial," but Lovett remained firm, and Baker explained to the distraught father that the Board entrusted student affairs to Lovett. As a trustee, he could not interfere.[49] When G. Martel Hall and some accomplices were caught in a prank that involved setting a fire on a residence hall roof in November 1914, his parents each vigorously protested their son's suspension from the residence hall. They wrote to Lovett and Baker and leaked the uproar to the press. Once again, Baker stood by Lovett's actions, evaded a personal call from the father, and suggested in his final letter to the parents that the stunt and its punishment would not reflect on the boy's adult reputation.

More serious were insurrections from professors. Lovett usually handled faculty demands for better equipment, more staff, and increased pay, but when he hired William Franklin Edwards to set up the chemistry lab and department in 1914, he soon learned he had chosen a troublemaker. A native of Houston, Edwards held only a BS degree, so was not as well trained as much of the staff. As events transpired, he proved to be a master of hyperbole rather than a scholar of chemistry. By June 1914 he was sending complaining letters to Baker about Lovett's leadership abilities and faculty choices. In January 1915 the Board chairman decided to grant the grumbling professor a conference. Edwards dismissed as an "untenable assumption" Baker's comment that "many mistakes and even blunders were to be expected" in a young institution. The professor concluded, mistakenly, that Baker's conversation indicated the chairman was "aware of many of the shortcomings" of Dr. Lovett. In February, Baker tried to settle the matter by firmly backing Lovett's actions, but in April and May he received two more lengthy screeds. In one letter, Edwards claimed, "Dr. Lovett has treated the Institute somewhat as if it had passed entirely into his hands and is for the future, therefore to be treated only as a private affair," a "feudal policy" supported by the Board although "finally abandoned by nearly all civilized peoples, even in politics." In the other letter, he told the patient chairman he had hoped to build a chemistry department "in a peaceful way" but was forced to fight "with a boy architect and a misfit president" to get a suitable laboratory for the students. Tired of this overheated harangue, Baker passed on the letters to Lovett and set up a meeting with his president to discuss the matter. A citation in the June 9, 1915, minutes authorizing payment to Edwards through September 1915 suggests that the professor had been relieved of duty but would be paid for the summer months. In July Edwards leaked the story to the *Chronicle*, hoping for justification. Instead, the editor exclaimed that the article was printed by a neophyte reporter without his knowledge, and the public sided with Lovett and Baker in general outrage against Edwards's intemperate language. By August the feisty chemist had quit the fight and moved to Philadelphia.[50]

Another student controversy, which reached the Board in February 1918, concerned the case of senior Errol Middleton, found guilty of breaking Rice's honor code following a complaint made by chemistry Professor Harry Boyer Weiser. Lovett informed the Board that he explained the honor system at a public meeting at the beginning of each school year; that the regulations were published in the *Thresher* every fall; that Middleton underwent a proper trial; and that he had met at length with the senior, his mother, and the accusing professor. Weiser "expressed a most kindly feeling toward Middleton" and hoped rules would not require his dismissal, but the Student Honor Council voted 7 for dismissal to 1 for suspension. Finding Baker and Lovett unresponsive to parental protest, the student's father, E. Middleton, wrote an impassioned letter to the Board on February 26, pleading that "this awful blight against his young life," which had been "rendered by a bunch of boys and girls who have no knowledge of the Rights of the Accused," would be removed from his son's record. In reply, the trustees informed the devastated parents that "the action of the Honor Council, approved by the President, is final and conclusive and there is nothing further [the Board] can do."[51]

WORLD WAR I COMES TO HOUSTON

When the guns of August 1914 brought turmoil to Europe's vast world empires, Houston soon felt the effects. Blockades and U-boats impeded free trade with Europe. Germany's invasion of neutral Belgium horrified those like Edgar Odell Lovett and Ima Hogg, who loved German music and revered German academic innovation. At the Institute, several professors of European origin returned home to defend their countries. Ironically, the Houston economy boomed: its port received goods shipped through the new Panama canal, oil production soared, cotton prices rose, and workers poured into the city. Texans used their ties to the Wilson administration to secure training camps for army troops and air squadrons. Public opinion turned against the Germans when a U-boat sank the passenger liner *Lusitania* on May 17, 1915. Woodrow Wilson prevailed on the Kaiser to declare a moratorium on submarine warfare against commercial traffic, but tense relations continued. After the Germans resumed unrestricted submarine warfare in January 1917 and torpedoed seven US merchant ships, Wilson asked Congress to declare war against Germany on April 6, 1917. Houston immediately assumed a war footing, and hundreds of young volunteers began training for overseas service at Leon Springs, not far from San Antonio.

Baker, Botts, Parker & Garwood immediately felt the stress of war. Of thirteen men appointed to the national Priorities Committee for the Council of National Defense, three were associated with the firm. Former partner Robert S. Lovett, then running the Union Pacific system at its New York headquarters, was called to Washington to serve as Priorities Commissioner.[52] He turned to his former law partner, the supremely organized Edwin B. Parker, and asked him to be chairman of the War Industries Board, and thereby responsible for restructuring industrial plants to equip the armed forces. Ralph B. Feagin spent three years in New York and Washington, DC, as secretary of the national Red Cross and then as assistant to Robert S. Lovett. Edwin B. Parker and his wife left for Washington, where he worked for Woodrow Wilson's administration through 1922, first with Lovett and then as head of the Liquidation Commission, formed in 1919 to round up and sell off all US war supplies in Europe. With barely a gap between assignments, Parker next accepted Warren G. Harding's call to arbitrate the United States' settlement claims against the defeated German coalition (1923–1926) and finally to preside over the United States Liquidation Commission and the Mixed Claims Commission, posts he held until his early death in 1929 at age sixty-one.

Mayor A. Earl Amerman mobilized Houston for war work and called on all civic organizations to support President Wilson's crusade to "make the world safe for Democracy." He asked Houstonians to begin each day with prayer and a "moment of quiet." Former Mayor Ben Campbell accepted leadership of the local Red Cross chapters and oversaw dozens of committees and hundreds of volunteers, who prepared surgical dressings, knitted clothing, blankets, and scarves, and raised over $860,000. Clarence Wharton, premier litigator at Baker, Botts, Parker & Garwood, became chairman of the local Red Cross Social Services Committee and an active member of Houston's War Service Commission. Institute trustee Edward A. Peden took on statewide responsibilities when named Federal Food Administrator of Texas' eight districts. Houstonians enthusiastically purchased liberty bonds and served on committees to entertain troops stationed in the area.

Captain Baker, sixty years old in 1917, immediately took action to support the war effort. As chairman of the Institute trustees, he helped secure an army training camp for the city. On May 17, 1917, he wrote to J. W. Link, chairman of the Cantonment Committee, to say the Institute would cooperate with other owners of land north of Buffalo Bayou who were willing to lease the area at a below-market rate of $10 an acre for two years, with an option to extend the lease; Board members ratified his action at the annual meeting on May 25. Baker then worked out the best mechanism to convey use of the land to the government and asked lawyers at Baker, Botts, Parker & Garwood to prepare a lease between the Institute and the Chamber of Commerce, who would rent 115 acres of Institute land lying north of Buffalo Bayou and west of city limits. The chamber, in turn, would sublet the land to the US government for two years, with an option to renew for three more years, so the Army could build a training ground, which was called Camp Logan.

In July 1917 Baker asked the Institute Board, in its capacity as a major stockholder, to approve the South Texas Commercial National Bank's donation of $5,000 to the Red Cross Fund. On October 31, Baker and the trustees unanimously granted Institute Professor Stockton Axson leave of absence, at full pay, so he could serve as secretary of the Red Cross War Council in Washington. Baker told Axson and the Red Cross chairman that the trustees would regret losing the professor's services temporarily but took "pleasure in being able to make this contribution to the great work being done by said War Council." Baker and his fellow trustees also granted leave of absence to professors who wished to enlist in the US military. The Board promised to meet any difference between military pay and Institute salary and to hold soldiers' positions "provided they are then in condition physically and mentally to perform the duties now performed by them."[53]

Alice threw herself into war work. As a leading organizer of the city's social service sector, she offered invaluable advice to lonely soldiers, families whose fathers were away at war, and war workers looking for housing. Clarence Wharton, executive chairman of Houston's War Service Commission, asked Alice to serve on the Executive Committee for War Camp Community Service. The Commission organized community programs to welcome soldiers stationed at Camp Logan. During Hospitality Week October 17–24, 1917, nearly every church, club, and lodge participated on one or more of twenty committees. The Thalian Club converted to a soldiers' club, the Houston Light Guard armory became a recreational canteen, and volunteers from twenty-eight women's clubs acted as hostesses under Estelle Sharp's direction. Alice Baker, Harriet Levy, and others with large gardens entertained groups of one hundred at their homes, while six hundred soldiers feasted on watermelons at Hermann Park. A housing bureau found thousands of homes for military families and inspected each to make sure it was suitable.

Alice also joined the YWCA War Council and was one of three Houston women named to the National War Work Council of the YWCA in the summer of 1917 when she, Mrs. Harris Masterson, and Agnese Carter Nelms attended the National Conference in New York City. As chairman of the YWCA War Council, Alice and a committee of twenty-four leading women mustered two thousand young women to do Red Cross work and to serve in the Hostess Houses (duly chaperoned by older women) at Camp Logan and at Ellington Field, which had been constructed near Houston to train army air force pilots. These Hostess Houses provided light airy rooms for relaxing and sponsored concerts and dances. To honor Alice's commitment to the war effort, Red Cross volunteers filled the Alice G. Baby Chest with layettes for women whose husbands were serving in the armed forces. At war's end, Mayor Amerman asked those who had formed war committees to unite in a Welcome Home Committee to greet returning soldiers at Union Station and fete them with bands, cannonades, food, flags, and flowers.[54]

Captain and Mrs. Baker were visiting New York City on Thursday, August 23, 1917, when one hundred African American soldiers of the 3rd Battalion, 24th US Infantry, marched toward downtown Houston to protest harassment by the local police. The battalion, led by seven white officers and previously stationed in New Mexico, arrived in Houston July 27 to guard construction crews building Camp Logan. Almost immediately, soldiers experienced heckling and harassment if they left camp. When a rumor that police had shot a black military policeman reached the base, men seized arms and marched toward town. Fifteen white men and four black soldiers died in a disorganized riot before the soldiers drifted back to camp. At 7:30 the next morning municipal authorities clamped a curfew on black neighborhoods, and white citizens organized at the Criminal District Court to help military authorities and local police restore order. Leading citizens, including Baker's partner Hiram M. Garwood and Chamber of Commerce President Joseph Cullinan, deplored the "unfortunate affair" and organized volunteer squads to fan out through the African American neighborhoods to search for military equipment or renegade soldiers. A banquet committee that included several Baker, Botts, Parker & Garwood partners canceled a Saturday dinner at the Rice Hotel, planned to honor officers from area training camps, "due to the disturbed conditions." The army hustled the battalion out of town that weekend and later held courts martial in New Mexico. That Sunday, the *Chronicle*, on page 1, reassured Houston's African American population that their fears were "unwarranted," that no Houstonians had harbored the rioting criminals, and that the soldiers and officers in charge of them were solely responsible for the "scene of carnage, of rioting and of terror." If the Bakers reacted to the disorganized and quickly quelled weekend of rage, they left no written record. Only the actions of his partners and friends suggest how Captain Baker may have felt.[55]

THE WAR YEARS AT RICE

As war closed over Europe and drew several professors, graduates, and even students to military service, the Institute faced new problems. As so often happens in times of tension, some who fear what they do not understand questioned academic freedom and those who espoused its tenets. On January 20, 1918, President Lovett received a communication from the Houston Ministers Alliance asking him to explain the Institute's stance regarding atheism and the boundaries, if any, of academic freedom. Couched in respectful language, the group recognized the authority of the Institute to employ people of all beliefs, but its members still felt "well within the bounds of courtesy, fairness and right in asking that a statement be made as to the character of teaching and instruction to be given in the class rooms."[56] Lovett immediately consulted the Board, which asked him to acknowledge the resolutions by telephone. After considerable discussion, Lovett formulated the Institute's position, which Baker reinforced in his own writing on the subject. The Institute, Lovett reminded the Ministers Alliance, did support freedom of choice but did not approve or disapprove courses taught by the professors it hired. Believing "it is only in an atmosphere of freedom that learning thrives," Lovett, with the Board's blessing, also outlined the many ties between the Institute and religious institutions such as the YMCA, and reminded the ministers that "plans for the development of the Rice Institute have . . . been informed by a broad and generous spirit."[57]

Most explosive was the student protest launched early in 1918 against an intensified military training program that had turned the campus into a military post in September 1917. In his annual matriculation address, President Lovett welcomed the freshman class in September 1917 with solemn words. Reminding the students that the Institute's founders "set about deliberately, five years ago, to train men and women in science and scholarship and citizenship," he noted that the school would continue this mission, but that he had to "recognize the imperative call of the nation." The Institute would also "do our part in training soldiers for the country's service and in the coming year . . . will be converted into a military camp."[58] Lovett's effort to answer his country's call backfired, but led to closer relations between the students and Captain Baker.

As recounted in the *Thresher* and reprised in the *Houston Chronicle*, the confrontation between Lovett and the faculty on one side and the student body on the other was so "serious" it caused Edwin B. Parker, serving in Washington as chairman of the War Industries Board, to write a letter of encouragement to Baker. Wishing he could be there to help, Parker told his partner, "I have . . . every confidence in your ability to pour oil on the troubled waters and restore the cordial relations which have heretofore existed between the Rice faculty and its students."[59] President Lovett and Chairman Baker viewed the United States declaration of war on April 6, 1917, with one mind. "We enter" the war, Lovett told the seniors in May 1917, "because some things are worth dying for." As soon as war was declared Lovett traveled to Washington to request that a Reserve Officers Training Corps (ROTC) be established at Rice, and in May 1917 Major Joseph Frazier was assigned to the campus. When students arrived that September they discovered Frazier had introduced military camp regulations complete with taps, bugle calls, inspections, and drill. Most deplorable, if the students were to be believed, was the food. Protest mounted: students claimed Lovett refused to listen, parents and students pelted trustees with letters, and communication channels clogged. Vitriol replaced reasoned discourse when the students published a protest paper, *Tape*, its criticisms heavily highlighted in red.

Finally, on Saturday morning January 26, 1918, Captain Baker and the Board met with the cadet leader, who produced a long list of complaints. Immediately, the trustees realized they needed to hold a meeting open to all students, and they arranged to visit the campus on Monday morning. For the first time since the Institute's founding, trustees listened for over three hours and seemed, according to *Thresher* reporters, to be "surprised" by the conditions on campus. Baker presided as the cadets, fearful of trustee reaction, declared they were not "insurrectionists." Baker responded with a little talk about his own college days, "at the end of which we would have done anything in the wide world for him," said the *Thresher* reporter. On Saturday, February 9, the Board again came to campus, and Captain Baker announced the results of the Board's deliberations: nearly all student requests were gracefully met, and the "military regime was replaced with the Rice of old," but with an ROTC program also in place. Baker led the students in a cheer, calling on them to yell "Yea-a-Rice" over and over again. "Boys," he declared, "that is the sweetest music I have ever heard in my life." The students, he told the crowd, had kept faith with the trustees, so the trustees would keep faith with them.[60]

The near rebellion and the charges that Dr. Lovett was an uncaring autocrat reached men and women all over the state. Baker mollified one concerned writer from El Paso by explaining that the trustees "have thoroughly investigated the existing conditions, and are satisfied that these charges are not true. Dr. Lovett is not an autocrat . . . but a straightforward, unpretentious gentleman of democratic ideas and practices." The students, he added, "had misconstrued" some of the rules they were protesting, and the Board modified others. He also stated that there was no pro-German sentiment on campus, that several professors and students were serving their countries, and that he saw no reason to dismiss foreigners on staff "whose services are acceptable and conduct unobjectionable to anyone."[61] Baker more than fulfilled Parker's prophecy that he would pour oil on troubled waters. His charm, his tact, and his ability to listen allowed him to calm the students' fears, support his chosen president, but resolve seemingly opposing opinions. Rice Institute would continue its tradition of liberal education while at the same time supporting the war effort and training young men and women for military service by encouraging voluntary participation in the ROTC program.

Baker's interaction with the students in January and February heightened his understanding of undergraduate life and reinforced his wish to strengthen the Institute. At the Annual Meeting on June 12, 1918, Baker announced that he and his wife Alice would establish the first Institute scholarship for outstanding student performance with an initial donation of $6,000. To be named for his son who had died sixteen years earlier, the Graham Baker Studentship of $270 a year would honor the Rice student who maintained the highest grades. On March 6, 1919, the *Thresher* published an interview with Chairman Baker that mentioned the importance of this gift, made by a man recognized as the "Students' Friend," one who always considered the interests of undergraduates.

At the June 12, 1918, Board meeting, Baker also read a letter from Estelle Sharp, who was transferring her sponsorship of the Texas School of Civics and Philanthropy to Rice to form a department where students could be trained for "careers of civic usefulness." She pledged $3,000 annually for the next five years to create the Institute's first endowed chair and to pay for the lecturer's salary. Her letter explained that four citizens, William C. Hogg, Joseph Cullinan, Abraham Levy, and John T. Scott, had pledged $250 each to create four scholarships for students who would train to be social workers in the South. In 1920 John Willis Slaughter began his long career at Rice as the new program's resident lecturer. To complete this sudden outpouring of generosity, Will Rice announced that as executor of the estate of Lionel Hohenthal he would be creating a charity foundation to benefit Rice and honor the donor's parents and brother. Dr. Lovett wired a summary of the third annual commencement to his old mentor, now President Woodrow Wilson, and included a description of these welcome gifts.[62]

In 1919 Will Hogg proposed that Rice establish a Student Loan Fund endowment similar to the fund he had set up at the University of Texas. Hogg would eventually establish funds to help students "in distress" pay for small expenses during their college years at every institution of higher learning in Texas. After several conversations with Lovett and Baker, Hogg announced in 1919 that he would donate $1,000 in Liberty Bonds to establish the fund and challenged Baker to raise an endowment of $25,000. Baker responded with a $1,000 match to get the drive started. He also drew up a charter based on the prototype Hogg used throughout the state.[63]

The turmoil of the war years ended with expressions of hope for the future when Captain Baker, Governor William P. Hobby, and Houston leaders welcomed British educators on Monday November 25, 1918, at the Rice hotel. The British Mission toured the United States immediately after the armistice to cement ties between Great Britain and the United States through exchange of professors and students. Baker extended the emissaries "a most cordial welcome . . . to the homes and hearts of our people" and reminded the audience of the common language and heritage shared by the two nations. As he inaugurated a week of lectures and events at Rice Institute, he predicted a "glorious future" with the flags of England and America "entwined" in friendship.[64] In December the Lovetts welcomed members of the French Educational Mission to campus. Mission participants, guests of the American Council on Education, traveled across the country to explain French culture, customs, and countryside to American audiences.

Baker's leadership during the ROTC crisis and his generous studentship endowment so impressed the students that they began to see him as their spokesman and friend, a leader who possessed an "unmeasured ability" to handle student problems. The March 6, 1919, issue of the *Thresher* devoted a long article to the trustees and to Baker's role as Board chairman. Highlighted by a large photograph of the Captain, who was then sixty-two years old, the article declared the "future success of our youthful university will be a lasting tribute to the man who has labored so diligently in her behalf." Baker, the undergraduate writer reported, was "consistently working for Rice" and "keeping our [student] interests from being trampled on." The student reviewed Baker's visit to campus the previous year and hoped he would make another visit to campus in 1919.[65] His wishes were granted when the Institute celebrated its first alumni homecoming on Thanksgiving Day in 1919. Captain Baker and President Lovett led an academic procession, attended a sermon in the quad, and watched the Rice football squad trounce Arkansas 40 to 7. That evening alumni, faculty, and trustees gathered for a holiday feast. Captain Baker welcomed the guests and called on professors and graduates to share their war experiences. The somber day of remembrance and gratitude ended at midnight as everyone gathered around a bonfire.[66]

The alumni gathering rallied factions who had split over remarks made by sociologist Lyford Paterson Edwards at a Sunday school class in May 1919. At a time when postwar economic conditions were unsettled and Red Scare rumors a staple of national news, the trustees faced a crisis of loyalty themselves. While addressing members of the First Congregational Church on the subject "Russia and the Soviet Government," Edwards tried to analyze how he saw the progress of revolution in that turbulent nation. "If," he said, "the Soviet system was successful and became permanently established, then . . . Lenin and Trotsky would be considered in Russia in the same way that Washington and Jefferson are now considered in the United States." One attendee jumped up, incensed, before the lecture was over, and repeated what he considered ominous and unacceptable Communist propaganda to the press. The media seized the story and were joined by local patriotic societies and some churches in a vicious personal attack on Edwards. Mayor A. Earl Amerman denounced the dangerous doctrines and pernicious "-isms" sullying the tender ears of Rice students. Most trustees and President Lovett were out of town when the story broke. By May 23, they had returned, read all the letters and press accounts, and counseled at length with Edwards.

On May 24 the Board made public a report that was motivated by a paternal desire to protect the Institute's good reputation but that reflects a confused understanding of academic freedom and freedom of speech. Statements about the case were "contradictory," the report began; those who attended did not see anything "to shock or otherwise disturb their patriotic sensibilities." Moreover, Edwards, a British subject, was well-known for his support of the Allied cause and had spoken on many occasions at Camp Logan and elsewhere. Nonetheless, he "possesses certain views in respect to the political conditions in Russia . . . so at variance with the prevailing sentiment of the people of this and the Allied countries, as, in the opinion of the Trustees, [to] utterly destroy his further usefulness to the Institute." In asking for and accepting Edwards's resignation, the trustees had "not been unmindful of the freedom of speech that should always be permitted to the teacher and searcher after truth," but rather than defend their professor's right to express his opinion, they instead focused on the reputation of the Institute, which they believed had been harmed by the way the case had been handled in the press. Condemning the actions of the complainant, the local press, Mayor Amerman, and "some of the citizenship at large," the Board stated that the Institute "is one of the greatest, if not the greatest asset of Houston not only from an educational standpoint but from a business point of view as well." How could the Institute fulfill its mission if "charges are published widecast by press and pulpit alike"? Instead of rushing into print, Edwards and other complainants should have laid the matter before the president and trustees, who "are administering a great public trust" and need "the generous and helpful co-operation of the Press, of the public officials and of the citizenship as a whole."

Edwards, who later taught at Saint Stephen's College in New York, described the witch-hunt that drove him from town. His friends warned him not to appear in public. "For three days before my flight I dared not go down town." On the day he departed, colleagues warned him a mob was forming to drive out to the campus and "get" him; he was "hustled away and eventually put on a train at a subordinate station at an uncomfortable hour." Writing to a Yale colleague years later, Edwards concluded, "The essential point is that I made the statement about Lenin and Trotsky and had to get out of town for fear of mob violence." While it is perhaps understandable that the trustees, including Dr. Lovett, saw the Institute's reputation as paramount, it is unfortunate that they bowed so easily to popular opinion.[67] The faculty supported Edwards vigorously and released a statement two days later in which they condemned "any action which seems to limit the freedom of thought or to check the proper expression of beliefs." Claiming no privilege "which we do not ask for every citizen," the faculty cited First Amendment rights as "the very essence of true Americanism" and pledged its "loyal desire to co-operate" with the president and board of trustees "in service to this community and to the broader cause of education." National newspapers condemned Edwards's dismissal, but the trustees' action found broad support in Texas. Noting that Edwards had been a faithful employee whose loyalty was never in question, the trustees agreed to continue his salary for six months beyond the expiration of his yearly contract.[68]

MILITARY SERVICE

Captain and Mrs. Baker devoted untold energy to their war work in part because they believed deeply in the allied cause and its determination to "put down forever the Prussian spirit of domination and control."[69] Captain Baker's military training and sense of civic responsibility ensured his active participation in the city's response to Wilson's crusade; Alice Baker's devotion to the well-being of Houston families naturally drew her to service. But closer to their hearts was the knowledge that their son was serving in France. Although immersed in his law studies at the University of Texas and deeply in love with his college sweetheart, Bonner Means, young Jim had been one of the first Houstonians to offer his services after war was declared. In quick succession he completed his law course, departed for training at Camp Travis in San Antonio, became engaged and then married, and received his commission as lieutenant in the army. By August 1918 Jim was facing the Germans on the western front. The few letters that survive from this time of anxious separation reveal the profound love and concern Jim's parents felt for their son and new daughter-in-law.

The family's war experience began with a rush of excitement. On May 9, 1917, Bonner's friends celebrated the young couple's engagement at an elegant luncheon given by her cousin, where Bonner announced plans for a winter wedding. The gathering of twenty-four ladies consumed an elegant six-course meal at two tables adorned by pink and lavender sweet peas set in fern-filled wicker baskets tied with pink and lavender tulle. Mints in the bonbon dishes were embossed with sweet peas, and place cards were shaped like bridesmaids, each hand-painted. Miss Means's place was marked by a miniature bride and groom. The final "cream course" featured lavender and pink ice cream and "individual cakes embossed with sweet peas." One fashion writer opined that "no engagement of the season will be of more cordial interest to society" than the announcement joining "two of Texas' most representative families."[70]

When Jim learned that he would receive his commission in August, plans for the wedding changed. A ceremony of "beauty and simplicity" celebrated their marriage at Christ Church at eight-thirty in the evening on Saturday, August 4, 1917. "In keeping with the summer season and the strenuousness of the times," the event, although attended by a large gathering of Houston's most prominent citizens, was considered "quiet"

Bonner Means (Mrs. James A. Jr.) Baker, 1917. Private Collection.

and "informal." Palms and ferns filled the chancel, and the groom and his ushers wore full military dress. The bride, her three attendants, and her mother wore white, while the groom's mother was quietly attired in grey tulle over gray satin. Bonner's parents, the J. C. Meanses, received the bridal party and family members at their Rossonian apartment, and two days later Jim and Bonner departed for a brief wedding trip to the Grand Hotel on Mackinac Island in Michigan.

On August 8 Captain Baker sent a loving letter to his son and new daughter, who had left Houston at nine-thirty the night before. He could not sleep after their departure and had several suggestions for their trip; he also enclosed a check for $500, the same amount he had given to Alice for her wedding trip. "As I told you, it is my purpose to be absolutely impartial as between my children as far as it is possible for me to do. Please accept this check with my warmest devotion. As Jim will be in camp when this letter reaches you, I have drawn the check in favor of Bonner." He then suggested a bank in San Antonio and enclosed a letter of introduction to its president and cashier. He closed with his "fondest love . . . in which Mrs. Baker and the children join," and signed the missive "Daddie." A handwritten postscript to Bonner explained to her, "Jim always calls me Daddie & Walter B. calls me Dad, so I sign this letter as I usually do when writing to Jim." By late August the young couple had settled at Leon Springs near San Antonio, where Lt. Baker enrolled in Quartermaster School.[71]

The Bakers wrote their son several letters full of advice while he was in camp, visited him on the Sunday after his birthday in San Antonio, and begged him to spend Thanksgiving Day in Houston. Enticements beyond the holiday feast included a Rice football game against A&M at which President Wilson's daughter would be the honored guest.[72] While on a business trip to New York, Captain Baker proffered more advice to his son about "the delicate points that should be borne in mind in your dealing with army people" and stressed that the "bearing and deportment of a young soldier" were critical to a favorable impression. Finally, he admitted, "I expect you and Bonner will think that I am overflowing today with an abundance of advice, but the truth is that Mrs. Baker and I have been thinking and talking of you both very much in the last few days and are wondering what the future holds in store for you. I know you both realize that my advice is prompted by my love and devotion for both of you and my anxiety to see you both well started on the road to success and happiness."[73]

Lt. Baker and the 90th Division, the "Pride of Every Texan," embarked for Europe at the end of June 1918 and reached the Western Front by late July. On the eve of his son's departure, Captain Baker sent "a fathers blessing": "I want you to know," he reassured his son, "I happily approve your course. . . . Your life has been a constant joy to your mother and me. I know you will be brave and consciensiously [sic] discharge every duty. May God in His mercy watch over you and keep you from all harm and bring you back in safety shall be my constant prayer until I see your dear face again."[74] Communication proved difficult. Waiting anxiously for word from the front, the family often received a batch of four or five letters after a long break.

Lt. Baker and his Company I of the 359th Infantry participated in the St. Mihiel Offensive (September 12–16, 1918) and remained in the trenches until pulled back on October 10, 1918. The next day the lieutenant was far enough away from action to read letters from his wife, sister, and parents and to pen replies. To his sister Alice, he confessed he cried when he saw the letter from his three-year-old niece; five of Alice's let-

Lt. James A. Baker Jr., August 1917–November 1918; promoted to captain November 1918; discharged April 1919; served with US Army 90th Division at St. Mihiel and Verdun. Private Collection.

ters had arrived at the same time, each "another ray of sunshine in my somewhat lonely existence over here." He told Alice he had been twice on patrol in Noman's Land and had captured four prisoners. "We are the 'shock troops,'" he explained, "which means that we get more fighting and a better chance of getting killed than the others."[75] Later Col. E. K. Sterling, who commanded Baker's unit, specifically described the "aggressive spirit" of the young soldier's nightly patrols, noting that on one occasion Lieutenant Baker went out at 3:00 a.m., returned before daylight with prisoners, and was sent out again the next night and again returned with captives.[76]

Letters to his mother were more circumspect. On the same day that he wrote his sister, Jim explained to his mother that he had been in the front lines and had received her letters, but the "difficulties of writing are stupendous" because no pencils or pens are allowed as a precaution against revealing troop location. He told his mother he appreciated his father's letters of introduction "very much but have had absolutely no opportunity to use them." While officers were supposed to have ten days leave every four months, he saw no chance of moving from the area. Her news of Bass Rocks "makes me mighty home-sick. Do you think we can ever get there together once more? I believe Houston is about as near Paradise as I ever want to be again."

On October 22, 1918, his unit moved back to the front near Verdun, where it relieved the 5th Division and remained until fighting ceased.[77] Lt. Baker's division was under fire from August 20 until November 4, except for a few days when changing sectors—seventy-five days with no relief.[78] A few days before the armistice, Jim wrote to his father: the captain of his company lay dangerously wounded, two lieutenants had been killed and two gassed, and he was the only officer who had escaped unharmed.[79] From October 20 until November 21, 1918, Lt. Baker commanded this depleted company. In later years, Jim Baker described the appalling experience of life in the trenches to his son, the danger of arresting two German soldiers found cowering in a command post, the tragedy of losing a buddy, shot on Armistice Day while cleaning his gun. He also passed on his patriotism and his core belief in service to the nation.[80]

Hoping to provide Christmas cheer for his son, Captain Baker wrote to a former business acquaintance, M. A. Mitaranga, on November 5, 1918, to ask him a favor. Mitaranga had lived in Houston many years earlier but was then a resident of Marseilles, and Baker wanted his old friend to put together jams, knickknacks, cakes, chocolates, and similar things "you would prepare for your own son" for a "nice bountiful Christmas box" and send the Captain a bill. Restrictions on shipping gifts from Houston were so great the Bakers could not send their son any luxuries for Christmas. Despite several letters and minute instructions, Lt. Baker never received the gift conceived with so much care by both older men.[81] On November 11, 1918, guns lay quiet on the western front after the Germans signed armistice terms at 11:00 a.m. By December 29, 1918, the battle-seasoned lieutenant had been cited for bravery and promoted to captain. He was now with the army of occupation in Wehlen, Germany, as aide to Gen. Ulysses Grant McAlexander, 180th Brigade, 90th Division. Letters home indicated his post along the Moselle was relaxing, almost fun, except that Jim was trying to find a way to get home as quickly as possible. On February 10, 1919, his father counseled patience, although on February 3 he had written to Gen. John J. Pershing, American Expeditionary Force commander in Paris, asking him "to expedite" Jim's return. Reassured by the general early in March that Gen. McAlexander had already ordered Jim back to the United States on February 17, the Bakers and Bonner anxiously awaited news in Baltimore, where Mrs. Baker was being treated for high blood pressure that spring. The war-weary captain made his way from Germany to Camp Mills, Long Island, where he arrived on April 4. "Crazy to see you," telegraphed Bonner as she rushed to New York to welcome Jim home.[82] Capt. Jim Baker, now a decorated war hero, could return to civilian life and the practice of law at his father's firm. Jim's younger brother Walter B was still seventeen when the United States declared war, so he finished the Hill School and matriculated at Princeton. When he turned eighteen in January 1918, he volunteered for the navy as a seaman, but armistice was declared before his orders arrived. His parents were overjoyed when Walter B resumed his studies at Princeton.

CHAPTER SEVEN

Leader of Men

HOUSTON'S ECONOMY GREW significantly during the 1920s. While other parts of the country suffered serious labor strikes in 1919, a deep recession in 1921, and a prolonged drought in the 1920s, Houston became a major industrial city because oil gradually replaced lumber and cotton as the city's economic foundation. Captain Baker's three great enterprises—his Institute, his law firm, and his bank—flourished during this expansion, sustained by his careful oversight.

BOOMTOWN HOUSTON

By 1920 the town that had reported 78,800 citizens in 1910 was now a small city of 138,276; by 1930 Houston had 292,352 residents, second only to New Orleans in the South. To house these immigrants, subdivisions spread in all directions beyond Houston's commercial and industrial zones. Ten skyscrapers defined the skyline in the 1920s, including the sixteen-story Houston Cotton Exchange Building (1924), the Gothic-style Medical Arts Building, also sixteen stories (1926), the twenty-two-story Petroleum Building (1927), Mellie Esperson's Italian Renaissance-

Illustration: Rice Institute Campus, aerial view 1920s. Early Rice Collection, Woodson Research Center, Rice University.

style memorial to her husband Neils (1927), and Jesse Jones's handsome thirty-seven-story Gulf Building (1929), the tallest in the city for more than thirty years. In 1920 Oscar F. Holcombe held sway at the mayor's office, as he would do intermittently for more than thirty years. Hospitable hosts were looking for alcohol substitutes with the initiation of Prohibition (1920 ratification of the Eighteenth Amendment), women had earned the vote (1920 ratification of the Nineteenth Amendment), biplanes delivered air mail, and motorized fire trucks sped to disasters.

Independent oil operators brought new fields into production just as the black gold they pumped became the energy fuel of choice for heating homes, firing industry, and operating automobiles. The Gulf Company, funded by Pittsburgh's Mellon family, opened offices in Houston in 1916, and Humble Oil and Refining Company, backed by local entrepreneurs and New York banks, set up headquarters in the city in 1917. Numerous small producers joined the larger corporations, and by 1919 three-quarters of the oil produced in the Gulf region was drilled in Houston-area fields. Between 1918 and 1929 Humble's fixed assets climbed from $13 to $233 million in value, in part because Standard Oil, which had become majority owner in 1919, put capital into the Houston company while giving considerable independence to the local entrepreneurs. In the 1920s Humble's huge Baytown refinery rivaled Sinclair Oil's pioneering operation. City statisticians counted forty-six millionaires.[1] Yet horse-drawn carts still delivered milk and ice to family homes, and the streetcar still stopped several blocks short of Rice Institute.

Three men stood at the apex of this growth in the 1920s: William Clifford Hogg, Jesse Holman Jones, and James Addison Baker. Each man had admirers who considered their exemplar the city's most influential citizen. Will Hogg, the son of popular Texas Governor James Stephen Hogg (1891–1895), was a brilliant, outspoken, but complex man of mercurial temperament. He envisioned Houston becoming a great city and used his money, connections, and determination to ensure that his dreams became reality. An inveterate world traveler who maintained an apartment in New York City during the 1920s, Will was recognized nationally for his successful efforts to create Memorial Park, build the first municipal art museum in the state, develop a plan for the city of Houston, and fight for excellence in public education as a University of Texas regent and the originator of his alma mater's Texas Exes alumni association. Best known as a "Tender Tempest" who gave millions to promote learning, support social service and civic projects, and protect natural beauty, Will detested Jesse Jones. In a letter he distributed to friends throughout the state, Hogg told Governor Dan Moody that Jones was an "ill-fitted pseudo-statesman who . . . is always using the other fellow's chips to his own advantage."[2] Will Hogg's death in September 1930 at age fifty-five removed the city's greatest advocate of urban planning and park creation from the civic scene.

While Jesse Jones did not enjoy Will Hogg's personal popularity and was well-known to be ruthless in business and card-playing, many considered him Houston's most representative citizen.[3] Depicted in photographs as tall, stiff, and humorless, Jones built downtown Houston. By late 1929, when he was called to Washington to help restructure the economy after Wall Street's collapse, Jones had moved the commercial district south by erecting thirty commercial structures, generally with borrowed money. In 1956, when he died, he still controlled forty-nine of his fifty Houston buildings. In the 1920s Jones shifted his gaze beyond Houston and built ties to capital markets in Chicago and New York. He also became a power in national Democratic Party politics, brought the national nominating convention to Houston in 1928, and served in Washington as chairman of the Reconstruction Finance Corporation (1932–1945) and Secretary of Commerce (1940–1945), where his ideas and administration slowed the flood of failing businesses. Even while absent from the city, Jones exerted influence in Houston through ownership of the *Houston Chronicle* and through the flow of government-sponsored projects to his home state. The endowment he established in 1937 continues to shape the city's civic culture.

Captain Baker may have been the unsung "Mr. Houston" in the interwar period. Will Hogg, albeit unwillingly, was often the subject of newspaper columns written by O. D. D. McIntyre and Irving Cobb, nationally syndicated humorists and close friends who hunted and traveled with Will and his younger brother Mike and delighted in the older brother's personality, escapades, and vision. Jesse Jones was never bashful about taking credit for enterprises he touched, and journalists appreciated his capitalist drive; his opinions were easily ascertained by reading the *Chronicle*. But it was to Captain Baker that men and women turned when they wanted a civic project to succeed; it was through his associates in Washington and New York that Houstonians linked their city's success to national sources of capital and influence; and it was from his Institute that they sought financial support for local construction projects and educational resources for their families. A congenial man, Baker conceded he had business competitors but wasted no time fostering enmity. Baker benefited from being the first Houstonian to form a law firm–banking connection, and his control of the Institute endowment cemented his role as a powerful economic leader, but the quality that set Captain Baker apart from his peers was his ability to inspire trust. If he gave his word that a cause was just or a business deal fair or a legal principle sound, people accepted his judgment.

CIVIC ICONS

In the 1920s civic leaders devoted as much energy to improving their city's quality of life as they did to building their personal fortunes. In an era of small government, city and county officials teamed with private citizens to pave roads, extend utilities, light pathways, and build hospitals, schools, playgrounds, and parks. Social service organizations enlarged their programs, and volunteers raised funds to build the first municipal art museum in Texas (1924) and to construct a handsome public library (1926), both designed by Ralph Adams Cram and William Ward Watkin, who had created the campus for Rice Institute. Sponsors of new ventures valued the Bakers' support, and Captain and Mrs. Baker appear on the rosters of many civic and business projects. The Bakers and their circle were progressive reformers. They did not challenge the parameters of their segregated society or the tenets of their political heritage, but they treated all people with dignity and respect. They believed that humanity could progress, that social and civic institutions would steadily improve, and that those who had been blessed by good fortune should help those who had not. In the great enterprises of their lives—Rice Institute and the Settlement Association—the Bakers moved beyond the traditional paternalism of many contemporaries. Captain Baker aspired to create an innovative, internationally acclaimed educational institution, where the search for new knowledge reigned, and he supported cultural and commercial initiatives that promoted Houston nationally. Mrs. Baker introduced a novel and inclusive concept of neighborhood where she saw everyone who lived in Houston as her neighbor; she taught newcomers English, sewing, and cooking, and she shared pleasures that delighted her—maypole dances, Christmas trees, parties, and athletic contests. She fostered interaction among Houstonians and promoted a decent standard of living for all. Neither the Captain nor his wife left behind diaries, letters, or documents that explain their thoughts. Only their actions and associations illuminate their nonjudgmental humanitarian concern for their community.

During the last decade of her life, Alice Baker continued to be the outstanding figure in the settlement house movement, even after administration of the program had passed from her hands to the city's Social Service Bureau. In the 1920s Alice recruited Rice faculty wives for her committees and Rice undergraduates to work with boys and girls clubs organized at the settlements. She continued to promote fellowship programs, health facilities, and training classes, and to expand Boy Scout troops and job placement services. More than ever the settlement houses had become community centers that drew support from all across Houston.[4] By 1931 Rusk Settlement reported nearly sixty-eight thousand visits to its facility. Alice and her friends also continued to promote the Recreation Department and to coordinate settlement programs with recreation activities under Corinne Fonde's expert management.[5] Originally, recreation programs relied on the Community Chest and other private sources for support, but Director Fonde relentlessly advocated for public, tax-payer support. Fonde and her dedicated phalanx of female advocates successfully pressured the mayor and council. Grudgingly, city officials began to finance playground construction and programs.

In 1929 Alice and two other members of the First Presbyterian Church Ladies' Association asked her nephew Alvis Parish, chairman of the Board of Deacons, and Institute Professor John Willis Slaughter, director of the Houston Foundation, to speak to the City Council about the association's desire to build a unit for the Houston Tubercular Hospital. Tuberculosis was usually incurable in the 1920s, and doctors often dismissed those patients who were considered hopeless after a nine months' stay in the hospital. Alice and her committee wanted to provide a home for these unfortunate victims. When the city gave permission to add a unit for the terminally ill to its Tubercular Hospital, the Ladies' Association hired an architect and raised over $20,000 to provide twenty-four beds, a living room, dining facilities, two treatment rooms, and suitable bathrooms. Initial pledges, announced at First Presbyterian Church's Sunday worship service on Mother's Day 1929, commemorated fifty years of "golden deeds . . . by these good mothers of the church, who have labored so zealously, so cheerfully, so devotedly, and so efficiently." To complete the capital campaign, Mrs. Baker and five friends compiled *Old and New Cookery* and raised $4,000. The book included recipes for old favorites found in the church's earlier editions, as well as new ideas like pimiento consommé and nonfattening mayonnaise. Alice also hosted two garden parties at her home with puppet shows and pony rides for the children and Indian dances performed by a Boy Scout troop. Ellison Van Hoose directed two hundred singers and a fifty-piece orchestra for a concert of religious and patriotic music in the City Auditorium, and the ladies' guild held a rummage sale. The parties, concert, and sale netted another $5,000 for the hospital, which was dedicated on October 26, 1930. Alice's daughter Alice and her fifteen-year-old granddaughter, another Alice, memorialized Mrs. Baker's "beautiful life and worthy example" on a tablet in the living room, which they furnished.[6]

After World War I, friends asked Captain Baker to support numerous worthy causes. In 1918 he served on a committee with Will Hogg, Sam Streetman, Joseph C. Hutcheson Jr., M. D. Anderson, and others to raise money for the Houston Public Health Counsel. In May 1920 he joined the Advisory Finance Committee charged with finding funds to expand the Young Women's Christian Association (YWCA) facilities and to provide the Blue Triangle building for African American citizens. Serving with him were Will Hogg as chairman, Edward A. Peden as campaign director, William A. Wilson as building committee chairman, the Carter brothers, and Baker, Botts, Parker & Garwood partner Clarence Wharton. This high-powered committee raised $500,000 to ensure that women and African American citizens had access to facilities and programs long popular with Houston's white male population. Seven years later in June 1927, Baker approved a request from the Young Men's Christian Association board for a $72,000 loan from the Institute, secured by the organization's headquarters property between Fannin and San Jacinto at McKinney.[7] In 1938–1939, Baker joined John T. Scott, chairman, and other Houston notables on the Citizens Committee to raise $1.375 million for a new YMCA building on Louisiana Street.

Captain and Mrs. Baker were among the most generous donors to the Community Chest when it sponsored its first Houston campaign in 1923. A nationwide institution established in most urban areas after

World War I to organize charitable fund-raising, the Community Chest steadily gained advocates among Houston corporations and individuals during the 1920s. Captain Baker continued his support in the 1930s and served on the board during that decade. He made sure his firm employees supported the community drive and encouraged his sons and their wives to make their own contributions.[8] In January 1924 Baker agreed to be chairman of a fifteen-man committee to fight community income tax legislation, although he stated his firm would not be employed or paid a fee to work on the issue.[9]

In 1924 Will Hogg drew Captain Baker into four pivotal civic projects: the Museum of Fine Arts of Houston, Memorial Park, plans for a Civic Center, and support for a Women's Club headquarters. In March Hogg announced he would take over the flagging fund-raising effort from John T. Scott and others who were trying unsuccessfully to raise $200,000 to build a municipal art museum. Hogg reviewed previous donations and made three lists: those who had given, those who had not given, and those who had not given enough. Then he bought a subscription book and began calling on his friends. If someone could not be found in his office, Hogg sent him a letter; if prospects were on vacation, Hogg sent telegrams to them. In three weeks Hogg had raised more than enough money to complete the project and furnish the building. On April 12, 1924, the much-anticipated Museum of Fine Arts of Houston opened to great fanfare and huge crowds.[10] Captain Baker at first refused to support Hogg's campaign, pleading real estate expenditures and estate planning in a letter April 2. Will responded immediately: "It is not in my heart to rebuke you, or to hurt your feelings, or to imply the slightest personal resentment, but your declination disheartened me so grievously, I can't close the case without this further appeal." Of all men in Houston, Hogg declared, Baker had "the most incentives to share in this gift": family name, his position as Institute chairman, his role as head of a nationally known law firm and head of the largest commercial bank and largest trust company, all commanded his compliance. "You are more completely identified with the commercial, financial, educational and realty development of Houston than any other man, bar none." Hogg urged Baker "to consider carefully the moving points above indicated." At noon on April 11, Hogg listed Captain and Mrs. James A. Baker as $5,000 subscribers on the final donor roster. Founders dedicated the state's first museum building the next day. Will Hogg knew his man, appealed to his civic pride, and pried loose the money needed to complete his campaign.[11]

When Will Hogg, his sister Ima, and his brother Mike conceived the idea to develop a forest park for Houston on acreage north of Buffalo Bayou, they turned to Baker, Botts, Parker & Garwood for legal advice. In July 1910 Jesse Andrews, James Baker, Clarence Carter, Clarence Wharton, and five other investors had chartered the Reinerman Land Company and purchased 654 acres of pine forest from the John Reinerman League. During the war this land and neighboring property had been leased to the United States Army for a training camp, and after the war the investors considered developing the Camp Logan tract. Will Hogg and his siblings, through their Varner Realty Company, purchased over eight hundred acres abutting the Reinerman Land Company land and persuaded Baker and the company investors to sell their property to Varner Realty. The Hoggs then conveyed the entire 1,500 acres to the City of Houston on easy terms over a ten-year period for a Memorial Park commemorating the fallen of World War I. Baker and his colleagues explored problems facing the transfer of the land, agreed to sell Reinerman Land Company to Varner Realty at a low price, and developed the option contract under which the transfer to the city could be made. "The acquisition of Memorial Park . . . is of great moment to its citizenship, the importance of which will be better appreciated in the years to come than it is now," concluded Clarence Carter's report of the lengthy transaction.[12] Ninety years later the park remains one of Houston's natural gems.

Captain Baker and Will Hogg also exchanged ideas about the value of a civic center. For some time Hogg had been trying to make the citizens of Houston understand the importance of a professional comprehensive plan to control Houston's rapid, disorganized development, which was, in Hogg's opinion, destroying property values and preventing the city from growing in "a logical, healthy way." In a letter to Kansas City urban planner Herbert Hare, Hogg explained he had recently purchased six acres downtown for a civic center. Hogg sent copies of the letter to Captain Baker, to Hugh Potter, with whom he was developing the subdivision of River Oaks, and to J. C. Nichols, at the time the country's most well-known proponent of planned communities. Baker responded, "Your plan is an ambitious one, but I believe is fully justified by the promising outlook for Houston."[13] When Will Hogg established his Forum of Civics "to coordinate civic effort, bring together information, digest proposals, and present programs to make more effective the cooperation of organizations engaged in civic development," he asked Baker, in his role as chairman of the Institute's Board of Trustees, to serve on the Forum's board of directors. Other directors included the mayor, the heads of Houston's major civic and government agencies, the president of the bar association, and the president of the City Federation of Women's Clubs.[14]

In 1926 Will Hogg got out another of his subscription books to help Huberta Garwood and twenty-five women structure a fund-raising campaign to build a Women's Building as headquarters for all the civic groups catering to women's interests. Captain Baker, banker Maurice McAshan, and Huberta's husband Judge Hiram Garwood joined Hogg on an advisory board and in 1928 pledged to raise $500,000. Will promised a site near his planned development of River Oaks, but the ladies wanted property on Main Street. Press coverage suggests that the long-debated but unconstructed clubhouse fell victim to squabbles among rival female factions. With the onset of the Depression and the failure to agree about location, the project faltered despite its impressive roster of supporters.[15]

LAWYERING IN THE 1920S

About two hundred lawyers practiced in Houston at the end of World War I: four civil district courts (the 11th, 55th, 61st, and 80th) and one criminal district court dispensed state justice in Harris County, and Woodrow Wilson's appointee, Judge Joseph C. Hutcheson Jr., was beginning his celebrated career on the federal district court.[16] Baker, Botts, Parker & Garwood retained its position as Houston's leading law firm, but in the 1920s its hegemony was challenged by the continuing prosperity of Andrews, Ball & Streetman (founded 1902) and two newcomers with aspirations to build large legal practices: Vinson & Elkins (founded 1917) and Fulbright & Crooker (founded 1919). In the next decades all three newer firms would adopt Baker Botts's paradigm of centralized organization, recruitment from top law schools, affiliation with a bank, and specialized expertise tailored to the varied needs of corporate clients. Yet each would adapt these modern ideas in ways reflective of the founding partners. In broad strokes the firms seemed similar; in details they were very different, but all of them prospered by their association with Houston's fast-growing corporate community.

Frank Andrews kept a strong grip on the firm he founded, although his first partners, Congressman Tom Ball (1902–1914), Judge Sam Streetman (1904–1933), Bankers Trust Company counsel William Bailey (1911–1918), and former assistant attorney general John Allen Mobley (1912–1933) were talented attorneys. They regrouped as Andrews, Streetman, Logue, & Mobley (1919–1933), when land lawyer and litigator John Logue joined the firm. The partners hired only top recent graduates from the nation's best law schools, and Andrews took great pride in his personalized practice where "the client is dealing with his particular lawyer and not the firm machine."[17] In 1905 the firm helped organize Union Bank & Trust, and when the bank nationalized as Union National Bank in 1910, the firm continued to handle its legal business. Although never an officer, Frank Andrews sat on the bank's board until his death in 1936, and his law firm moved its offices to the top floor of the Union Bank Building (1914–1929). The link between lawyers and bankers was clear.[18]

William A. Vinson of Sherman and James A. Elkins of Huntsville seemed an improbable pair to form a partnership. Vinson, tall and slim, dignified and cerebral, a pious man who yet believed his material rewards should be commensurate with his religious practice seemed quite unlike the hot-tempered Elkins, described by one biographer as "erratically chummy, occasionally coarse, and frequently imperative," and by a younger observer as a "driver of men." Yet both lawyers grew up in small Texas towns and prospered by helping the clients of large-city law firms solve regional problems or obtain justice in local courts. Both decided in middle age that their small towns did not offer sufficient scope for their talents. In 1917 they formed a general law practice and challenged the entrenched Houston firms.[19] A year later they invited Andrew Cox Wood, who specialized in insurance litigation, to join them. Vinson, Elkins, & Wood adopted several policies that more established firms avoided: they accepted contingency clients, no matter how small, and would take shares of a business or land as payment; and they sought clients in new industries, especially companies exploring for or producing oil and natural gas resources. Vinson became one of the state's most accomplished lobbyists, while Elkins cultivated oil and banking ventures.

From his early days as director of a Huntsville bank, Elkins exploited his legal and banking expertise, and he helped establish Guaranty Trust. He aggressively advertised his banking facilities, a practice almost unknown at the time, and through a series of mergers and purchases, built the full-service commercial City Bank & Trust (1928) that became six years later the City National Bank, which catered to risk-taking small oil producers, entrepreneurs, and savings depositors.[20] Some believed Judge Elkins's bank was more important to him than his law firm. Certainly, he made it clear to his clients that they should use his law firm's legal services and his bank's fiduciary facilities.[21]

R. Clarence Fulbright and John H. Crooker brought different backgrounds and talents to their partnership when they decided to work together. Fulbright grew up in comfortable circumstances and attended Baylor University and the University of Chicago School of Law. Upon graduation he accepted a job with Andrews, Ball & Streetman but withdrew to associate with John Crooker on October 1, 1919: Fulbright would handle corporate matters, Crooker would build a litigation practice. John Crooker's childhood had been hard; his widowed mother struggled to support her family, and he worked at the Southern Pacific yards as an iron molder's apprentice and then as a switchman. Too poor to acquire much formal education, he read law, obtained a license to practice in Texas in 1911, and was elected district attorney of Harris County at a young age. He proved a tough prosecutor and in 1917 closed down Houston's red light district, the "Reservation" that stretched south of the Buffalo Bayou west of town, so Houston could comply with US Army guidelines that demanded cities close vice districts before bidding to build training camps. During World War I Crooker served with the Judge Advocate General's office in Washington, DC, until his discharge in 1919 at age thirty-five. On January 1, 1924, John H. Freeman joined the pair as an equal partner in the firm of Fulbright, Crooker & Freeman. Freeman had grown up in Houston, where his father was a foreman with the Southern Pacific. Life in the 5th ward near the rail yards was rough, but Freeman worked hard to pay his way through college and law school at the University of Chicago. After graduating in 1912, he built a real estate practice and brought the State National Bank account to his new firm. Shortly after he signed on, the partners moved their offices to the top floor of the State National Bank Building, where they remained until after World War II.[22]

BAKER, BOTTS, PARKER & GARWOOD

Baker, Botts, Parker & Garwood business grew during the war and soared during the 1920s. The firm had a reputation for lucidly explaining the eccentricities of Texas law to non-Texas corporations wishing to do business in the state; after World War I, an exploding Texas oil and gas industry allowed Baker Botts to demonstrate leadership at the national level as council to Houston-based firms with national markets. Through the good offices of former partner Robert S. Lovett, who remained one of Captain Baker's closest friends until his death in 1932, the firm developed close ties to powerful Wall Street investment bankers. The firm offered legal expertise and access to Rice Institute funds as well as to New York's financial markets when underwriting major business expansion.

The firm continued to guide long-time clients like Rice Institute, the Southern Pacific System, Houston Lighting & Power, and the Texas Company. In June 1920 Clarence Wharton and Edwin B. Parker successfully completed a charter amendment for industry leader Peden Iron & Steel, allowing the company to more than double its capital stock. Writing to Edward A. Peden, Wharton noted, "Our firm has been connected with your enterprise since its first organization (ca. 1890), and we have watched [it] grow from a modest beginning to one of the great trading concerns of this country." Not "a matter of chance," the company's success was due to "the unfaltering guidance of men of character, courage, capacity and never failing industry."[23] Following Captain Baker's lead, younger men promoted Houston's real estate boom. In 1923 one junior lawyer reported several "miscellaneous" loans totaling nearly $10 million and noted that other clients—Sinclair Oil, Atlantic Oil Producing, and several lumber companies—invested "far in excess of $10,000,000.00" in real estate on Baker Botts's recommendation of title.[24]

To keep pace with business demands, the partners hired several new men, including Walter Walne and James L. Shepherd Jr. (1917), Rodman Cosby and Baker's son-in-law Murray Jones (1918), Captain Joseph C. Hutcheson's son Palmer, James A. Baker Jr., and two other men who did not stay long (1919).[25] Four more lawyers joined the staff in 1920, and by 1925 the firm comprised twenty-six lawyers, including Malcolm Lovett, the older son of Rice Institute President Edgar Odell Lovett; Brady Cole, an indefatigable workhorse who kept a diary of the incredible schedule that led to his early death in 1953; and University of Texas Law School

Esperson Building (firm offices 1927–1971), ca. 1927. Early Houston Collection, Woodson Research Center, Rice University.

graduate Dorothy Most, who was hired that year to supervise the library and occasionally assist with research. In 1925 seventeen stenographers served eleven partners, five associate members, and ten younger lawyers; 568 clients remitted $723,000 in gross revenues; and the partners split $487,000 after expenses. The firm distributed a daily cash balance of about $64,000 among Captain Baker's South Texas Commercial National Bank and Guardian Trust and the Carter family's Second National Bank.[26] Firm offices in the Commercial National Bank Building, once thought to be gleaming and modern, were now cramped even though they spread over the entire sixth floor and most of the fifth; files were stored in a pitch-black, filthy, rat-infested attic accessed only through a trap door. One lawyer recalled that anyone who had to find old files was "immediately ready for the shower" afterwards.[27]

In February 1925 an agent for Mellie Esperson approached Baker with a proposal: if Baker Botts and Guardian Trust would move into her new Niels Esperson Building as major tenants, she would allow Guardian to administer her estate and would turn her legal business over to Baker Botts. Judge Garwood said S. F. Carter wanted the firm to consider the

Second National Bank Building, and Wharton confessed he had committed to support relocation to the Sterling Building. Captain Baker and Mellie Esperson carried the day, and in 1927 the law firm and Guardian Trust moved into the Niels Esperson Building, the city's finest at the time, with its Roman temple atop twenty-six stories on the corner of Travis and Rusk. The well-lighted, ventilated storage in the new building's basement earned immediate praise. The firm took over the sixteenth floor and would remain in the Esperson Building until the 1970s, when it moved to its present quarters at One Shell Plaza. Young lawyers remembered Captain Baker's "tidy" office on the northeast corner and noted that Guardian Trust president Clarence M. Malone frequently rode the elevator up from the bank's spacious ground-floor quarters to counsel with his company's chairman. Rice Institute maintained its business office on the fifth floor, where the trustees usually held their meetings.[28]

Despite his many duties in Washington, DC, and as general counsel of Texaco in New York City, Edwin Parker continued as managing partner of the firm for several years after World War I. In 1920 Ralph Feagin, not yet thirty, agreed to be the older man's surrogate as Assistant Managing Partner (1920–1927); Feagin had worked with Robert S. Lovett and Parker during the war, and his organizational skills mirrored Parker's centralizing style. He was named Managing Partner in 1933 and led the firm until his death in 1946.[29] Parker and his successors continued to consolidate firm organization. Lawyers met every second and fourth Saturday evening at the Parker home or at Baker's Main Street address, and on January 27, 1920, Parker inaugurated the first issue of the Office Review, a "medium to advise of the rules and regulations for conduct of business and information of general interest."

Parker used the Office Review to offer homilies on lawyerly conduct and hints to "improve work product." If lawyers had failed to read Parker's Plan for each year, they could find important points reprised in the Review. "If we do not make a dollar," repeated Parker on December 21, 1922, "we must so conduct ourselves and discharge the duties and responsibilities undertaken by and imposed upon us, that the name 'Baker, Botts, Parker & Garwood' will stand throughout the country as a synonym for character, integrity, honesty, promptness, accuracy, resourcefulness, initiative, tact, diplomacy and ability to produce results. Professional recognition and pecuniary rewards will follow." Parker praised Brady Cole for devoting himself "entirely" to a case for nearly eight months and admonished his colleagues to pursue civic affairs and thereby "constantly enlarge our sphere of influence." Wives, he announced, must "be real partners of their husbands and . . . wholeheartedly assist them in carving out success."[30]

Captain Baker commended the Office Review enthusiastically and contributed his own advice, couched in his usual conciliatory language. When lawyers began to grumble that the Review was too long or took too much time to assemble or was not relevant, Baker defended it as an important mode of communication. Its entries reflect the keen attention firm members paid to court decisions, to the growing body of state and federal regulations, and to the increasingly complex realm of tax law. Baker also supported wholeheartedly Parker's annual Plan of Organization. The 1925 Plan, he noted, "is really an inspiration to me." Every member of the organization should read the Plan several times a year, he suggested, and "follow more scrupulously its suggestions and directions" so "the Organization will move along like a new, well-regulated, perfectly running machine."[31]

THE SENIOR MAN

Captain Baker, sixty-three in 1920, had been his law firm's respected senior man for nearly three decades. Younger men turned to him for counsel, and he continued to manage legal business for important clients of long standing, although he spent several months each year away from the office. Even clients like Houston Lighting & Power and Southern Pacific, whose legal work had been handled by others for years, viewed Baker as the attorney of record, the wise counselor whose judgment they valued. After the war, Baker spoke more often of the need to balance professional demands and personal growth. At the end of an important lawsuit that raised intriguing legal questions, he complimented a colleague: "In this day of materialism, when nearly everyone, including lawyers, is engaged in a mad chase for the almighty dollar, it is delightful and elevating to have had the experience I have had with you . . . in this litigation."[32] He admonished his Bass Rocks neighbor, oil man Robert Lee Blaffer, in the summer of 1922, "I often feel like lecturing you about confining yourself so closely to business when you have already accumulated far more than you and yours will ever need. Why not take life more easily," he asked the younger man, "and get better acquainted with your wife and children?"

He admitted "trying all my life to learn this lesson but believe I have learned it at last though I would have been better off in health if I had learned it earlier."[33]

In 1920 Baker called a meeting with Garwood, Walne, and Feagin because he wanted to study all the trust agreements the firm had prepared over the years to see if any should be revised to reflect recent interpretations of Income Tax statutes.[34] Considered the leading expert on trust and estate management, Baker counseled Rosa Allen about her real estate developments and helped art patron and suffragist Annette Finnegan and her two sisters create a corporation to take title to real property in the state so that its value could be distributed equally among them.[35] When his friend Hugh Hamilton died August 5, 1922, Baker, with assistance from Wharton and Feagin, took on the complex management of the estate's extensive enterprises. A "great engineer of artificial ice," the Scot had operated the Houston Ice and Brewing Association, built large ice plants, and moved fresh fruits and vegetables from the Rio Grande Valley in refrigerated cars. His Houston plant had been the first artificial ice operation in Texas.[36] When Houston Ice and Brewing Association could no longer compete during Prohibition, Baker led the complex negotiations that preceded its liquidation.[37]

Baker also consulted colleagues at other law firms. While receiver of the International & Great Northern Railroad, he asked his friend Sam Streetman to represent him in major litigation against Pierce Oil Corporation. During Baker's receivership, I&GN signed contracts with Pierce Oil at $.83 and $.70 a barrel; when prices skyrocketed in 1920, Pierce Oil reneged, forcing I&GN to pay $3.00 a barrel on the open market. Baker demanded the difference, and Streetman secured a great victory and a $2 million judgment—unheard of at the time. While awaiting appeal, Pierce Oil offered $1,555,425 to settle. "Take it," said Streetman, "That's all the money there is in the world."[38] The Captain agreed. In May 1921 Baker spent two weeks in Washington negotiating settlements on behalf of I&GN with the Railroad Administration, and during the rest of the year oversaw the process of evaluating the company. By February 20, 1922, he and S. B. Dabney, general counsel for the railroad, personally appeared before the Texas Railroad Commission to file a valuation of the additions and improvements to I&GN property since 1913. With the company's value established, proceedings moved forward to foreclose on the properties and sell them at public auction. A newly chartered company under the same name acquired the assets for a group of New York investors, and the entire process was approved by US District Judge Joseph C. Hutcheson Jr. on August 31, 1922.

Baker extended lavish hospitality to his clients. On June 23, 1925, he and the firm hosted the retiring and incoming managers of the Houston Electric Company and the new district manager for Stone and Webster, Boston engineering and management consultants who specialized in street railway administration and had first worked with Baker, Botts, Lovett & Parker in 1901–1902, when Houston Electric was refinanced and placed under Stone and Webster management.[39] Baker welcomed the guests, including Mayor Oscar Holcombe and Harris County Judge Chester Bryan, "in a manner that won the commendation and friendship of the press" and the gratitude of the honorees. Parker reprinted a news story in the August 15 Office Review: "The Press," claimed the reporter, "is at liberty to say what would have been inappropriate for any of the speakers. . . . Baker, Botts, Parker and Garwood exercise a tremendous influence when it comes to shaping public utility policies in this city. Captain Baker is at the head of the gas company. While Judge Parker is at the head of the light company, and the firm acts as counsel for the street car company. . . . Very few law firms in the United States wield such power and at the same time enjoy such general respect as Baker, Botts, Parker & Garwood."[40] The reporter also noticed the place cards shaped like miniature streetcars and the bouquets of flowers set in huge blocks of ice on each table.

While Baker's association with inventors, bankers, and investors continued to drive the firm's success, his most important role lay as public ambassador for the firm. Always active in the Houston and Texas bar associations, he also attended American Bar Association meetings, served as vice president, and was appointed to the Committee on Supplements to Canons of Professional Ethics for its January 1928 meeting. The politics of the meetings, "controlled" as they were "by those who are noted for their constant attendance upon the annual meetings of the Association rather than for any special ability in their own states" disappointed him, and he found greater rewards in the visits he made to friends in New York and other cities.[41] To Baker, New York contacts were critical: "I think our experience will show that we get more business out of New York in a year than from all other sources in five years. . . . There is no firm in Texas, and I may say in the South, that has so wide an acquaintance among the leading firms of New York as ours."[42] Baker's charm enabled him to operate in Houston's Southern culture, but his clear-sighted, cosmopolitan outlook allowed him to seize opportunities in the nation's financial capital.

When in Houston, Baker spent much of his time mentoring younger lawyers and addressing difficult firm issues. For six years Captain Baker worked closely with Rodman Cosby, a bright young man who performed "valuable and satisfactory work" but whose stressful schedule had led to bouts of heavy drinking. In May 1923 Cosby's doctor told him to take a leave of absence, although Cosby made it plain he did not want a sabbatical from the office. After a particularly disastrous binge, the partners held two long meetings to discuss the issue. Captain Baker reported he had investigated the situation and talked at length with Cosby, who was "very appreciative of our generosity in giving him a second chance." Baker recommended the young man be allowed to resign but be retained on a consulting basis while he tried to regain his health. Baker had learned that Cosby was the sole support of his wife, mother, and sister and feared his "future would be entirely ruined if [the firm] threw him overboard now." Even though this humane viewpoint was "not the best thing to do from the standpoint of the Firm," Baker convinced his colleagues to let Cosby try again. Unhappily, later minutes reveal that Cosby could not control his drinking, and the second chance had failed.[43]

Baker's nephew Alvis Parish, who had come to the firm from his native Huntsville in 1910, spent a year in partnership with Murray Jones (1919–1920) and two years with Vinson and Elkins but returned to Baker, Botts, Parker & Garwood on September 1, 1922, to take over work for Guardian Trust and Rice Institute that had been handled by the recently deceased Thomas Botts. Parish's decision to leave in 1919 had been difficult, one he discussed at length with his Uncle Jimmie. The younger man was "just not happy and contented" and felt he had been treated unfairly; with great regret and appreciation for his uncle's many kindnesses, Parish decided to try another path. On his return, Parish became one of the country's leading utilities lawyers, joined the partnership in 1923, and from 1927 to 1933 served as managing partner.[44] He remained close to Captain Baker and looked upon him as a father figure: "I do know and can say that no father could have or would have done more for a son than you have done for me and mine. We all do appreciate . . . the thousand kindnesses you and yours have shown us and the thousands of favors

Alvis Parish, son of Captain
Baker's sister Minnie Baker Parish.
Courtesy of Baker Botts L.L.P.

you have rendered us."[45] Parish often wrote to his uncle about the older
man's rheumatism and relationship with his son Jim.

Captain Baker enjoyed mentoring the young men who began their
careers at the firm; Tom Botts had consulted him daily—sometimes
"many times a day." When Jim Baker did not ask his father for advice, the
Captain was puzzled and confided his confusion to Alvis Parish. Why,
he asked his nephew, did Jim not call on him as other young men had
done? Was his son "too self-reliant"? He told Parish, "you can help me
now by helping Jim. . . . Naturally, my heart is wrapped up in the boy and
I hope he will some day take my place in the firm, as I took my father's. If
you will help me to help him, and I know you will, I will be your life long
debtor." Parish promised to work with his younger cousin and to get him
started on Institute and Guardian Trust business.[46]

The Captain loved his children deeply and believed that he should
oversee and direct the progress of his sons as his father had guided him.
Baker never demanded that his sons follow his professional path, but he
hoped that they would, and they felt the pressure of this expectation.

Friends always mentioned Captain Baker's twinkling eyes, charm, amusing stories, and many kindnesses, but his opponents had often felt the steel behind the smile. A formal man of strong principles and imposing build, Captain Baker brooked no nonsense and often seemed stern to young family members. Jim, who joined his father at Baker Botts and at South Texas Commercial National Bank, and Walter Browne, who began at Guardian Trust and was named vice president there in 1928, regarded their father with great respect and considerable affection but struggled to do what they thought he wanted done while forging career paths of their own. Contemporaries of all three men used similar words to describe them: many remembered their kindness, their outstanding mentoring skills, their great interest in young people, and their ability to recognize talent. But his peers acclaimed Captain Baker Houston's leading citizen, and it was not always easy for his two older sons to escape this shadow. Malcolm, the youngest child, born when his father was forty-nine, entered banking in the 1930s, but after service in World War II, he pursued an independent investing career.[47] Alice and Ruth, as was typical in their era, were expected to follow their mother's domestic and civic path; with no pressure to compete in the professional world, they found it easy to adore both parents.

PARKER'S DEPARTURE

Edwin B. Parker and Captain Baker were close personal friends. Baker saw his partner as "an indefatigable worker," who possessed "an unusually analytical mind, an attractive and pleasing personality, and . . . was an executive of outstanding ability."[48] Parker's railroad practice was the largest in the state before World War I. Year after year he enforced an organizational plan that transformed a small partnership into an enduring institution. His prodigious energy enabled him to work late, lead civic projects, and participate in his wife's cultural activities. In 1919 he wrote to his partners that he had not taken a vacation in four years but felt a rest was unnecessary because his work varied and he traveled so much. Feeling "well and strong and fit as ever," he hoped to "labor up to the limit of my capacity" for twenty more years.[49] Like the Bakers, the Parkers enjoyed widespread popularity and an active social life.

When Woodrow Wilson and Robert S. Lovett called Parker to Washington to serve his country during World War I as a "dollar a year man," his absence forced the lawyers who remained in Houston to redouble their efforts. Parker's contacts with national figures like financier Bernard M. Baruch, mortgage bond expert Clarence Dillon of Dillon, Read & Co., and J. P. Morgan executive Edward Reilly Stettinius proved invaluable to the firm.[50] In 1920 when Parker was offered the post of General Counsel to the Texas Company, headquartered in New York, his commuting schedule did not reduce his zeal for office management in Houston. His colleagues saw this triple responsibility of Texas Company officer and director, Baker Botts managing partner, and national civic figure as "a decided step forward in the progress of our Firm—an advancement . . . which . . . redounds to the benefit of the Firm as a whole."[51] Then, in 1922, President Warren G. Harding and Secretary of State Charles Evans Hughes asked Parker to accept appointment as the American Commissioner "to sit with the German Commissioner to hear and determine claims of American nationals against Germany." Some Baker Botts lawyers began to worry about Parker's continued leadership at the firm.[52] In a letter to his partners, Parker explained he was able to withstand the financial sacrifice and wanted "to make such use of the remaining years of my life as will most contribute to the common good." Parker's motives could not be disputed, but Ralph Feagin asked Captain Baker for "the benefit of [his] counsel and advice." Feagin estimated Parker would be gone one to three years and might also continue as Texas Company counsel. Baker advised patience, but at the end of 1923, Parker told his partners he had not made a report of his accomplishments for the Gates Estate or the Mixed Claims Commission "on account of extreme stress" of his work load. He explained how that year he had handled 12,500 cases pending before the commission involving about $1.5 billion.[53] By 1925 everyone realized Parker could not continue to shoulder so many responsibilities without harming the firm.

On October 23, 1925, Parker wrote to Ralph Feagin from Washington that he believed his continued absence from Houston, his inability to outline future plans, and his failure to give priority to firm business were having "a disturbing effect on the morale of the organization" even though his varied duties had brought "pecuniary profit" to firm members. Clarence Wharton, who had been "continuously engaged in Court for several weeks" and would not be in Houston for several more, wrote Parker that he felt "it is a great mistake" for Parker and Jesse Andrews, who maintained headquarters in Kansas City, to be away from the firm.

Wharton was "mindful of the many years of pleasant and profitable association with you" and hoped his partner would choose the firm over continued service in Washington. After years of juggling tasks, Parker decided to focus his energy on promoting international arbitration because he believed that his decisions would have a permanent impact. Though withdrawing from pecuniary participation in Baker Botts, his "personal interest in the growth and prosperity of the Firm will in no wise abate." In his final message as managing partner, Parker reiterated the importance of the firm's creed, which had placed Baker Botts on the highest professional plane, and he reminded his friends, "The function of the profession of the law is service." On December 31, 1925, after twenty-five years as a partner, Edwin B. Parker ended the association he had begun in 1896.[54] The Office Review continued to chronicle Parker's movements. He resigned from the Texas Company and was still handling claims and other issues for the government when he died, childless, in Washington on October 30, 1929, at age sixty-one.[55] He was buried in Houston's Glenwood Cemetery. Parker provided "handsomely" for his widow and left his considerable estate to a board of trustees to found the Parker School of Foreign and Comparative Law. With his usual precision, he laid out plans in detail and named the men he wished appointed trustees: an associate justice of the US Supreme Court, a secretary of state, an attorney general, and the president of the Texas Company. The trustees chose Columbia University as recipient of Parker's foresight and largesse.[56]

INSTITUTE EXPANSION

As chairman of Rice Institute, Captain Baker confronted critical challenges in the 1920s. With peace restored, Rice supporters and Houston boosters wanted their Institute to begin building again, and they demanded new facilities, faculty, and programs. Undergraduate enrollment surpassed one thousand in 1923, and over twenty graduate students demanded deeper commitment to high-level courses. Yet, Baker and his Board had pledged not to acquire debt. Even with a healthy regional economy and a surging stock market, Institute leaders began to realize that their dream to provide free tuition and pursue excellence might exceed their ability to live within endowment income. During Baker's lifetime, Rice trustees, like board members of most universities, initiated no formal fund development plan.[57] Unlike older institutions that could rely on a large, wealthy alumni base to support special projects and programs, the Institute's young graduates were not able to bolster investment income. Nor could Houston's donors compete with the wealth accumulated over generations in Boston, New York, and several older cities of the Northeast. Baker and his fellow trustees continued to earn income by underwriting Houston's growth through loans to commercial and residential developers and to major corporate friends, but Baker began to examine ways the Board might expand the Institute's income stream.

First, the trustees strengthened their Board. When Emanuel Raphael died in 1913, the Board quickly named his successor at that year's annual meeting. John T. Scott (1913–1946) had long worked with Baker and the other trustees as president of First National Bank and as an active civic leader. In April 1916 James E. McAshan, for many years the Board's vice chairman, passed from the scene. Remembered by his colleagues as a prudent man of independent thinking and untiring devotion to the founder's "monumental enterprise," he was not replaced on the Board for six years. Cesar Lombardi, who had been living outside Houston for many years but continued to take a keen interest in the Institute, died in July 1919. His fellow trustees mourned his gentle manner, quiet humor, and loyal devotion and recalled the humanitarian interest and forward-looking deliberations he provided William M. Rice, when the philanthropist was considering how best to use his fortune for the public good. But they did not fill his spot.

In the fall 1919, Edwin B. Parker told Baker he knew his partner wanted to fill the Board vacancies with "strong unselfish men of broad visions" and recommended Edward A. Peden and himself as possible trustees. Recognizing Baker might not think it "very good taste . . . to urge my own appointment," Parker stated plainly, "The fact is that I very much want to become a member of the board not for any selfish reason but because I believe I am equipped to tender . . . very real service."[58] Despite this strong expression of interest, the five remaining trustees made no attempt to replace McAshan and Lombardi until the annual meeting held May 24, 1922. Then Baker, the Rice brothers, Lovett, and Scott elected Edward Andrew Peden (1922–1934) and Alexander Sessums Cleveland (1922–1954) to fill the vacancies.[59] Captain Baker knew both men well. Peden had been a client of his law firm for over thirty years and served with him on the board of Glenwood Cemetery. Cleveland ran important cotton brokerage and wholesale grocery businesses.

Monitoring the Institute's endowment continued to occupy the trustees' agenda in the 1920s. Although Arthur B. Cohn and his staff handled business and investment details and analyzed loan requests, Board members studied financial reports thoroughly and made all investment decisions. In 1908 auditors reported net assets of $6.7 million; at the annual meeting in May 1912, trustees announced growth to $9.8 million; and when the United States entered World War I, the Institute's endowment stood at $11.8 million. From 1919, when the endowment registered $12.2 million until 1929, when it stood at $14.7 million, growth continued steadily. During the 1920s Captain Baker supervised about $10 million in Rice Endowment real estate loans at 6 to 8 percent interest, with a standard security double the loan value. Guardian Trust, where W. Browne Baker handled Institute business for his father, administered most of these loans. The trustees also invested in high-quality corporate bonds and treasury notes, earning as much as 7 percent on Anaconda Copper, Swift, and Southwestern Bell Telephone bonds.[60] Through conservative investment, careful management, and constant attention, Captain Baker closed the books in 1941, the year of his death, with a report of $17.942 million. The ability to maintain endowment growth through war and depression provided a commendable legacy, but other figures highlight the difficulties facing the Board. Income rose steadily from $240,000 in 1908 to a peak of $764,470 in 1923, but salary and program expenses climbed more quickly. More telling, the surplus of income over expenses, more than $348,000 in 1914, shrank to $36,494 in 1926 and remained fairly narrow during the 1930s.[61]

The press, in its zeal to support Houston's greatest asset, led the public to believe the Institute had unlimited funds to build new programs quickly, but by April 1923 Edgar Odell Lovett expressed concern that revenues were not adequate to fulfill the Board's dreams for a top-ranked university. On June 8, 1924, Captain Baker told the graduating class and their guests that the endowment, generous as it was, "is insufficient to keep the university growing as fast as we want it to grow," and he made the "first formal request for aid" when he urged men of wealth to donate funds for the Institute's operations.[62] Friends who agreed with Lovett that the leaders of the next generation would come from "those brave youngsters of ours who have the vision and the courage to face the long pull for the best . . . training the world can offer" did step forward. Will Hogg established a student loan fund with an initial gift of

$1,000, matched by Chairman Baker. In subsequent years, this fund grew steadily with numerous modest gifts, but in 1929 student aid funds expanded suddenly. Cora Jordan, a Houston resident, bequeathed over $56,000 for student loans, while Libbie A. Richardson, the widow of founding trustee Alfred S. Richardson, left $51,000 to the Institute for scholarship endowment.[63] The Daughters of the American Revolution, the Association of Rice Alumni, three campus literary societies, and the Edith Ripley Scholarships for "self-supporting scholars at the Rice Institute" all provided funds in the 1920s to students who were "impelled by their own ambition" to seek a college education.[64]

Houstonians also underwrote new programs. At a dinner party honoring a visiting lecturer in 1922, Ima Hogg told Captain Baker she wanted to endow, anonymously, a music lectureship to elevate music taste and understanding among the students and residents of Houston. For six years, about $1,500 annual interest from a trust she established for the purpose supported the Institute's music department by sponsoring lecturers and concerts. Ima discussed her "musical adventure" with Mary Lovett, helped choose performers, and built the audience for these popular lecture-concert evenings at the City Auditorium.[65] Estelle Sharp underwrote the salary of sociologist John W. Slaughter, who gave courses in civics and philanthropy for several years. Sharp funds also supported a visiting lecturers' series on citizenship.[66] In 1927 Friends of Architecture offered traveling fellowships. These gifts, while generous, did not enable Lovett to build solid academic departments; indeed, the donors themselves saw their sponsorship as temporary until formal departments could be properly funded.[67]

Baker and the Board began discussing alternative methods of funding by 1924. In March 1927 the alumni proposed raising money for a Memorial Building to house classrooms. They launched a drive to raise $500,000 as an endowment for the complex, which they projected would be in service for the 1937–1941 class.[68] Architects Ralph Adams Cram and William Ward Watkin drew speculative plans for a library, classroom building, and fine arts group, hoping the sketches would appeal to donors. When Democrats descended on the city for the national convention in 1928, local committees wanted to rent dormitory space, to set up a rodeo on the athletic fields, and to hold meetings and other events in the academic buildings. The trustees were not enthusiastic but grudgingly said rooms could be used to house delegates and visitors if the Democrats paid high rent, insured against all damages, and furnished linens and attendants to keep the rooms clean. Reminded that there was nowhere in Houston but the Rice athletic complex to hold a rodeo, Baker and his Board charged the convention $2,000 for four days and demanded the politicians cover all damages and build a proper fence to protect the track and other structures. Baker asked his law firm to draw up a contract and told J. T. McCants "to induce [the organizers] to build a permanent fence enclosing the Athletic field," which would keep those without tickets from sneaking into the rodeo and into football games during the school year.[69] But renting facilities during the summer was not viewed at the time as a steady source of income.

In January 1929 Baker proposed another idea to the trustees. For some time Baker, an avid fan of Institute team sports, and William Ward Watkin, chairman of the Committee on Outdoor Sports, had discussed the quality of the athletes who matriculated at Rice. Athletes, Baker felt, were unable to produce winning seasons in the Southwest Conference, which Rice had joined in 1914, or to maintain good academic standing. Ticket sales did not cover expenses of the athletic program, and the Captain was tired of the Institute's "puny" teams. The Board agreed more funding and a full physical education curriculum might address both issues. Baker invited prominent citizens to a dinner at the Houston Club in February 1929 and asked them to make five-year pledges to establish and underwrite a Physical Education Department at the Institute, paid for entirely by private subscription. These pledges, accruing to $20,000 each year, plus ticket receipts would, the Board believed, support the athletic program and provide a curriculum attractive to serious football players and other athletes. Captain Baker, William Marsh Rice II, Will Clayton, Jesse Jones, William Stamps Farish, and Mellie Esperson Stewart immediately pledged $1,000 a year for the five-year trial period. Citizens of Houston rallied to the cause, and the new program, pending faculty appointments, was included in the course brochure for 1929–1930.[70] Not everyone felt that more athletic victories would ensure more applicants or improve the education received at the Institute. Anderson Clayton and Company president Lamar Fleming Jr., since 1924 an "interested spectator" at Rice games, believed that young men "whose principal purpose at college is athletics are a liability to their college." Not even the combined charm and argument of Baker and Lovett that "athletic sports are an indispensable adjunct of academic life" could sway Fleming, who concluded, "I am utterly out of step with current ideas . . . and must ask you count me out" of the fund-raising scheme.[71]

Baker and the trustees generally agreed that campus expansion to accommodate more students and new programs should continue, but the pace slowed in the 1920s and halted altogether in the 1930s. Harris Masterson Jr., an Episcopal priest who had worked with young people during World War I, was the first to fill an important need for postwar students when he proposed that the Episcopal Diocese of Texas build a community center and gathering place for Rice undergraduates across the street from campus. The Episcopal Diocese acquired property and Masterson hired Institute architects Cram and Ferguson to design the facility in 1920. In 1921 Allie Kinsloe Autry, the recent widow of Judge James Lockhart Autry and mother of Rice student James L. Autry Jr., agreed to donate $50,000 for a memorial to her late husband. At Captain Baker's suggestion, Rice Institute worked with Mrs. Autry, her attorney Joseph S. Cullinan, and the diocese to execute a construction loan for $50,000.[72] Allie's son James laid the cornerstone at commencement in 1921 but died of appendicitis shortly after his graduation in 1922.[73] William Ward Watkin supervised completion of the project, and Autry House quickly became the Institute's recreational center. The upstairs Girls' Lounge provided the only refuge for female students, who had no on-campus residence or dining hall. In 1927 Daphne Palmer Neville donated $100,000 in memory of her brother Edward Albert Palmer to build a collegiate chapel adjacent to Autry House. She commissioned architect William Ward Watkin, who created a small gem that recalled a favorite Venetian church. Within two years the Episcopal Diocese established a parish there but continued to welcome Rice students.[74]

Spurred forward by all the activity surrounding Autry House, in May 1920 the Board voted to accept William Ward Watkin's plans and construction bids for an Athletic Field House, and the following fall Watkin reported that construction was complete according to the final estimates. Lovett requested additional appropriations for roads, walkways, gates, and infrastructure improvements to link the new structure to the campus grid.[75] In 1923 the trustees authorized Watkin's plans and $1 million budget for the Chemistry Building, promised to be the "best in the South." Projected to open in September 1924 and to house a newly formed Geology Department, the project was delayed a year when the factory supplying the bricks foundered financially. The Board agreed to provide financing to the factory, the bricks were manufactured, and the handsome fireproof building of limestone, marble, and brick opened its doors in April 1925.[76] The Board also raised the value of its plant by investing in neighboring development projects and improving access to the site. When Will Hogg offered to lobby County Commissioners for an "ample thoroughfare around the Institute grounds," the Board joined adjacent landowners and allocated funds to pave roads along the campus perimeter.[77]

Two construction projects took shape in 1926–1927. Always keen to improve athletic facilities and attract a crowd to football games, Baker was particularly interested in Watkin's design for a steel grandstand to replace the old seats. Debate raged about cost versus quality, but in the end the Board dispensed with Watkin's cost-cutting efforts and adhered to the architect's original plan.[78] In 1926 George S. Cohen, president of Foley's Department Store, began talking to Board and faculty members about a gift to Rice. After many meetings, he provided funds to build a faculty club to honor his parents, Robert and Agnes Cohen of Galveston, on their seventieth birthdays. He was "desirous that they, while living, may witness a son's expression of love and reverence, and of symbolizing in enduring fashion before the eyes of youth on the campus . . . the divine injunction of filial devotion."[79] George Cohen made a donation of $25,000 and borrowed $100,000 from the Institute's endowment to construct the handsome faculty refuge designed by William Ward Watkin. Six months after the trustees accepted Cohen's gift, they dedicated the Italian Romanesque structure of concrete, brick, and hollow tile on Thanksgiving Day. A boost to faculty morale, the club's lounge — with its stone fireplace and polychromed wood ceiling, and the various dining, meeting, and game rooms — became a popular gathering place when completed in 1928.[80]

Captain Baker oversaw only one other construction project on campus during his lifetime: the memorial statue of William Marsh Rice. In 1922 Baker asked Lovett and the Rice brothers to explore an appropriate memorial and final resting place for the founder's ashes, and in November 1928 the Board appropriated $25,000 for the project. Ralph Adams Cram selected a site; Will and Ben Rice visited the sculptor, John Angel, in his New York studio to approve plans for a seated figure of their uncle as a middle-aged man; and William Ward Watkin coordinated production of a granite pedestal and casting of the bronze statue. Once the ashes had been interred on May 22, 1930, workers placed the statue, which the Board unveiled Sunday morning, June 8. Rev. Dr. James Gordon Gilkey of Springfield, Massachusetts, the founder's birthplace, gave the benediction at the unveiling before addressing those attending the Institute's fifteenth Baccalaureate, and Ralph Adams Cram explained the sculptor's goals before speaking to the graduating class of 1930 at commencement the next day.[81]

CAMPUS CONCERNS

Inevitably, money issues affected Lovett's ability to build a faculty and student body of the highest caliber. Following the tumultuous years of World War I, Lovett and the trustees recognized the Institute needed more administrators, programs, and professors if it wanted to increase student applications and retain faculty. In 1919 the trustees approved three critical appointments. Popular English Professor Stockton Axson, Woodrow Wilson's brother-in-law, persuaded Captain Baker that a dean of the college "would be an excellent 'shock-absorber'" who could relieve Dr. Lovett from "petty annoyances" and release his energies "for the larger constructive policies of the Institute."[82] Baker and Lovett named Dean Robert Granville Caldwell to run interference between Lovett and the students and faculty. Additional relief came when Registrar Samuel G. McCann and Bursar John T. McCants began to manage the mechanics of academic life.

In March 1924 the Board agreed to add the geology curriculum and to make admission competitive so only qualified students would be selected "to take advantage of the opportunity" offered by Rice.[83] Each year during the 1920s the educational department grew—from 58 faculty and staff in 1919 to 108 in 1927. The budget also rose from $129,706 in 1914 to $236,487 after the armistice to $493,548 in 1926 and $502,514 in 1928. It peaked at over $581,000 in 1931 and remained in the $400,000s during the 1930s. Every spring Baker, Lovett, and Cohn spent hours examining each entry of the General Office and Educational Department budgets, often meeting in the evening at Baker's home. Generally supportive, Baker did, however, question both men closely and sometimes requested cuts.[84]

Even without budget restraints, Lovett found recruiting and retaining faculty for a young institution challenging. During the 1920s, he was often absent from the campus for five or six months on trips to the Northeast or to Europe in search of scholars willing to join him in remote Texas. Living conditions were difficult. Single men could find accommodations in the residential hall or at local boarding houses for reasonable rates, but married men, who needed homes for their families, discovered that Houston's population boom had pushed the cost of housing beyond the means of junior faculty. The Board studied this issue in 1921 and again in 1924. One young recruit wrote Arthur Cohn in despair on November 13, 1921: "After almost two months of a fruitless search for decent living quarters at a reasonable cost," he finally found a four-room furnished apartment, far from the Institute, with "no adequate provision for heating" and a price "out of proportion to my income."[85] By 1929, several professors, whose employment Lovett valued, had secured loans from the Institute at "a low rate of interest" to help them build homes near the campus.[86]

Lovett offered generous salaries in 1912 to attract good scholars to the new enterprise, but the pay scale at Rice lagged behind national trends after World War I. Baker focused so intently on preserving the endowment that he failed to see the importance of raises—to reward talent, to attract academic leaders, and to compete with wealthy institutions in the Northeast and Midwest. Baker never suggested increasing Lovett's compensation package, which grew slowly—and only when the president threatened to leave—from $12,000 salary plus $3,500 travel and house allowance in 1919 to $16,000 plus $7,400 in expenses by 1928. Faculty retention was a serious problem. Morale plummeted when beloved French Professor Albert L. Guerard and founding German Professor Lindsey Blayney left in 1924 for more prestigious posts with better salaries. In January 1926 when Professor Griffith C. Evans, who held the Chair of Mathematics, received a call from Harvard, Lovett met with the Board to discuss ways to keep Evans at Rice. Lovett had conferred with him and knew he would stay for $9,000 a year, effective September 1, 1926, and the Board authorized this expenditure, provided it "not be construed as a precedent for similarly increasing the compensation of others." Popular professors like Stockton Axson and Radoslav Tsanoff did command good salaries and became important members of Houston's leadership circle. The Board also encouraged faculty members to improve their financial positions by pursuing dual careers.[87] Architect William Ward Watkin built a substantial private practice while leading the Institute's architecture department and managing its athletics committee. Architecture Professor James H. Chillman Jr. served as director of the Museum of Fine Arts, perceived by its board to be a part-time job until the 1950s. Lewis B. Ryon earned extra income by providing engineering services to the City of Houston, while sociologist John Willis Slaughter held numerous paid and volunteer posts in Houston's growing nonprofit sector.

Salary, housing costs, and distance from East Coast centers of higher education were not the only problems. Baker had never been enthusiastic about the system of tenure being introduced in some universities. Throughout his years as chairman he resisted this method of ensuring faculty loyalty. Seen by professors as a way to protect their academic freedom from interference by donors or administrators, tenure was viewed with disfavor by many nonacademics who preferred a business model and year-to-year contracts. Still opposed to the idea in the fall and winter of 1935–1936, Baker discussed the issue at length with Lovett; at the chairman's request, Lovett wrote to presidents and officers of sister institutions and realized that "no uniform policy" was in effect, although some prominent faculty members held life tenure in other institutions. In March 1937 Baker again suggested that the trustees "adopt a policy that no one whomsoever be employed, directly or indirectly, for life."[88] For most of his presidency, Lovett could not use this perquisite to attract outstanding men.

Although Baker preferred a business model for managing Rice, he sincerely enjoyed his friendships with Institute personnel. He entertained faculty, encouraged them to join Houston's civic and social groups, and attended high table, lectures, and concerts on campus. He often helped faculty families with personal gifts and paid their unexpected health-care costs himself. Baker also addressed campus societies and participated in the Houston Philosophical Society and the Town and Gown Club, founded by professors to nurture closer relations with Houstonians.[89]

The Institute's prestige improved nationally in 1928 when the National Council of Phi Beta Kappa (PBK) named Rice the Beta Chapter in Texas, following earlier approval of a chapter at the University of Texas. Meeting the honor society's stringent requirements affirmed the high quality of Rice's academic programs. On March 1, 1929, chapter President Stockton Axson and Secretary Radoslav Tsanoff signed papers naming Captain Baker their chapter's first honorary member. Delighted by this recognition, Baker had his portrait painted wearing the Phi Beta Kappa key.[90] In 1929 the Engineering Department produced its first public exhibit of student research projects. Sponsored by local industries and corporations, the show demonstrated the practical uses of scientific research and cemented ties between the Institute and Houston's business community. In recognition of student accomplishment, the aptly named Samuel Rhodes Dunlap became the Institute's first Rhodes Scholar in 1934.[91] Even with these marks of recognition, Baker continued to worry about financing improvements. By May 1929 he was exploring the legal hurdles overcome by Stanford when that university, whose original charter also forbade charging tuition, inaugurated some student fees.[92]

Board minutes in the 1920s reveal that Baker and his fellow trustees focused on investment decisions and the athletic program. Rarely did they address issues relating to student life or faculty retention; nowhere did they debate the need for female housing or dining facilities on campus. Nor is there any record that the Institute's leaders took an official stand on controversial issues, even when their silence affected donations. In 1921–1923 a revived Ku Klux Klan generated enough support in Houston to affect local elections and mount a terror campaign. Civic leaders Joseph Cullinan and John Kirby answered with an Anti-Klan Association, which quashed the movement by 1924. When Cullinan discovered in September 1922 that a small klavern had formed at Rice, he was "greatly chagrined" and refused that November to contribute to the Student Loan Fund, declaring he would not support any church or organization that did not proactively denounce the Klan. On November 13, 1922, he resigned as president and member of the Chamber of Commerce because that organization also failed to take a firm stand against the Klan.[93] Captain Baker was away from Houston for the last six months of 1922, and his well-known reverence for the Constitution and respect for the rights of all citizens would have presumably made Klan activity repugnant to him, but neither he nor Lovett answered Cullinan's call for proactive denunciation. *Thresher* editors lampooned the "Ku Klucks" on November 25, 1921, and the 1922 *Campanile* included a Klan spoof, but Institute authorities remained silent.

REAL ESTATE INVESTOR

During the nineteenth century, Houston's residential neighborhoods expanded gradually, moving slowly away from the commercial center to the south and east, filling city lots platted by the Allen Brothers. In the 1870s when Judge Baker moved to town, most people still walked to work. The steady population expansion after 1900 changed the scope of residential development dramatically. Investors purchased large swaths of ranch and farmland north, south, and east of the commercial area. Many of these rural properties outside city limits had not been subdivided since their original owners received land grants from Mexico or from the Republic of Texas, but streetcars and rail lines meant speculators could develop satellite suburbs several miles from the center of town. By the 1920s the automobile and extensive road paving projects initiated by the city and county brought renewed interest in South End properties between downtown and the Institute, where speculators began purchasing blocks of farmland to develop high-end residential enclaves in the early twentieth century. They advertised these early projects as rural alternatives to high-density urban living, protected by deed restrictions and high price tags to keep them safe from industrial encroachment. Plans incorporated gardens, boulevards, stables, and open spaces.[94]

From his Victorian mansion on Main Street, within walking distance of most of his friends, Captain Baker observed these developments and by 1905 began representing William A. Wilson, a realtor, entrepreneur, and proponent of several civic projects. Baker helped Wilson organize the Woodson Realty Company, capitalized at $30,000, to purchase a thirty-five-acre addition north of Buffalo Bayou. In 1907 the two men chartered William A. Wilson Company to develop 106 acres of sparsely populated but nicely wooded rural land on high ground near White Oak Bayou, north of the city, which they named Woodland Heights. Wilson, who rented an office in the Commercial National Bank Building, had already built custom homes in the South End and in Houston Heights northwest of town, but his Woodland Heights development was a fully conceived community of six hundred lots laid out on graded streets bordered by sidewalks and shaded by hundreds of live oak and sycamore trees. Wilson himself chose a prime lot and built a substantial home for his family. A 1910 promotional brochure listed investors James A. Baker, William A. Wilson, and three others; the officers and directors were men of "keen business judgment and ability"; and the attorneys, Baker, Botts, Parker & Garwood "gave their careful attention to every legal point," including title search and contract approval. In *Homes* magazine, which Wilson published in 1911 and 1912, he explained that lot owners could build innovative bungalows, Victorian cottages, or two-story American foursquare houses, "sold to white people only." Wilson marketed Woodland Heights to middle-class "men of character and standing in the community." The development was far enough from downtown "to ensure the quiet and repose of an ideal residential district." Streetcars served this "picturesque woodland," which also boasted gas and electric utilities, a school, and fire protection. Protective property restrictions preserved each homeowner's investment. All businesses of any kind were forbidden, and no liquor of any description could be sold in the subdivision.[95]

At the same time Baker was investing in Woodland Heights, he and Will Rice were amassing property for the Institute campus (1908–1909). Baker also quietly purchased nearly forty acres west of Main Street along the county's Poor Farm Road (later renamed Bissonnet Street) outside city limits, which he did not develop for more than a decade. A few years later in July 1915, Baker purchased lot 12 in Courtlandt Place. Anticipating the birth of his first grandchild, Captain Baker handed title of the property to his daughter Alice Baker Jones so she and her husband Murray Brashear Jones could build a family home in the friendly, protected enclave. Three men had formed the Courtlandt Improvement Company in 1906 and had purchased fifteen and one-half acres to create "a district restricted to the erection of residences of good class and to surround . . . the locality generally with conditions assuring . . . freedom from noise, dust, constant traffic and other annoyances incident to location upon public streets in a populous city."[96] Architect Birdsall Parmenas Briscoe, already known for his use of high-quality materials and his attention to architectural details, designed a two and one-half story house for Captain Baker and his daughter in 1915–1917. Briscoe practiced in Houston from 1909 until 1955 and designed over fifty homes in the city's most beautiful neighborhoods. Number 22 was one of five he built on Courtlandt Place. A Georgian revival structure featuring a classical central bay, the house was built of stuccoed hollow tile, a rare construction method for private homes but a boon in Houston's long hot summers. The outer walls, from 12 to 24 inches thick, provided insulation and were an early example of energy efficiency. In 1919 Alice moved the little playhouse she and her sister Ruth had shared from Main Street to the Courtlandt Place garden, where she had it refurbished in stucco with handsome fluted pillars for her own daughter.[97] Alice Baker Jones owned 22 Courtlandt Place until April 1938, when she sold the property to Ralph B. Feagin, then managing partner of her father's law firm.[98]

In the summer of 1922 Captain Baker began talking to his son Jim about developing the property he had purchased north of Rice Institute in 1908. The open country around the Institute had become prime residential land, and Baker's property, which was protected by the Rice campus, Hermann Park, land secured for a museum of art, and other upscale enclaves, lay well removed from the commercial activity along Montrose Boulevard that was spoiling older developments. By 1919 Joseph Cullinan had established a trust to oversee construction in Shadyside, a gated enclave of thirty-seven acres west of Main Street and north of the Institute campus where twenty substantial homes sat in large, landscaped gardens.[99] Attorney John H. Crooker invested in Shadowlawn, a small enclave of twelve well-designed houses across Poor Farm Road from Baker's land. Herbert A. Kipp and William Ward Watkin platted Southampton in 1922 along two boulevards situated on 162 acres northwest of the Institute and advertised homes there for middle-income buyers.

The Bakers conceived their Broadacres enclave as a public amenity distinguished by fine architecture and distinctive planting but limited in ownership to personal and professional friends invited to invest in the project. By late 1922 seventeen investors, including law partners Walter Walne and Clarence Carter, had agreed to purchase the oversized lots. On January 31, 1923, Captain Baker, Guardian Trust, and the lot owners signed an agreement of sale, and the investors deposited $150,000 with Guardian Trust to finance infrastructure improvements. Captain Baker turned management over to his son, who served as chairman of the supervisory committee and handled all details. In February 1923 City Engineer Herbert A. Kipp platted the rectangular site with two long boulevards, crossed by two shorter avenues, all to be planted with oak trees. Kipp placed utilities in underground conduits, laid out sewers, and specified twenty-five lots—three reserved for Captain Baker, his daughter Alice, and his son Jim. Captain Baker had consulted with Rice Institute architect William Ward Watkin, who apparently suggested the name Broadacres for the new enterprise. After the plat was approved January 30, 1923, Watkin designed four pairs of entry posts at the four entrances, and Bonner Means Baker, Jim Baker's wife, proposed a landscaping plan of trees and shrubberies. Captain Baker also asked Watkin to design a home for him and Mrs. Baker to be constructed on his oversize lot number 9. Just as plans to build the Spanish-Mediterranean style house were moving forward, the large estate owned by his partner Edwin B. Parker became available, and Baker purchased that property instead.

Typical of the finest homes being constructed in Houston during the 1920s, the houses in Broadacres represent the eclectic style favored by the country house movement prevalent in the era. Taking Tudor, Norman, Mediterranean, Georgian, and Colonial antecedents as models, Houston's best residential architects produced gracious homes set in manicured gardens to create a sense of country living and leisurely repose as a haven from the stress felt in a fast-paced industrial economy. In 1903 owners built homes at 1309 North and 1310 South Boulevard. In 1924 Baker Botts attorney Palmer Hutcheson hired John Staub to design his house at 1405 North Boulevard, and Walter Walne chose Birdsall Briscoe to build a Tudor-inspired brick residence. Briscoe also designed two other houses that year. In 1925 Watkin produced a Spanish-Mediterranean design for one home while Staub chose English Tudor for another. Between 1926 and 1929 Staub produced four more designs and Briscoe five, including a French Breton model for Baker Botts partner Clarence Carter.

On September 24, 1924, Jim Baker wrote the lot owners that improvements were complete and the charge to each lot owner would be less than estimated because he had cooperated with neighboring developers to share infrastructure costs. Between 1922 and 1926 Jim Baker, John Crooker (who was improving his Shadowlawn project), and engineers from the city and county argued over cost-sharing to extend water and gas mains, pave the county road out past Broadacres, install lighting along the roadways, and build sidewalks and curbs. John Crooker importuned Jim to move more swiftly as he was anxious to push his project along. Jim's caution was prescient because two weeks after a "rather long talk" when Jim was "unable to view the matter as I did," Crooker wrote to say that "upon investigation" he discovered the figures he had given were more than double what they should have been. In the end, contractors installed the standardized improvements to everyone's satisfaction.[100] Broadacres owners were leading professional and business men, ambitious to succeed and active in city-building projects; they wanted their homes to be places where they and their families could enjoy compatible neighbors and relax in the outdoors. The boulevards and gardens beckoned strollers and visiting; the park at the eastern end of the enclave allowed children to play games. The men and women who conceived Broadacres and other planned neighborhoods in the 1920s also advocated city planning, created parks and playgrounds throughout the city, and sponsored the municipal recreation department to improve the quality of Houston's living spaces.

Construction in Broadacres stopped during the Depression, although many homeowners hired the best landscapers of the era to create their gardens. Ironically, James A. Baker Jr. never did move to Broadacres. Feeling he could not afford the $20,000 down payment for a lot, he purchased a smaller property owned by his father in the Turner Addition adjacent to Broadacres and asked Sam Dixon to design and build a "temporary" house in 1926–1927. Jim and Bonner Means Baker never moved from this home that faced a bend in Poor Farm Road. Behind them, Browne and Adelaide Lovett Baker, Adelaide's brother Malcolm Lovett, and family friend William Kirkland built comfortable homes that faced Berthea Street, where the young families raised their children.

By the 1920s the community developing around the Institute included several public buildings: Autry House, the Edward Albert Palmer Memorial Chapel, a parish house designed by architect John Staub, and Hermann Hospital (1925), the charity hospital designed by Berlin & Swern of Chicago and provided to the city in George Hermann's will. All adopted the Mediterranean vocabulary first introduced to Houston at Rice Institute. Cram and Watkin turned to classical examples when they built the Museum of Fine Arts (1917–1924) on a triangle of land between Main and Montrose at the entrance to Hermann Park. Planners placed the public and residential buildings at the end of Main Street in a setting that harmonized residential and public spaces and created a "center of learning, culture and the humanities" noted favorably by contemporary journalists.[101]

THE OAKS

On July 12, 1923, Alice Baker was vacationing at Rockhaven Cottage on Grape Vine Road in Bass Rocks, Massachusetts, when she received an exciting telegram. "Believe I can get the Oaks for $125,000, which is cheap," wired her husband, who wanted to know if she could rearrange the dining and breakfast rooms to suit her. He continued in choppy telegram shorthand, "do you think we can purchase at price named wire prompt." Two days later on July 14, Captain Baker wired again: "I have bought and now tender you the Oaks with my heart's best love. I wish you may be as happy in its possession and enjoyment as I expect and hope to be all well and send love Jimmie."[102] So the dignified, sixty-six-year-old civic leader wrote with boyish excitement to tell his beloved wife of forty years that he had finally acquired Edwin B. Parker's admired home and garden. He must have been pleased since rumors abounded that Parker had spent $250,000 to build the house in 1907.

When the Parkers went to Washington during World War I, they rented their residence, The Oaks, and continued to lease it while Parker served on postwar commissions. By the summer of 1922 the Bakers were considering leaving their home on Main Street because commercial buildings and traffic noise were destroying the pleasure of their old neighborhood. That August, when he and son Jim were discussing plans for Broadacres, Baker turned down an offer to purchase a home in Shadyside, saying if he were to build a home, he would rather "build one according to my own ideas."[103] By September another plan to escape urban sprawl materialized. While in New York to enroll Ruth at Manhattan's Spence School and take Malcolm to school at the Hill in Pottstown, Pennsylvania, Alice Baker and the Parkers agreed that she and Captain Baker would rent the Parker home for two years, taking possession on December 1, 1922.

The next few months challenged Alice's executive abilities. Captain Baker, who had suffered severe pain all summer, was undergoing treatments for sciatic rheumatism in Boston during the fall. Alice returned home without him to undertake two monumental tasks: moving her household from their home of twenty-five years and making wedding plans for Browne and Adelaide Lovett, who had announced their plans to marry on December 23. With much-appreciated help from Jim and Browne, Alice moved the household in mid-December, just in time to receive Captain Baker home from the hospital, serve a grand dinner to the men Jim had invited to invest in Broadacres, and entertain Browne's friends and groomsmen at a stag dinner on December 21.[104] Six months later Parker realized he might never return to Houston and began discussions with his partner that culminated in Captain Baker's July 1923 telegram. When Baker learned The Oaks was for sale, the consummate

The Oaks, Baker family home 1922–1941. Private Collection.

lawyer hired a surveyor to check out the tract.[105] Apparently satisfied, Baker wired Alice and Parker and acquired the maturely landscaped estate. Architect John F. Staub, who helped the Bakers remodel their library and the troublesome dining spaces, remembered the Captain's displeasure when his builder, Chris Miller, submitted a cost-plus contract far higher than Baker had calculated. Staub, who built many of Houston's finest homes during the 1920s, gained Baker's respect when he explained to the lawyer that remodeling costs were higher per square foot than new construction and was frank about all expenses.[106]

The Bakers handsome new home was set on 6.73 acres of landscaped gardens at Baldwin and Hadley streets, sixteen blocks southwest of the central business district and three miles from the Institute.[107] In 1908 Parker had asked the city to close certain streets and reroute others so he could build a main house, servants' quarters, and carriage house in the modern Prairie Style made famous by Frank Lloyd Wright and adapted for the Parker family by Sanguinet and Staats of Ft. Worth. The greenhouse, controlled winter and summer to protect tender seedlings, provided plants and flowers for the reception rooms and garden beds. For years Parker held firm meetings in The Oaks' basement game room, which accommodated a large pool table at one end and enough chairs for the Thursday night gatherings. Captain Baker continued the firm tradition enthusiastically until his death. The full basement, which ran

The Oaks, dining room arranged for a reception. Private Collection.

beneath the large house, also housed a heating system, wine cellar, and laundry room. The main floor, designed for entertaining large groups, boasted gracious reception and dining rooms; a library, where Captain Baker housed a carefully organized collection of books with the case, shelf, and division number noted on each flyleaf; a music room, where Mrs. Baker placed her piano; galleries, a breakfast room, and extensive kitchens. Like most homes built before air conditioning tempered Houston's hot spring and summer months, the second floor contained bedrooms, screened sleeping porches, and bathrooms. The Parkers had named their home The Oaks for the estate's eighty oaks and many specimen trees. In 1909 they had planted shrubbery and plotted garden paths that led to a Japanese tea house, a huge rose garden, a vegetable garden, and a chicken yard. Planter boxes under the windows, sunken flower beds, and a breezeway covered with sweet honeysuckle completed the showplace while the Bakers lived there.[108]

Visitors who stayed at The Oaks and guests arriving for a party approached the house by a long circular drive. Under the porte cochere, they "first came under the scrutiny of Captain Baker," who would often answer the door. Grandchildren remember the house as large, dark, and redolent of the cigars their grandfather habitually smoked. When in a teasing mood, he would send his small grandsons into the dining room and offer a nickel or dime to those who could walk all the way around the banquet-sized table in the darkened room without bumping into the chairs—or running away in fright. Clarence Wharton and other partners owned houses near The Oaks, and when Baker's two youngest children, Ruth and Malcolm, married, their father offered them homes at 207 and 211 Bremond Street on the grounds of The Oaks.[109]

Commercial development had marched out Main Street by the time the Bakers moved to The Oaks. Captain Baker decided to develop the city block on which his family had lived happily for more than two decades. He chartered Graham Realty, a family corporation created to hold the property on Main Street and other properties he had acquired over the years, several in lieu of legal fees. The Main Street block and a block on the west side near City Hall were the most valuable, but Graham Realty also owned a dress shop at Louisiana and Prairie, property at San Jacinto and Bell where Southwestern Bell built a large building, and the site of a Chevrolet dealership. In addition to his other legal work, Jim Baker was handed the thankless and time-consuming task of managing these diverse pieces of real estate. Graham Realty paid a retainer to Baker Botts, and Jim found himself collecting rents, interviewing prospective employees, and overseeing maintenance. After Captain Baker's death, the five children inherited undivided interest in the property and a family headache. As could have been predicted, family members had different needs and opinions; some wanted to follow the course established by their father; others wished to sell poorly performing properties and reinvest in areas of town where real estate was booming. Finally, in the early 1980s one grandson was handed the task of liquidating the properties and distributing the assets—much to everyone's relief.[110]

In the late 1920s Captain Baker was involved in two other real estate ventures through his role as chairman of Guardian Trust Co. He had helped W. W. Baldwin, an investor from Chicago, incorporate the South End Land Company in 1908 and purchase over 9,000 acres of the old Rice Ranch, willed to the Institute as part of William M. Rice's estate. Baldwin had tried to generate interest in the suburb of Bellaire planned for the site by advertising "Truck farms and suburban homes within sight of Houston" on his South End Land Company letter head, but sales were very slow. Time and again he sought new loans from the Institute and then requested numerous extensions on the payments. Despite frequent refinancing, he had trouble meeting his obligations. By 1926 Baldwin still owned 4,760 acres he was trying to sell to developers. That year Guardian Trust President Clarence M. Malone, Munroe D. Anderson, James A. Baker, and others organized the Westmoreland Development Company, capitalized at $200,000; Baldwin sold the Westmoreland investors over 1,000 acres, with a year's option to purchase the remaining lands.[111]

In 1927 Baker, Botts, Parker & Garwood helped C. M. Malone and two investors with interests in the Rio Grande Valley charter Progreso Development Company to develop 6,300 acres in Hidalgo County. The capital stock was owned by the three incorporators, Captain Baker, and four Houston investors; Malone was elected president and Captain Baker vice president of the new company. Guardian Trust would act as agent in executing deeds and collecting notes. Most early investors in Progreso lived in the Middle West, and Baker and his partners soon discovered Wisconsin and Illinois had "very exacting laws" regulating out-of-state land purchases by their residents. In January 1930 Baker and a young lawyer traveled to Milwaukee on Progreso's behalf. The company had been organized to develop residential properties and then citrus orchards, but the 1929 crash, the end of railroad service in 1931, and a hurricane in 1933 drove the enterprise into bankruptcy. The investors retained the property, and Baker's partners and younger lawyers remembered firm hunting trips there in the 1930s and 1940s. A small hotel and clubhouse used to entertain potential buyers proved perfect for shooting parties during the fall dove season.[112]

FAMILY MATTERS

In the 1920s Captain Baker's children finished school, married, and settled in Houston. Every summer found the family at Rockhaven in Bass Rocks, Gloucester, Massachusetts, where the Palmer Hutchesons and oil man Robert Lee Blaffer joined the Bakers, George V. Rotan, and other Texan vacationers. Captain Baker and Alice usually opened Rockhaven after Baker had fulfilled his Institute Commencement duties in June and closed the house in late October. Children arrived, well-chaperoned, from colleges and schools in the northeast and stayed until school reopened in the fall. The Baker boys enjoyed sailing and tennis while their

Summertime at Rockhaven in Bass Rocks, Massachusetts, 1920s. Private Collection.

father puttered on the golf course. Alice and the girls gardened, walked along the rocky shore, and welcomed guests. Doctors had diagnosed Mrs. Baker with high blood pressure in the early 1900s, and her husband believed the sea air and relaxed schedule were beneficial during Houston's hot summers. By the 1920s the Bass Rocks guest list included the Bakers' married children and the friends and fiancés of their younger sons and daughter. In the fall of 1922 Adelaide Lovett recuperated at Rockhaven from some unnamed malady and wrote long letters to her mother that provide a glimpse of the Bakers' hospitality.[113] Mrs. Baker spoiled her, showered little gifts upon her, and took her on shopping sprees, while Captain Baker read Lord Chesterfield's *Letters to His Son* aloud to the assembled guests in the evening. Adelaide thanked Captain Baker "for the rare privilege of living in your lovely home. . . . You are so thoughtful and generous to those who have the good fortune to know you.[114] Malcolm and his fiancée Anita Stewart remembered the halcyon summers of their courtship in the late 1920s for the rest of their lives.

In 1922 the Baker family was plagued by ill health. Alice Baker Jones spent weeks in Baltimore where her husband Murray underwent a serious operation and slow return to health. Captain Baker was glad advice he had given his son-in-law proved helpful and assured him "you are as dear to me as my own boys are . . . I will always do for you as much and as cheerfully as I would for them."[115] That summer Baker was sufficiently troubled by his health problems to write his oldest son a letter with instructions to follow in the event of his death. For months he struggled to alleviate chronic pain in his shoulder that had made his right arm almost useless. Baker had been diagnosed with diabetes several years before and felt he should not subject himself to an anesthetic. In the fall of 1922 when Alice closed Rockhaven Cottage and returned to Houston, her ailing husband remained in Boston to try new treatments he hoped would make an operation unnecessary but would restore use of his arm.

Loving letters from this period of enforced separation attest to an enduring marriage between two devoted soul mates. Each kept the other informed about activities, and both yearned to be together again. Although a sister astutely remarked, "You are always happiest when you have some big and great plan to work out," Alice assured her "Dearest husband" she was "extremely happy" to know he missed her and but for her duties at home she "would be with you every minute of the time." Despite her disappointment that they would not be together for Thanksgiving, Alice concluded, "we have so much to be thankful for in our children & the boys in particular and then when I think of our great & abiding love for each other, my gratitude knows no bounds." These heartfelt messages sent "with more love than I can ever express," survived a pact made early in November to destroy all their letters "from now on." After nine weeks in the Boston hospital, Captain Baker met Malcolm and Ruth in New York, purchased appropriate wedding clothes so they could all attend Browne's wedding in style, and returned to Houston, his happy wife, and his new home.[116]

For some years it had been clear that the childhood friendship between Adelaide and Browne had evolved into romance. When Browne followed Adelaide to Paris in 1921 after he finished Princeton, no one was surprised, and both families welcomed the engagement announced after Adelaide's return. Their wedding on December 23, 1922, united the son and daughter of the Rice Institute's chairman and president and gave the faculty chamber of the Administration Building a new role. Not since the opening ceremonies a decade before had the room looked so splendid. Large jars of calla lilies defined the aisle, and the simulated altar held cathedral candles whose "luminous rays" provided subdued lighting for the palms and smilax garlands. Enhancing the romantic scene were "unusual touches of sentiment." The bride had selected her parents' twenty-fifth wedding anniversary for her own celebration and wore her mother's gown embellished by a tulle veil and coronet of orange blossoms. She carried the prayer book her maternal grandmother had used in 1865. Alice Baker Jones, seven, held the ring while Adelaide's younger brother Alexander, eleven, served as trainbearer in the full dress of a student at Eton. Mrs. Lovett adorned the Institute banquet hall with holiday greens, and Institute chefs created the wedding cake, a six-foot confection of graduated tiers "decorated with gold and silver leaves, doves, bridal blossoms and woven ribbons and topped with a home scene." During the evening the bride and groom slipped away for a month-long wedding trip.[117]

The friendship between the Baker and Lovett families intensified during the 1920s. Alice and Mary wrote frequently during the years Mrs. Lovett spent in Paris while her daughter Adelaide studied at the Sorbonne (1920–1922), following her graduation from Rice Institute. Alice helped Edgar Odell Lovett entertain Institute visitors and dignitaries during his wife's prolonged absence, while Captain Baker and President Lovett moved beyond a cordial business partnership to a relationship based on shared interests, personal concern, and family ties. Typical of these strong bonds were Captain Baker's actions in the summer of 1928, when Lovett was so seriously ill that his doctors and friends recommended he consult specialists at Johns Hopkins Medical School. Baker kept apprised of developments and rushed from Bass Rocks, Massachusetts, to Baltimore to supervise his friend's care. When the train carrying Lovett, his doctor and nurse, and his wife and son pulled into Baltimore station on August 22, Baker was standing on the platform. He escorted his ailing friend to a waiting ambulance, rode with him to Union Memorial Hospital, where members of the Baker family had received treatment in the past, and remained in Baltimore until satisfied that Lovett was receiving good care.[118]

Every few years found the Bakers in Europe visiting spas or enjoying the metropolitan delights of London and Paris. In 1924 the Bakers sailed in September to visit Ruth, who had finished the Spence School and was studying in Paris. While there Captain Baker and Robert S. Lovett toured Western Front battlefields to see where their sons had served during World War I. Moved by the scene, the admiring father wrote to his daughter-in-law Bonner: he was ending the fifth of a six-day trip "through the War Zone of France and a marvelous and wonderful trip it has been too. Today we were at Verdun in the Argone [*sic*] Forest, and all day the sweet face of dear Jim has been before me. I wish I knew where he was in the Argone, so that I might see the very things his eyes saw. . . . The beauty of this poppy plucked from the battle scarred field of Verdun recalled sweet thoughts of you, my dear child, and I enclose it with my hearts devotion to you & Jim. Lovingly, Mr. Baker." These tender words evoke the rose petals enclosed in a letter five-year-old Jimmie sent his own father, who was away on another front during the American Civil War.[119]

Jim and Bonner settled quickly into postwar patterns of family and civic life. In 1920 Jim was named director of the South Texas Commercial National Bank and started along the dual legal-banking career path taken by his father. Browne began work as a clerk at Guardian Trust, was a vice president by 1928, and remained in banking for the rest of his life. Adelaide, following the example set by her mother and mother-in-law, gathered twelve friends to found the Junior League of Houston in 1925 as a "leading force in helping those in need." She served as the League's first president and raised funds for a health center for the underserved, the first project undertaken by League volunteers. Alice Baker Jones, with encouragement from her father and brother Jim, began to support the Kinkaid School, which her daughter Alice attended for eight years. In 1928 Captain Baker, Alice Baker Jones, and Robert Lee Blaffer urged school founder Margaret Kinkaid to expand her school. They helped raise funds for the project and encouraged William Ward Watkin to donate his design services to construct a handsome Spanish Renaissance-style complex at Graustark and Richmond.[120]

When Ruth returned from Paris, she made her debut at dances held by two new clubs with Baker family affiliations. Alice Baker Jones and Mrs. Edgar Odell Lovett were founders of Assembly in 1920, and Ruth's brothers Jim and Browne helped organize Allegro (1925), where she and seven friends celebrated at a Cinderella ball. Malcolm completed four years at the Hill School in the spring of 1924 and matriculated at Princeton that fall. During the winter of 1925, he fell ill with flu. His parents, fearing the tragedy that had befallen their family in 1902, rushed him home to Houston, where they supervised his recuperation personally. When he returned to health, there was no more talk of Princeton and its long, cold winters; Malcolm enrolled at Rice and was graduated with the class

Bonner and Jim Baker, 1920s.
Private Collection.

of 1929. Following his graduation, Malcolm began his business career at South Texas Commercial Bank.[121]

Society page reporters considered Baker weddings important news. Readers of the Sunday *Chronicle* on October 24, 1926, learned that the coming week's social calendar "holds no more interesting date" than the wedding of Ruth Baker to Preston Moore, scheduled to take place on Tuesday evening at 7 o'clock in the First Presbyterian Church. Baskets of chrysanthemums set against banks of ferns and palms embellished the "impressive and stately" candlelight ceremony celebrated by Dr. William States Jacobs. Ruth's sister Alice and her young niece, Alice Baker Jones, attended the bride. Her three brothers served as groomsmen and ushers. The bride's rose point lace veil made a "sweeping train," and she carried "white orchids with a shower of lilies of the valley falling to the hemline of her skirt." Afterwards Mrs. Baker, wearing "a handsome creation" of blue gray velvet sparkling with beads and rhinestones, received her

Anita Stewart Baker
on her wedding day,
November 15, 1929.
Private Collection.

guests at The Oaks. Roses filled every room, and the ring-shaped wedding cake was "embossed with azaleas." The happy couple left the reception bound for New Orleans, Havana, and New York, where they would attend the Yale–Princeton football game, "the groom being a Princeton man." They would soon receive friends "in their own picturesque home" at 207 Bremond, adjacent to Ruth's parents.[122]

When Malcolm married his college sweetheart, the beautiful Anita Dee Stewart, on Thursday, November 15, 1929, Palmer Memorial Chapel was the setting for an "impressive service" of "statewide interest." White roses, shaggy chrysanthemums, palms, and smilax adorned the church with ivory candles in floor candelabra "lending a luminous glow to the scene." The bride, daughter of widowed Mrs. John S. Stewart, had been Queen of the May at Rice Institute. She was given in marriage by her brother John and wore "an exquisite costume of ivory satin . . . made along princess lines." Orchids and lilies of the valley "cascaded along the length of the skirt." Sisters of the bride and groom attended the bride, Jim Baker served as best man, and Browne was a groomsman. The bride's mother entertained the bridal party and family members after the 5:00 p.m. service before the couple left for a honeymoon trip to New Orleans, Havana, and Florida. The evening before this "leading event," Captain and Mrs. Baker had entertained the wedding party after the rehearsal at The Oaks, where "flowers of the Southland season were basketed and vased." When they returned, Malcolm and Anita moved to a house next door to Ruth and Preston Moore on The Oaks grounds.[123]

CHAPTER EIGHT

Final Passages

AS THE DEPRESSION tightened its grip on the world economy in 1930, Captain Baker turned seventy-three. For over half a century he had guided his law firm, and for nearly forty years he had loyally guarded William Marsh Rice's Trust. At a time when many men relinquish their influence to others, Baker stood firm. During the last years of his life he resolved crises by finding common ground among warring parties, he imagined new ways to move Rice Institute forward, and he helped Houstonians weather financial hard times. Despite economic uncertainty, more and more investors in the oil industry made Houston their headquarters, and newcomers added over ninety thousand residents, pushing the city's population to 384,514 by 1940.

SAVING THE BANKS

Captain Baker played a critical, behind-the-scenes role in October 1931, when he persuaded doubting colleagues to step in and control a poten-

Illustrations: Alice Baker, James A. Baker, paintings on glass, ca. 1930. Private Collection.

tial banking crisis. Rapidly expanding credit and increased money supply fueled the booming 1920s in Houston and across the United States. Oil drilled in Texas filled the gas tanks of cars bought by young women who bobbed their hair and raised their hemlines, and by young men determined to launch a new era after the old world's collapse in the trenches of World War I. Jazz banks, as Roy M. Farrar, president of Houston's Union National Bank (1924–1943), disparagingly called small banks that proliferated before the Depression, attracted consumers who wanted car loans or speculators in high-risk ventures who thought the market would never stop climbing. Many customers of these banks could not meet the stricter qualifications of Houston's established financial institutions. When the broader economy weakened and the New York Stock Market crashed on October 24, 1929, Houston bankers and businessmen faced a regional crisis. Cotton sat unwanted in warehouses around the globe; oil prices sagged because of booming production; shipping at the Port of Houston stalled. As they had done during dark times before World War I, Houston's business leaders overcame personal ambition or animosity to stabilize the financial foundations underpinning Houston's economy.

Jazz banking held no charms for James Baker and his colleagues at South Texas Commercial National Bank or at Guardian Trust, two of the three major depositories for Rice Institute funds. During the 1920s, these banks controlled by the Baker family followed a conservative path and continued to serve stable corporate clients and large estates, but Baker did make some changes in response to customer demand. In 1924 Baker helped the South Texas Commercial National Bank amend its charter to take advantage of new banking laws that empowered national banks to add trust departments to their commercial business. Baker explained to his law partners that "it is not the purpose of the Bank at this time to enter actively into the Trust features of the banking business," but the bank wanted the option to act "whenever it was called upon to do so."[1] In February 1927 Baker supervised amendment of the Guardian Trust charter to increase the company's capital stock from $300,000 to $600,000. The next month he organized the South Texas Commercial Company, capitalized at $150,000, to make loans on real estate security, purchase real estate notes, and subscribe to stocks and bonds—all functions not allowed under South Texas Commercial National's charter. Baker told his law partners, "It was deemed advisable that the stock . . . be held by the stockholders of the bank" and "distributed pro rata among" them. The officers of the bank and its commercial arm comprised Baker as chairman, S. Maurice McAshan as president, and twenty-one directors, including Robert Lee Blaffer, Edwin B. Parker, and James A. Baker Jr.[2] In 1929 South Texas Commercial National's directors even dabbled in more risky ventures when they decided that "call loans" to finance stock purchases were "proper" if handled by reputable New York brokers; this speculative mechanism that allowed investors to pay only a portion of the stock price were later cited as a cause of the 1929 crash.

By 1929 bank deposits in Houston reached $106 million; the port was third in US exports; and money in circulation was twice the national average. South Texas Commercial National Bank held deposits of $26 million, with $1 million capital stock and $1 million surplus; its net earnings of $420,000 in 1929 reached an historic high mark. But rumblings of distress were growing: too many new banks had opened, too many rural banks had already failed, real estate development was stalling, oil and gas prices had dipped, and warehoused cotton, worldwide, depressed the commodity's price. When the Wall Street markets crashed, Houstonians grasped for causes of the worst financial collapse in history. One Houston banker noted that bankers of the day lacked reliable credit information, they were slow to press old customers for loan payments, and the value of their security pledges could not support the loans. Almost at once, Houston bank assets began to deteriorate. Depositors made withdrawals or hoarded cash in safety deposit vaults, and stockholders called for stern measures. As unemployment rose, bankers reduced overhead, collected debts with renewed energy, and introduced service fees—all measures that increased depositor distress.[3]

Houston's established banks weathered the storm at first, but by October 1931 bankers realized two important institutions were facing failure: Public National Bank, organized in 1921 and owned primarily by W. L. Moody III and Odie R. Seagraves, who were major speculators in natural gas fields and pipeline construction, and Houston National Bank, repository for Governor Ross Sterling's oil-based fortune. By late October, the public had learned that Moody and Seagraves were borrowing heavily from their own bank, and depositors began withdrawing funds. Captain Baker was on vacation in Bass Rocks and did not immediately take action to avert the looming disaster, but Jesse Jones, with assets in several banks, knew Public National and Houston National could not continue much longer. In 1930 he had absorbed the struggling Marine Banking and Trust state bank into his fast-growing National Bank of Commerce. Now he saw another opportunity to add to his bank portfolio.

On Sunday afternoon, October 25, 1931, Jones called officers from Clearing House banks, executives of major Houston utilities, and important oil investors to a meeting at his office on the thirty-third floor of the Gulf Building. Guardian Trust's Clarence M. Malone, First National Bank's John T. Scott, South Texas Commercial National's S. Maurice McAshan (president 1927–1941), attorney and Union National Bank director Frank Andrews, Second National Bank president B. D. Harris, cotton broker Will Clayton, and oil men Harry Weiss and William Stamps Farish responded, while other businessmen came and went during a marathon debate that continued through the night until nearly dawn the next morning. Jones explained the dire situation at Public and Houston National, he suggested that the books of all Houston banks be examined, and he tried to forge a plan that would include the city's major corporate and financial players. Nothing was settled when the meeting broke up, but the group decided it would not let either bank fail and would supply funds if necessary. Then they went home to change clothes, shave, and return to their offices. When Public National opened its doors on Monday, business proceeded as usual, although one employee remembered looking down at the tellers from a mezzanine balcony and fearing they would run out of cash.

At 5:00 p.m., the group reassembled in Jones's office, where negotiating began in earnest. McAshan and Union National Bank President Roy M. Farrar at first argued the two banks should fail but finally agreed that the strong banks had to save the weak to prevent "a black eye to Houston, and the loss of business . . . due to the panicky feeling prevailing throughout the city generally." But, they did not trust Jesse Jones and wondered what advantage he was pursuing. Jones contended a run on the banks would ruin everyone and proposed a guaranty fund, financed by twelve banks and five major corporations, whose officers would promise to raise $2.4 million to bail out the two failing banks. Real estate investor Joseph Meyer and his sons agreed to take over Houston National Bank, with which Meyer had been associated for nearly half a century, if others would assume $800,000 of the outstanding notes. Humble Oil & Refining agreed to purchase Houston Oil Terminal Company from Governor Sterling for $400,000, which Sterling would apply to his bank debt, and the guarantors promised to raise the remainder. Jesse Jones's National Bank of Commerce pledged to purchase Public National Bank, if the cooperating banks would guarantee $1.2 million and the Gas Company, Houston Lighting & Power, Southwestern Bell, and Anderson Clayton would make additional contributions. Jones told the bankers that guaranty fund contributions were not only "patriotic acts, but good business as well," but still Farrar, McAshan, and Malone balked. Knowing Jones well, the bankers feared he would "ask for a little additional protection" when the "trade was closed," and he did try to squeeze more from each bank.

Finally, Jones roused Captain Baker at his home in Bass Rocks at two o'clock Tuesday morning, October 27, and "prevailed upon him to raise the South Texas' subscription." More important, Baker convinced McAshan and Malone that he stood behind the deal and that they should support it, too. By 3:00 a.m. frightened directors and officers awaiting their fate at Public National signed documents approving Jesse Jones's takeover of their bank. Later in the day, McAshan wrote Captain Baker that he realized allowing the banks to fail was not an option: "it was a really frightful thing to contemplate twenty-odd thousand of our fellow-citizens and countless thousands of others in the interior towns having their funds tied up by these failures."[4] Jones hoped to persuade Southern Pacific to provide $250,000 for the guaranty fund, but instead National Bank of Commerce, Second National Bank, Union National Bank, and South Texas Commercial National Bank each added $25,000 to their shares. In the end, the compliant contributors each received a refund of $4,500.

On Tuesday October 27, 1931, local papers delayed their morning editions so they could calmly announce that Houston National was operating under new management and that Public National was now part of Jesse Jones's National Bank of Commerce. The consortium had averted a run on the banks, and in the next few days, Jones wrote the depositors at Public National to explain that their money was now safe in "one of the strongest and largest financial institutions in the South." He also wrote the presidents of Chase National Bank, the Bank of America, and other New York investors to explain what Houston bankers, working together voluntarily, had accomplished. On October 29 Jones wrote Baker that his telephone call "gave us real courage after several days and nights of a very harrowing experience. I felt that none of us had a right not to stop the tragedy that would have followed our failing to do that which we did." Jones concluded his brief letter by saying "we want your assistance in getting [Southern Pacific] to come along with the rest of us."[5] How hard Baker tried to sway his longtime client is not recorded. Many believe that without the famous 2:00 a.m. telephone call, Jones would never have convinced McAshan, Farrar, and Malone to accept a deal that stabilized Houston's financial base but substantially increased the size of Jesse Jones's bank.

ALICE

Economic upheavals increased the importance of Captain Baker's ability to analyze problems and bring people together to develop creative solutions, but the disastrous business conditions did little to change the Baker family's domestic life. The generous couple continued to entertain friends of the Institute at The Oaks and to hold gala garden parties to benefit local charities. Captain and Mrs. Baker retired to Bass Rocks for several months every summer as they had done for many years and now welcomed their married children and a growing bevy of grandchildren. On September 23, 1931, as Edgar Odell Lovett was greeting the class of 1935 in Houston, Captain Baker and Alice "were reading [the matriculation address] about the hour you were delivering it." Robert S. Lovett, long referred to as Judge Lovett to honor his judicious demeanor, was a guest and "also had the pleasure of hearing me read it." In this chatty letter thanking Edgar Odell Lovett for sending him a copy of the speech, Captain Baker mentioned the delightful autumn weather, a visit with the Lovetts' son Alexander, and plans he and the Judge had for a ten-day motor trip through New England, New York, and Quebec.[6]

For ten years after the birth of Alice Baker Jones on September 30, 1915, the Bakers had eagerly awaited another grandchild. Finally, on November 13, 1925, Walter Browne Baker Jr. (Brownie) arrived, to the delight of his parents Adelaide Lovett and Browne Baker. Five years later, in a joyous eighteen months, five girls and boys who would be constant playmates and lifelong friends, joined their two older cousins. After thirteen years of happy married life marred only by their unfulfilled wish to have children, Jim and Bonner welcomed "their hearts desire," a son James A. Baker, III, to his carefully furnished nursery on April 28, 1930.[7] Known from that day forward to his family and friends as Jimmy, the new arrival

Captain and Mrs. Baker with Alice Jones and Brownie Baker, c. 1930. Private Collection.

was joined eighteen months later on November 6, 1931, by his sister Bonner Means. Between the siblings came Lovett Baker, the second son of Adelaide and Browne, born on September 21, 1930. Malcolm and Anita Baker's daughter Shirley hailed the new year on January 18, 1931, while Ruth and Preston Moore greeted their son Preston Jr. on August 7, 1931.

While her siblings were beginning their families, Alice was struggling with her marriage to Murray Jones, which dissolved by 1931, when she and young Alice were living with Captain and Mrs. Baker at The Oaks. Although a hard passage for everyone, Grandfather Baker could hardly contain the delight he felt to have Alice Jones, his "dear Sweet Child," in his home. Alice had finished eight years at Kinkaid School in June 1931 and was attending the Spence School in New York City. During Christmas vacation in 1931 she had made herself "agreeable to everyone about you, including the servants [who] always have words of commendation for your consideration for and kindness to them."[8] Alice Baker Jones returned home at a time when her mother's health had been declining. For many years Mrs. Baker had treated her high blood pressure through diet and lifestyle choices, and at this time her eyesight was beginning to fail. After their marriages, the Baker children had participated in their parents' civic and social activities; now Alice Baker Jones began to play a greater role in household management.

Since her marriage forty-nine years earlier, Alice Graham Baker had remained close to her three sisters, and each year the four affectionate women celebrated a reunion at one of their homes. In May 1932 the group gathered in Houston for their annual festivities. During the afternoon of Monday May 10, Mrs. Baker "appeared to be in the best of health" as she sat in the garden with her sisters and other family members. A few minutes after she went inside about 5:30 p.m., she was "stricken by a heart attack" and died that evening. Her death was a shock to family and friends, who eulogized her help to "those in poverty and distress." Her life "as a great civic leader . . . was an inspiration to all who knew her," and "she was the embodiment of Southern hospitality and graciousness."[9] Reverend Charles L. King of the First Presbyterian Church officiated at funeral services on Thursday afternoon at her home, and Alice was laid to rest in Glenwood Cemetery beside her beloved son Graham, with whom she had shared a birthday. Rice Institute and Baker's law firm closed for the day "as a mark of respect to Captain Baker during his bereavement." On her tombstone Captain Baker requested the well-known words of seventeenth-century English Bishop Jeremy Taylor: "A good wife is Heaven's last best gift to man—his gem of many virtues, his casket of jewels; her voice his sweet music, her smile his brightest day, her industry his surest wealth, her lips his faithful counselor." To her memory, he dedicated a garden at the Museum of Fine Arts of Houston and provided copies of six old master paintings to Sam Houston State Teachers College in Huntsville.[10]

Although the beautiful woman who looked youthful even as her hair turned a soft white was no more, her grieving husband decided to carry on traditions she had begun. On August 4, 1932, he wrote to Jim and Bonner to celebrate their anniversary. "One of my keenest pleasures now is to continue, as long as I can, her beautiful and unselfish customs. Accordingly . . . I hope you will accept as a gift from her and me" an enclosed check.[11] Christmas had long been special for the Baker family and for the families of their household employees. The Bakers supported a large domestic staff, often hiring Southern Pacific workers no longer able to toil in the rail yards to do household and gardening chores. At Christmas everyone gathered at the Baker home for carols, refreshments, and fun. Alice, the Captain, and the Baker children distributed gifts to all their guests, a custom continued by Alice's children and grandchildren after her death. Alice Baker Jones remained at The Oaks and served as her father's hostess and household manager until his death in 1941. Friends rallied his spirits, and his surviving sisters and sisters-in-law paid him long visits. One visitor in the spring of 1933 spoke warmly about the "delightful memory" of Captain Baker's hospitality and the privilege of being "drawn into the inner circle of such a family" of caring sons and daughters.[12] In his last decade Captain Baker lost no opportunity to invite his children and grandchildren to spend time with him at The Oaks.

After Alice's death, Captain Baker also introduced traditions of his own. On November 4, 1932, he wrote a lawyerly but fond letter to his children. He noted that his grandchildren had been "brought into pleasant contact with each other in the grounds of The Oaks" while their parents were all staying there for a few days. The happy experience made him realize "the importance of your children seeing more of each other and coming to know one another better as the years come and go." He and Alice decided they would like to set aside one afternoon each week as "Grandfather's Day," when "your little ones with their attendants will be free to spend the hours from two to six p.m. in the grounds and

Captain Baker with his grandson Preston Moore Jr. Private Collection.

Captain Baker with his son Jim (James A. Baker Jr.) and his grandson Jimmy (James A. Baker, III). Private Collection.

gardens of The Oaks." The thoughtful grandfather assured his children "there will be no obligation on any of the children to attend unless . . . they feel like doing so," and he emphasized, "it goes without saying that the parents are included in the invitation." After urging the children to wear their "everyday" clothes so they can "run and frolic with the greatest freedom," he concluded: "Beginning next Tuesday, the 8th, all of you will be welcome, and each Tuesday afternoon thereafter until further notice." His plan worked; the cousins remained lifelong friends.[13]

BAKER, BOTTS, ANDREWS & WHARTON

It was not just Captain Baker's family life that underwent change in the 1930s. His law firm, too, faced important decisions. On May 15, 1930, Judge Hiram Garwood, then sixty-six, passed from the legal scene. Frank Andrews, himself a noted scholar, praised the Judge as "the most scholarly and polished gentleman in all avenues of cultivated attainment" it had been his "good fortune to intimately know." Garwood, Andrews noted, "through the process of omnivorous reading and intelligent acquisition" became a great historian and a master of ancient and modern literature, a man who frequently delivered "an instructive and accurate lecture of the highest literary merit with the briefest preparation."[14] Garwood's death left a leadership gap at the firm that was difficult to fill, but with both Parker and Garwood now deceased, the senior partners decided to recognize the contributions of Jesse Andrews and Clarence Wharton and renamed the firm Baker, Botts, Andrews & Wharton, made official January 1, 1931.[15] Baker, now dean of the Houston bar, hosted the annual meeting of the Executive Committee of the American Bar Association when it met in Houston that year. As in former times, Houston lawyers and their wives feted the visitors warmly with elaborate banquets and a tea for the wives.[16] In December 1931 the Captain was elected president of the Houston Bar Association by four votes in a hotly contested race.[17]

Jesse Andrews, who came to Baker Botts in 1899, had for many years managed an office in Kansas City that handled a major firm client, the Long-Bell Lumber Company. Like Captain Baker, Andrews was an active businessman who served on the boards of several banks and other enterprises during his career, and like Baker, Andrews attracted clients for the Kansas City office. Clarence Wharton, who joined the partnership with Andrews in 1906, was a short, combative man whose fiery oratory held juries spellbound. He mentored younger men, was a real team player happy to take on any trial task, and had a good sense of humor. Despite maintaining a demanding trial docket for utility companies, railroads, and oil companies, Wharton published several history books, including a text used in Texas public schools and a five-volume history of the state. Wharton died in 1941, just months before Captain Baker; Andrews could not match Baker's sixty-four years but remained in harness until his death in 1961, a tenure of sixty-two years.

Considered a brilliant and capable lawyer, Jesse Andrews left a mixed legacy. He quickly took the senior position after Captain Baker died, and he enhanced Baker, Botts, Andrews & Wharton's national stature through friendship with Harry Truman and important political and business leaders in the Midwest. Yet he was not personally popular; he could be tough on his legal peers, even as he was kind to many social acquaintances. He was an indefatigable worker, clocking 30,000 miles of business travel one year, and he wrote the federal bankruptcy provisions that allowed his longtime client Long-Bell to weather the Depression and merge favorably with International Paper. Despite the wealth he brought to his law firm, his determination to run a satellite office in Kansas City became a real problem for Captain Baker and the senior partners in the depressed 1930s.

Long-Bell Lumber Company, headquartered in Kansas City, had been a client of Edwin B. Parker's since the early 1900s. Until he went to Washington in 1918, Parker visited Kansas City frequently, and Judge Garwood handled a number of trials for the company, which in 1915 was the largest lumber company in the United States. On January 24, 1918, Jesse Andrews made his first trip to Kansas City. Over the next forty years he developed a close relationship with the company, serving as an executive and director. At the company's fiftieth anniversary in 1925, Andrews hosted a dinner for one thousand guests that was broadcast by radio to mills in Kansas City, Dallas, Portland, and Oakland. That year Long-Bell was the largest lumber manufacturer in the world, with 128 lumber yards and 12 large mills that produced 800 million feet of lumber a year.

By 1919 Andrews had opened a satellite office of Baker, Botts, Parker & Garwood in Kansas City. The next year he moved his family there and began to build a staff that peaked at fifty-five lawyers. In 1922, Andrews tried to get his Houston partners to authorize a second satellite office near Kelso, Washington, where Long-Bell was building the town of Longview to house an enormous production plant, its workers, and their families. The partners would not consent to opening another office, but they did agree that Cornelius Lombardi, a young attorney recently sent to the Kansas City office, could go to Kelso to look after Long-Bell interests there.[18] In 1924, when Andrews mentioned increasing office expenses, he was told that Ralph Feagin, Walter Walne, Palmer Hutcheson, and Captain Baker had formed a committee to consider "ways and means of reducing the overhead expense of the firm."[19] Andrews must generate enough business to cover the Kansas City expenses.

The idea that Andrews was building a legal empire in Kansas City while simultaneously reaping benefits as a Houston partner was deemed "illogical" and was meeting a good deal of resistance in Houston by 1925. Parker felt Long-Bell would probably keep Baker, Botts, Andrews & Wharton as its legal counsel regardless of Andrews's place of residence. Baker accepted the satellite office only if the Kansas City operation did not drain assets from Houston. Armed with data comparing the costs of running the two offices, Wharton and Garwood expressed serious reservations; between 1921 and 1925, the firm had spent $41,000 supporting the office and had lost the benefit of Andrews's participation in Houston. Even Parker, despite his absences in Washington and his tenure with the Texas Company, stressed that branch offices destroyed a law firm's cohesiveness. Baker promised to tell Andrews that his partners could only justify keeping the office open if it were self-sustaining.[20] In a face-to-face meeting, Baker explained that the firm "needed strength at the top" and wanted Andrews to return to Houston. Andrews, of course, saw things differently: he was needed in Kansas City, and his work reflected well on the Houston firm, he was active in Kansas City civic life, his client base was expanding, and Long-Bell was a major source of fees for his law firm. Moreover, Andrews, who had articulated the concept of a depletion allowance as applied to timber lands, was building a national reputation as an expert on federal tax law. It was clear he liked being head of his legal fiefdom, which he continued to dominate for another decade. Baker reluctantly conceded to his wishes.

By 1935, his partners had lost patience with Andrews's position. Lumber prices fell during the Depression; Andrews had reorganized Long-Bell and guided it back "to solid financial ground" in 1932–1933, but his Houston partners demanded he choose between Kansas City and Houston. Andrews stalled all year, but at 11:00 p.m. December 31, 1935, Jesse

Andrews wired that he would return to Houston. The Kansas City office was reorganized as Lombardi and Robertson, while Andrews continued as general counsel to Long-Bell and in 1952 was elected chairman
of the board. In 1956 Long-Bell merged with International Paper Company. The firm's fee resulting from this merger was the largest received by
Baker Botts up to that time.[21]

PRACTICING LAW DURING THE DEPRESSION

Statistics compiled by Ralph Feagin to measure the progress of Baker,
Botts, Andrews & Wharton during the depressed 1930s show the firm
continued to grow even as revenues fell. Economic trials did not bring
any abatement in legal work. In 1929 Baker Botts was handling so much
business that Walter Hillman Walne, the de facto hiring partner for many
years, added eight attorneys to the firm's roster. On a trip to the Dallas-
Ft. Worth area, he persuaded four outstanding lawyers to move to Houston. Gaius Gannon and Francis Graham Coates, Alice Baker's nephew,
transferred as partners; Tom Martin Davis and William M. Ryan became
partners after the Depression waned. Walne also hired the three best
graduates from the University of Texas Law School and the firm's second
Yale Law School graduate, trial specialist Dillon Anderson. This team
joined their new colleagues in Houston only to witness the spectacular
crash of 1929.

Although the number of clients rose slightly in the 1930s, gross income fell from $750,000 in 1930 to $575,000 in 1931 and down to $525,000
in 1933, after which it began to grow steadily. Employees also increased:
in 1933 Baker Botts employed sixty people, half of them lawyers; in 1939,
ninety were on the payroll, forty-two of them lawyers. Partners' shares
rose between 1933 and 1935, then they went up and down through the
end of the decade, with a pullback in 1939 for all but the youngest men.
By 1938 offices had spread from the sixteenth to the seventeenth floor of
the Niels Esperson building. Miss Willie A. Rowell, grown formidable
in middle age, commanded her support staff from a glass-enclosed office that overlooked the receptionist and telephone operators and was
strategically placed near the offices of Captain Baker and the managing
partner.

Effects of economic depression were apparent not so much in the
quantity of work or in the number of lawyers kept busy as in the kinds

of cases they handled. In some respects Houston continued to prosper: despite overproduction and low prices, demand for oil stayed high; the port began to expand; and in 1937 building permits capped $25 million. The firm developed a significant patent practice and enlarged its oil industry clientele, but many clients now sought help on tax defaults and salary litigation or were victims of bankruptcy. Baker Botts helped companies refinance through the federal Reconstruction Finance Corporation run by Houstonian Jesse Jones, and they reorganized several businesses entirely. New Deal legislation generated legal battles to interpret the expanding body of laws regulating utility rates, controlling industry and agricultural products, overseeing securities and banking, outlining social security, and redefining bankruptcy. In several cases, Baker Botts helped local businesses spin off from large out-of-state holding companies and then became lead counsel for major independent corporations headquartered in Houston. As it had since its founding, the firm adapted its talents to the needs of the clients and managed to survive the severe economic conditions without terminating anyone's employment involuntarily.

Depression did stall those on the track to partnership. No new places opened between 1929 and 1940, although between 1930 and 1939, the firm hired eight attorneys who eventually attained partner rank. In January 1938 Captain Baker sent a memo to Managing Partner Ralph Feagin to compliment him on his forceful presentation of objectives for 1938. He then noted that "for some time . . . my activities in the office have been gradually diminishing and my outlook for this year for opportunities to render substantial service to the Firm is not encouraging." He next listed his several responsibilities as chairman of Rice Institute's trustees, of South Texas Commercial National, and of Guardian Trust as well as director of various companies. He noted he would like to travel or spend time abroad but concluded he would always be in his office during regular business hours when in town. Nonetheless, it was time, he had decided, to limit his share.[22] Records show that in 1936 Baker's partner share was $41,400, $48,000 in 1937, and $20,100 in 1938. In 1939 his share dipped to $17,100, and in 1941, the year of his death, he received $7,500 (January through August). Tom Martin Davis, who became a partner in 1940, believed that Baker cut back his share so Davis, William M. Ryan, and Dillon Anderson could join the firm. In those days, Davis recalled, "everybody had a percentage and whenever a partner came in, somebody had to give up a percentage. . . . Captain Baker was generous enough and thought enough of the firm and was that interested to give up all of his percentage to permit us to come in."[23]

Although he reduced his workload and decreased his share of the firm's net income, Captain Baker continued to advise his major clients, to maintain cordial relations with lawyers throughout the country, and to observe closely corporations like Westinghouse and Shell Oil to assess their potential for the firm.[24] He often invited lawyers and executives to stay at The Oaks when legal business called them to Houston and continued to host firm meetings in his home. Ralph Feagin cited Baker's compliance with office procedure in a long memo admonishing each lawyer to "record his time of arrival . . . and departure . . . and time out for lunch," so that client time could be correctly documented.[25] Baker's curiosity did not diminish with age. On March 6, 1940, Baker and two younger lawyers visited the Houston plant of their client, Continental Can Company, situated in the Industrial District at Canal Street and Navigation Boulevard. They "followed the [lithographed] cans through the machinery and conveyors from the insertion of the tin sheets to the several points of outlet of the finished product." The mechanical setup of the plant and the "high type of employees" impressed the visitors favorably.[26] At the regular firm meeting, held at his home on Thursday evening, October 24, 1940, Baker prepared an illuminating homily. In describing at length young Joseph C. Hutcheson III's work for Mrs. Jessie P. Keller, a divorcee, he not only praised a colleague but also showed how the story was important "as an illustration of what can be accomplished for your client by thoroughly ascertaining the facts going to establish the client's claim, and then pushing the litigation with vim and energy, with a clear understanding of the legal questions involved."[27]

In a rare interview, the media-shy Captain spoke at length with journalist Ed Kilman for a *Houston Sunday Post* magazine story published October 3, 1937. Headlined in red and blue, the article quoted the dean of Houston's bar, "Work hard, study and apply yourself closely, stay on the job, and—keep out of politics." Well illustrated with pictures of Baker in youth, in middle age, and during his distinguished later years, the article reprised the Captain's great triumphs—the defeat of Albert Patrick, the creation of Rice Institute, the growth of his law firm—and recorded his musings on the practice of law. His father, Baker told the reporter, kept him out of politics while he was alive, "and after that I've had good enough judgment to stay out." Seated casually behind his desk in shirt sleeves and suspenders, Baker was soft-spoken, quiet-mannered, "a remarkably well preserved and active man" but "rather stout, solid-looking with short gray hair, short gray mustache and eyes to match." Baker talked about his youth and grew enthusiastic about the Institute's football team. He explained the dilemma of enlarging the school: "with the growth of the school and the depression, with the reduction of interest rates and so on, while the principal of the estate has not decreased, it is becoming increasingly difficult to operate the school under the present income from the endowment. We ought to have an increase of the endowment so that the student body could be enlarged." He recalled his time reading law when Houston "was a muddy town of about 15,000 population and Galveston was the emporium of Texas." He then predicted Houston would double its population of 400,000 by the 1950s and declared, "In my opinion there is no place of greater opportunity in the country for lawyers—or anyone else, for that matter."[28]

Baker was certain Houston would prosper, and he convinced the directors of twelve banks to establish the Houston Community Trust in 1938. To make charitable trusts "more flexible," the Community Trust provided a mechanism to invest funds and distribute income "only for educational or charitable purposes." Individuals would place some portion of their estate in trusts overseen by the twelve member banks; the banks would invest funds and cooperate in a trustees' committee composed of an officer from each bank; but a special distribution committee of seven would "determine how the net income shall be disbursed." Institute Sociology Professor John W. Slaughter, formerly director of the Houston Community Chest and active in several nonprofit organizations, accepted Captain Baker's invitation to direct this new community foundation. James A. Baker Jr. served on the distribution committee.[29]

DEPRESSION YEARS AT THE INSTITUTE

Captain Baker's enthusiasm for Rice Institute never slowed. He invited young Baker Botts lawyers, family members, and friends to athletic events, lectures, and concerts; he marched in the academic procession at Commencement and entertained Institute dignitaries in his home and at his clubs. In 1931 when the commencement speaker failed, he stepped in at the last moment to detail the story of the Institute's founding. From time to time he addressed the students about the legal profession and the Institute's history and aspirations, and he continued to sit at high table in the faculty chamber. Year after year he toiled with city officials to share costs of road paving, utility installation, and area planning.[30]

As economic conditions soured in the late 1920s and early 1930s, Baker turned full attention to stabilizing the endowment and finding the income needed to allow the young institution to grow. Board minutes follow the trajectory of economic depression and recovery in Houston as large investors and Houston builders scrambled to survive the decline. In 1929–1930 Institute investments produced income of $733,890; slight decreases followed with a dip to $652,500 in 1932–1933. Income jumped to $712,000 in 1933–1934 but sank to a low of $616,284 two years later. In 1933 Business Manager Arthur Cohn revealed average interest on Rice investments had dropped from 6 to 4.5 percent as interest rates nationwide kept falling and Institute customers requested lower rates.[31] At the time of Baker's death in 1941, income had not recovered its 1929 high.[32]

Throughout the Depression, the Board had difficulty with borrowers who could not make timely payments and sought extensions or refinancing plans. Rather than lose the income altogether or foreclose on land of little use to the Institute, Baker worked with customers who made serious attempts to fulfill their obligations. He granted extensions and carried unpaid interest as "past due" in an effort to avoid foreclosing on borrowers he felt would survive. He also made fewer loans with real estate or a house as collateral.[33] The business office began providing lists of defaults at almost every Board meeting, and not until 1939 could the business manager report he had begun to resell defaulted properties.

Other sources of income also declined. Startled to discover student housing was filled only to 60 percent of capacity in 1933, Baker held informal discussions with the dean and business manager and concluded that beginning in 1933–1934 all men "registering for the first time will be expected to live in the residential halls on the campus for not less than one year."[34] The same year, several donors who had made five-year pledges to the Athletic Program fell behind in their payments or canceled their pledges altogether. Baker and the Board decided to advance money from the Institute's general fund to cover the delinquent payments, hoping donors would be able to fulfill their obligations when economic conditions improved.[35]

Even before the Depression's full effects curtailed growth, Baker and the other trustees had realized that they could not continue to rely on investment income and the handful of scholarships and lectureships given by friends in recent years. New proactive approaches would be needed if Rice were to fulfill its promised goals and expand its academic programs. On May 20, 1929, Captain Baker called a special Board meeting to discuss two funding proposals and to confirm that, after lengthy negotiations, the Institute had sold the remainder of its property on Louisiana Street to the Houston Independent School District for a school and playground.[36] First, the trustees heard from Estelle Sharp, who wished to discontinue funding lectures in Civics and Philanthropy and instead to donate property to the Institute to support a traveling fellowship for postdoctoral petroleum engineering candidates. After agreeing to establish the Walter B. Sharp Memorial Fund for Research in Pure and Applied Sciences (funded 1931), the Board welcomed Will Hogg.

Hogg submitted a plan he had discussed five days earlier with Edgar Odell Lovett to secure funding from the City of Houston for a period of ten years. "In view of the benefits conferred by the Institute upon the City"—the free advice professors provided civic projects, including the Museum of Fine Arts, the Houston Foundation, and the Planning Commission—the city should, in Hogg's view, provide funds for those Houston men and women who could not pay for board, books, and fees. The trustees asked Baker to appoint a committee (Baker, Lovett, and Will Rice) to confer with Hogg and refine the proposal.

Professor John W. Slaughter, executive secretary of the Houston Community Chest at the time, approached Captain Baker about Hogg's proposal. Slaughter wondered if accepting public funds was legal and was particularly concerned about political pressure on the Institute that would inevitably arise if Rice accepted public money. Pleased by Slaughter's interest, Baker asked him to investigate further the problems associated with accepting taxpayers' money and to prepare his report before the plan went to City Counsel in late 1929 or early 1930.[37] The Board also asked Hogg to proceed with his efforts to secure support for a Rice Memorial Endowment. In October 1929 Hogg purchased one of his leather-bound books, made famous in previous fund-raising efforts. He made a list of businesses and individuals owning real property assessed at $50,000 or more and began making calls. Three newspapers tacitly committed to Hogg's program and promised zealous endorsement.

Over eight hundred donors, including Captain Baker, President Lovett, Estelle Sharp, and Palmer Hutcheson, signed his book and pledged to champion his request to the city.

Shortly after his blitz, Will Hogg turned the project over to his brother Mike and a Protective Campaign Committee and departed for a trip around the world.[38] In September 1930 Will died following surgery while touring with his sister Ima in Baden-Baden.[39] Will's absence, Slaughter's concern about political problems inherent in public money, the sagging economy, and a nascent plan to create a publicly funded university affiliated with the Houston Independent School District Board of Education conspired to kill the proposal.[40] Will Hogg had not forgotten Rice, however. When executors probated his will, the public learned that he had bequeathed the Rice Student Loan Fund he had established in 1919 another $25,000; in fact, he had left similar amounts to student loan funds at every institution of higher learning in Texas. Rice finally received the bequest in February 1933.

Other friends came forward to expand the number of endowed fellowships, including the Samuel Fain Carter Fellowship, the Rockwell Fund, and the Texaco Fellowship in Chemistry. On a visit to Houston, probably in 1929, Robert S. Lovett told his old friends, Captain Baker and Edgar Odell Lovett, that he wanted to establish a memorial to his wife Lavinia Abercrombie Lovett to promote "the intelligence, gentleness, 'quietness and confidence,' manifested in diction of precision, dignity, and elegance" reminiscent of her legacy to Houston's cultural scene. President Lovett appointed a committee of fifteen colleagues to discuss scholarship and lectureship alternatives. The project stalled when Robert S. Lovett did not find it "convenient to provide the cash required" because "the financial earthquake has been so disturbing and upset so many plans that I have felt safer to wait until business conditions become more settled."[41] Before he died on June 20, 1932, Lovett provided a substantial bequest to Rice in his will. In 1933 Baker and the trustees tried a new approach to underwrite curriculum improvements when they created the Institute Fund for New Courses and called on individual subscribers to pledge $1,000 (six including Baker, William M. Rice II, and Jesse Jones) or $500 (fifteen supporters) each year for five years, payable semiannually.[42]

These gifts, though gratifying, could not make up for the loss in investment income, and Baker also considered new investment strategies. At first he hired his old friend Robert S. Lovett's son Robert A. Lovett of Brown Brothers Harriman to give the Institute access to New York's bond market. Brown Brothers analyzed the Institute's needs at the January 15, 1931, Board meeting and made numerous suggestions, but Baker was frustrated by the difficulty of doing business at long distance. By the spring of 1932, he was consulting George V. Rotan, whose brokerage business was headquartered in Houston. Rotan was a summer visitor to Bass Rocks and a close friend of the Baker family. He came to most Board meetings through the Depression years, made detailed reports, and guided the Board's investments in corporate and government bonds, even getting them to consider some carefully selected stocks by 1941.

Still, income barely covered expenses, and at a specially called meeting on June 2, 1932, Baker explained the Institute's budget crisis. Everyone but President Lovett was present, and the other members reluctantly resolved "because of the distressing economic conditions existing through the world," that Rice "in common with most if not all other similar educational institutions, and all business enterprises of every kind and character" must "reduce materially its operating expenses." To begin May 1, 1932 in the General Office and July 1, 1932 in the Educational Department, "total compensation of all on the payroll" would be reduced 10 percent, unless the individual made $100 or less a month. No one would receive less than $100 a month. Three days later, Dr. Lovett presented a petition from the faculty asking that married men on the faculty receiving $3,750 or less be given only a 5 percent reduction. The Board agreed.[43] These reductions remained in effect until the trustees restored salaries in June 1936.[44] Physics Department Chairman Harold A. Wilson requested that the Institute fulfill its salary contract with him for $8,000 per year, but he promised in writing that he would contribute 10 percent of his salary to the Physics Department and would use his donation to defray department expenses.[45] Baker wrote Lovett a reflective letter explaining the Board's "deliberate judgment, reached after careful consideration of every argument for and against" salary reduction. Noting that the Institute's capital structure had been reduced by nearly $1 million, that Rice alumni were neither numerous nor well-established, and that the charter forbade the Board from creating indebtedness, he explained that the Board had acted "most reluctantly and regretfully" with the hope that Institute employees would cheerfully make the sacrifice "in a great crisis like this, when every government in the world seems tottering to its fall."[46]

Two years after Baker had made the wrenching decision to cut salaries, he received a welcome telephone call from George Hamman on December 6, 1934. Hamman explained he was executor of Eugene Bender's estate, and Bender had bequeathed $200,000 to Rice, to be paid within five years of notification. Hamman said Bender wanted his executors to liquidate the estate at the "best values possible," and they would hope for a rising market before December 1939.[47] In December 1936 Baker believed the Institute's fortunes might be turning around at last when William Marsh Rice II stepped forward to increase the endowment with the largest donation since his uncle had created the Institute in 1891. In a handwritten letter on December 21, Will told his old friend Jim Baker that he was giving 10,000 shares of Reed Roller Bit Company stock to the endowment, that the gift's value was $320,000 and that the shares should produce annual income between $8,000 and $20,000. Baker emphasized the "magnitude and importance" of the donation, and Will Rice's fellow trustees spoke warmly of his "unwavering loyalty . . . and steadfast devotion," of his "wisdom" and "understanding" during nearly forty years. "The action is beyond all praise, and adequately to express its significance to the Rice Institute is beyond our powers," Baker told the *Houston Chronicle*. "This will certainly make it a merry Christmas for Rice," he smiled. With the generosity of individuals like William M. Rice II, Baker told the *Thresher*, the Institute could "look forward to the . . . future with a great deal of pleasure and confidence."[48]

The Board itself had undergone change in the mid-1930s. On July 10, 1934, Edward Andrew Peden, trustee since 1922, died, and Baker asked President Lovett and John Scott to draft resolutions expressing the Board's sorrow. His fellow trustees noted Peden's leadership skills, his "simple religious faith," and his desire to serve others. Characterized as gentle, kindly, and friendly "toward all conditions of men," Peden could "mix a little frivolity with [his] wise counsels" and steadfastly promoted the goals of the founder.[49] On March 21, 1935, the Board elected Robert Lee Blaffer to fill Peden's place. President of Humble Oil & Refining Company and a friend of the Baker family who spent his summers in Bass Rocks, Blaffer brought knowledge of Houston's petrochemical industry to Board investment discussions.[50]

During these years Baker called many special meetings to review budget demands and investing strategy, and he never ceased to study new ways to finance the Institute's programs and ensure its future.[51] In 1929 Baker asked Edgar Odell Lovett to explore ways Rice could require fees for various activities on campus without contravening the free tuition provision of William Marsh Rice's will. Through the Depression decade, Baker continued to investigate the issue of fees, tuition for out-of-state students, and possible amendments to the 1891 Charter to provide additional revenue. He also talked to business associates about the feasibility of oil and gas exploration on the Institute's Texas lands. By 1932 Arthur Cohn was meeting with Humble Oil & Refining Company, Shell Petroleum Corporation, and the Texas Company to discuss conducting geophysical surveys of Rice land in Waller County and elsewhere.[52]

In April 1941 Baker reported that he had asked Baker, Botts, Andrews & Wharton lawyer Dillon Anderson to see if the Institute could "secure some relief through the courts." Anderson had researched the possibility of charging tuition. He argued, and Baker agreed, that the facts justified action: Baker and Anderson found that if "the general object of the trust will be greatly hampered and in part defeated unless the change is made" and if "a strong and convincing showing" could be made that circumstances not anticipated at the time the trust was drawn had developed, then it would be possible to charge tuition without overturning the trust. In his last actions for Rice Institute, Baker sought permission to prepare for trial. Because the original charter was due to expire on May 18, 1941, he and Benjamin Botts Rice, secretary, signed a resolution asking the Texas secretary of state to extend the charter, pending resolution of the tuition matter.[53] Baker's death precluded further action, and Rice did not begin charging tuition until the fall of 1965.

When the economy began to improve in 1938, Dr. Lovett and the Board considered making major campus improvements for the first time in a decade. Lovett explained that Rice must hire three instructors and update its Mechanical Laboratory in order to meet national accreditation standards for university engineering programs. The Board authorized his proposals after lengthy discussion, and in July William Ward Watkin presented final plans for the needed improvements.[54] Rice alumni initiated the first public campaign undertaken by their alma mater, and four hundred contributors donated over $200,000 to build a new stadium. Again the Board asked Watkin to prepare plans and specifications.[55] Although the program was put on hold in 1939 because of war clouds gathering in Europe, the ability of alumni and friends to support Rice expansion encouraged the trustees.[56] In 1941 Baker asked Watkin to make an architectural study for a library and for Bender Hall, to be supported by the Bender bequest, and Lovett discussed a library project with Ralph Adams Cram.

Other positive actions cheered Baker's last years. Although the Institute struggled financially in the 1930s, its athletes excelled. Teams won conference championships in football, basketball, track, and golf—and the Cotton Bowl in 1938. By 1940 the Alumni Association, proud of its efforts to raise funds for a new stadium and for a memorial classroom building, appeared several times before the trustees to request a place on the Board for an alumni representative and to suggest that the alumni group and the trustees communicate more often and coordinate activities. Twenty-four classes had passed through the Sallyport by 1940, and the alumni now constituted an important support constituency. Since June 1939 Baker had been researching the issue and compiling bylaws of other institutions, and he assured the group's leaders the Board wanted to join other leading universities whose governing boards included alumni representatives. The next time a Board vacancy occurred, Baker promised, the trustees would consider alumni candidates.[57] In the last months of his life, Baker and Assistant Secretary Arthur Dwyer reviewed the forty-two endowment gifts that had been given to the Institute since its founding. Baker asked Dwyer to compile a complete record of each donation and make it available to the donors or to their representatives and to the trustees and president of the Institute at all times.[58]

END OF AN ERA

Baker continued to support Alice's settlement house initiative during the 1930s. In April 1932, after nearly fourteen years as part of the Houston Social Service Bureau, the settlement committee reestablished Alice Baker's original Houston Settlement Association as an independent nonprofit agency because it wanted to focus attention on community welfare service at Rusk, Parkside, and Bethlehem Settlements. Faced with municipal funding cuts and increasing demand for services, the Association turned to private citizens for support. Encouraged by her father, Alice Baker Jones agreed in 1934 to be cochairman of Friendship House, a new initiative located on Navigation Boulevard east of downtown. She enlisted volunteers from Palmer Memorial Church to organize clubs for mothers, children, and teenagers; recruited musicians from the Houston Symphony to develop a music program; and provided Thanksgiving and Christmas feasts for area residents.[59] On May 10, 1935, Captain Baker, Samuel Maurice McAshan, and William D. Cleveland incorporated the Ripley Foundation for Baker's longtime client Edith Hudson Ripley to protect the nearly $2 million legacy of her husband Daniel. Edith Ripley named Baker, McAshan, Cleveland, F. C. Proctor, William L. Clayton, and Herbert Godwin as foundation trustees and requested that, after her death, they create a memorial "that would benefit women and children." The Ripleys were longtime friends of the Baker family and held a huge block of shares in South Texas Commercial National Bank.

In 1938 William Cleveland and Herbert Godwin approached Settlement Association president Corinne Tsanoff to discuss ways the Edith and Daniel Ripley Foundation and the Association could work together. By May the Association board announced that the trustees of the Foundation would spend $200,000 to build, furnish, and maintain a large recreation and health center east of downtown. Dedicated on April 14, 1940, by Charles King, minister of the First Presbyterian Church, Ripley House transformed the Association's ability to serve Houston neighborhoods.[60] While the record does not explicitly outline Captain Baker's role in these discussions, the outcome suggests his heart and mind were engaged. Ripley House expanded his wife's pioneering initiative to address broad social issues, and the Ripley Foundation enabled his client to protect her heritage for the public good and thereby promote civic responsibility through her generosity, support that continues today.

Demonstrating his Texas roots, Captain Baker agreed in 1935–1936 to serve as one of eleven advisors to the San Jacinto Centennial Association, organized by Jesse Jones to raise funds for a monument celebrating the Texas Centennial in 1936,[61] but more and more, he turned his attention to his children and grandchildren. Alice Baker Jones proved a model hostess who welcomed her father's partners at their monthly meetings and set her lunch table with extra places so he could bring young lawyers home whenever he wished. She organized special events in The Oaks' extensive gardens to support civic causes, and she traveled with her father or accompanied him to Institute commencements, lectures, and receptions. In September 1936 Alice and her father represented the Institute at Harvard's Tercentenary Celebration.[62]

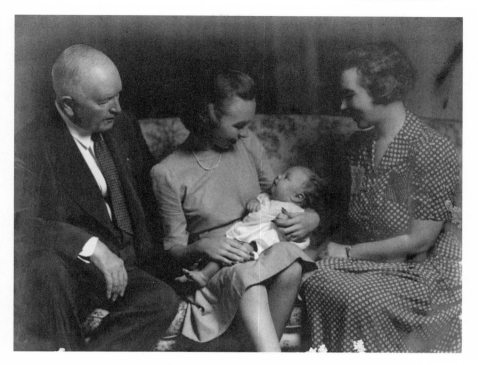

Four generations: Captain Baker, Alice Jones Meyers holding Alice Graham (Graeme) Meyers, Alice Baker Jones, 1940. Private Collection.

Grandfather Baker kept a fatherly eye on young Alice, who was pretty, petite, and popular with those youthful attorneys who haunted the house. The brave young men had to pass the Captain's scrutiny at the door and adhere strictly to his curfew demands—or they would not be invited to return. Young people held Captain Baker in respect and affection, but he could be stern and rather regal in his bearing when making a point. Even his grandsons found him "fearsome" and were not spared a whipping if they failed to be truthful about their pranks.[63] One handsome young man, attorney John Harris Meyers, was not deterred by the Captain's steely stare, and on June 10, 1938, he and young Alice Baker Jones married at Palmer Church. Her flower-filled wedding, in the Baker family tradition, preceded a festive reception in The Oaks' gardens. On April 30, 1940, the happy couple presented Captain Baker with his first great-grandchild, Alice Graham (Graeme) Meyers, a milestone her great-grandfather proudly announced in letters to friends.[64]

Alice Baker Jones also convened family dinners on Sunday, and the Captain's grandsons remember he teased the older children, asked them to recite or perform after the meal, rewarded them with small gifts, and bounced the babies on his knee. Three more grandchildren expanded the family after their grandmother's death: Browne's daughter Graeme (June 30, 1935) and Malcolm's sons Malcolm Jr. (February 5, 1936) and Stewart Addison (October 5, 1938). Sundays were lots of fun. Sometimes Alvin Billy, Captain Baker's chauffeur, would drive the grandsons and their grandfather downtown to look at the trains arriving at Union Station. Or the big black touring car might putter out to Rice Institute, where Grandfather Baker pointed out the trees. "Pick it up, Alvin, pick it up," he would command, tapping his cane on the glass that separated the driver from his rambunctious passengers. Captain Baker never learned to drive a car, and at least two of his sons were notoriously bad drivers, frequently caught in harmless but annoying fender benders.

Friends recall magical birthday parties for young grandchildren at The Oaks, where Captain Baker was the favorite guest. The honoree's mother placed small tables and chairs in the dark basement game room or, weather permitting, on the spacious lawn surrounding the house. The young guests, dressed in their party clothes, can still describe the linens and miniature flower arrangements, the surprise favors, and the specially molded ice cream. Often the party had a theme—exotic Japan was a favorite—and there were magic tricks, pony rides, and Captain Baker's riddles. Older grandchildren accompanied their parents and grandfather in a special observation car hitched to a Sunset Lines train that would take them to Texas A&M football games at Thanksgiving or to out-of-town Rice games during the fall. Six-year-old Preston Moore Jr. sailed on the *Gripsholm* for a Scandinavian Cruise with his grandfather, parents, Auntie Alice, and Cousin Alice Baker Jones in July and August 1937, the last voyage Captain Baker made to Europe.[65]

As war shadows fell across Europe and his eightieth birthday passed, Captain Baker acknowledged to his daughter Alice, "Life is, as we know, uncertain." In the last years of his life, Baker maintained his usual office routine and was impatient if his sons offered a helping hand as he descended from his car or climbed the stairs, but he also prepared papers for each child that clarified his estate plan, and he corresponded with relatives about family genealogy.[66] Captain Baker viewed his sixty-year legal and banking career as an enterprise undertaken for the benefit of his family. Like his own parents, he wanted to give his children a loving home and to provide the best education available; like the Judge and Rowena, Captain Baker hoped his children's worlds would reach beyond Houston's horizon, so he sent them to schools in the Northeast and to study or travel in Europe. Having built his career on his father's solid foundation, Captain Baker launched his sons from the platform he had prepared. Time and again his comments and actions reflect a "policy . . . to distribute his estate equitably": each child received the same monetary gift for a wedding trip; each had help purchasing a family home. During his lifetime, Captain Baker began to equalize cash advances to his children and to distribute his interest in Graham Realty, his stock in Guardian Trust, and his other assets so that his children could enjoy the benefits of the family's good fortune during his lifetime and, undoubtedly, so they could benefit from his astute understanding of the nation's evolving tax and estate laws.

Some family stories, if known to him, Captain Baker never shared with his children and grandchildren. His cousin Andy (Andrew Gabriel), born in Huntsville in 1864 to Gabriel and Julia Pippin Baker, was a bachelor who frequently visited the Bakers in Houston and was buried in the Glenwood family plot after his death in January 1924. As a young man Andy had a relationship with a freedwoman, Emma Curtis. In an era when racial mixing was banned by white Texans and feared by blacks, neither family approved. Their son Jesse Baker married Fannie Willis and was the father of eleven children. One of these children, Herbert, and his wife Mackie lived at The Oaks, where Mackie worked as a cook for twenty years. At her funeral in May 1940 Captain Baker gave a "heart-touching eulogy," so moving that a reporter reproduced it in full the following day: "My Friends," the Captain began, "We are gathered here this evening to . . . pay tribute of affection to one, whom to know was to admire and love. . . . Mackie Baker . . . was a patient soul . . . diligent and faithful in the performance of her duties." She "loved my children with a devotion almost equal to a mother's love. . . . Her spirit . . . has gone to join those of our friends and loved ones who have already passed on; my son Graham . . . my faithful wife. . . . May we meet them again in the sweet bye and bye."[67]

1941

In February 1940 Jim Baker was in his father's thoughts "continuously, morning, noon and night" as he underwent a major operation at Union Memorial Hospital in Baltimore. Typical of "naturally healthy, husky people" who "have never learned how to be sick," Jim was anxious to leave the hospital and return to his office immediately, but his father admonished him strongly to obey his doctor. Captain Baker was "continuously in a state of uncertainty" about his son but delighted to have the company of Jimmy and Bonner Means, who came to live with their grandfather and Auntie Alice during their father's ordeal. Alice reported that the well-behaved children were captivating, that she "let them do everything they wish," and that their grandfather was "in great spirits" in their company.[68] Captain Baker told his son he had "never known two more interesting, intelligent and well-behaved children" who were "no trouble whatever" despite the terrible cold weather and a widespread flu epidemic that prevented several members of his household crew and Baker Botts's staff from working.[69] His delight in his grandchildren contrasted with the sober daily reports from Europe.

Realizing that war was once again threatening his Institute, Baker reconsidered the investment strategy for endowment funds and rented much of the Louisiana timberlands to the army for war maneuvers (April–September 1940). He also began disheartening talks with Edgar Odell Lovett. Thirty-three years had passed since the trustees called Lovett to build Rice Institute, and the president was approaching his seventieth birthday. He believed it was time to pass the burden of leadership to a younger man and took up the subject of his retirement "individually and collectively" with the trustees. After "wrestling with the problem" for some time, the trustees reluctantly accepted their friend's request that he be allowed to resign. They applauded his suggestion that he continue to perform his administrative responsibilities until the Board could find a successor and agreed he should remain on the Board of trustees for as long as he wished. With many expressions of gratitude and regret on both sides, the trustees praised Lovett's "wise counsel and sage advice so frankly and freely given," and placed the announcement of his retirement in the press on May 18, 1941.[70] A few days later, Captain Baker told a *Thresher* reporter that the Board would contact and interview "a great number of" candidates during the summer. He intimated the replacement would be "a man less than forty years of age" and told the student interviewer he would announce the next president as soon as a choice had been made, "were it to be four, six, eight, or twelve months hence."[71] Clearly Baker anticipated a busy summer of hard work, but his death in August and the nation's declaration of war in December kept Lovett in harness until physicist William Vermillion Houston from California Institute of Technology accepted the Board's invitation to become the Institute's second president in January 1946.

Leadership at Baker, Botts, Andrews & Wharton was also changing. On May 1, 1941, Clarence Wharton, age sixty-eight, died. Remembered by colleagues for his "unfailing wit and endless repartee," his prodigious energy, and his kindly help, Wharton had, for forty years, been the firm's preeminent trial lawyer, feared "as the most dangerous adversary" in trial or appellate court. The printed briefs of his cases on appeal filled seventy volumes. Wharton had also played a critical leadership role within the firm, counseling clients about business policy, public relations, and matters of law. "Lots of men have been great. Mighty few have been funny, too," remarked one colleague. Wharton, he continued, "was both and while the world at large will remember his greatness, those of us who knew him well will treasure his memory even more highly for the way he made our lives lighter and gave us laughter with our work."[72] A "brilliant, busy lawyer, advocate and counselor, he amazed his closest associates" because he was also a fine humanitarian who amassed "the greatest library on Texas history in the world." With Wharton's death, Jesse Andrews took the lead as senior partner.

Through the spring of 1941, Captain Baker maintained his usual schedule. On May 8 and June 7 he hosted long meetings of the Baker Botts partners at The Oaks. As he had done every year since 1916, Baker participated in the Institute's June commencement exercises. On Sunday June 8, the Captain was host at a luncheon for the baccalaureate and commencement speakers at the Houston Country Club and attended a large dinner at Cohen House with guests, faculty, and Board members. On Monday morning, June 9, at 8:30 a.m., he called at the Warwick Hotel to escort Johns Hopkins President Isaiah Bowman, the honored speaker, to the campus, and he entertained him and other dignitaries at The Oaks for luncheon afterwards. Adelaide Lovett Baker took Dr. Bowman to an afternoon reception and stood in the receiving line beside her father and sister-in-law Alice Baker Jones, who acted for Captain Baker.

On June 10, 1941, Captain Baker wrote his last letter—to eleven-year-old Jimmy, who was away at Camp Rio Vista in Ingram, Texas. After thanking his young grandson for writing and congratulating him for passing his swimming test, the fond grandfather offered some advice similar to words he had received more than sixty years before from his father. "You must mingle freely with your companions," he wrote, "learn to know all of them intimately, sufficiently so to call each by his first name, where they live . . . take good care of yourself, don't eat too much, nor play too hard, but do everything within reason, necessary or desirable to improve your physical condition, and come home fully prepared to continue your studies here." That day Captain Baker fell ill.[73] On August 2, 1941, this deeply respected elder statesman died at his home, amidst the family he treasured.

EPILOGUE

The Legacy

NEARLY ONE THOUSAND RELATIVES, friends, partners, business associates, and citizens "from every walk of life" crowded into The Oaks or filled the green lawns surrounding the house when Dr. Charles L. King, pastor of the First Presbyterian Church, began his simple service for Captain James A. Baker at 5:00 p.m. on Sunday, August 3, 1941. Respectful of Baker's request, Dr. King read a Bible chapter and led the mourners in a song and prayer.[1] Standing by the casket covered with brilliant red roses were his three sons, Jim, Browne, and Malcolm, his two daughters, Alice and Ruth, his sisters Minnie Parish of Huntsville and Anna B. Thompson of Ft. Worth, and his ten grandchildren and one great-granddaughter. Eight nephews—Nettie's sons Frank, Bruce, and Baker Duncan, Minnie's son Alvis Parish, Anna B.'s sons George and Beverly Thompson, and Alice's nephews Frank Coates and Ed Stewart—bore the casket from the house. Six carloads of flowers and eleven family cars led a procession that was two miles long and required six police officers to control traffic.

When the mourners reached Glenwood Cemetery they found the family plot already covered with flowers. There beside his wife and his son, and with his brother Robert (1867–1939) and his cousin Andrew Gabriel (1864–1924) nearby, mourners laid this civic icon and family patriarch to rest. His family later placed a marker that read: "Citizen, lawyer, husband and father, friend, the record is well written and on memory's altar will ever glow a wealth of love and affection for one who through life was loyal to every trust, and measured up to the full stature of man."[2]

Captain Baker signed his last testament on June 14, 1941, and named his sons Jim and Browne executors; in his final written words, he urged all his children to cooperate "with each other in that spirit of loyalty and affection which should always characterize the relations between brothers and sisters." His executors filed the document for probate in mid-August, and Houstonians learned Captain Baker had bequeathed his home to Rice Institute. If the Institute did not turn The Oaks into a residence for its president, then Baker requested that the trustees sell the property and endow the Jas. A. Baker and Alice Graham Baker Bequest. Baker's will further stipulated that the trustees use the bequest's income for student scholarships or fellowships and for faculty salaries. The remainder of the estate, valued in December 1941 at $1.6 million, was divided evenly among Baker's five children after his executors had funded small memorials to each of his domestic employees, thoughtful gifts to his sisters, and modest trusts for each child and grandchild.[3] The Institute trustees preferred Captain Baker's second option, sold The Oaks to the M. D. Anderson Foundation for $62,500 on May 16, 1942, and established the Baker bequest. The Foundation launched Houston's first cancer research hospital in the estate's buildings.[4]

Friends, associates, and those whose lives Captain Baker had touched realized the magnitude of their loss. With "profound wisdom and unfailing judgment," Baker had labored tirelessly for Houston "during the city's most fruitful period of expansion, toward the perfection of the city," whose fortunes he had linked with his own.[5] Remembered as "kindly in his nature, democratic in his manner," many agreed "no other citizen" was held in "deeper respect. The closing of his rich career of service and leadership, after a period of three score years, leaves a vacancy in the life of this community that will not soon be filled."[6] An editorial writer praised the Captain's forceful character and powerful influence; Houston, he believed, "would never have been the city it is without him, and it probably will never outgrow his influence."[7]

The Captain's children sent telegrams, wrote notes, and placed telephone calls to dozens of friends. For two weeks they kept a list of visitors who called at The Oaks to comfort the family, and three volumes contain the stream of letters from mourners, who spoke often of the dead man's generosity, kindliness, and consideration for others. Alvis Parish told his cousin Alice, "Uncle Jimmie was my and Mother's constant

pilot. Whatever I have attained in my professional and other life, he de-
serves . . . the full credit. . . . Never a word of censure; never a moment
of anger; but always with infinite patience, and an understanding sym-
pathy with the problems of youth and young men, did he meet me and
help me to overcome and solve my problems."[8] Baker, Botts, Andrews &
Wharton, the Houston Bar Association, the trustees of Rice Institute,
the directors of the South Texas Commercial National Bank and Guardian Trust, the Texas Philosophical Society, the Chamber of Commerce,
and other associations proudly memorialized their affiliation with their
distinguished colleague in formal commemorative essays.

Noting feelings of "irreparable loss," the trustees of Rice Institute remembered their only leader "exhibited those qualities which marked all
the relationships of his long and distinguished career, namely, courage,
diplomacy, humor, sound judgment, and business intuition." Trustees,
faculty, and students all considered him a "venerable friend" because
"he shared fully their ambitions, their enthusiasms, their successes, and
their defeats."[9] President Lovett gave a short statement to the press expressing "an inconsolable sense of personal loss." Never, Lovett said, had
he "known [Baker's] equal as a trust officer."[10] James Baker Jr., speaking
for the family, assured President Lovett his testimonial expressed their
"Dad's hopes and wishes" for the Institute. Their father, wrote his son,
had "found much happiness in his service" to Rice because of its "steady
growth and development" as a national university.[11]

Jesse Andrews called frequently to ask about Captain Baker during
his last illness and sent flowers for the service. Jim expressed the family's
"grateful appreciation" and told his father's successor as senior partner
that there was no one for whom his father "had greater respect and more
affectionate personal regard." Andrews and the other Baker Botts partners asked Fifth Circuit Court of Appeals Judge Joseph C. Hutcheson Jr.
and a committee of ten members of the Harris County Bar Association
to express the legal community's admiration in resolutions on Captain
Baker's life and service. At 10:30 a.m. on October 17, 1941, their eulogy
was presented to the Supreme Court of Texas, and a short version was
reprised in the *Philosophical Society of Texas Proceedings* for that year. The
lengthy comments noted that "Captain Baker's was no commonplace
life." Baker was "rarely endowed to make the most of the great transi-
tions in which the old South became the new." The son and father of

lawyers, Baker was "essentially the advocate who made his client's cause his own.... Every aspect of his long and distinguished career was informed, directed and dominated by his attainments in and his devotion to the law." The resolutions noted that Baker was "as well known and respected in the financial and professional centers of the country as he was at home" and that he brought energy, imagination, vigor, strength, and balanced judgment to all his endeavors.[12]

*   *   *

In the early twentieth century three men brought advanced education at the highest level to Houston and recognized the centrality of knowledge to the economic life of a great city: William Marsh Rice, James Addison Baker, and Edgar Odell Lovett. Three men created the city's first modern law firm and realized the role law played in developing the economy and resolving civic problems: James Addison Baker, Robert Scott Lovett, and Edwin Brewington Parker. Three men imagined the great city Houston could become and built institutions to enhance the quality of urban life: James Addison Baker, William Clifford Hogg, and Jesse Holman Jones. Many Houstonians amassed greater fortunes, but few built as many successful partnerships as did Captain Baker.

In his long life he did not write down a philosophy of law, business, or education, and he never sought power through elective or appointive office. In a small city where individual, family, and community interests were entwined in interlocking relationships, Baker formed partnerships that brought him personal fulfillment and the admiration of his peers. In partnership with Edgar Odell Lovett, he laid a firm foundation for Rice University; in partnership with outstanding lawyers, he built an enduring law firm; in partnership with talented entrepreneurs, he nurtured banks, real estate ventures, and businesses vital to the city's life; and in partnership with his loving and beloved wife, he created a family whose commitment to community life has endured for four generations.

Leadership came naturally to Captain Baker. He grew up in an affectionate household with ambitious parents who imparted high standards and expected their children to excel. Rowena and Judge Baker helped their son set and achieve goals, and by example they instilled a strict moral code and a strong work ethic that never abated. They stimulated his inquisitive mind, channeled his high energy into positive action, and trained him to assume responsibility. Their belief in his abilities made him self-confident, self-assured, and emotionally secure. The young Baker eagerly followed his father to Houston and to a career in the law. At an early age the Captain inspired trust. He quickly showed William Marsh Rice and older men he understood economic and legal issues, was dependable, and could get things done. As he matured, Baker demonstrated good judgment of people and a sensitivity to his surroundings that enabled him to grasp opportunity. Personal setbacks—ill health and the loss of his son—made him resilient and determined. He was broad-minded and took the long view when making decisions.

A deliberate, logical thinker of unquestioned integrity, he was also charming, persuasive, and credible. He developed a wide acquaintance that provided access for his clients to partners across the country. He recognized talent and enabled younger men because he listened and probed and showed them respect. Although there is considerable evidence his viewpoint frequently prevailed, peers did not feel he forced his ideas on them. Some competitors resented his success, but he refused to recognize enemies. Baker had the instincts of a consummate back-room politician who favored a pragmatic approach. He knew the critical players in business and government circles and helped adversaries find common ground to resolve differences and achieve goals. Baker took a keen interest in public affairs, but his name, as one editor recalled, "resounded less often in public places than in the smaller halls where leadership performed its vital roles."[13] Usually unflappable, he restrained his temper— "unless he wished to explode" to carry his point.[14]

Captain Baker lived in an era when loyalty to friends and family, courtesy to others, and duty to community defined a successful life. He demanded excellence because he wanted to do his best for those who relied on him. Entrusted by William Marsh Rice to create a center for the advancement of literature, science, and art, he stayed in harness because he considered it was his duty to carry out the client's trust. Like his parents, Captain Baker believed, "The more you have, the more you have to give. And the more you give, the more you will grow."[15] He paved a path for family members because he wanted to guide them as his parents had guided him. His was a transformational and inspirational life: he steered his banks, his law firm, his businesses, and the Institute toward success, and he recruited and trained the next generation of leaders. All his life

Captain Baker worked hard to make every opportunity presented to him succeed; he studied carefully the problems he was asked to resolve; he stayed on the job until it was done; and he kept out of politics. By following the advice he gave to others, the Captain secured the respect and trust of contemporaries, who "held him in great admiration and deep affection."[16]

Appendix A

CHRONOLOGY OF CAPTAIN BAKER'S LIFE

1821	Mar. 3	James Addison Baker born in Alabama
1828	Apr. 8	Rowena Crawford born in Alabama
1835–1836		Pleasant and Ephraim Gray found Huntsville, Texas
1836–1837		Augustus Chapman and John Kirby Allen found Houston, Texas
1837	May	Col. William Fairfax Gray begins practice of law
1853	Sept. 27	Rowena Crawford and James Addison Baker marry
1855	Mar. 14	Beverly Crawford Baker born (d. Jun. 13, 1856)
1857	Jan. 10	James Addison (Jimmie) Baker born in Huntsville
1858	May 13	Mary Susan (Minnie) Baker born in Huntsville (d. Jun. 26, 1947)
1860	Sept. 13	Anna Bland Baker born (d. Dec. 20, 1952)
1861	Oct.	James Addison Baker enlists as private in Confederate Army (6-month tour Oct. 1861–Mar. 1862)
1862	Mar. 10	James Addison Baker elected judge, 7th District Court
1863	Jan. 26	Jane and Jeanette ("Nettie") Baker born (Jane d. in infancy; Jeanette d. Dec. 15, 1920)
1864	Oct. 18	Alice Graham born in Waco
1865	Jun.	Judge Baker removed from court by Reconstruction Government
1867	Jul. 27	Robert Lee Baker born (d. Feb. 2, 1939)
1870	HOUSTON POPULATION: 9,382 (3rd largest city in Texas)	
		Houston Bar Association founded; Peter Gray, first president
1872		Judge Baker, Peter Gray, and Walter Browne Botts form Gray, Botts & Baker law firm in Houston

1874	Fall	Cadet James A. Baker at Texas Military Institute
1875		Law firm renamed Baker & Botts
1876	Sept.	Baker family moves to Houston, 1104 San Jacinto at Lamar
1877	Spring	Cadet Baker graduates from Texas Military Institute
	Dec. 1	James A. Baker begins reading law with Judge Baker
1879	Aug.	James A. Baker Captain Houston Light Guard (year appointment)
	Oct. 7	Rowena Crawford Baker dies
	Dec.	Captain Baker admitted to practice law; joins Houston Bar Association
1880		HOUSTON POPULATION: 16,512
1881	Jul. 1	Baker, Botts & Baker formed, Captain Baker junior partner
	Jul. 14	Anna Bland McRobert Crawford dies
1882		Captain Baker helps organize Texas Bar Association
1883	Jan. 10	Captain Baker marries Alice Graham of Waco
	Oct. 18	Frank Graham Baker born
1884	May	Jane Saxton Baker Croft Cobb dies
		Captain Baker secures Houston Electric Light & Power franchise
1886	Jun. 10	Captain Baker and others found Commercial National Bank
1887	May 13	Alice Graham Baker born (d. Mar. 26, 1978)
		Captain Baker, vice president, Texas Rolling Mills Corp.
1890		HOUSTON POPULATION: 27,557
		Captain Baker, president, Texas Rolling Mills Corp.
1891	May 13–19	William Marsh Rice establishes trust; charter for Institute for the Advancement of Literature, Science, and Art
1891–1941		Captain Baker, chairman, Rice Institute Board
1892	Nov. 3	James A. Baker Jr. born (d. May 21, 1973)

		Captain Baker, founder, director, president Houston Abstract Co.
1893	Jan. 1	Baker, Botts, Baker & Lovett
	Mar.	Captain Baker writes charter for DePelchin Faith Home Association; Alice Baker volunteers
1894	Mar. 7	Col. Walter Browne Botts dies
		Captain Baker, president, Citizens Electric Light & Power; director, Houston Gas Light Co.; founding member, Houston Club
1895		Captain Baker, founder, Houston Business League
1896–1912		Captain Baker, director, Commercial National Bank
1896	Jul. 24	Elizabeth Baldwin (Mrs. William Marsh) Rice dies
	Sept.–1900	Litigation regarding Mrs. Rice's last testament
	Sept.	Captain Baker writes will for William Marsh Rice
1897		Captain Baker, vice president, Commercial National Bank
	Feb. 23	Judge Baker dies
1898		Baker family moves to 1416 Main Street
1900	HOUSTON POPULATION: 44,633	
	Jan. 23	Walter Browne Baker born (d. Nov. 17, 1968)
	Sept. 8	Hurricane decimates Galveston
	Sept. 23	William Marsh Rice murdered
	Sept. 23–1910	Litigation surrounding Rice's murder and estate
1901	Jan. 10	Spindletop inaugurates Texas oil industry
1902	Feb. 12	Graham Baker dies of influenza at the Hill School
	Jun. 27	NY Surrogate Court admits 1896 will of William Marsh Rice to probate
1903		Captain Baker helps Glenwood Cemetery reorganize
1904	Mar. 22	Captain Baker and friends found Houston Golf Club
	Apr. 29	NY Court directs distribution of William Marsh Rice estate in NY

	May 11	1896 will of William Marsh Rice admitted to probate in Texas
	Sept. 9	Ruth Graham Baker born (d. Aug. 11, 1982)
	to 1916	Captain Baker on Executive Committee of Glenwood
1906	to 1908	Captain Baker assists YMCA fund drive
	Feb. 18	Malcolm Graham Baker born (d. Mar. 9, 1994)
	Apr.	Captain Baker elected vice president, Texas Golf Association
1907	Jan. 9	Captain Baker names Rice Institute Search Committee for Academic Head
	Feb.	Alice Baker launches Houston settlement house movement
	to 1918	Alice Baker, president, Houston Settlement Association
		Captain Baker, president, Houston Industrial Club
		Captain Baker and partners develop Woodland Heights
	Nov.	Daughter Alice Queen of No-Tsu-Oh Festival
1908	Jan. 18	Edgar Odell Lovett accepts call to lead Rice Institute
		Captain Baker, founding member, Houston Country Club
	Jul. 24	Edgar Odell Lovett departs for global tour
	Summer	Captain Baker and Will Rice amass campus land
	Aug. 4	Houston Country Club founded; Captain Baker, member 30
1909	May	Edgar Odell Lovett returns from global tour
	May 8	Edgar Odell Lovett announces Institute site selection
	Sept.	Trustees hire Cram, Goodhue & Ferguson to design campus
		Alice Baker joins Chautauqua
	Nov.	Captain Baker is King Nottoc at No-Tsu-Oh Festival

1910		HOUSTON POPULATION: 78,800
		Alice Baker, president, First Presbyterian Church Westminster Guild
		Captain Baker, vice president, Texas Trust (1910–1911)
		Houston Chamber of Commerce established
	Jun. 1	Edgar Odell Lovett elected to Institute Board
	Jun.	Campus construction begins
1911	Jan. 25	Alice Baker hosts first meeting of Girls Musical Club; Young Alice elected first president
	Feb.	Rice-Land Lumber Co. organized; proceeds fund buildings
	Mar. 11	Cornerstone laid for Administration Building
		Captain Baker on Houston Music Festival Association board
		Bakers purchase Rockhaven, Bass Rocks, Gloucester, MA
	Sept. to 1915	James Baker Jr. attends Princeton
	Nov. 21	Alice Baker marries Murray Brashear Jones
		Captain Baker, president, Houston Gas Co.; vice president, Bankers Trust (1911–1912)
1912	Jan.	Commercial National Bank and South Texas National Bank merge to form South Texas Commercial National Bank; Captain Baker, director (1912–1941), vice president (1913–1914)
	Sept. 23	First class matriculates at Rice Institute
	Oct. 10–12	Academic Festival to inaugurate Rice Institute
		Houston Symphony Association founded; Bakers sponsors
1914		Houston Ship Channel opens
	to 1922	Captain Baker, president, STCNB
1915–1918		Captain and Mrs. Baker advocate City Recreation Dept.
1915		Captain Baker purchases 22 Courtlandt Place for daughter Alice Jones

	Sept. 30	First grandchild Alice Baker Jones born (d. May 15, 2008)
		Captain Baker, president, Houston Gas & Fuel; receiver, I&GN Railway
1916–1941		Captain Baker, president, Glenwood Association
1917	May	Captain Baker helps city create Camp Logan, World War I training camp
	Aug. 4	James A. Baker Jr. and Bonner Means marry
	Aug.–1919	Lt. James A. Baker Jr. war service, San Antonio, France
		Captain Baker, Clarence Malone et al. found Guardian Trust; Captain Baker, briefly president, then chairman until 1941
1918	Jan.–Feb.	Rice Institute student protests
	Jun. 12	Captain and Mrs. Baker establish Graham Baker Studentship at Rice Institute to reward top student
	Jun.	Lt. James A. Baker Jr. shipped to the Western Front
		Alice, volunteer chair, Houston Social Service Bureau Settlement and Social Service Department
	Summer	Alice named to YWCA National War Work Council; chairman, local council
	Nov.	Captain Baker, member, Harris County Patriotic League
1919		James A. Baker Jr. begins his career at Baker Botts
1920	HOUSTON POPULATION: 138,276	
	Jan.	Baker Botts Office Review inaugurated
	May	Captain Baker on YWCA Advisory Finance Committee to build YWCA and Blue Triangle (for African American citizens) branches
	Fall	Rice Field House opens
		Autry House dedicated as first student center
1922		Captain Baker and James A. Baker Jr. begin Broadacres
	Dec. 1	Bakers rent The Oaks from Edwin B. Parker

	Dec. 23	Walter Browne Baker marries Adelaide Lovett
1923		Bakers begin generous support of Community Chest
	Jul. 14	Bakers purchase The Oaks from Edwin B. Parker
1924		Captain Baker helps Hogg family organize Memorial Park
	Apr.	Captain and Mrs. Baker make major donation to Museum of Fine Arts of Houston building drive
	Fall	Ruth Baker studies in Paris
	Sept.	Captain Baker and Robert S. Lovett visit WWI battlefields
1925		Adelaide Lovett Baker founds Junior League of Houston
	Apr.	Chemistry Building opens
	Nov. 13	Walter Browne ("Brownie") Baker Jr. born (d. Aug. 30, 1994)
	Dec. 31	Edwin B. Parker resigns from Baker Botts
1926	Oct. 26	Ruth Baker marries Preston Moore
	to 1928	James A. Baker Jr. and Bonner Means Baker build home at 1216 Bissonnet
1927	to 1941	Captain Baker, chairman, STCNB
		Captain Baker on YMCA expansion committee; secures Rice Institute loan for new building
		Baker Botts moves to the Esperson Building
1928	Nov.	Cohen House faculty club opens
		Phi Beta Kappa chapter approved
1929		Alice Baker leads fund drive for the Houston Tubercular Hospital, dedicated Oct. 26, 1930
	Feb.	Captain Baker initiates fund drive to support Physical Education Department at Rice
	Mar.	Captain Baker named first honorary member of Rice's Phi Beta Kappa chapter
	Oct. 30	Edwin B. Parker dies in Washington, DC
	Nov. 15	Malcolm Baker marries Anita Dee Stewart
1930	HOUSTON POPULATION: 292,352	
	Apr. 28	James A. (Jimmy) Baker, III born

	May 15	Hiram Garwood dies
	Jun. 8	Memorial Statue of William Marsh Rice dedicated
	Sept. 21	Lovett Baker born (d. Feb. 7, 2010)
1931	Jan. 1	Firm becomes Baker, Botts, Andrews & Wharton
	Jan. 18	Shirley Baker born (d. June 8, 1993)
	Jun.	Captain Baker delivers Commencement Address at Rice
	Aug. 7	Preston Moore Jr. born
	Oct.	Houston Bank Crisis; 2:00 a.m. phone call to Captain Baker
	Nov. 6	Bonner Means Baker born
	Dec. 31	Captain Baker elected president, Houston Bar Association
1932	May 10	Alice Baker dies
	Jun. 20	Robert S. Lovett dies
1934	to 1935	Captain Baker one of eleven advisers to the San Jacinto Centennial Association
	Jun. 30	Graeme Baker born (d. Aug. 24, 1991)
1936	Feb. 5	Malcolm Graham Baker Jr. born
	Dec.	William M. Rice II makes gift worth $320,000 to Rice endowment
1938		Captain Baker organizes Houston Community Trust
	to 1939	Captain Baker on $1.375 million YMCA Building Committee
		Courtlandt Place house sold to Baker Botts managing partner Ralph Feagin
	Jun. 10	Granddaughter Alice Jones marries John Meyers
	Oct. 5	Stewart Addison Baker born
1940		HOUSTON POPULATION: 384,514
	Apr. 30	Great-granddaughter Alice Graham (Graeme) Meyers born
1941	May 1	Clarence Wharton dies at age 68
	May 18	Edgar Odell Lovett announces his intention to retire

Jun. 7	Last Baker Botts firm meeting at The Oaks
Jun. 8–9	Last Rice commencement
Jun. 10	Last letter, to grandson Jimmy Baker
Aug. 2	Captain Baker dies
Aug. 3	Funeral and burial in Glenwood Cemetery
Dec. 20	Last grandchild James Harrison Moore born (d. Jan. 1, 2011)

Appendix B

BAKER BOTTS L.L.P. AND ITS PREDECESSORS

The law firm known in the twenty-first century as Baker Botts L.L.P. originated when Colonel William Fairfax Gray began the practice of law in Houston, Texas, in 1837, within a few months of the city's founding. Name partners and their years with the firm (in parentheses) are listed below the firm name as it evolved from 1837 to 2012.

1837 COLONEL WILLIAM FAIRFAX GRAY

1840 SCOTT & GRAY
William Fairfax Gray (1840–1841), John Scott (1840–1842), Peter W. Gray (1840–1874)

1842 PETER W. GRAY

1865 GRAY & BOTTS
Peter W. Gray, Colonel Walter Browne Botts (1865–1894)

1872 GRAY, BOTTS & BAKER
Peter W. Gray, Colonel Walter Browne Botts, Judge James Addison Baker (1872–1897)

1875 BAKER & BOTTS
Judge James Addison Baker, Colonel Walter Browne Botts

1881 BAKER, BOTTS & BAKER
Judge James Addison Baker, Colonel Walter Browne Botts, Captain James Addison Baker (1877–1941)

1893 BAKER, BOTTS, BAKER & LOVETT
Judge James Addison Baker, Colonel Walter Browne Botts, Captain James Addison Baker, Robert Scott Lovett (1892–1904)

1904 BAKER, BOTTS, PARKER & GARWOOD
Captain James Addison Baker, Edwin Brewington Parker (1894–1926), Judge Hiram Morgan Garwood (1904–1930)

1931   BAKER, BOTTS, ANDREWS & WHARTON
Captain James Addison Baker, Jesse Andrews (1899–1961),
Clarence Ray Wharton (1902–1941)

1946   BAKER, BOTTS, ANDREWS & WALNE
Jesse Andrews, Walter Hillman Walne (1912–1947)

1948   BAKER, BOTTS, ANDREWS & PARISH
Jesse Andrews, W. Alvis Parish (1910–1953)*

1954   BAKER, BOTTS, ANDREWS & SHEPHERD
Jesse Andrews, James Leftwich Shepherd Jr. (1917–1964)

1962   BAKER, BOTTS, SHEPHERD & COATES
James Leftwich Shepherd Jr., Francis Graham Coates
(1929–1971)*

1971   BAKER & BOTTS

1993   BAKER & BOTTS L.L.P.

2000   BAKER BOTTS L.L.P.

*W. Alvis Parish was the son of Mary Susan Parish, Captain Baker's sister; Francis Graham Coates was the son of Eddie Graham Coates, Alice Graham Baker's sister.

Appendix C
GENEALOGICAL CHARTS

CHART 1: Descendants of ELIJAH ADAM BAKER

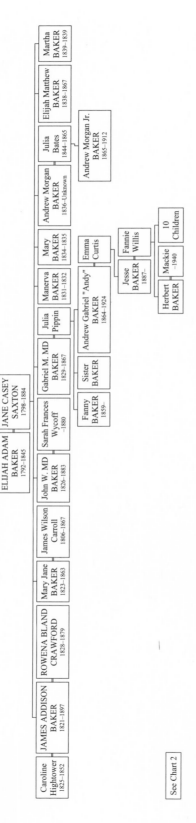

CHART 2: Descendants of JUDGE JAMES ADDISON BAKER

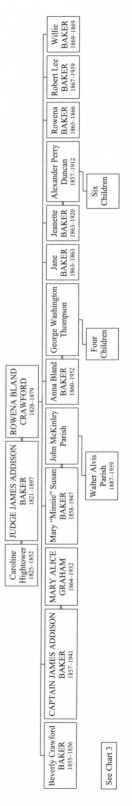

CHART 3: Descendants of CAPTAIN JAMES ADDISON BAKER

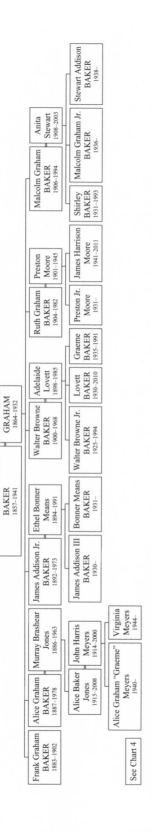

CHART 4: Relations of ROWENA BLAND CRAWFORD BAKER

CHART 5: *Relations of ALICE GRAHAM BAKER*

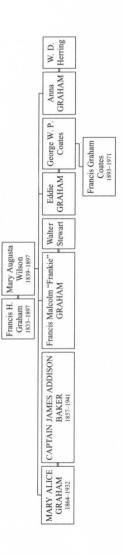

MARY ALICE GRAHAM
1864–1932

CAPTAIN JAMES ADDISON BAKER
1857–1941

Francis H. Graham
1833–1897

Mary Augusta Wilson
1839–1897

Francis Malcolm "Frankie" GRAHAM

Walter Stewart

Eddie GRAHAM

George W. P. Coates

Anna GRAHAM

W. D. Herring

Francis Graham Coates
1893–1971

Acknowledgments

BIOGRAPHY IS A TREACHEROUS ART. While biographers may be able to outline a subject's activities and accomplishments with some accuracy, their attempts to understand the inner mind—the feelings, emotions, intuitions, and passions that shape each person's essence and frame his or her actions—usually remain elusive, the realm of poets, novelists, and a few self-aware diarists and memoirists. Captain James Addison Baker and his wife Alice lived in a reticent era; they kept no diaries; and they did not retain their personal correspondence, as I discovered while reading one of their rare extant letters during the first week of research. Lawyers and bankers of Captain Baker's day respected their clients' trust, and their quotidian discussions and consultations go almost entirely unrecorded. Yet the delights of meeting figures from the past, of exploring bygone pathways, and of rummaging in archives and exhuming faded photographs far outweigh the perils of blind alleys and personalities forever shrouded in memory. Biography may be risky, but the rewards are great: only by absorbing stories from the past can we begin to understand our own.

I could not have undertaken this exploratory journey without the help of many colleagues and fellow travelers. Ray Watkin Hoagland Strange believed Captain Baker deserved a biography, pursued that goal with the Rice Historical Society, and provided underwriting for the project. To her and to the Society, I am deeply indebted.

Many members of Captain Baker's extended family provided enthusiastic, good-humored help during every phase of this project. I am especially grateful to James A. Baker, III for sharing memories, photographs, and private papers and for providing an inspirational foreword to celebrate his grandfather's life. Like his grandfather, Secretary Baker has practiced law, advised Houston's businessmen and bankers, and served his community, but he did not heed Captain Baker's admonition to "keep out of politics." During a successful career in politics, James A. Baker, III led campaigns for Presidents Gerald Ford, Ronald Reagan, and George H. W. Bush. During a distinguished career in public service, he served as 61st Secretary of State (G. H. W. Bush administration), 67th Secretary of the Treasury (Reagan administration), White House Chief of Staff for Reagan and Bush, and Under Secretary of Commerce (Ford administration). He returned to private life to become senior partner of his grandfather's law firm and Honorary Chairman of the James A. Baker III Institute for Public Policy at the university his grandfather founded. Stewart Addison Baker and Preston Moore Jr. devoted untold hours to sharing memories of their grandfather. Graeme Meyers Marston and Virginia Meyers Watt placed the archive of their mother, Alice Baker Jones Meyers, in my hands for the duration of my work. Betty Kyle Moore read an early draft with thoughtful care. She and Preston Moore Jr. made several important suggestions that expanded my understanding of Captain Baker the golfer and my appreciation of Alice Baker's humanitarian influence, and they discovered a trove of priceless photographs. Malcolm Lovett Jr. provided important insights and a map of the Baker/Lovett enclave on Berthea. Addison Baker Duncan, a descendant of Judge Baker's daughter Jeanette Baker Duncan, and Patricia Honea Schutts, a descendant of the Judge's daughter Anna Bland Baker Thompson, transcribed letters that broadened my understanding of the family's long held interest in higher education.

John B. Boles, Evelyn T. Nolen, Roy L. Nolen, and Charles Szalkowski read earlier versions of the manuscript, and their insights immeasurably improved final copy. They also proved to be clever archival sleuths who uncovered Baker's trail in unlikely places.

Baker's trail proved elusive, but numerous archivists illuminated the path. At Rice University Archivist Lee Pecht oversees the Woodson Research Center, ably assisted by Amanda Focke, Lauren Meyers, and Dara Flinn. For four years this outstanding team responded promptly to every request and, more important, made my archival visits fun. Joel Draut, archivist of the Photography Archives, Metropolitan Research Center, Houston Public Library, offered valuable help identifying and finding early scenes of Houston. In Huntsville Cheryl Spencer and Paul Culp of Sam Houston State University Special Collections; James D. Patton, Walker County Clerk and historian; and Linda Pease, city Cultural Services Coordinator, discovered important information about the family's Huntsville years.

This project would not have been completed without the efforts of generous colleagues and friends. Angela Blanchard, President of Neighborhood Centers Inc. made available records relating to Alice Baker's Settlement Association work and discussed her perception of Alice Baker's importance to Houston's heritage. Fellow writers and friends Elizabeth Hutcheson Carrell and Joanne Seale Wilson untangled the Hutcheson genealogy and provided critical details about life in Captain Baker's Houston. Françoise Djerejian redefined the meaning of a petit café and brought important family letters to my attention. Barbara Eaves tried to discover what happened to early banking records and shared her interest in local and banking history with me. J. Thomas Eubank, Roy L. Nolen, and Charles Szalkowski helped me understand the practice of law and Baker Botts culture, and John Cater illuminated Houston's banking history. Steven Fenberg discussed his research project with me and made the Jesse Jones Papers at Houston Endowment available. Joan Ferry gave me information about the windows at Palmer Church. Stephen Fox toured Baker landmarks with me and was, as always, a supportive colleague. Sandy Hatcher and John Williams smoothed the path at Baker Botts and provided invaluable assistance. Gary Nichols found early YMCA records that explained Captain Baker's affiliation. The late Martha Peterson provided archival material about Glenwood Cemetery and its Board of Directors. Director of Communications Cathy Skitko uncovered information about Graham Baker's years at the Hill School. My good friend Francita Ulmer, herself a natural-born historian, told stories of her childhood with the Baker clan, gave me archival records that revealed how Captain Baker built his law practice, and disclosed fascinating information about Houston's history. Janet Wagner not only took the Baker genealogical data and turned it into beautiful charts; but also she discovered when Captain Baker really became a name partner and unearthed other critical records that clarified family mysteries.

To all these friends and colleagues and to Texas A&M University Press editor Mary Lenn Dixon, who eased the editorial experience, I say, with gratitude, thank you.

Notes

ABBREVIATIONS

EOL	Presidential Records, Edgar Odell Lovett, WRC
ER	Early Rice Institute Records, WRC
HMRC	Houston Metropolitan Research Center, Houston Public Library
MS40	Baker Family Papers, MS40, WRC
MS487	Captain James A. Baker Papers, MS487, WRC
OR	Baker Botts Office Review, Baker Botts L.L.P., Houston
RU	Rice University
WRC	Woodson Research Center, RU

Please note: James Addison Baker refers to Judge Baker, father of Captain James A. Baker.

Jimmie Baker refers to Captain James A. Baker as a child and young man.

James A. Baker refers to Captain James A. Baker as an adult.

James A. Baker Jr. refers to Captain Baker's son, also cited as Jim Baker in the text.

James A. Baker, III refers to Captain Baker's grandson.

Jimmy Baker refers to James A. Baker, III as a child.

Certain documents in chapter 3 refer to Captain Baker as James A. Baker Jr., as he was sometimes called until about 1910.

PROLOGUE

1. Huxley, "Texas and Academe," 59.

2. Welcome remarks, EOL 46:2; also quoted in Boles, *University Builder*, 100.

3. Huxley, "Texas and Academe," 55.

4. Rice Institute Board Minutes, WRC, May 2, 1912, May 21, 1912. Hereafter cited as Board Minutes.

5. Letters, Edgar Odell Lovett to James A. Baker, Jul. 22, 1912 (in Bass Rocks), Jul. 26, 1912 (in New York about to sail to Europe), ER 90:1.

6. Quote in Boles, *University Builder*, 94.

7. Newspaper lists of delegates in ER, Opening Ceremony file. The invitation measured 18 x 23.75 (Boles, *University Builder*, 101). See also McCants, "Rice Institute," 68–76, for opening weekend events.

8. Boles, *University Builder*, 102.

9. *Houston Chronicle*, Oct. 10, 1912, clipping in ER, Opening Ceremony file.

10. McCants, "Rice Institute," 75.

11. *Book of the Opening*, Baker, 1: 26, passim, WRC.

12. *Houston Chronicle*, Oct. 9, Oct. 11, 1912.

13. Mary Hale Lovett to her mother Virginia Hale, Oct. 20, 1912, Lovett Family Papers, addendum, courtesy of John B. Boles.

14. *Book of the Opening*, 1: 84, WRC.

15. Huxley in Meiners, "Rice University Historical Commission Newsletter," 3; Cram and Lovett, in *Book of the Opening*, 1: 93, WRC.

16. Edgar Odell Lovett, "The Meaning of the New Institution" in Lovett, *Creation of Rice University*, 53, 66, 79, 134.

17. Mary Hale Lovett to Virginia Hale, Oct. 20, 1912, Lovett Family Papers, addendum.

18. Meiners, "Rice University Historical Commission Newsletter," 4; McCants, "Rice Institute," 76.

19. Mary Hale Lovett to Virginia Hale, Oct. 20, 1912, Lovett Family Papers, addendum.

20. *Houston Daily Post*, Oct. 14, 1912, p. 8. The entire sermon and Van Dyke's Bible readings are included. Charles Aked was a member of the Neutral Conference for Continuous Mediation that tried to broker a peace settlement among the European powers in 1916.

21. *Houston Press*, Mon. Oct. 14, 1912.

22. *Houston Daily Post*, Oct. 14, 1912, "Dr. Van Dyke in Unique Sermon Addressed Students."

23. Ibid.

CHAPTER ONE

1. Austin College was founded Oct. 13, 1849. Its charter was received in Nov. 1849. In 1876 the trustees voted to move the college to Sherman, Texas, and in 1877 they sold the campus to the city of Huntsville.

2. Rankin, *Texas in 1850*, 25.

3. Olmsted, *Journey through Texas*, 39.

4. Ibid., 27.

5. Ibid., 37.

6. *Houstonian*, Oct. 18, 1979, p. 8.

7. Rankin, *Texas in 1850*, 138. The precise date of Miss Rankin's stay in Huntsville is unclear, but some time between 1849 and 1851 she spent about twelve months there, teaching at the Brick Academy before continuing her missionary career.

8. Ibid., 122, 120.

9. Ibid., 138.

10. Ibid., 22.

11. Cummins, *Austin College*, 19.

12. During Texas' first decade as a republic and state, the seat of government moved several times. Several towns vied with Houston and Austin—the most ar-

dent contenders—to become the permanent capital city. By 1850 the argument had been settled decisively in Austin's favor after several elections.

13. Information about the family comes from genealogical studies provided by grandsons James A. Baker, III and Preston Moore Jr. and by great-granddaughter Virginia Meyers Watt; from court records provided by James D. Patton, county clerk of Walker County, Texas; and from visits by the author to Oakwood Cemetery, Huntsville, and Glenwood Cemetery, Houston. Beverly is spelled Beverley in some records.

14. Walker County Records. John Baker's diploma is in the Sam Houston Museum Collection, Huntsville. He practiced medicine in Madison County before emigrating to Huntsville, Texas, where he died in 1883 after a distinguished medical career. Carolyn (Mrs. Carlos) Hamilton to James A. Baker, III, Jul. 15, 1996, in Virginia Meyers Watt collection.

15. James Addison Baker to Anna McRobert Crawford, letter from Huntsville, Texas, Jun. 22, 1853; written on the back is Captain James A. Baker's note: "My father to Grand Ma Crawford asking for my mother," in James A. Baker, III personal collection, Baker Institute, RU; Anna McRobert Crawford to Rowena Crawford, letter from Raleigh, Tennessee, Aug. 29, 1853, MS 40.

16. Marriage license written into the county records as item 212 for 1853, Walker County Courthouse, Huntsville, Texas. Rev. Baker was beginning an illustrious career when he married Rowena and James. He is buried in Austin beside his father Daniel Baker. Red, *History of the Presbyterian Church in Texas*, 416–17. Notice also printed in *Texas Presbyterian*, Oct. 1853, published by Rev. A. J. McGowan in Huntsville for the Cumberland Presbyterian Synod of Texas.

17. Anna McRobert Crawford to Rowena Crawford Baker, letter from Raleigh, Tennessee, Oct. 20, 1853, MS 40.

18. Rowena Baker to Jimmie Baker, Jan. 18, 1877, MS 40, 1:7.

19. Davidson, "Making of a Judge," 11.

20. Olmsted, *Journey through Texas*, 414.

21. Names vary during the period; one letter of 1862 speaks of Bush and Baker; letters of credit in 1867 use Hightower and Baker or A. M. Baker & Co. Andrew and Matt are listed as grocers in the 1860 census for Walker County.

22. Jabour, "'Grown Girls, Highly Educated,'" 43.

23. Chancellor, *History of the Hill School*, 9. The so-called Academy Period of American education spanned the Revolution to the Civil War.

24. Red, *Presbyterian Church in Texas*, 223.

25. Brackenridge, *Voice in the Wilderness*, 9.

26. Ferguson, "Antecedents of Austin College," 240–53; also clipping of article in Baker Botts Papers, WRC.

27. Cummins, *Austin College*, 8.

28. Ibid., 9.

29. Red, *Presbyterian Church in Texas*, 89.

30. Cummins, *Emily Austin of Texas*, 184, 253 n. 4. Emily Austin Perry transferred legal title to 1,500 acres inherited from her brother Stephen F. Austin to Austin Col-

lege, donated $3,500 in the 1850s, and assigned to the college any payments the state of Texas might pay the estate of Stephen F. Austin as reimbursement for his 1836 diplomatic mission to the United States. Such payments were made to the college in the 1870s.

31. Ferguson, "Austin College in Huntsville," 387–402.

32. Austin College Board of Trustee Minutes, I, 76, in Virginia Meyers Watt collection.

33. Estill, "Old Town of Huntsville," 277; Rowena Baker to James A. Baker, Feb. 9, 1877, MS 40, 1:7.

34. Walker County Deed Records, 2: 377–81, 401–03.

35. All correspondence between James Addison Baker and Rowena Baker cited in this section is located in MS 40, 1: 2, 3, 4.

36. From James, *Biography of Sam Houston*, 410, citing Alfred M. Williams, *Sam Houston and the War of Independence in Texas*, 354.

37. James Addison Baker to Andrew Baker, Feb. 5, 1862, sent to Captain James A. Baker from George Thompson Jr., Dec. 21, 1921, in James A. Baker, III personal collection, Baker Institute, RU.

38. Estill, "Old Town of Huntsville," 276.

39. Walker County Census, County Courthouse, Huntsville, 1860.

40. Jimmie Baker to James Addison Baker, 1862, James A. Baker, III personal collection, Baker Institute, RU. This letter and the crushed petals are in an envelope sent from Fort Worth to Captain James A. Baker, Dec. 22, 1921, with "personal" written on the outside. Inside is a later description: Letters from Judge James A. Baker to his son James A. Baker Jr., 1862, and the note, "rosebuds were pressed 99 years ago."

41. Quoted in Davidson, "Making of a Judge," 12. Davidson mistakenly believes Baker to be "absent from the state" and thus not the author of this "leak." Rather, Baker's proximity to Houston and his presence in Galveston suggest that he or his friends clearly wrote the announcement.

42. Davidson, "Making of a Judge," 12; statistics and candidate information.

43. Rowena Baker to James Addison Baker, Mar. 31, 1862, MS 40, 1:3. All correspondence between James Addison Baker and Rowena Baker cited in this section is located in MS 40, 1:3, 4.

44. Mary Crawford had married Tennessee native Samuel R. Smith, owner of the second-largest plantation in Walker County.

45. Harris County Court Records, Vol. K, Minutes of District Court, Dec. 1863.

46. Ibid., May 1864.

47. Ibid., Jun. 1865, 185–86.

48. Kilman, "Work Hard, Study and Keep Out of Politics," 1.

49. James Addison Baker to Jimmie Baker, Jun. 7, 1868, MS 40, 1:6.

50. Rowena Baker to James Addison Baker, Aug. 8, 1866, MS 40, 1:4.

51. Secondary sources and some newspaper accounts incorrectly name John McParrish as one of the defendants. No such person is recorded in any Walker County census data of the period, although census records do confuse Parrish and Parish. John McKinley Parish was born in May 1850 to W. A. and Katherine Parish.

He was nicknamed Mac, and on April 27, 1880, he married Mary Susan (Minnie) Baker, daughter of Judge James A. Baker, in Huntsville. See census data, Walker County, 1850, 1860, 1870, 1880; marriage license, Walker County Courthouse.

52. Margaret Leigh Thornton to Cousin Emma, Mar. 1, 1871, Thornton Papers, Sam Houston State University, Special Collections. On February 15, Governor Davis ordered his adjutant general to Huntsville, where martial law was imposed on February 20.

53. "Complete Official History of the Troubles in Hill and Walker Counties," *Union*, Feb. 16, 1871; Report of the District Attorney of the 30th Judicial District of Texas; *Galveston Daily News*, Mar. 8, 1871; Jayne, "Martial Law in Reconstruction Texas," 40–58; Nunn, *Texas under the Carpetbaggers*, 80–86. Handbook of Texas Online, Walker County Rebellion, Jan. 10, 2010, misnames the defendant John McKinley Parish as John McParrish. I am indebted to Cheryl Spencer, Special Collections, Sam Houston University, and James Paton, Walker County Clerk, for checking census data and providing other materials that show John McKinley Parish was one of the defendants and later married Judge Baker's daughter Mary Susan (Minnie) Baker. According to the 1870 census, John M. Parish was head of a household that included himself, a black servant, and some mulatto children.

54. Clipping, "Old Swimmin' Hole Gang," 1936, in MS 40, scrapbook.

55. Rowena Baker to James Addison Baker, Jul. 10, 1866, MS 40, 1:4.

56. Woodall reference in *Houston Post*, Jul. 31, 1936, clipping, MS 40. Records and correspondence do not fully explain Jimmie's school enrollment. Austin College lists J. A. Baker for the 1872–1873 academic year, but report cards from TMI do not begin until the fall of 1874. Rowena and Judge Baker both write to Jimmie in September 1873 while he was enrolled in the Austin College Preparatory Department, MS 40, 1:6.

CHAPTER TWO

1. Fuglaar, "Streetcar in Houston," 36.

2. William A. Kirkland, *Old Bank–New Bank*, 12–14.

3. Some sources say Judge Baker built his house at San Jacinto and Lamar, although there is no archival evidence relating to the home's construction. Minor architectural details relating it to late nineteenth-century construction suggest the house was built after the Civil War. City Directories are missing for the years 1872, 1874–1876, and 1885. Houses were not numbered until 1880, when the Baker home was listed as 204 San Jacinto. In 1892 the house was renumbered 1104 San Jacinto. Correspondence supports a move sometime in 1876; Rowena Baker to Jimmie Baker, Sept. 17, 1876, MS 40, 1:7; *City Directory* 1877 lists Jas. A. Baker, attorney, at the San Jacinto address.

4. US Census 1880 lists residents at the San Jacinto address as Judge Baker, Jas. A. Baker Jr., Anna B as housekeeper, Janette (Jeanette), Robert, nephew Andrew (mislabeled as a son), Mrs. Crawford, and Mrs. Cobb, as well as twelve adult servants, two teenage workers, and six children. These employees had all been born in Alabama, Tennessee, or Texas and are clearly former bondsmen who remained with

family members during their various moves before, during, and after the Civil War. The servants are listed as unable to read or write, and only the judge's younger children are listed as attending school regularly. Andrew Morgan Baker began working for William D. Cleveland Co. in 1882, was named cashier in 1884, and had left Houston to establish his own business by 1890.

5. James Addison Baker to Rowena Baker, Jun. 1, 1865, MS 40, 1: 4.

6. Freeman, *People of Baker Botts*, 10, n. 3, citing *Morning Star* advertisement Jan. 7, 1840, for the firm of Scott & Gray comprising W. Fairfax Gray, John Scott, and Peter Gray.

7. 1850 census, quoted in Freeman, *People of Baker Botts*, 12.

8. Kroger, "Reconstructing Reconstruction," 29.

9. Freeman, *People of Baker Botts*, 16. See also Kelly, "Peter Gray," 29–35.

10. Memorial statement in Baker Botts Papers, 4.0B, WRC.

11. "Chronological Table of Representation of Southern Pacific Lines by This Firm and Its Predecessors," Baker Botts Papers, 5B, WRC.

12. Funeral report in Freeman, *People of Baker Botts*, 11. Gray left his considerable property to his wife, who left it to Christ Church; some years later, the vestry sold the property and used the proceeds to expand the parish church.

13. James Addison Baker to Jimmie Baker, Mar. 30, 1877, and Rowena Baker to Jimmie Baker, Apr. 2, 1877, MS 40, 1:7.

14. Correspondence, MS 40, 1:6. Correspondence does not include the name of Minnie's school, but Nettie later attended Notre Dame of Maryland, so I am assuming that her older sister did as well. Notre Dame of Maryland, founded in 1873, became the first four-year Catholic college for women in the United States in 1896. Information about the sisters' schooling, courtesy of Addison Baker Duncan.

15. Mary Sharp College offered algebra, geometry, and trigonometry; Latin and Greek; English literature, grammar, and composition; ancient, English, and American history; philosophy and rhetoric; botany, chemistry, astronomy, and physiology. Girls came from California, Texas, Vermont, and China.

16. Correspondence in MS 40, 1:6; Anna B. Baker to Nettie Baker, Jan. 28, 1877, private collection, courtesy of Addison Baker Duncan and Patricia Honea Schutts.

17. Rowena Baker to Nettie Baker, Sept. 28, 1878, private collection, courtesy of Addison Baker Duncan and Patricia Honea Schutts.

18. Harris County organized its first free or public school in 1871; in 1877 Houston passed an ordinance authorizing municipal control of county schools within city limits. Kate S. Kirkland, *Hogg Family and Houston*, 124.

19. Jimmie Baker to James Addison Baker, Feb. 2, 1875, Virginia Meyers Watt collection, letter folder.

20. TMI Superintendent John Garland James became president of A&M College and modeled its program after the TMI program.

21. Superintendent John G. James to James Addison Baker, Jan. 28, 1875, MS 487, scrapbooks 1:9.

22. MS 40, scrapbook.

23. Virginia Meyers Watt collection, letter folder.

24. Superintendent John G. James to James Addison Baker, Mar. 26, 1877, MS 40, 1:7; report cards, MS 40, 1:7; Virginia Meyers Watt collection, letter folder.

25. Jimmie Baker to Minnie Baker, Oct. 15, 1874, MS 487, 1:5.

26. Jimmie Baker to James Addison Baker, Mar. 24, 1875, Virginia Meyers Watt collection, letter folder; Apr. 8, 1875, MS 487, 1:1.

27. James Addison Baker to Jimmie Baker, Jan. 21, 1875, 8-page letter, MS 487, 1:2.

28. James Addison Baker to Jimmie Baker, Oct. 1, 1874, MS 40, 1:7.

29. Jimmie Baker to Rowena Baker, Feb. 26, 1875, slim box, James A. Baker, III personal collection, Baker Institute, RU.

30. James Addison Baker to Jimmie Baker, Jan. 31, 1877, MS 40, 1:7.

31. Rowena Baker to Jimmie Baker, Oct. 11, 1876, MS 40, 1:7.

32. Rowena Baker to James Addison Baker, Jan. 18, 1877, MS 40, 1:7.

33. James Addison Baker to Jimmie Baker, Sept. 18, 1873, MS 40, 1:6.

34. Rowena Baker to Jimmie Baker, Oct. 19, 1876, MS 40, 1:7.

35. Rowena Baker to Jimmie Baker, Apr. 2, 1875, MS 40, 1:7.

36. Jimmie Baker to James Addison Baker, Apr. 22, 1875, MS 487, 1:1.

37. Texas Military Institute Diploma, Baker family personal papers, courtesy of Susan Baker. "Cadet James A. Baker of Houston carefully examined in all the branches of the Arts, Sciences, and Literature taught in the Texas Military Institute has been judged worthy to be declared a Graduate of the same in token of which The Academic Board have awarded him this Diploma in Austin June 13, 1877."

38. Although Captain Baker later recalled pledging to work at TMI for one year, some amicable agreement must have been reached after the first semester so he could begin his legal studies in Houston.

39. James A. Baker, Memorandum to Clarence R. Wharton, Jan. 12, 1927, "historical statement in reference to the offices of the firm," Baker Botts Papers, WRC.

40. James Addison Baker to James A. Baker, Sept. 19, 1878, MS 40, 1:6; 4 pages of advice.

41. Rowena Baker to James A. Baker, Sept. 30, 1878, MS 40 1:6.

42. Harris County District Clerk's records, Vol. R, Part II, 623, for exam. Baker Botts Papers, RU, WRC, lawyers file, Length of Service, lists the name change as first occurring in 1887, a date that is copied by later chroniclers of the firm but is shown to be incorrect by archival evidence and court records: Baker, Botts & Baker listing in the city directory from 1882 forward; Baker, Botts & Baker stationery dated 1883 and 1885, in Baker Botts Papers, client correspondence, WRC; Proceedings in the 11th District Court, Harris County are signed Baker, Botts & Baker at least from Oct. 1881 forward. For years the firm made significant changes on July 1 and probably changed the name on July 1, 1881. Documentation provided by Janet Wagner; copies of documents in author's possession and at Baker Botts L.L.P. offices in Houston.

43. Plaque with state seal, in James A. Baker, III personal collection, Baker Institute, RU.

44. Jimmie Baker to Nettie Baker, Mar. 25, 1881, James A. Baker, III personal collection, Baker Institute, RU.

45. Inventory of William Marsh Rice Assets, ER 64:2.

46. The Houston Light Guard Files (HMRC) list Baker as Captain from Aug. 6, 1879 to Aug. 4, 1880. Bruce A. Olson's thorough study of the Guard says Baker commanded the first interstate drill team in 1881 ("The Houston Light Guards," 110).

47. *Houston Press*, Aug. 3, 1941, clipping "In Memoriam" vol. 1, MS 40.

48. Marriage license, Mr. John M. Parish and Miss Minnie S. Baker, Walker County Court Records.

49. Jane Cobb died in 1884, and youngest son Robert, a docket clerk at Baker, Botts & Baker, lived at home until 1895, after which he took bachelor rooms in town.

50. The playhouse was moved five times for the enjoyment of Captain Baker's daughters, granddaughters, and great-granddaughters. James A. Baker, III recalls that his sister Bonner "adored that playhouse," where she played with her favorite dolls and hosted tea parties for her friends. In 2010 it was given to the Harris County Heritage Society, where it explains childhood customs in Houston. James A. Baker, III, "Baker Playhouse Dedication," May 17, 2011; documents and time lines developed by the author, in the author's possession and in the files of the Harris County Heritage Society.

51. *City Directories*, 1872–1900. Robert is first mentioned as a clerk for the Texas Western Railway in 1886, when he was nineteen years old; Ballinger & Assoc. Papers, HMRC.

52. The wedding invitation for Jeanette Baker and Alexander Perry Duncan, courtesy of Addison Baker Duncan, provides this information and the only reliable spelling of her name, which is misspelled in several documents. See also, *City Directories*; Glenwood Cemetery Baker plot. Mr. Duncan, a descendant of Judge Baker's daughter Jeanette Baker Duncan and resident of San Antonio, has placed the invitation in the Woodson Research Center archives, Fondren Library, RU.

53. James A. Baker to Stewart Addison Baker (age two), Dec. 18, 1940, author's collection. I am indebted to Stewart Baker for sharing this touching letter.

54. Grandson Preston Moore Jr. recalls seeing Captain Baker's manservant administer insulin shots to Captain Baker in the 1930s. I am indebted to Philip S. Bentlif, MD, for comments about medical treatment prevalent during Captain Baker's lifetime. Addison Baker Duncan provided the information about nineteenth-century spas in Marlin and San Antonio (letter to author, Apr. 20, 2010).

55. Comments by Alice Baker Jones Meyers, courtesy of Virginia Meyers Watt.

56. Bylaws for music group, Faith Home Charter in Kirkland, *Hoggs and Houston*, 5683.

57. Malcolm Lovett, son of Edgar Odell Lovett, quoted in "The History of Captain Baker," copy in Virginia Meyers Watt collection.

58. *Houston Post*, May 20, 1894.

59. Contemporaries described his eyes as gray, brown, and blue; portraits and memories do not clarify this color distinction. Hazel seems to be the safest guess.

60. Baker, "Reminiscences of the Founder," 127. Some of Judge Baker's books remain in family collections today. In 1870 the original Allen brothers' town lot book was given to Baker Botts and is still in the firm's vault. Mrs. Gray's niece Marga-

ret Stone was married to Ebenezer Nichols, William Marsh Rice's partner in the mercantile Nichols & Rice, explaining the early and strong relationship of the two families.

61. John T. Maginnis, "Baker & Botts, 1866–1978," Baker Botts Papers, WRC.

62. OR Jun. 8, 1922, 18–19.

63. Correspondence between Captain Baker and George E. Dilley, May 1927, recorded in OR May 12, 1927, 166–71. Dilley discovered old correspondence with the Judge, which he sent to Baker.

64. "History of Captain Baker," Virginia Meyers Watt collection; also quoted in Freeman, *People of Baker Botts*, 27.

65. James A. Baker to the President and Directors of the Houston Loan & Building Association, May 31, 1879, MS 487, Box 3.

66. Purpose quoted in Pollard, "History of the Texas Bar Association," 31. See also "Centennial History of the Texas Bar, 1882–1982," 1–3, Baker Botts Papers, 8A, WRC.

67. Sheppard, "Nineteenth Century Bench and Bar in Harris County," 7.

68. "Statement of James A. Baker Jr., in connection with the . . . Last Will and Testament of William M. Rice, Deceased," ER 91:1, p. 2.

69. William Pitt Ballinger was Texas counsel for the Santa Fe Railroad and had long argued that railroads were good for local business. He offered free rail passes and election support to secure favorable rulings in the hundreds of court cases that resulted from railroad expansion and was Galveston's leading attorney in the late nineteenth century. He helped many Houston-based clients with legal issues related to their Galveston investments. Ballinger & Associates Papers, HMRC.

70. Thomas, *Lawyering for the Railroad*, 139; Handbook of Texas Online Feb. 13, 2010, Huntington, Gould, Transcontinental Railroad. See White, *Railroaded*, for a critical examination of the transformation brought to western North America by the "transcontinental" railroads.

71. See correspondence of International & Great Northern Railroad (1888), Houston & Texas Central (1888), Missouri Pacific Railway Company (1887), Galveston, Harrisburg & San Antonio Railway Company/Texas & New Orleans Railroad Company (1897), Baker Botts Papers, Southern Pacific client file, WRC.

72. G. G. Kelley to Baker, Botts, Parker & Garwood, Dec. 4, 1915, Baker Botts Papers, Southern Pacific client file, WRC.

73. *Southern Mercury*, Aug. 21, 1888, p. l.

74. Norvell, "Railroad Commission of Texas," 466; Cotner, *James Stephen Hogg*, 155–245; Thomas, *Lawyering for the Railroad*, passim.

75. James A. Baker to William Marsh Rice, Feb. 23, 1900, ER 98:4.

76. Baker, "Reminiscences of the Founder," 127.

77. Hyman, "William Marsh Rice's Credit Ratings," 91–96. Only John Hunter Herndon, a sugar planter in Brazoria County, had greater antebellum wealth, mostly in land, slaves, and sugar processing equipment.

78. List of Assets, ER 64:2; James A. Baker Jr., "Enterprises in which Mr. Rice Was Interested," ca. 1901, ER 22:10.

79. Records in ER 98:2. At the time it cost $.25 or .30 to notarize a document; $.35 to send a messenger across town; $50–$75 to draw a deed of trust; and $150–$250 to try a lawsuit. Between May 26, 1896, and April 1, 1897, Baker, Botts, Baker & Lovett collected $2,477.95 to try five lawsuits and handle other Rice business.

80. Correspondence, James A. Baker and William Marsh Rice, ER 98:3, 4; ER 99:2; ER 101:3.

81. Houston Electric Light & Power, which also became a Baker Botts client, received its franchise in 1884 and by 1900 had brought electricity to most homes. Houghton et al., *Houston's Forgotten Heritage*, 278.

82. Freeman, *People of Baker Botts*, 44–47.

83. Correspondence with J. Kruttschnitt, Jul. and Aug. 1894, Baker Botts Papers, 11L (2), WRC.

84. Memo to Mr. Freeman from Mr. Andrews, Dec. 27, 1957, Baker Botts Papers, 4A; Maginnis interview, Baker Botts Papers, 3, WRC.

85. James A. Baker to Edwin Brewington Parker, Nov. 28, 1900, ER 79:1.

86. Baker Botts Papers, Box 4A, WRC.

87. Houghton, *Houston Club*, 7. Edwin B. Parker was one of eight men who signed the charter. Captain Baker's instructions regarding his funeral, written shortly before his death, suggest he was no longer active in the Elks. See *Makers of Houston, 1912* (James A. Baker); MS 40, In Memoriam, vol. 3.

88. Grandchildren of the Baker, Duncan, and Thompson families still recall these family visits fondly. I am indebted to the recollections of Addison Baker Duncan, letters Apr. 20, 30, 2010; Patricia Honea Schutts, e-mail Feb. 8, 2010; Georgeann Johnson, e-mail and telephone, Feb. 10, 12, 2010; family photographs.

89. James Addison Baker to Mrs. A. P. (Nettie) Duncan, Waco, Nov. 11, 1896, Jan. 4, 1897, James A. Baker, III personal collection, Baker Institute, RU.

90. "Tribute of Reverence and Affection," Mar. 18, 1897, James A. Baker, III family papers, courtesy of Susan Baker.

91. Clipping, in several family collections.

92. After 1885 Captain Baker represented Union Trust Company of New York, trustee of the mortgage securing the debt of Houston East & West Texas Railway Company during its receivership, and he was personal attorney for E. S. Jemison, who acquired the railroad property through foreclosure. When Jemison died, Baker represented his widow during New York probate proceedings and served as secretary of the company in the late 1890s.

93. Houghton et al., *Houston's Forgotten Heritage*, 84, 136.

94. *Houston Post*, Jan. 2, 1899, clipping, Virginia Meyers Watt collection.

CHAPTER THREE

1. US Census, summer 1900: San Antonio, 53,321, up 41.54 percent from 1890; Houston, 44,683, up 61.97 percent; Dallas, 42,638, up 12.01 percent; Galveston, 37,789, up 29.93 percent. Cited on the front page of the *Houston Post*, Sept. 28, 1900.

2. *Houston Daily Post*, Thursday morning, Sept. 13, 1900.

3. Turner, *Women, Culture, and Community*, 17–39. Dr. Turner's dramatic retell-

ing of the United States' worst natural disaster of the twentieth century is followed by an equally moving story of the way citizens working together brought order out of chaos.

4. Horace Baldwin Rice, grandson of Mayor Horace Baldwin, was mayor from 1896–1898 and again from 1905–1913.

5. *Houston Daily Post*, Sept. 27, p. 2; Sept. 29, p. 2; Oct. 5, p. 4; Oct. 6, p. 2.

6. Morris, ed., and Muir, *William Marsh Rice and His Institute*, 60. The biography includes details of Rice's second marriage, which are based on court records found in several ER files. McCants, "Rice Institute," 4, quotes Muir as saying that the Rices' marriage was "stormy" in the 1890s when she consulted divorce lawyer A. G. Allen.

7. Baker, "Reminiscences of the Founder," 135.

8. Baker, "The Patrick Case," 4, pamphlet prepared for Baker's law partners, in Baker Botts Papers, 10A, WRC; and in MS 487, scrapbook.

9. Baker, "Reminiscences of the Founder," 131.

10. Charles Boston, a lawyer with Hornblower, Miller & Garrison who worked on the legal case stemming from W. M. Rice's death, believed Mrs. Holt was a cousin of Mrs. Rice. "Memorandum of Charles Boston," Rice University File, Baker Botts Papers, 5 B, WRC.

11. "Statement of James A. Baker, Jr., of Houston, Texas, in connection with the Litigation that may follow the offer for probate of the Last Will and Testament of William M. Rice, Deceased," ER 96:1. Statements over the years from Baker and others also use the terms "stroke" and "illness" to describe Mrs. Rice's condition and variously estimate the amount of her bequests from $1–$2.5 million. Although details vary, the basic narrative remains consistent. William Marsh Rice to W. S. Campbell, n.d., in response to letters of Dec. 29, 1899, ER 76:4, 5 mentioned the presence of Mrs. Huntington and Mrs. Holt.

12. Wills of Elizabeth Baldwin Rice, ER 41:1.

13. Boston, "Memorandum," see note 10.

14. *Houston Post*, Feb. 8, 1913, clipping in "Oran Holt," *Mayors' Book*, HMRC. Documents and printed material from the era refer to O. T., Oran T., and Orren Thaddeus Holt.

15. Marian Seward is identified as the present Mrs. O. T. Holt in a photograph of Captain Baker with Alice Graham and three of her closest friends, taken in 1887 just before the Bakers' marriage (Sunday *Houston Post Magazine*, Oct. 3, 1937, p. 1). Original photograph in Baker family collection. Mrs. Holt, as a former mayor's wife and lifelong friend, assisted Mrs. Baker as a hostess at the Opening Garden Party of Rice Institute, Thursday, October 10, 1912, and Mr. and Mrs. Holt assisted the Edgar Odell Lovetts at their farewell reception October 12. *Houston Chronicle* clippings, ER, File of the Opening.

16. "Statement of James A. Baker," ER 96:1, p. 4. The executors of William Marsh Rice's will were to receive "five pr cent upon the aggregate value of the whole of my estate" (Par. 10, 1896 will, ER 41:1).

17. Wills of Elizabeth B. Rice, ER 41:1.

18. Emanuel Raphael to James A. Baker, Jun. 20, 1899, ER 1:4. This letter out-

lines the property W. M. and E. B. Rice executed and delivered "as a gift to and for account of the William M. Rice Institute for the Advancement of Literature, Science & Art" in Jones County, in the Obedience Smith survey, in Louisiana, and at the Capitol Hotel, and further states that "On Sept. 30th, 1892, Mr. Rice instructed E. Raphael and James A. Baker to publish and put on record the deed to the 6½ acres of the Obedience Smith survey."

19. 1896 Will, ER 41:1.

20. ER 41:2 (William Marsh Rice response, March 1897); 43.1 (depositions of Dr. Wiggonton, superintendent of Wisconsin State Hospitals for the insane, friend Mary C. Brewster, maid).

21. James A. Baker, "Patrick Case," 5; letter Sept. 15, cited in testimony, ER 115, p. 143; ER 77:1, p. 774.

22. Rice Will, 1896, ER 21; "Statement of James A. Baker . . . W. M. Rice Deceased Probate," ER 9:4, p. 10. See also, William Marsh Rice to James A. Baker, Sept. 15, 1896, letter outlining wishes for his will; and William Marsh Rice to James A. Baker, Sept. 26, 1896, telling his lawyer he has "completed" the will (signed it) and placed it in a vault at the New York Deposit Company; only he and Baker will have the combination. Unfortunately, Rice never sent the combination to his lawyer, ER 77:4.

23. Will, ER 41:2, 41:4; James A. Baker, "Patrick Case," 5; suits listed in Report to the Board of Trustees, Oct. 1, 1906, ER 82:1.

24. "Statement by James A. Baker," ER 90:3, p. 3.

25. "Statement of James A. Baker," ER 96:1, p. 5. This statement, apparently made earlier than a similar statement found in ER 90:3, is longer and more detailed, setting forth a nuanced legal argument that is summarized in the statement of ER 90:3.

26. Robert S. Lovett to James A. Baker, Oct. 14, 1900, ER 26:1; "Statement of James A. Baker," ER 96:1, p. 8.

27. Kate S. Kirkland, *Hogg Family and Houston*, 51–53.

28. There is considerable evidence that Hutcheson and Baker discussed ways to lessen the animosity between Holt and Rice. In June 1899 Baker wrote Rice that "Capt. Hutcheson has informed us that he intends . . . to institute suit against you to recover supposed value of one-half of all personal property." Armed with this information, Baker worked with South Texas Bank and First National Bank to help Rice close his accounts in Houston and move his cash to a retainer account held by the law firm and to banks in New York City so that Rice would not "be annoyed . . . by having your funds in the local banks tied up for some months," although Baker felt sure he would be able to get the case dismissed for want of jurisdiction. Letters, Baker, Botts, Baker & Lovett to William Marsh Rice, Jun. 6, 10, 16, Oct. 4, 1899, ER 98:4.

29. Ella Stuart (Mrs. George W.) Heyer as told to her nephew, Robert C. Stuart. Recollections provided by Francita Stuart Ulmer.

30. James A. Baker to William Marsh Rice, Sept. 10, 1898, ER 98:3.

31. James A. Baker to William Marsh Rice, Oct. 11, 1898, ER 98:3. See also contract between O. T. Holt and A. T. Patrick, where Patrick agrees to "render and perform such legal service" as required by Holt, ER 4:7.

32. Charles Adams to William Marsh Rice, Sept. 22, 1899, ER 99:2, notes he would have invited the Captain for a "good long visit" had Baker not had his family with him in New York.

33. Edwin B. Parker to James A. Baker, Oct. 8, 1900, ER 96:1.

34. "Statement of James A. Baker," ER 96:1, p. 9.

35. "Statement of James A. Baker . . . W. M. Rice Deceased Probate," ER, 9:4, p. 5; James A. Baker to Robert S. Lovett, Feb. 2, 1901, ER 79:4. "Mr. Rice never spoke to me about any of his wills until he wrote me in the summer of '96 that . . . it [was] proper" to make one. Baker testified that New Yorker John C. Tomlinson worked on the *Rice v. Holt* litigation, under Baker's direction, *New York Evening World*, Apr. 10, 1901, ER 30, clipping.

36. James A. Baker to William Marsh Rice, Aug. 29, 1899; James A. Baker to Spencer Hutchins, Aug. 29, 1899, ER 4:6; Baker, Botts, Baker & Lovett to Hornblower, Byrne, Miller & Potter, Jun. 12, 1901, ER 75:3.

37. "Statement of James A. Baker," ER 96:1, p. 7.

38. Ibid., p. 8.

39. On Patrick's father, "Memorandum of Charles A. Boston," Baker Botts Papers, Box 5B, WRC; Morris, ed., and Muir, *William Marsh Rice and His Institute*, 110; on Hutcheson defamation, clipping, *Galveston News*, Nov. 5, 1893, ER 30, manila folder; Muir, "William Marsh Rice, His Life and Death," 37.

40. Robert S. Lovett to James A. Baker, Oct. 9, 1900, ER 78:1.

41. *Dallas Morning News*, Nov. 11, 1893.

42. "Mr. Patrick's Legal Career," *New York Times*, Sept. 28, 1900, clipping, ER 38. There is no hard evidence where the leak came from, but Patrick and Jones were in touch by then, if not actually conspiring.

43. The summary of events surrounding Rice's death and the ensuing legal battles is based on correspondence, trial transcripts, Baker's summaries, Jones's confessions, and newspaper stories found in Early Rice Institute Papers, Series I: Court Cases, Boxes 1–50; Series II: WMR will and estate, Boxes 51–87; and Series III, Rice Institute, Boxes 88–91; and in *People v. Patrick* file, Baker Botts Papers, 10A, WRC; MS 487, scrapbook. "Murder on Madison Avenue," in Morris, ed., and Muir, *William Marsh Rice and His Institute*, 84–109, recounts Rice's last days in some detail, again using Early Rice records. Friedland, *The Death of Old Man Rice*, presents a well-researched step-by-step account of the murder case, its appeals, and Patrick's eventual pardon. Friedland's sources include the Early Rice Papers (which have been renumbered since his book was published, so his notes are now hard to follow); transcript and appeal documents, Association of the Bar of the City of New York Library; Hill Papers, New York State Library, Albany; District Attorney files, Municipal Archives, City of New York. Unfortunately, Friedland ignores the logic of his own story and instead accepts the Defense attempt to shift blame to Baker and implicate him as a possible villain. Friedland fails to support his charge against Baker by analysis of Baker's life, personality, or career before, during, or after the events described in his book.

44. Memorandum summarizing Jones's first confession, n.d., ER 11:45, p. 1. Ac-

cording to Jones, Patrick and Jones first met in November 1899 when Patrick called at Rice's apartment, using an assumed name, although they already had been exchanging letters.

45. Henry Oliver Jr. to William Marsh Rice, Sept. 11, 1900; William Marsh Rice to Henry Oliver Jr., Sept. 15, 1900, ER 80:6.

46. Baker, Botts, Lovett & Parker to Hornblower, Byrne, Miller & Potter, Jan. 13, 1902, ER 80:6.

47. Letter, William M. Rice to James A. Baker and T. W. House, Sept. 19, 1900, quoted in Summation, ER 8, p. 5089.

48. Chronology of Facts, ER 25:3; First Confession, ER 11:45, p. 8.

49. *New York Sun*, Sept. 26, 1900, clipping, ER 38. Details first mentioned when New York City papers unleash a flood of news stories. See also, *New York World*, *New York Times*, *New York Press*, Sept. 26, 1900, ER 38.

50. Telegrams, ER 77:3, 78:5; Testimony of N. S. Meldrum, ER 6:5, p. 1008. Meldrum had recently taken the New York job and was staying at the Waldorf Astoria.

51. Testimony of James W. Gerard, wire, ER 9:4, p. 34.

52. Telegrams, ER 77:3, 78:5. It took more than twenty-four hours to heat the crematorium, enough time for police action to avert the cremation plan that would have destroyed critical evidence.

53. Norman S. Meldrum to Robert S. Lovett, Tues., Sept. 25, 1900, ER 77:3.

54. Baker, Botts, Baker & Lovett, letters, Sept. 1900; Norman Meldrum to James A. Baker, telegram, Sept. 24, 1900, ER 77:3.

55. Charge to the Jury, ER 8, p. 5190.

56. Ibid.

57. Not until 1914 could a telephone call be made coast to coast, and only in early 1915 was commercial long-distance calling introduced, a tedious process of patching calls through a series of special long-distance operators.

58. Robert S. Lovett to James A. Baker, telegram Sept. 26 (a.m.), Lovett to Baker, letter Sept. 26 (p.m.), ER 77:3 (Baker, Botts, Baker & Lovett Letters, Sept. 1900 folder).

59. James A. Baker to Captain J. E. Whittlesay, Oct. 6, 1900, ER 75:1.

60. Statement of N. S. Meldrum, ER 9:4. The first tunnel from Jersey City, New Jersey, to Manhattan was opened for commercial railway traffic in February 1908, and Penn Station began receiving railroad traffic in 1910.

61. Chronology, ER 25:3, p. 352; *New York Evening World*, Apr. 10, 1901, summary of Baker's testimony, clipping, ER 30.

62. James A. Baker to Robert S. Lovett, Oct. 2, 1900, ER 77:4.

63. Baker Statement, ER 11:1, p. 6; Meldrum Statement, ER 9:4.

64. Malcolm Lovett interview with Joe Pratt and Chris Castaneda, May 1, 1986, Baker Botts Papers, WRC.

65. Exhibit A, ER 53:4.

66. Chronology, ER, Box 25:3, p. 357.

67. See for example, *New York Tribune, New York World, New York Journal, New York Times*, Sept. 28, 1900, ER 38.

68. Patrick did not know that Baker and the Assistant District Attorney had agreed that the papers could not be removed without consent of the District Attorney's office. Meldrum Statement, ER 9:4, p. 11; Testimony, ER 6, p. 404.

69. Baker's testimony, telegram, ER 6, p. 927.

70. Robert S. Lovett to James A. Baker, Hotel Normandie, Sept. 28, 1900, ER 77:3.

71. Eula Gray to James A. Baker, Sept. 27, 1900, ER 77:3.

72. Robert S. Lovett to James A. Baker, Nov. 26, 1901, ER 75:5.

73. *New York Times*, Sept. 28, 1900.

74. Jones's Statement, ER 12:2, p. 14. Jones says Patrick began talking about a will around Christmas 1899.

75. Patrick had Short made commissioner to "furnish an excuse for introducing him" to Rice. Memorandum as to the Admissibility of a Deed . . ., ER 73:2.

76. Abstracts of Testimony, ER 9:1, pp. 47, 48, 54–56; Report of William A. De Ford, Assistant District Attorney in the People of the State of New York against Albert T. Patrick, Morris Meyers and David L. Short, Mar. 1910, ER 68:10.

77. Charge to the Jury, ER 8, p. 5182.

78. ER 8, p. 5185.

79. James A. Baker to William Marsh Rice II, Nov. 7, 1900, ER 78:5; Charge to the Jury, ER 8, p. 5183.

80. Charge to the Jury, ER 8, p. 5187.

81. Jones Testimony, ER 71, p. 2335; in Charge to the Jury, the Judge mentions Sapolio or baking powder to weaken him, ER 8, p. 5185.

82. W. L. Jones Statement, Mar. 22, 1901, ER 25:2.

83. Charge to the Jury, ER 8, p. 5186.

84. Muir, "William Marsh Rice, His Life and Death," 3.

85. Boston, "Memorandum," 54, see note 10.

86. "Memorandum of Matters to Which Capt. Baker's Attention Should Be Called," n.d., ER 70:1; Statement of Frederick A. Rice, ER 25:2, p. 1; Statement of N. S. Meldrum, ER 9:4, p. 5.

87. James A. Baker, Testimony, vol. 1, p. 323, ER 6.

88. Baker Statement, ER 90:3, p. 5.

89. E. B. Parker to James A. Baker, Oct. 8, 1900, ER 96:1.

90. Osborne, Closing Statement, ER 8, p. 5042.

91. Ibid., 5043.

92. James A. Baker to Robert S. Lovett, Oct. 25, 1900, ER 78:2, p. 4.

93. James A. Baker to Robert S. Lovett, Jun. 27, 1902, ER 81:3. In addition to the legal teams hired for Patrick and Jones, the following law firms represented heirs disputing the 1896 or 1900 will: Eugene L. Bushe (Nina Belle Rice); Ward, Hayden & Satterlee (A. E. McKee); Davis, Stone & Auerbach (Charles W. Rice); Nicoll, Anable & Lindsay (Joseph Blinn); William P. Dewey Jr. (Charlotte S. McKee).

94. Time Sheets, ER 22:2; James A. Baker Statement, ER 11:1; James A. Baker to Robert S. Lovett, Oct. 22, 1900, ER 78:4; Nov. 7, 1900, ER 78:5; James A. Baker to Judge J. D. Bartine, Jan. 30, 1901, ER 79:3.

95. James A. Baker to Robert S. Lovett, Oct. 3, 1900, ER 77:4.

96. Emanuel Raphael to James A. Baker, Oct. 6, 1900; J. E. McAshan to James A. Baker, Oct. 6, 1900, ER 75:1; Board Minutes, Oct. 16, 1900, WRC.

97. Board Minutes, Oct. 16, 1900.

98. Board Minutes, Jan. 5, 1901.

99. Letter, Oct. 16, 1900, ER 78:2.

100. Robert S. Lovett to James A. Baker, Nov. 12, 1900, ER 78:5, p. 6.

101. Letter, Oct. 16, 1900, ER 78:2.

102. Robert S. Lovett to James A. Baker, Oct. 30, 1900, ER 78:4.

103. James A. Baker to Ruth A. Watrous, Oct. 20, 1900, ER 78:1.

104. James W. Osborne to James Byrne, Dec. 12, 1900, ER 75:1; Baker, Botts, Baker & Lovett to Francis P. Garvan, Deputy Assistant District Attorney, Dec. 18, 1901, Dec. 31, 1901, ER 76:5.

105. Edwin B. Parker to James A. Baker, Oct. 8, 1900, telegram, ER 77:3; and letter, ER, 9:4.

106. *New York World*, Sat. Oct. 4, 1900, ER 39.

107. James A. Baker to Capt. J. E. Whittlesay, Washington, Conn., Oct. 6, 1900, ER 75:1, example of letters sent asking if addressees knew of any conferences between Patrick and Rice. Robert S. Lovett to James A. Baker, Oct. 6, 1900, regarding Cohn letters; Robert S. Lovett to James A. Baker, Oct. 6, 1900, regarding willingness of bankers Root and McAshan to supply documents signed by Rice; both in ER 77:4.

108. E. B. Parker to James A. Baker, Oct. 8, 1900, ER 96:1, p. 6; Robert S. Lovett to James A. Baker, Oct. 9, 1900, ER 78:1 and 96:1; E. B. Parker to James A. Baker regarding Raphael letter, Nov. 16, 1900, ER 79:1; Cesar Lombardi to James A. Baker, Nov. 20, 1900, ER 79:1. See also James A. Baker to William Marsh Rice II, Nov. 7, 1900, ER 78:5.

109. Statement of Joseph Mayer, Berlin, Germany, Oct. 30, 31, Nov. 1, 1901, ER 12:15; Pinkerton reports, ER 75:1.

110. James A. Baker to Robert S. Lovett, Oct. 2, 1900, ER 77:4, pp. 5–6.

111. Some months earlier Baker had asked Jones to get the 1896 will from the safety deposit box so Baker could examine it. Instead of returning the 1896 will promptly to the vault, Jones showed it to Patrick. Boston history, ER 22:4, p. 27; James A. Baker, Testimony, vol. 1, p. 323, ER 6, set value at $2.75 million.

112. *New York Evening World*, Oct. 5, 1900, p. 1, in ER 39; letters in ER 75:1.

113. James A. Baker to Norman Meldrum, Oct. 19, 1900, ER 78:1. The will was offered for probate by Judge Bartine because Baker and Will Rice II were listed as executors in both wills, Bartine benefited most by the 1896 will, and the team wanted the option for Baker and Rice to object to the 1900 will should it prevail in probate court. James A. Baker to Robert S. Lovett, Oct. 22, 1900, ER 78:4.

114. Edwin B. Parker to James A. Baker, Nov. 13, 1900, ER 78:5, p. 7.

115. Clippings, ER 35.

116. Clippings, Oct. 27, Oct. 6, 1900, ER 35.

117. Clippings, Nov. 1, 1900, ER 39; Nov. 2, 1900, ER 30.

118. Statements and Confessions of Charles Jones, ER 9.

119. *New York Times,* Oct. 28, 1900, p. 1, ER 35.

120. Full account in James A. Baker to William M. Rice II, Nov. 7, 1900, and James A. Baker to Robert S. Lovett, Nov. 1, 1900, ER 78:5. "Osborne was kept busy writing [the confession] from quarter to nine o'clock until four o'clock in the morning," Baker told Lovett. Trial statements say 8:00 p.m. until 3:00 a.m., ER 15.

121. Statements and confessions of Charles Jones, ER 9:5 and 12:2.

122. James A. Baker to Robert S. Lovett, Nov. 1, 1900, ER 78:5.

123. Letters from James A. Baker to Robert S. Lovett and to William M. Rice II (p. 5), Nov. 7, 1900, ER 78:5.

124. Millikin first resisted efforts by Patrick and House to secure his support but finally bowed to his wife's pressure. James A. Baker to Robert S. Lovett, Nov. 7, 1900, p. 7, ER 78.5.

125. ER 17:3; 70:1;14.8; Patrick Testimony, ER 13:17.

126. *New York Herald,* Feb. 28, 1901; telegrams, Hornblower, Byrne, Miller & Potter to James A. Baker, Feb. 26 and 27, 1901, ER 75:2.

127. "Judge Jerome The Man with a Sledge," clipping, ER 36. Justice Jerome's first cousin, Lady Randolph Churchill, was a famous beauty and heiress and the mother of future Prime Minister and World War II leader, Sir Winston Churchill.

128. *Evening Telegram,* Apr. 1, 1901; *Herald, Evening Telegram,* Apr. 2, 1901, clippings, ER, Box 30; descriptions in clippings, ER 36.

129. *Morning World,* Apr. 3, 1901; *Daily News,* Apr. 3, 1901, ER 37.

130. *Daily News,* Apr. 3, 1901; *New York Journal,* Apr. 3, 1901, ER 37.

131. *New York Journal,* Apr. 3, 1901, ER 37.

132. *Evening World,* Apr. 10, 1901, ER 30; *New York World,* Jan. 29, 1902, ER 31, says Baker had a "small, curly brown mustache and frank brown eyes." Other sources note Captain Baker's gray or blue eyes.

133. *New York Evening World,* Apr. 10, 1901, clipping, ER 30.

134. "Memorandum of Examination Made of Signatures to the 1900 Rice Will by George W. Wood, Expert, of Pittsburgh, Pa., April 29, 1901, at the Surrogates' Court," ER 17:3.

135. The glass plates are stored in ER 19 a, b.

136. James A. Baker to Robert S. Lovett, Nov. 30, 1900, ER 79:1.

137. *New York Tribune,* Oct. 14, 1900, ER 39.

138. James A. Baker to Robert S. Lovett, Dec. 6, 1900; James A. Baker to Robert S. Lovett, Dec. 4, 1900, ER 79:2.

139. John Bartine, In the Matter of Rice Will Case, ca. Apr. 1902, ER 81:2.

140. A statement of expenses on August 5, 1902, shows Baker charged $10 a day for his living expenses, $154.50 for Eula Gray's expenses, and $55 for travel. James A. Baker to Emanuel Raphael, Aug. 5, 1902, ER 81:5.

141. James A. Baker to Norman S. Meldrum, Nov. 26, 1900, ER 79:1.

142. For example, Robert S. Lovett to James A. Baker, Feb. 3, 1900, ER 79:4.

143. *Houston Daily Post,* Mon. Jan. 20, 1902, ER 30, p. 1.

144. *New York Herald,* Jan. 24, 1902, ER 30.

145. Baker Testimony, ER 6, p. 914.

146. Ibid., 842–1007.

147. Chancellor, *Hill School*, 1.

148. Ibid., 30.

149. James A. Baker to Edgar Odell Lovett, Jun. 13, 1925, EOL 42:5.

150. Meigs ideal in Bowie, *Biography of John Meigs*, 155; other information in Chancellor, *Hill School*, 42, 81, 97; comments of Addison Baker Duncan, Jan. 20, 2011.

151. Chancellor, *Hill School*, 34.

152. *Houston Chronicle*, Feb. 7, 8, 12, 1902, front page.

153. Bowie, *Biography of John Meigs*, 305.

154. *Houston Chronicle*, Feb. 13, 1902, pp. 1, 2.

155. *Houston Chronicle*, Feb. 18, 1902, p. 4.

156. I am indebted to Cathy L. Skitko, Director of Communications, The Hill School, for this information.

157. James Byrne to James A. Baker, Feb. 21, 1902, ER 80:7.

158. James A. Baker to James Byrne, Feb. 21, 1902, ER 80:7.

159. James Byrne to James A. Baker, Feb. 26, 1902, ER 80:7.

160. I am indebted to Preston Moore Jr. and Stewart Baker for these insights.

161. Address of Captain James A. Baker before the Rice Institute Engineers' Society, Nov. 13, 1929, p. 30, EOL 36:3.

162. Defense Summary Statement, ER 8, pp. 4764–4940. Quotes, in order, 4765, 4775, 4773, 4779, 4783, 4817, 4909.

163. Prosecution Summary Statement, ER 8, pp. 4942–5748. Quotes, in order, 4944, 4945, 4943, 4946, 4961, 4958, 5026, 5083–84, 5138, 5144.

164. Charge to the Jury, ER 8, pp. 5162–5253. Quotes, in order, 5164, 5168, 5173.

165. Friedland, *Death of Old Man Rice*, 235, explains the contract process in detail.

166. Captain Baker to Engineer's Society, Nov. 13, 1929, EOL 36:3.

167. Walter P. Stewart, Edward A. Peden, to James A. Baker, ER 81:1.

168. James A. Baker to Robert S. Lovett, Mar. 29, 1902, ER 81:1.

169. Ibid.

170. Letter from Patrick about starting proceedings, quoted in Aston, *Promiscuous Breed*, 26.

CHAPTER FOUR

1. William B. Hornblower to James A. Baker, Feb. 22, 1900, ER 75:1; Hornblower, Byrne, Miller & Potter to Baker, Botts, Baker & Lovett, Mar. 2, 1901, ER 79:5.

2. Harris County Court #2402, ER 56:7.

3. Robert Lovett to James A. Baker, Apr. 11, 1901, ER 55:4.

4. Robert S. Lovett to James A. Baker, ER 75:3, notes appeals filed Apr. 10, 1901 by Mrs. McKee opposing Baldwin Rice. Rice was appointed Permanent Administrator on May 8, 1901; the appeal was dismissed Dec. 7, 1906, ER 83:1.

5. Memorandum of Lands Sold by Administrator, ER 64:7.

6. Mark Potter to James Byrne, Jan. 24, 1901, ER 75:2.

7. Baker, Botts, Lovett & Baker to Hornblower, Byrne, Miller & Potter, Jan. 27, 1903, ER 77:1.

8. James A. Baker to Robert S. Lovett, Feb. 7, 1901, ER 79:4.

9. Trustee request (Mar. 18, 1901) and resolution, ER 56:9, 79:5.

10. James Byrne to James A. Baker, Dec. 28, 1901, ER 83:1.

11. Baker, Botts, Baker & Lovett to Hornblower, Byrne, Miller & Potter, Mar. 4, 1901, ER 75:6; James A. Baker to Robert S. Lovett, Feb. 7, 1901, ER 79:4.

12. Robert S. Lovett to James A. Baker, Oct. 14, 1900, ER 75:4.

13. Robert S. Lovett to James A. Baker, Nov. 9, 1900; James A Baker to Robert S. Lovett, Nov. 13, 1900, ER 78:5; Edwin B. Parker to James A. Baker, Nov. 17, 1900; James A. Baker to Edwin B. Parker, Nov. 22, ER 79:1.

14. Baker, Botts, Lovett & Baker to Hornblower, Byrne, Miller & Potter, Jan. 9, 1901, ER 79:3. At Christmas 1900, an unnamed party told Baker that Patrick wired Holt after Rice's death to revisit the $250,000 settlement offer. According to the source, Patrick also wrote to Holt about Sept. 15 to urge the settlement, saying Rice's "days were numbered." Foolishly, Holt replied through A. M. Francis, Patrick's landlady.

15. Robert S. Lovett to James A. Baker, Nov. 12, 1900, ER 78:5, p. 3.

16. Edwin B. Parker to James A. Baker, Nov. 13, 1900, ER 78:5, p. 3.

17. Ibid., p. 4.

18. Hutcheson, Campbell & Hutcheson to O. T. Holt, May 15, 1901, ER 4:9.

19. Baker, Botts, Baker & Lovett to Hornblower, Byrne, Miller & Potter, Jan. 20, 1902, ER 77:1; James A. Baker to Joseph C. Hutcheson, Jan. 21, 1902, ER 80:6.

20. Correspondence, Feb. 1, 1902–Sept. 11, 1902, ER 80.7, 81.2, 81.4, 83.1, 83.2. Good summary of issues, Baker, Botts, Baker & Lovett to Hornblower, Byrne, Miller & Potter, Apr. 7, 1903, ER 77:1.

21. Correspondence, Jun. 5, 1902–Sept. 13, 1907, ER 41:4, 67:5, 77:1–2, 83:2–3; Agreement between Trustees of William Marsh Rice Institute for the Advancement of Literature, Science and Art and Mary Turnure, Marian Roberts Robinson, Julia Roberts, Lola Morton Seybel, Diet Kitchen Society of New York City, and Belle Wallace Perkins, ER 82:4.

22. Robert S. Lovett to James A. Baker, Feb. 6, 1901, ER 79:4.

23. James A. Baker to William M. Rice II, Nov. 7, 1900, ER 78:5.

24. James A. Baker to Robert S. Lovett, Nov. 22, 1900, ER 79:1.

25. Robert S. Lovett to Frank H. McKee, Nov. 13, 1900, ER 78:5.

26. James A. Baker to Baker, Botts, Baker & Lovett, Jan. 30, 1901, ER 79:3.

27. B. F. Rice to Hornblower, Byrne, Miller & Potter, from Radical, MO, Nov. 30, 1900, ER 79:1.

28. William Dewey Jr. (quoting Gibbs's letter to him) to Hornblower, Byrne, Miller & Porter, Dec. 26, 1901, ER 76:5.

29. James A. Baker to Robert S. Lovett, Nov. 2, 1901, ER 80:5; James A. Baker to David, J. S., W. M., H. Baldwin, and B. B. Rice, Jun. 1, 1901, ER 80:3.

30. Board Minutes, Dec. 11, 1901.

31. James A. Baker to Edward B. Cushing, Jun. 25, 1902, ER 81:3. Cushing must

have been a close friend because Baker addresses him as My Dear Ed, a rare use of someone's first name.

32. Baker, Botts, Baker & Lovett to Hornblower, Byrne, Miller & Potter, Mar. 28, 1903, ER 77:1.

33. *Syracuse Herald*, Dec. 17, 1910; *Albany Journal*, Dec. 19, 1910; *New York Times*, Dec. 19, 1910, ER 30 (manila folder).

34. William M. Rice II to James A. Baker, Jul. 21, 1902; Judge John D. Bartine to Mark Potter, Jul. 23, 1902, ER 81:4.

35. The Surrogate granted letters testamentary Sept. 11, but he required bond of $7 million, which was arranged with the National Surety Company and deposited in Blair & Co. by Oct. 22. Blair & Co. had been of "great assistance" to Baker during the controversy so he was particularly pleased they would hold the deposit. Board Minutes, Sept. 12, 1902 (copy in ER 88:7); James A. Baker to William Marsh Rice II, Sept. 23, 1902, ER 81:6.

36. Judicial Settlement, Dec. 15, 1903, ER 62:6; Inventory showed starting balance of $3,355,202.96 plus $287,223.24 interest/income for total $3,642,426.20, less expenses of $161,395.48, for the $3,481,030.72 figure. Instructions regarding authorization failed to reach the executors because the telegraph lines were not open and messages were delayed. James Byrne to James A. Baker, Dec. 6, 1902, ER 81:9.

37. Telegrams, Mar. 26, 30, 1903, ER 77:1.

38. Settlement decree, Apr. 29, 1904, ER 66:4. Cash $1,082,408.62; securities and notes $2,333,400,46.

39. Byrne & Cutcheon to Baker, Botts, Parker & Garwood, Aug. 27, 1907; John Brooks Leavitt to James A. Baker, Aug. 29, 1907, ER 82:4.

40. Hornblower, Byrne, Miller and Potter to Julius Offenbach, Sept. 4, 1904, ER 65. William M. Wherry Jr. to James A. Baker, Nov. 18, 1904, ER 85:1.

41. McCants, "Rice Institute," 13; Board Minutes, Sept. 25, 1906, indicated all funds and securities would be turned over about Oct. 1, 1906. Final report in Board Minutes, Oct. 23, 1906.

42. Baker, Botts, Baker & Lovett also received about $100,000 for services performed during Rice's last year of life, to fight Mrs. Rice's will, and to assist the temporary and permanent administrators in Texas.

43. Full account to the Rice Institute Board, Oct. 1, 1906, ER 82:1; information in Statement to Judge Bartine, Sept. 18, 1907, ER 82:2; and in documents, ER 41:5; 65; 68:11; 77:1, 2; 80:3, 5; 81:3, 7; 82:4; 83:1; 85:1.

44. Account of Cesar Lombardi, 2–3, ER, Lombardi file; Morris, ed., and Muir, *William Marsh Rice and His Institute*, 37.

45. James A. Baker to Rice Institute Engineer's Society, Nov. 13, 1929, EOL 36:3.

46. In the late nineteenth century, an "orphan" referred to a fatherless child.

47. Arey, *Girard College and Its Founder*, last testament, 57–85. I am grateful to Dr. Melissa Kean for alerting me to this comparison.

48. 1882 Last Will and Testament, ER 88:1.

49. City Directories, 1880s–1890s; Kate Sayen Kirkland, *Hogg Family and Houston*, 124.

50. Baker, "Reminiscences of the Founder," 133–34.

51. Cesar Lombardi to James A. Baker, Nov. 20, 1900, ER 76:4.

52. "History of Rice Institute," Baker Botts Papers, 5B, p. 6, WRC. One high school served the Houston Independent School District (HISD) in 1912.

53. Cesar Lombardi to James A. Baker, Nov. 20, 1900, ER 79:1.

54. Statement of Emanuel Raphael, ER 96:1.

55. Morris, ed., and Muir, *William Marsh Rice*, Appendix 5.

56. Brief, ER 115:19.

57. Malcolm Lovett, son of Edgar Odell Lovett and senior partner of Baker & Botts, maintained that Baker had told him Raphael did most of the work on the charter. Other sources, including Raphael's statement for the Patrick trial (ER 9:5), give Baker more credit, and some note that he checked over all related materials. The Rice Institute charter so closely resembles the Cooper Union charter that it must have served as the model for Raphael, Rice, and Baker. I am indebted to J. Thomas Eubank and Dr. Melissa Kean for these insights.

58. Certificate of Incorporation, ER 22:3; Charter reprinted in Morris, ed., and Muir, *William Marsh Rice*, Appendix.

59. Documents (charter, indenture, certificate of incorporation, deed of gift) in ER 88:1, 2, 3; Board Minutes, vol. 1, front matter.

60. Memorandum from James A. Baker to James Byrne, in *Rice v. Holt*, ER 4:5.

61. Emanuel Raphael to James A. Baker, Jun. 20, 1899, ER 1:4. The actual deed specifies 8 acres, although sworn testimony and several letters mention 6.5 to 7 acres. Deed, Jun. 20, 1892, ER 88:3; Board Minutes, Jul. 14, 1892.

62. Testimony, ER 6, p. 276.

63. Statement of Emanuel Raphael, ER 9:5.

64. "The Wm. M. Rice Institute," *Houston Daily Post*, Oct. 21, 1900, pp. 10–11.

65. Stockton Axson to Mrs. James A. Baker, Mar. 16, 1929, MS 487, miscellaneous; letters and lists, ER 97:1; Summary of Educational Institutions, ER 96:2.

66. Edwin B. Parker to James A. Baker, Jun. 13, 1902, enclosing "Daniel Coit Gilman" by G. Stanley Hall, *The Outlook*, Aug. 3, 1901, pp. 818–21.

67. J. J. Pastoriza to James A. Baker, Oct. 28, 1905, ER 88:7. Pastoriza was elected Houston mayor in 1917 and died in office. Many establishment businessmen regarded Pastoriza as an impractical visionary because of his single tax proposals. The *Chronicle* editor Marcellus Foster and arch-conservative Rienzi M. Johnston, editor of the *Houston Post*, strongly opposed his campaign, which was as vehemently supported by the *Houston Press*. During his three months in office, Pastoriza investigated the Houston Police Department and the Houston Lighting & Power Company, a Baker, Botts, Parker & Garwood client.

68. Board Minutes, Dec. 14, 1905.

69. Committee Minutes, Oct. 10, 1892, ER 88:3; Board Minutes, Oct. 10, 1892; Emanuel Raphael to Robert S. Lovett, Apr. 9, 1901, ER 80:1.

70. Motion by Alderman O'Leary, ER 88:7; Boles, *University Builder*, 27.

71. ER 5:7.

72. Board Minutes, Sept. 19, 1907. Cohn and H. H. Lummis were to be paid

$2,500 a year in monthly installments and were required to deposit $10,000 surety bonds in the Institute vault. The Institute headquarters were convenient to Captain Baker's offices during these years: 1907–1909 the Heitmann Co. building; 1909–1912 the Scanlan Building; until 1927 the Commercial National Bank Building; and from 1927 to about 1963 the Esperson Building.

73. Board Minutes, Feb. 20, 1907.

74. See Boles, *University Builder*, 39–45; letters in ER 88; Board Minutes.

75. James A. Baker to Prof. Harry Estill, May 4, 1907, ER 88:10.

76. Henry F. Estill to James A. Baker, May 6, 1907, ER 88:10; Jones, *Southwestern University*.

77. James A. Baker to Sidney E. Mezes, Jul. 2, 6, 1907, ER 5:10.

78. Emanuel Raphael to James A. Baker, Jul. 9, 1907, ER 88:10.

79. James A. Baker to William Hayne Leavell, Mar. 15, 1907, ER 88:9.

80. "William Hayne Leavell, 1850–1930: An Autobiography," 156, printed by Alec Bayless and Larry Noble, 1979, MS 384, WRC.

81. Arthur LeFevre to Edgar Odell Lovett, EOL 13:3.

82. Board Minutes, Dec. 28, 1907.

83. Board Minutes, Jan. 22, 1908.

84. Summary from histories in EOL 28:10, 29:2, 36:2.

85. Boles, *University Builder*, 43.

86. Board Minutes, Mar. 11, 1908.

87. James A. Baker to Edgar Odell Lovett, Apr. 16, 1908, ER 89:2.

88. EOL 1:2; letters in ER 89:3.

89. Board Minutes, Oct. 8, 1908.

90. Board Minutes, Apr. 10, 1907.

91. Henry F. MacGregor to James A. Baker, Feb. 4, 1908, ER 89:2.

92. Kate Sayen Kirkland, *Hoggs and Houston*, 49–53. Hermann donated a large area of land on May 30, 1914; he also bequeathed to the city a square block downtown for a "breathing space" park and $2.6 million for a public hospital. In 1915 the city purchased additional land for the nature park from the Hermann Estate. Exploration of the Humble Oil Field began tentatively in 1902–1903 with real development from 1904 on.

93. Weber drove a hard bargain; when he finally agreed to sell, he demanded that he be allowed to stay on for another three and one-half years. Unfortunately, his pig sties and other farm buildings abutted the Administration Building and location designated for opening ceremonies. Just days before the October 10–12, 1912 Academic Festival began, Institute personnel finally persuaded Weber to move his animals and buildings off the property.

94. Correspondence between James A. Baker and Senator Joseph W. Bailey in ER 89:6. See also Board Minutes 1908–1909; ER 89:2, 3; McCants, "Rice Institute," 18–19.

95. Board Minutes, May 12, 1909; news accounts, *Houston Post, Houston Chronicle*, May 9, 1909.

96. Edgar Odell Lovett, "Historical Sketch of Rice Institute, A Gift to Texas Youth," EOL 46:27; Institute Announcement, 1915–1916, p. 9, WRC.

97. EOL 4:1, p. 2.

98. Executive Meeting, Board Minutes, Jul. 14, 1909.

99. Lovett, "Historical Sketch," 8.

100. Ibid., 6. Ralph Adams Cram was consulting architect to Princeton from 1906 to 1929, created the school's first master plan, and mandated Collegiate Gothic as the predominant style.

101. Cram, *My Life in Architecture*, 124–26.

102. Board Minutes, Dec. 1, 1909.

103. Ralph Adams Cram to Edgar Odell Lovett, Jan. 19, 1910, EOL 4:2.

104. Lovett, "Historical Sketch," EOL 46:27, p. 7.

105. Edgar Odell Lovett to James A. Baker, Nov. 1, 1910, James A. Baker to Thornwell Fay and G. Radetzki, Nov. 8, 1910, ER 89:8.

106. "The Laying of the Cornerstone," Press Release, EOL 46:1.

107. Institute Announcement, 1915–1916, p. 13, WRC.

108. James A. Baker to Edwin B. Parker, Aug. 4, 1909, ER 89:7.

109. Board Minutes, Dec. 23, 1910. Cesar Lombardi and Ben Rice each took five shares, and the others four shares apiece.

110. Lovett family papers, addendum, courtesy of John Boles.

111. Table, ER 89:3.

112. Resolutions Adopted by Houston Bar Association, Oct. 3, 1941, As a Tribute to the Memory of Captain Baker, written by J. C. Hutcheson Jr., in several family collections.

CHAPTER FIVE

1. Lovett, *Creation of Rice University*, 56.

2. Lindsey Blayney to Lindsey Blayney Jr. and J. M. Blayney, Feb. 10, 1959, Lindsey Blayney information file, WRC.

3. Spratt, *Road to Spindletop*, 274.

4. Introduction of "modern" law firm practice is attributed to Paul Drennan Cravath, who joined associates in 1899 to form the firm that became Cravath, Swaine & Moore. Cravath and Parker were inaugurating their systems at about the same time, but New York was considered the legal and financial capital of the country, so Cravath's name has long been associated with prototypical large law firm organization.

5. Thomas Phillips, Interview, Baker Botts Papers, 7B, WRC.

6. Freeman, *People of Baker Botts*, v; James A. Baker, III, and J. Thomas Eubank, interviews with author.

7. Freeman, *People of Baker Botts*, 49.

8. In 1919 Parker assumed the title Managing Partner, a position invented in the early twentieth century to help larger firms organize legal talent and assign client business.

9. Freeman, *People of Baker Botts*, 65.

10. Ibid., 73. Baker also acted as a surrogate parent for Tom Botts's siblings; shortly after her parents' deaths, he escorted Hester Botts down the aisle when she married Arthur Cargill on October 21, 1894.

11. Robert S. Lovett was chairman of the executive committee and president of the Southern Pacific and Union Pacific from 1909–1913. After the two properties separated, he was chairman of the executive committee of Union Pacific from 1913–1918; CEO of Union Pacific 1919–1924; and chairman 1924–1932, when he died in 1932. Lovett was settled in offices at 120 Broadway at least by June 3, 1904 (letter James A. Baker to Robert S. Lovett, Jul. 31, 1904, ER 85:1).

12. Hiram Garwood, OR, Jun. 16, 1921, reprise of a speech delivered in 1913.

13. Baker Botts Papers 4A, WRC (Railroad Lawyers); Freeman, *People of Baker Botts,* 55–58. Garwood tried the "Shreveport Rate Case" (234 U. S. 342), still considered one of the firm's major triumphs.

14. OR, Sept. 23, 1936, p. 177.

15. Freeman, *People of Baker Botts,* 70.

16. Ibid., 81.

17. Firm Contracts, Baker Botts Papers, 4A, WRC. In 1919 the firm averaged deposits of $41,000 in South Texas Commercial National Bank, over which Baker presided; $7,000 in S. F. Carter's Lumberman's National Bank (Second National after 1923); and $2,000 in Guardian Trust, organized by Baker to facilitate real estate development.

18. Robert S. Lovett to James A. Baker, Dec. 4, 1900, ER 79:2.

19. OR, Nov. 10, 1927, p. 321.

20. Edwin B. Parker to W. B. Scott, Dec. 23, 1913, Baker Botts Papers, Southern Pacific client file, WRC.

21. James A. Baker to Jesse Andrews, Memorandum, Baker Botts Papers, 3, WRC.

22. E. B. Parker, Memorandum, Jul. 29, 1916, Baker Botts Papers, 3, WRC.

23. Cipher books and telegrams in Baker Botts Papers, client files, WRC; telegrams in ER 80:5 (1900–1901) and ER 69:2 (1910).

24. Creed, cited in Parish History, Jan. 16, 1954, Baker Botts Papers, WRC.

25. 1911 Plan in Baker Botts Papers, WRC, quoted in Freeman, *People of Baker Botts,* 49.

26. Memorandum, Jul. 21, 1916, with handwritten, signed note from Clarence Wharton to Jesse Andrews, Baker Botts Papers, 3, WRC.

27. General information about Texas' banks is found primarily in Buenger and Pratt, *But Also Good Business;* Logan, *Houston Heritage Collection;* William A. Kirkland, *Old Bank–New Bank.* Unfortunately, since Buenger and Pratt published their thorough study in 1986, the South Texas Commercial National Bank (STCNB) Directors' Minutes and other archival material cannot be found, despite extensive detective work by Barbara Eaves, to whom I am much indebted for information about the banking industry.

28. A series of federal laws passed during the Civil War encouraged formation of nationally chartered banks but required heavy initial investment unavailable to most businessmen in the cash-poor postwar South.

29. Federal laws (1863–1865) required $50,000 capital outlay and allowed banks to issue notes up to 90 percent of the face value of their bonds on deposit with the US Treasury. Typical charters were for twenty years. In 1882 banks were allowed to

issue notes up to 100 percent of the value of their bonds on deposit. Logan, *Houston Heritage Collection*, 9, 11.

30. Handwritten articles of organization signed by the six stockholders are reproduced in Freeman, *People of Baker Botts*, 17. President Decimus et Ultimus Barziza, the largest investor at $1,500, was, as his name implies, the tenth and last child of parents well-versed in the classics.

31. Board Minutes, Dec. 20, 1901; also Mar. 30, 1901.

32. Emanuel Raphael to James A. Baker, Jun. 4, 1902; James A. Baker to William B. Chew, Jun. 25, 1902; James A. Baker to Emanuel Raphael, Jun. 25, 1902, ER 81:3.

33. James A. Baker to Robert S. Lovett, Aug. 5, 1902, ER 81:5.

34. Board Minutes, Aug. 4, 1905.

35. Except for a few years during Reconstruction, the State Constitution explicitly excluded state banks.

36. Logan, *Houston Heritage Collection*, 65, 70; OR, Nov. 3, Feb. 8, 1923.

37. The House bank also made some huge loans, including $500,000 to lumberman and investor Jesse Jones. See Fenberg, *Unprecedented Power*, 45.

38. William B. Chew to Jesse Jones, Sept. 20, 1907, Jesse H. Jones Collection, Houston Endowment, quoted in Fenberg, *Unprecedented Power*, 45.

39. Kate Sayen Kirkland, *Hogg Family and Houston*, 14; Sibley, *Port of Houston*, 136–37; Fredrickson, *Andrews & Kurth*, 4, 8–9, 12.

40. Figures in Buenger and Pratt, *But Also Good Business*, 59.

41. According to a Union National Bank employee, Carter believed Jones was "trying to pad his own pocket at the expense of Union National." Story in Buenger and Pratt, *But Also Good Business*, 54.

42. Ibid., 88.

43. OR, Feb. 10, 1927, p. 63. Baker served as vice president of Bankers Trust (1911–1912), whose officers included J. S. Rice, president, and W. T. Carter, S. F. Carter, Abe Levy, and others as vice presidents, but he is best known for his investment in and supervision of Guardian Trust.

44. James A. Baker to D. K. Cason, Feb. 15, 1918, EOL 36:2 (Trustees 1918–1947).

45. Stockton Axson to Alice Baker, Mar. 16, 1929, MS 487.

46. James A. Baker to Florence T. Griswold, Dec. 14, 1915, ER 91:2.

47. Board Minutes, Jul. 1941.

48. James A. Baker Jr., Captain Baker's son, reported on one such transaction that occurred in 1919 when Baker Botts acquired the permits for National Biscuit Company, a New York Corporation doing $55 to $85 million in business nationwide, and then was hired by the firm as regional representative. OR, Mar. 8, 1923, p. 87.

49. Baker Botts Papers, 5.0 B, WRC.

50. Board Minutes, Dec. 2, 1903, Jun. 8, 1905, Apr. 8, 1907; James A. Baker to Col. I. M. Standifer, ER 88:10.

51. Board Minutes, Mar. 25, 1908, Jul. 22, 1914; "The James A. Bakers and Austin College," in family collection, based on Austin College Trustee Minutes and George Landolt, *Search for the Summit*.

52. Photograph in Montgomery, *Rice Institute, 1913*, 98; Board Minutes Mar. 10, 1909, Jun. 23, 1909, Nov. 17, 1909. The caption calls attention to this important embellishment.

53. Correspondence and deeds in Jesse H. Jones Collection, Box 81 (Rice Hotel folder), Houston Endowment, courtesy of Steven Fenberg. One subscriber dropped from 250 to 100 shares in December 1906, noting that first investors in hotel projects "either lose out or . . . donate their original subscription." Harris Masterson to Jesse Jones, Dec. 16, 1906, Jesse H. Jones Collection, Box 81, Houston Endowment.

54. Edwin B. Parker to James A. Baker, Aug. 9, 1909, ER 89:7.

55. Fenberg, *Unprecedented Power*, 51.

56. Hotel Association information in Jesse H. Jones Collection, Box 81; Board Minutes, Jun. 7, 22, 1911; Oct. 13, 1911; May 1, 1912; Jun. 5, 19, 1912; Nov. 6, 1912.

57. Board Minutes, Feb. 6, 1918.

58. Biographical material about Harriet Elizabeth Palmer Milby Hutcheson courtesy of Elizabeth Hutcheson Carrell. See also, Board Minutes, Jan. 14, 1914; Feb. 16, Mar. 1, 15, 29, Apr. 4, 1916; Feb. 20, 1925.

59. Board Minutes, Jul. 22, 1914.

60. I am indebted to Francita Ulmer for the information about her great-grandmother, Rosa Lum Allen. Mrs. Allen's professional advisers kept meticulous records, which have been preserved by her family. Her business records, Allen, Mrs. Samuel E., (Rosa) Papers, 1862–1945 and Undated; Allen, Mr. and Mrs. S. E. Papers, 1870–1978 and Undated, Southwest Collection, Texas Tech University, were provided to me on CD by Mrs. Ulmer. Information relating to Mrs. Allen's transactions is also found in Baker Botts Papers, WRC; in Board Minutes, Jul. 22, 1914; and in the Stuart and Allied Families Papers, WRC. Camp Allen is now located in Navasota and is a full-service conference center and camp facility. For more information, see Brown, *Episcopal Church in Texas II*. Rosa Allen's grandson Robert C. Stuart Jr. learned about the summer camping movement so popular in the eastern United States while a student at Harvard and encouraged his grandmother to make the original offer.

61. OR, 1927, p. 254. Deeds in Stuart and Allied Family Papers, WRC. I am indebted to Francita Stuart Ulmer for information relating to Robert Stuart.

62. *Standard Blue Books of Texas*, "Houston Society"; Federation of Women's Clubs, *Key to the City of Houston*, 11.

63. Freeman, *People of Baker Botts*, v.

64. Houghton, *Houston Club*, 20. Houghton provides a thorough history of Houston's early club movement.

65. Reminiscences of James A. Baker, III and Preston Moore Jr. to author; Trimble, *Houston Country Club Centennial*, 10.

66. Mayo, *American Country Club*, 1, 2; Wind, *Story of American Golf*, 216, 221.

67. I am indebted to Ira Gruber for information about golf in America; e-mail 6/5/2011. See Ira Gruber, *John Peebles' American War: The Diary of a Scottish Grenadier, 1776–1782*, Army Records Society, 1997.

68. Mayo, *American Country Club*, 71; Wind, *Story of American Golf*, 19, 33, 51.

69. The club was located along what is now West Dallas where the Federal Reserve Building stands.

70. Trimble, *Houston Country Club Centennial*, 10.

71. Alexis J. Colman, "Golf in Texas," 93. Article courtesy of Nancy Stulack, United States Golf Association Museum Librarian.

72. Ibid., 94. George V. Rotan of Waco and Houston was a five-time Texas champion from 1912–1915, gained an international reputation, and was on the 1923 Walker Cup team that won at Old Course St. Andrews, Scotland.

73. Houston Country Club Charter, article II, cited in Trimble, *Houston Country Club Centennial*, vii.

74. Will C. Hogg suggested issuing an additional $25,000 of non-interest-bearing bonds.

75. Trimble, *Houston Country Club Centennial*, 23; Mayo, *American Country Club*, 2, 7.

76. Trimble, *Houston Country Club Centennial*, 29–34.

77. Chautauqua Minute Book, Chautauqua File, HMRC.

78. Chautauqua File, HMRC; Chapman, "Chautauqua Study Club," 24–28.

79. Boles, *University Builder*, 148.

80. Photograph Album, courtesy of Virginia Meyers Watt.

81. These portraits were displayed for many years in family homes. In 2010–2011 all were reunited in the Baker College Library, Rice University, the gifts of Graeme Meyers Marston and Virginia Meyers Watt and the bequest of James Harrison Moore. Elizabeth Gowdy Baker (1860–1927) lived in Keokuk, Iowa, Boston, New York, Palm Beach, and Lake Placid. She painted many prominent contemporaries, landscapes, and seascapes and specialized in children and watercolors. She trained in New York, Philadelphia, Rome, Florence, and Paris and was married to Daniel B. Baker.

82. Robert Lundberg, Bass Rocks Golf Club historian, speculates that the Rotans introduced Bass Rocks to the Bakers. It is also possible that the families' summer friendship spurred Baker to hire Rotan as investment adviser in the 1920s. Lundberg, *Bass Rocks Golf Club*, 36.

83. *Houston Post*, Nov. 8, 1909.

84. "The Echo of the Ball," n.d., clipping courtesy of Virginia Meyers Watt.

85. "Elegant Reception," Dec. 2, 1907, clipping courtesy of Virginia Meyers Watt.

86. H. Malcolm Lovett, partner interviews, Baker Botts Papers, WRC.

87. "In Society" column, *Houston Chronicle*, Nov. 20, 1911, p. 8; Nov. 21, 1911, p. 10; Nov. 22, 1911, p. 11; Nov. 22, 1911, p. 12.

88. Alice Baker, Bass Rocks, to Bonner Means, the Rossonian, Houston, Jul. 25, 1915, MS 40, 2:1; Interview with Mrs. James A. Baker Jr., 1985, Marguerite Johnston Papers, 1:8, p. 4, 12, WRC.

CHAPTER SIX

1. Kate S. Kirkland, *Hogg Family and Houston*, for an exploration of this Progressive-era ethos.

2. Leavell, " Autobiography," 138, MS 384, WRC.

3. Board Minutes, Sept. 3, 1915.

4. OR, Sept. 17, 1937, p. 183, reprising Plan of Organization.

5. "Capt. Baker's Address," *Texas World*, clipping courtesy of Virginia Meyers Watt.

6. A. J. Downing, *Horticulturist* (Jan. 1847), quoted in Turner and Wilson, *Houston's Silent Garden*, 1, 9–15.

7. Information comes from the Glenwood Minute Book, Glenwood Cemetery office; a time line, courtesy of the late Martha Peterson, Glenwood Cemetery staff; Heitman Collection, MS 42, 1:6, WRC. For a full account of Glenwood Cemetery, see Turner and Wilson, *Houston's Silent Garden*.

8. Committee members included YMCA Board President William A. Wilson, Baker, Wm. D. Cleveland (the first Y president), E. W. Taylor, J. Lewis Thompson (a good friend of the Baker family), S. F. Carter (whose bank became the depository of YMCA funds), J. B. Bowles, and J. V. Dealy. Information in Pamphlet of the Campaign; YMCA Board Minutes, Apr. 14, 1906, May 24, 1907, Jan. 27, 1908, Jun. 10, 1908; Arnold, "History of the YMCA of Greater Houston," 49–59. I am indebted to Gary Nichols for making these materials available to me and for his insights about the YMCA.

9. YMCA Board Minutes, Feb. 5, 1908. Rice Institute Board Minutes, Jan. 22, 1908, Feb. 19, 1908. Early Rice Land Deeds Collection UA 222, 59:5.

10. YMCA Board Minutes, Jun. 10, 1908.

11. Houston clubwomen formed the Federation of Women's Clubs in May 1897 and received a charter affirming its nonprofit corporate status in 1902.

12. Beard, *Woman's Work*, x (quote), 10, 11, 44, 45, 64, 131, 143, 182, 220–21, 283.

13. Ione Peden was the first wife of Captain Baker's friend, the industrialist Edward A. Peden. She died in 1902, and he later married Cora Root, also a lover of music and supporter of the Houston Symphony.

14. Federation of Women's Clubs, *Key to the City of Houston*, 152.

15. Tuesday Musical Club File, HMRC; Kate Sayen Kirkland, *Hogg Family*, 165–66.

16. For information about the Houston Symphony, see Kate Sayen Kirkland, *Hogg Family*, 158–98; Roussel, *Houston Symphony Orchestra*.

17. *Houston Chronicle*, Jul. 13, 1912, clipping, Estelle Sharp Papers, 5:4, WRC, reviews the debate. Early social service work in Kate Sayen Kirkland, *Hogg Family*, 83–93.

18. Kate Sayen Kirkland, *Hogg Family*, 83.

19. Faith Home Year Book, 1927; Kate Sayen Kirkland, *Hogg Family*, 83–93, discusses pre-WWI social services; Chung, Levit, and Linseisen, "DePelchin Children's Center," 9–12.

20. First Presbyterian Church Records, HMRC.

21. Neighborhood Centers Inc., *100 Years*, 2.

22. Tsanoff, *Neighborhood Doorways*, 1–3.

23. Neighborhood Centers Inc., *Heart of Gold Yearbook*, 1997, 5.

24. Estelle Sharp (1873–1965), widow of drill-bit inventor Walter Benona Sharp

(1870–1912), was a woman of exceptional humanitarian and intellectual power who believed her wealth should be used to help others. A person of great moral courage and broad insight, she worked for the cause of lasting world peace, was influential in planning Texas social welfare programs, and remained on the board of the Houston Settlement Association and its successor, Neighborhood Centers Inc., until her death. See Estelle Sharp Papers, WRC; NCI Papers, brown binder, courtesy of Angela Blanchard. Roxalee (Mrs. Frank) Andrews served briefly as vice president, but Mrs. H. R. Akin replaced her sometime in 1908.

25. Federation of Women's Clubs, *Key to the City*, 62–63.

26. Tsanoff, *Neighborhood Doorways*, 3.

27. Olivia Sage founded the Russell Sage Foundation as a memorial to her husband in 1907 to influence social welfare policy. The foundation supported pilot projects, trained professional social workers, and focused on problems of childhood.

28. Settlement Association, *Year Book*, 15.

29. Ibid., cover page.

30. Ibid., 5.

31. Neighborhood Centers Inc., *100 Years*, 8.

32. This settlement became a day nursery and nursery school under private management within a few years of its organization.

33. Tsanoff, *Neighborhood Doorways*, 9–12.

34. *Houston Daily Post*, Aug. 6, 1916, p. 27.

35. Tsanoff, *Neighborhood Doorways*, 4.

36. "The History of Captain Baker," courtesy of Virginia Meyers Watt.

37. Bylaws of the Houston Foundation, William C. Hogg Papers, 2J371, folder 1.

38. Diary entries Feb. 12, Feb. 27, Jun. 27, 28, Jul. 5, 11, 12, Sept. 3, 1917, William C. Hogg Papers, 2J399.

39. Board Minutes, Apr. 17, 1915.

40. Radoslav Tsanoff file, WRC.

41. Edgar Odell Lovett to James A. Baker, Jun. 24, 1915, ER 91:1.

42. Marked article, *Princeton Alumni Weekly*, vol. XVII, no. 13, 307–08, in MS 40; survey in ER 91:1. Although critics have felt the Board held back Rice's expansion, during the 1912–1929 period, slow growth was due in large part to the difficulty of getting buildings finished in a timely manner and to the challenge of finding faculty willing to move to Houston.

43. Board Minutes, Jan. 11, 1917. Tony Martino signed a contract to provide all labor for the grounds and a vegetable garden from Jan. 8, 1917 to Jan. 1, 1918, at a monthly salary of $4,910.

44. Edgar Odell Lovett to Marcellus E. Foster, Jun. 19, 1914, ER 91:1.

45. A. L. Guerard to James A. Baker, Jan. 21, 1918, EOL 91:6.

46. Correspondence S. B. Houx to James A. Baker, James A. Baker to Edgar Odell Lovett, May 12, 17, 1913, EOL 90:5.

47. McCants, "Rice Institute," 41.

48. For a detailed account of the drama surrounding the design and building of Rice Institute, see Fox, "Rice Institute and Its Architectural Development."

49. Correspondence, Jan. 4, 1913, EOL 15:5.

50. Board Minutes, Jun., 1915; EOL 42:5. These anecdotes about parent and faculty issues are covered in Boles, *University Builder*, 117–45.

51. Board Minutes, Feb. 20, 1918, Apr. 24, 1918; letters read into the minutes.

52. Robert S. Lovett was chairman of the Executive Committee and President of the Union Pacific and Southern Pacific Systems (1909–1913). After the properties were split, he was Chairman of the Executive Committee of the Union Pacific (1913–1918). During the war he held several offices: Chairman of the Committee on Cooperation of the American Red Cross (1917–1918); Priorities Commissioner; War Industries Board member; Allied Buying Commission; Director of Capital Expenditures for American Railroads under Federal Control (March to December 1918). Firm History File, Baker Botts Papers, 10A.

53. Board Minutes, Oct. 31 (first quote), Apr. 30 (second quote), May 25, Jul. 11, 25, 1917. Jesse H. Jones moved to Washington to lead the Department of Military Relief for the Red Cross. Fenberg, *Unprecedented Power*, 68–69.

54. Baines, *Houston's Part in the World War*, 59–104; Benda, *War Service Memorial*. The YWCA War Council is also referred to as the YWCA War Work Council.

55. Haynes, *A Night of Violence*, provides an excellent account of this brief but bloody race riot. "Unfortunate affair" in Joseph Cullinan Papers 55:12; other quotes in *Houston Chronicle*, Aug. 24, 25, 26, 1917.

56. EOL 7:7, Ministers Alliance. This anecdote is discussed in Boles, *University Builder*, 127–32.

57. First quote in Boles, *University Builder*, 130; second in reply, EOL 7:7.

58. Edgar Odell Lovett, Matriculation Address, EOL 46:12.

59. Baker Botts Papers, 5B; ER 91:6.

60. *Thresher*, Feb. 2, 16, 1918, Mar. 6, 1919. The incident is covered in Boles, *University Builder*, 136–41.

61. James A. Baker to D. K. Cason, EOL 36:2.

62. Board Minutes, Jun. 12, 1918; donation correspondence, EOL 35:6; Telegram Edgar Odell Lovett to Honorable Woodrow Wilson, Jun. 12, 1918, EOL 91:6.

63. EOL 30:32.

64. *Houston Post*, Nov. 26, 1918, p. 14.

65. *Thresher*, Mar. 6, 1919.

66. Melissa Kean, www.ricestorycorner.com, Nov. 25, 2010.

67. Report of the Board, EOL 7:7; Lyford P. Edwards to Professor Jerome Davis, Nov. 17, 1931, EOL 7:3. This incident is covered in Boles, *University Builder*, 227–32.

68. Correspondence and memos, EOL 42:5.

69. James A. Baker to M. A. Mitaranga, Marseille, Nov. 5, 1918, James A. Baker, III personal collection, Baker Institute, RU.

70. News clippings, MS 40, scrapbooks.

71. Letter to Lt. James A. Baker Jr., Quartermaster School, Officers Reserve Corps, Camp Travis, Ft. Sam Houston, Texas, Sept. 15, 1917, James A. Baker, III personal collection, Baker Institute, RU.

72. Correspondence, MS 40, Box 2.

73. James A. Baker, Waldorf Astoria, New York, to James A. Baker Jr., Camp Travis, Leon Springs, Aug. 27, 1917, James A. Baker, III personal collection, Baker Institute, RU.

74. Telegram, 3:30 a.m., James A. Baker to Lt. James A. Baker Jr., Jun. 16, 1918, MS 40: 6, scrapbook.

75. Lt. James A. Baker Jr. to Alice Baker Jones, Oct. 11, 1918, James A. Baker, III personal collection, Baker Institute, RU.

76. Col. E. K. Sterling, Apr. 15, 1919, "History of the 90th Division," MS 40, Box 6, manila file.

77. Dorothy Fly to Bonner Means Baker. The writer's husband, Montgomery Fly, took Lt. Baker's place when Baker was reassigned and was killed in action. Lt. Fly spoke often of his friend and "was so devoted to him." Both men would write letters to their wives at the same time, MS 40, Box 2:1.

78. Division History, MS 40, Box 6, manila folder.

79. James A. Baker to Eddie Coates, Nov. 15, 1918, MS 40, folder 1; Lt. James A. Baker Jr., statement, MS 40, Box 6. Captain Baker wrote to his sister-in-law speculating about their son's service on the front lines when neither parent had heard from them. Baker quotes from Jim's letter about the devastation to his company in the last days of the war.

80. James A. Baker, III, interviews with author.

81. James A. Baker to M. A. Mitaranga, Nov. 5, 1918, James A. Baker, III personal collection, Baker Institute, RU.

82. James A. Baker to Gen. John J. Pershing, American Expeditionary Forces, Paris, Feb. 3, 1919; correspondence and telegrams, MS 40, manila folders.

CHAPTER SEVEN

1. Clipping, MS 487. E. F. Woodward (oil) at $12 m. was Houston's richest resident, followed by Jesse Jones (real estate) at $10 m; Will C. Hogg (real estate and oil) at $4 m.; and James A. Baker (public utilities and real estate) at $3.5 m.

2. William C. Hogg to Governor Dan Moody, Austin, Jun. 19, 1928, Joseph Stephen Cullinan Papers, 12:2, University of Houston Archives, also quoted in Kate Sayen Kirkland, *Hogg Family and Houston*, 35.

3. I am indebted to the "ruthless in business and cards" insight to Steven Fenberg, whose biography about Jesse Jones (*Unprecedented Power*) is the latest study of this important Houstonian and national figure. Will C. Hogg quote in William C. Hogg to Governor Dan Moody, Jun. 19, 1928, EOL 43:10; the letter is also found in several other local collections and was widely distributed.

4. Tsanoff, *Neighborhood Doorways*, 12.

5. *City Book of Houston*, 143, HMRC; "Premeditated Pleasures," Mar. 10, 1929, "Recreation a la Mode," Mar. 31, 1929, "The Work of Play," Jun. 9, 1929, *Gargoyle*, RU.

6. King, *Except the Lord Build*, 90–92.

7. Board Minutes, Feb. 15, 1939, shows that the YMCA was having difficulty meeting its obligations by 1939 and had rearranged its remaining indebtedness.

8. Information on the YM/WCA and Community Chest in collections at

HMRC. I am grateful to Gary Nichols for sharing additional materials from the YMCA archive. The Community Chest bulletin shows the Bakers gave $2,000 in 1923 and 1928, $1,500 in 1924–1927, and $1,800 in 1929–1930. The Community Chest was organized in Houston in 1922 after a 1921 Chamber of Commerce study group recommended it carry on United Charities work.

9. Minutes, Firm Conference, Jan. 12, 1924, Baker Botts Papers, 3, WRC.

10. Kate Sayen Kirkland, *Hogg Family*, 206–09.

11. William C. Hogg to James A. Baker, Apr. 2, 3, 11, 1924, William C. Hogg Papers, 2J337. The Hogg family gave $50,000 to the city for its 1924 down payment.

12. OR, Oct. 23, 1924, 336–38a.

13. Correspondence in William C. Hogg Papers, 2J299, folder 2.

14. Pamphlet, Forum of Civics, William C. Hogg Papers, 2J317.

15. *Gargoyle*, Jan. 29, 1929; William C. Hogg Papers, 2J395. In 1949 fund-raising began again. Milford House opened November 11, 1953, but the membership declined and disbanded in 1988, when the Italian Cultural and Community Center of Houston purchased the property. Woman's Building of Houston-Milford House papers, WRC, "Historical Note."

16. Hyman, *Craftsmanship and Character*, 45, says 198 lawyers were practicing in 1917. Crooker and Gayle, *Fulbright & Jaworski*, 2, say 168 lawyers were practicing at the end of the war. By 1926, according to the *Houston Chronicle*, 500 lawyers practiced in the city. *Houston Chronicle*, Oct. 24, 1926.

17. Fredrickson, *Andrews & Kurth*, 7.

18. Ibid., 6, 14. Andrews, Streetman, Logue & Mobley clients during this period included international cotton brokers Anderson, Clayton & Company, Standard Oil of New Jersey, Kirby Lumber Company, and inventor Howard Hughes.

19. Hyman, *Craftsmanship and Character*, quote p. 63, see also pp. 23, 61, 62.

20. Clients and friends included natural gas investor Odie R. Seagreaves, Gus Wortham, Jesse Jones, and Governor William P. Hobby. In 1926 Elkins, Wortham, and Jones needed only to shake hands—and invest $75,000 each—to create American General Insurance Company.

21. I am indebted to J. Thomas Eubank for the phrase "driver of men"; he described Baker as a leader of men, Elkins as a driver of men, and Parker as a pusher of men. Others have suggested to the author that Elkins was a bully with a bad temper and strong language. Information from Hyman, *Craftsmanship and Character*, 24, 25, 45, 50, 60, 61, 70, 71, 72.

22. Crooker and Gayle, *Fulbright & Jaworski*, 2, 5, 6, 7, 10, 12, 13, 15–18; Macon, *Mr. John H. Freeman and Friends*, 15, 16; Fredrickson, *Andrews & Kurth*, 12.

23. OR, Jun. 17, 20, 2–3. In 1929 Baker Botts helped Peden Iron & Steel reorganize as Peden Co. by another charter amendment.

24. Minutes, Dec. 21, 1923, p. 11, Baker Botts Papers, 3, WRC.

25. Murray Brashear Jones stayed at Baker Botts only one year. He later served as Harris County Judge, ran for mayor of Houston, and practiced law independently. Political opponents accused him of close association with the Ku Klux Klan during

his mayoral campaigns, and his marriage to Alice Baker ended in divorce in 1931. Greene, "Guardians against Change," 14, 15; Harris County Court Records, research courtesy of Janet Wagner.

26. Firm statistics found in Baker Botts Papers, 3, 4A, WRC.

27. Baker Botts Papers (partner interview), WRC.

28. Interview, John T. McCullough to Joe Pratt, May 29, 1985, Baker Botts Papers, 7B, WRC.

29. Feagin served as assistant managing partner from 1920–1927, when he withdrew from the firm to become vice president of Electric Bond & Share Co. in NY and then president of United Gas Corporation in 1930. Freeman, *The People of Baker Botts*, 83.

30. Quotes in order, OR, Dec. 21, 1922, p. 395; Feb. 9, 1922, p. 39; Mar. 13, 1924, p. 98; Aug. 16, 1927, p. 24; Dec. 7, 1922, p. 377; Jan. 25, 1923, p. 26; Sept. 21, 1922, p. 286.

31. OR, Mar. 12, 1925, p. 94.

32. OR, May 22, 1924.

33. James A. Baker to R. Lee Blaffer, Aug. 2, 1922, MS 40, 2:2.

34. OR, Jun. 17, 1920.

35. OR, Jan. 24, 1924, p. 37. Annette Finnigan was named by her father to run his business but fell ill with a mysterious disease that forced her retirement; in the 1930s she traveled widely and provided the first treasures of antiquity to enter the collection of the Museum of Fine Arts, Houston.

36. OR, Aug. 17, 1922.

37. Minutes of meetings show that Baker, a member of the board, tried to secure new management and reorganize the company but that the company was "in a bad state" and had "made no money since prohibition became effective." The owner of its controlling interest, the Estate of Hugh Hamilton, was not in a position to control board members who could not agree among themselves. Minutes and memos Mar.–Apr. 1924, Baker Botts Papers, 3, WRC.

38. Fredrickson, *Andrews & Kurth*, 7. Case information, *Dallas Morning News*, Sept. 24, p. 1; Oct. 4, 1922, p. 3; *Ft. Worth Star*, Mar. 8, 1914; Nov. 6, 1914, p. 6.

39. Baron, *Houston Electric*, chap. 5.

40. OR, Aug. 15, 1925, p. 249.

41. ABA comments, OR, Nov. 24, 1927, p. 336; OR, Apr. 26, 1928.

42. OR, Jan. 13, 1927, p. 5.

43. Minutes, May 5, May 28, 29, 1923, Baker Botts Papers, 3, WRC.

44. OR, Aug. 17, 1922, announced Parish's return.

45. Alvis Parish to James A. Baker, Oct. 14, 1922, MS 40.

46. Correspondence James A. Baker to Alvis Parish, Oct. 20, 1922; Alvis Parish to James A. Baker, Sept. 29, Oct. 14, Nov. 24, 1922, MS 40.

47. My interpretation is based on correspondence and on comments made by Captain Baker's grandsons, James A. Baker, III, Preston Moore Jr., Malcolm Baker Jr., and Stewart Baker. Malcolm Baker Jr. noted that primogeniture played a role, with great pressure on oldest sons to succeed their fathers; Stewart Baker sensed a generational split, with the older children adhering more closely to their father's ideas.

48. OR, Apr. 12, 1933, Captain Baker on Edwin B. Parker, p. 108.

49. Edwin B. Parker to Baker, Garwood, Andrews, Wharton, Carter, Tallichet, Botts, and Walne, Sept. 3, 1919, MS 40, 5:1.

50. OR, Feb. 3, 1921. Rice Institute used Dillon Read and Brown Brothers Harriman to invest Rice endowment funds and underwrite business expansion of client firms. Parker believed Dillon Read was a financial house "of very high standing." Parker was an associate of Edward R. Stettinius, a J. P. Morgan executive and war production official under Woodrow Wilson. His son, E. R. Jr. (1900–1949), served in Franklin D. Roosevelt's administration, became secretary of state, and helped organize the United Nations.

51. OR, Apr. 9, 1920, p 77.

52. OR, Jun. 8, Oct. 12, 1922. At this time he was a National Councilor to the Chamber of Commerce of the United States, a trustee for the Carnegie Endowment for International Peace, and a member of the Council on Foreign Relations.

53. 1923 Meeting Minutes, Baker Botts Papers, 5:2, WRC.

54. OR, Jan. 7, 1926, pp. 17–25.

55. OR, Jan. 11, 1923, p. 4; Apr. 12, 1933, p. 109.

56. Freeman, *People of Baker Botts*, 53. Parker's 8 percent share was divided ³⁄₇ of 1 percent to Baker, Garwood, Andrews, Wharton, Carter, and Walne; 1³⁄₇ percent to Tallichet; 1⅓ percent to Hutcheson, Feagin, Parish to total 8 percent. Feagin to Neilson, Dec. 31, 1925, Baker Botts Papers, WRC.

57. Johns Hopkins, Princeton, and Harvard were three leading institutions that did mount fully staffed, modern fund-raising campaigns, but the professional program was exceptional rather than standard.

58. Edwin B. Parker to James A. Baker, Sept. 3, 1919, MS 40.

59. Board Minutes, Special Meeting, Jul. 14, 1919; Annual Meeting May 24, 1922.

60. Board Minutes, 1920–1929.

61. Figures from Board Minutes, annual meeting reports, 1908–1941.

62. Edgar Odell Lovett to James A. Baker, Apr. 2, 1923, cited in Boles, *University Builder*, 161; clipping, *Dallas News*, Jun. 10, 1924, EOL 16:2.

63. P. B. Timpson, Houston Land and Trust, to J. T. McCants, Jun. 6, 1929, EOL 20:8.

64. Scholarships, press release, EOL 16:4.

65. Ima Hogg to Mary Hale Lovett, Sept. 1, 1922, Lovett Family letters, courtesy of John B. Boles; letters, Edgar Odell Lovett to Ima Hogg, May, Jun. 1922, Feb., May 1923, Jun. 1924; list of City Auditorium box holders, EOL 24:1; William C. Hogg Papers, 4W271.

66. Sharp Lectures, EOL 23:9, 10.

67. Lovett in EOL 51:6; funds in EOL 16:6, 16:8, 20:8, 23:15, 24:1, 43:10; William C. Hogg Papers, 2J367.

68. This project flagged in the 1930s. Board Minutes, May 31, 1928, show $13,000 collected when the group requested permission to hire a secretary. Board Minutes, Nov. 20, 1940, record that alumni had raised $32,500 plus $9,540.09 interest.

69. Board Minutes, May 22, 1928.

70. Board Minutes, Feb. 27, 1929; EOL 16:7.

71. Lamar Fleming correspondence, Feb.–Mar. 1929, EOL 35:8. Lamar Fleming (1892–1964) worked for Anderson Clayton for several years before coming to Houston in 1924 as the company's president and later chairman. He transformed the international family-run cotton brokerage into a publicly traded agricultural corporation and served on the boards of the University of Houston, Rice Institute, Kinkaid School, Baylor Medical Foundation, and the Federal Reserve Bank of Dallas.

72. Ferry, "Autry House," 3, 4; A. B. Cohn to Edgar Odell Lovett, May 26, 1921, EOL 35:7.

73. *Thresher*, Feb. 23, 1935; the writer believed young James suggested the project to his mother. James's death following dengue fever, two operations for an appendicitis, and gangrene in the intestine, shocked his acquaintance and devastated his mother. More shocking to his parents' friends was the appearance of known members of the Ku Klux Klan (which also sent a memorial wreath) at his funeral. Joe Cullinan was "greatly chagrined" to learn that young James had been a member of the Klan, which he attributed to the influence of Mrs. Autry's brother, a prominent Klan member in Jefferson City, Texas. Joseph S. Cullinan to Judge W. W. Moore, Sept. 27, 1922, Joseph S. Cullinan Papers, 32:12.

74. Edward Palmer drowned in 1908 trying to rescue his sister Daphne, who had fallen overboard. Alice Baker Jones became a member of Palmer Church and dedicated the stained glass rose window, "Christ Crucified," to her parents' memory. The window has since been obscured by the installation of a large organ and is no longer visible to worshippers inside the church.

75. Board Minutes, Apr. 16, May 22, Oct. 20, 1920.

76. Fox, "Rice Institute and Its Architectural Development," 65; *Thresher*, Nov. 29, 1923; Board Minutes 1923, 1924.

77. William C. Hogg to James A. Baker, Mar. 9, 1922, EOL 35:7.

78. Board Minutes, Jul. 2, 6, 1926.

79. Letter of donation read by Captain Baker at a special meeting, Board Minutes, Mar. 21, 1927.

80. Board Minutes, Mar. 16, 21, Jun. 2, 1927; Nov. 28, 1928; W. M. Rice Institute to J. T. Watson, IRS, Jul. 12, 1932; Nicholson, *Watkin*, 186–87; Boles, *University Builder*, 166–67.

81. Press Release, Jun. 9, 1930, EOL (commencements section); Board Minutes, Nov. 28, 1928; Nicholson, *Watkin*, 232–36; Boles, *University Builder*, 186.

82. Stockton Axson to James A. Baker, Jun. 24, 1918, EOL 35:6.

83. Board Minutes, Mar. 5, 1924.

84. Board Minutes, budget sections, 1920s.

85. Erwin Escher to A. B. Cohn, Nov. 13, 1921, EOL 35:7.

86. A. B. Cohn to Edgar Odell Lovett, Feb. 15, 1929, EOL 35:8.

87. When Tsanoff was offered $7,500 from the University of Southern California, the Board authorized Lovett to counter with $8,000 to keep the popular professor, whose wife worked on civic projects with Alice Baker. Board Minutes, between Jun. and Oct. 1928.

88. James A. Baker to Edgar Odell Lovett, Mar. 10, 1937, EOL 8:23.

89. *Thresher*, Nov. 13, 1929; EOL 15:8, 22:1.

90. *Thresher*, Oct. 5, 1928; Recognition in James A. Baker, III private collection, courtesy of Susan Baker. Photograph of the portrait, courtesy of Stewart Baker; whereabouts of the portrait not currently known.

91. Lists of corporate sponsors EOL; Boles, *University Builder*, 196.

92. Correspondence, May 1929, EOL 36:3.

93. Joseph S. Cullinan to Judge W. W. Moore, Sept. 27, 1922; to Frank Andrews, Chairman Student Loan Fund, Nov. 1, 1922; to Board of the Chamber of Commerce, Nov. 13, 1922, Joseph S. Cullinan Papers, 32:12.

94. Houston Subdivision Collection, 2:6, HMRC. Westmoreland Addition, Houston's first private place subdivision, organized in 1902 by Wilmer Waldo, the civil engineer who developed Rice Institute's infrastructure; Montrose, planned between 1902 and 1906; and small enclaves organized by Humble Oil company founder Ross Shaw Sterling (Rossmoyne, 1914) and the Hogg family (Colby Court, 1923–1924) were absorbed into the surrounding mixed-use district by the mid-1930s. Sterling published the *Post Dispatch* (1925–1932), was president of the Houston National Bank (1925–1932), commissioner of the Port of Houston and head of the State Highway Commission (1927–1930), and governor of Texas (1931–1932); *Houston Architectural Survey*, 819–20.

95. Woodland Heights, Houston Subdivision Collection, 1, HMRC.

96. Statement of purpose, pamphlet on the Baker/Jones Residence, courtesy of Virginia Meyers Watt. Baker gave half the lot to his daughter and sold the other half to Sara Brashear Jones, mother of Murray Jones. The original Jewet icebox and ceiling fans are still in the house.

97. Photograph album made by Ruth Baker (Moore) in 1917–1919 shows toddler Alice scampering across the Courtlandt house lawn and standing proudly on the playhouse porch. Courtesy of Preston Moore Jr.

98. The homes on Courtlandt Place have been placed on the National Register of Historic Places in 1979 and look today very much as they did in the 1920s.

99. Shadyside, Houston Subdivision Collection, 2; 26, HMRC; Fox, "Shadyside," 41.

100. Correspondence in Broadacres and Milroy Place/Subdivision Papers, WRC.

101. *Houston*, Jun. 1922, p. 18; *Houston Architectural Survey*, 960–62, 986–87, 1008–09, 1026–28.

102. Telegrams, Jul. 12, 14, 1923, MS 487, A 1–3, scrapbook.

103. James A. Baker to Robert L. Blaffer, Aug. 2, 1922, MS 40, folder 2.

104. Correspondence, Alice and James A. Baker, Oct.–Dec. 1922, MS 40, folder 2. Walter Browne Baker became known as Browne or W. Browne in his professional career. Through his teens, family referred to him as Buster, and his father mentioned him as Walter B. For clarity, I have decided to adopt W. Browne or Browne for references after his graduation from college.

105. *Houston Post*, Aug. 3, 1941, clipping in Baker Botts Papers, 10 A, WRC.

106. Barnstone, *Architecture of John F. Staub*; I am also indebted to Stephen Fox for his comments about Captain Baker.

107. Harris County Deed Records, vol. 542, p. 579. The field notes describe the property, which includes .92 acre later deeded in 1938 to Captain Baker's five children (vol. 1043, p. 417), on which stood homes for Ruth and Malcolm at 207 and 211 Bremond. At his death, Baker bequeathed 5.81 acres to Rice Institute. Harris County Records Search courtesy of Janet K. Wagner, JK Wagner and Company Inc.

108. Houghton et al., *Forgotten Heritage*, 54–55, citing *Houston Post*, Sept. 5, 1909.

109. *Cornerstone*, Summer 9:3; Baker Botts Papers (title search); books in collection of Preston Moore Jr., each denoting section and shelf for placement; Preston Moore Jr. and James A. Baker, III, interviews.

110. Recollections of James A. Baker, III, Stewart A. Baker, and Preston Moore Jr.

111. OR, Apr. 8, 1926, pp. 154–55.

112. OR, Aug. 16, 1927, pp. 246–47; Nov. 28, 1930, pp. 112 ff.; interview, John T. McCullough to Joe Pratt, May 29, 1985, Baker Botts Papers, 7B, WRC.

113. Neither the Baker nor the Lovett papers reveal the nature of this ailment, although its symptoms suggest a onetime spell of extreme fatigue and depression following studies in Paris. I am indebted to comments by John B. Boles about this illness. Adelaide pursued an active family and civic life after her marriage.

114. Adelaide Lovett to James A. Baker, Oct. 10, 1922, MS 40, 2:2.

115. James A. Baker to Murray B. Jones, Oct. 15, 1922, MS 40, 2:2.

116. Correspondence in MS 40, 2:2.

117. *Houston Chronicle*, Dec. 24, 1922, "In Society" page.

118. Episode recounted in Lovett Family Papers, addendum; information made available by John B. Boles.

119. James A. Baker to Bonner Means Baker, The Savoy, Houston from Reims, Marne, Sept. 22, 1924, James A. Baker, III personal collection, Baker Institute, RU.

120. Nicholson, *Watkin*, 138. Kinkaid was founded in 1904. The Watkin building served the school from 1924–1957, when the campus was moved west of Voss at Memorial and San Felipe.

121. Malcolm remained at the bank until World War II erupted. In 1941, at age thirty-six, he signed up with the Air Force and attended officer training school. He was stationed in East Anglia (1943–1945), where due to his age, he was assigned on-base administrative duties. After the war Malcolm left banking to become an independent investor. Recollections of Stewart Baker.

122. *Houston Post-Dispatch*, Society, Oct. 24, 27, 1926; *Houston Chronicle*, Oct. 24, 27, 1926.

123. *Houston Chronicle*, Nov. 14, 15, 24, 1929; *Houston Post-Dispatch*, Nov. 15, 1929.

CHAPTER EIGHT

1. OR, Feb. 7, 1924, p. 61.

2. OR, Mar. 24, 1927, p. 112.

3. William A. Kirkland, *Old Bank–New Bank*, 74–75.

4. Letter, Jesse Jones to A. D. McDonald, Southern Pacific Lines, Oct. 29, 1931, Jesse H. Jones Collection, Houston Endowment, courtesy of Steven Fenberg. Secondary sources on the banking crisis include Buenger and Pratt, *But Also Good Business*, 90–108; Logan, *Houston Heritage Collection*, 107–08. Quote, McAshan to Baker, TCB Minutes, now missing, quoted in Buenger and Pratt, *But Also Good Business*, 98.

5. Letters to customers and to James A. Baker, Jesse H. Jones Collection, Houston Endowment.

6. James A. Baker to Edgar Odell Lovett, Sept. 26, 1931, EOL 36:3.

7. Anna Graham Herring to Alice Graham Baker, Apr. 30, 1930, MS 40, 2:3.

8. James A. Baker to Alice Baker Jones, Jan. 12, 1932, MS 487, 1:7.

9. MEFO (Marcellus E. Foster), *Houston Press*, clipping, notebook on death of Alice Graham Baker, MS 487; *Houston Press*, May 10, May 11, 1932; *Houston Chronicle*, May 10, 1932; *Houston Post* May 11, May 13, 1932.

10. The paintings, given in 1935, were copies of *Madame Le Brun and Daughter* by Louise Elizabeth Vigée Le Brun (French, 1755–1843); *Magdalen* by Carlo Dolci (Florentine, 1616–1686); *The Milkmaid, The Broken Pitcher,* and *The Dead Bird* by Jean Baptiste Greuze (French, 1725–1805); and *Immaculate Conception* by Bartolommeo Esteban Murillo (Spanish, 1618–1682). Information courtesy of Preston Moore Jr.

11. James A. Baker to James A. Baker Jr. and Bonner Baker, Aug. 4, 1932, MS 40, 2:3.

12. Robert A. Falconer to James A. Baker, Apr. 3, 1933, EOL 36:2.

13. Jas. A. Baker to Mr. and Mrs. Jas. A. Baker Jr., Mr. and Mrs. W. Browne Baker, Mr. and Mrs. Preston Moore, Mr. and Mrs. Malcolm G. Baker, Nov. 4, 1932, private collection, courtesy of Bonner Means Baker Moffitt and James A. Baker, III.

14. Frank Andrews's eulogy quoted in Freeman, *People of Baker Botts*, 56.

15. OR, Jan. 21, 1931, p. 2–5.

16. Ibid., 7

17. EOL 36:3.

18. OR, Oct. 12, 1922. Information regarding Andrews also in Baker Botts Papers 7A, WRC; Freeman, *People of Baker Botts*, 59–64; Lipartito and Pratt, *Baker & Botts*, 122–25.

19. E. B. Parker to Ralph Feagin, Baker Botts Papers, 11 L1, folder 1, WRC.

20. OR, Feb. 7, Oct. 27, 1925.

21. J. H. Freeman to Joe Pratt, memo, Dec. 28, 1987, Baker Botts Papers, 7A, WRC.

22. James A. Baker to Ralph Feagin, Jan. 18, 1938, Baker Botts Papers, 10 D 2, WRC. The letter makes plain that Feagin and Baker have already come to an agreement.

23. Interview, Tom Martin Davis, Baker Botts Papers, 7A, WRC.

24. OR, 1938, p. 52; 1939 passim. These corporations proved to be lucrative clients in later years.

25. OR, Jan. 11, Jun. 11, 1938, memo, Feagin to all lawyers.

26. OR, Mar. 13, 1940, 59–60.

27. OR, Oct. 23, 1940, 202–04. Joseph C. Hutcheson III was the son of Federal District Judge Joseph C. Hutcheson Jr. and nephew of Palmer Hutcheson.

28. Kilman, "Work Hard, Study and Keep out of Politics," 1, 6.

29. OR, Mar. 1, 1938, p. 7.

30. Seating charts in Lovett Papers, addendum, courtesy of John B. Boles; EOL 35:7

31. Arthur Cohn to Edgar Odell Lovett, May 12, 1933, EOL 36:14.

32. Income/Expense data, Board Minutes, Apr. 16, 1941, p. 242.

33. Board Minutes, Feb. 24, 1932.

34. James A. Baker to Trustees of Rice Institute, Apr. 3, 1933, EOL 25:5.

35. Board Minutes, Mar., 4, May 1, 1931, and through 1939.

36. The Board discussed selling the property at Louisiana and Jefferson to the school district in March 1927, and Baker announced the school district was ready to close the sale of the Louisiana Street property at the annual meeting, June 13, 1928, but the process was not completed until May 15, 1929. Board Minutes, Mar. 9, Mar. 16, 1927, Jun. 13, 1928, May 20, 1929; deeds in Early Land Deeds, Contracts, and Related Records.

37. Board Minutes, May 20, 1929; Baker-Slaughter correspondence, Jun. 19, 20, 1929, EOL 35:8; William C. Hogg Papers, 2J399, 1929 diary entries, May 15, May 20.

38. Ima Hogg Papers, 3B122, folder 3, Dolph Briscoe Center for American History, University of Texas.

39. William C. Hogg Papers, 2J367.

40. Houston School Superintendent E. E. Oberholtzer and Board of Education Chairman R. H. Fonville appeared before the Institute Board March 9, 1927, to describe the plan to create a junior college under school board auspices. Public demand for a four-year institution quickly followed the successful junior college experiment. Board Minutes, Mar. 9, 1927.

41. Edgar Odell Lovett to Robert S. Lovett, Feb. 18, 1930; Robert S. Lovett to Edgar Odell Lovett, Jun. 3, 1931.

42. List of Subscribers and Potential Subscribers, EOL 36:14.

43. Board Minutes, Jun. 2, 5, 1932.

44. Board Minutes, Jun. 3, 24, 1936.

45. A. B. Cohn to Edgar Odell Lovett, Jul. 18, 1932, EOL 36:1; Board Minutes, Jun. 29, 1932.

46. James A. Baker to Edgar Odell Lovett, Jun. 6, 1932, EOL 36:1.

47. Board Minutes, Dec. 19, 1934.

48. *Houston Chronicle*, Dec. 23, 1936; *Houston Press*, Dec. 23, 1936; *Houston Post*, Dec. 24, 1936; Board Minutes, Dec. 24, 1936; *Thresher*, Jan. 8, 1937, p. 1.

49. Board Minutes, Sept. 5, 1934, p. 27; Jul. 24, 1934.

50. *Thresher*, Mar. 29, 1935.

51. Board Minutes, Jul. 7, 1933.

52. Board Minutes, Apr. 29, 1932; Jun. 22, 1933; Jul. 12, Aug. 23, 1933; James A. Baker to Trustees of Rice Institute, Jul. 12, 1933, EOL 36:5; Robert L. Blaffer to Edgar Odell Lovett, Jun. 20, 1940, EOL 36:2.

53. Board Minutes, Apr. 16, 1941.

54. Board Minutes, Apr. 20, Jul. 20, 1938.

55. Stadium Fund, EOL 16:16; Board Minutes, Feb. 2, 1938.

56. EOL 16:16.

57. James A. Baker to Edgar Odell Lovett, Jun. 1939, EOL 36:15.

58. James A. Baker to C. Arthur Dwyer, Feb. 12, 1941, EOL 37:1.

59. Tsanoff, *Neighborhood Doorways*, 22–24, 30–32; Neighborhood Centers Inc., *100 Years*, 17.

60. Tsanoff, *Neighborhood Doorways*, 44–55; Neighborhood Centers Inc., *100 Years*, 65; Neighborhood Centers Inc. Minutes, Box 1, courtesy Neighborhood Centers Inc.; *Houston Post*, clipping, Apr. 15, 1940, MS 40.

61. Cullinan Papers 20:1.

62. Edgar Odell Lovett to James A. Baker, Mar. 17, 1936, EOL 36:2.

63. Interview, James A. Baker, III with Pratt, Barnett, Freeman, and Doty, Aug. 22, 1985, Baker Botts Papers, 7B; James A. Baker, III, interviews with author.

64. Alice Jones Meyers later changed the spelling of Graham to Graeme. Information courtesy of Graeme Meyers Marston.

65. Recollections of James A. Baker, III, Preston Moore Jr., and Francita Stuart Ulmer, one of the frequent party guests; riddles in "History of Captain Baker," courtesy of Virginia Meyers Watt; *Gripsholm* ship's list in scrapbook, courtesy of Betty Kyle Moore: Mr. and Mrs. Preston Moore, Captain James A. Baker, Alice Baker Jones, Miss Alice Baker Jones, Preston Moore Jr.

66. Contract with and letter to Alice Baker Jones, May 28, 1938, courtesy of Graeme Meyers Marston; reminiscences of Stewart Baker.

67. "Long Time Houston Resident Expires; Paid Lofty Tribute," clipping courtesy of Virginia Meyers Watt; Mackie Baker death certificate (May 24, 1940), Harris County Records; family genealogy tables. James A. Baker, III, *"Work Hard, Study . . . and Keep Out of Politics!"*, 419–25, traces the Jesse Baker story.

68. Correspondence, Feb. and Mar. 1940, MS 40, 2:3. Jim Baker had his appendix removed and an obstruction in his intestinal tract repaired. He and Bonner were in Baltimore and then in Bermuda to recuperate for more than two months. Ella and Rufus accompanied the children to their grandfather's.

69. James A. Baker to James A. Baker Jr., Feb. 21, 1940, James A. Baker, III personal collection, Baker Institute, RU.

70. James A. Baker to Edgar Odell Lovett, May 17, 1941, EOL 36:2; Board Minutes, May 14, 1941; *Thresher*, May 23, p. 3.

71. *Thresher*, May 23, 1941, p. 1.

72. Bill Ryon in OR, May 29, 1941, p. 74; other tributes, pp. 69–79.

73. James A. Baker to Jimmy Baker, Jun. 10, 1941, James A. Baker, III personal collection, Baker Institute, RU. On the envelope in pencil is the information that the letter was written the day Captain Baker became sick.

EPILOGUE

1. In penciled remarks on the last page of his will, Baker had written "Wishes of the Deceased." These included that no one but the undertaker and nurse would see him after his death so that everyone could remember him "as a living man." He did not want eulogies or a reprise of his life at the funeral since "remarks at my funeral cannot change the consequences of my own acts." He also did not want the funeral ceremony to follow rituals of any secret order of which he might be a member because he felt the "show of tinsel" seemed out of keeping with the solemnity of the occasion. MS 40, In Memoriam, vol. 3.

2. *Houston Post*, Aug. 4, 1941, MS 40; Glenwood Cemetery grave site.

3. The trust for each grandchild was $10,000; Ruth, who was pregnant with her second child when Captain Baker wrote his will, received $20,000 for her children. *Houston Post*, Aug. 14, 1941, MS40, 4:4; James A. Baker and Alice Graham Baker Bequest, EOL 30:7.

4. Early Land Deeds, Contracts and Related Records, UA222, 59:4.

5. Description, Houston Lighting and Power tribute, in Palmer Hutcheson remarks, MS 40, 4:1; quote, *Houston Press*, Aug. 4, 1941, MS 40, 4:4.

6. *Houston Post*, Aug. 3, 1941, editorial, In Memoriam vol. 3, MS 40, 4:4.

7. *Houston Chronicle*, Aug. 3, 1941, MS 40, 4:4.

8. Alvis Parish to Alice Baker Jones, MS 40, 4:3.

9. "A Tribute to the Memory of Captain James Addison Baker, 1857–1941, President of the Board of Trustees of the Rice Institute, 1891–1941, from His Associates on the Board," Oct. 2, 1941. On February 16, 1942, a copy of the testimonial in a leather case was carried by messenger to Baker, Botts, Andrews & Wharton, Guardian Trust, South Texas Commercial National Bank, to each of Captain Baker's children, to his two surviving sisters, and to Mr. and Mrs. H. Malcolm Lovett. President Lovett presented the copy to Alice Baker Jones personally. EOL 35:3.

10. Statement to the Saturday papers, Aug. 2, 1941, EOL 36:2.

11. James A. Baker Jr. to Edgar Odell Lovett, Oct. 11, 1941, courtesy of Virginia Meyers Watt.

12. "In the Supreme Court of Texas, Proceedings Incident to Presentation of Resolutions and Addresses on the Life and Service of Captain James A. Baker, Friday, October 17, 1941, at Ten Thirty A. M.," in several places including pamphlet in Baker Botts Papers, 10 A, WRC.

13. *Houston Press*, Aug. 4, 1941, MS 40, 4:4.

14. "Captain Baker," MS 40, 4:1. His son Malcolm recounts an amusing anecdote of a shopping mix-up that caused his father to chastise a hapless salesman "for half an hour."

15. Belief of Captain Baker, courtesy of Virginia Meyers Watt.

16. Owen D. Young, quoted in "Captain Baker," MS 40, 4:1.

Works Consulted

ARCHIVAL SOURCES
Baker Botts L.L.P.
    Office Review, 1920–1941
Glenwood Cemetery Foundation, Glenwood Cemetery Office
    Minute Book and Records
Harris County Court Records
Houston Endowment
    Jones, Jesse H., Collection
Houston Metropolitan Research Center, Houston Public Library
    Ballinger & Associates Papers
    Chautauqua File
    City Book of Houston, 1925
    Community Chest Files, 1928–1931
    First Presbyterian Church Records
    Holcombe, Oscar, Papers
    Houston Light Guard Files
    Houston Social Service Bureau Records
    Houston Subdivision Collection
    Junior League of Houston File
    Mayors' Book (Houston)
    YWCA Collection
Neighborhood Centers Inc., Offices, Houston, Texas
    Centennial Records
Rice University, Woodson Research Center, Fondren Library
    Baker & Botts Law Firm Archive, 1840–1990
    Baker, Captain James A., Papers, MS 487
    Baker Family Papers, MS 40
    Blayney, Lindsey, Information File
    Broadacres Milroy Place Subdivision Papers, MS 371
    Early Land Deeds, Contracts and Related Records, 1830–1969, UA 222
    Early Rice Institute Records, UA 101
    Eisenlohr Rice Institute Letters, 1913–1921, MS 536
    Heitman Collection, MS 42
    House, Edward M., Correspondence, 1925–1934, MS 263
    Hutcheson Family Papers, MS 496
    Leavell, William Hayne, autobiography typescript, MS 384

Lovett Family Papers, MS 494
Merchants and Planters Oil Company Records, MS 260
Muir, Andrew Forest, Papers, MS 17
Presidential Records: Edgar Odell Lovett, 1912–1945, UA 14
Rice University Opening Ceremony Files
Ryon, Lewis B., Information File
Sharp, Estelle, Family Papers, 1883–1965, MS 271
Stuart and Allied Families Papers, MS 553
Tsanoff, Radoslav, Information File
Watkin, William Ward, Papers, 1903–1953, MS 332
Woman's Building of Houston-Milford House papers, 1894–1976, MS 388
Sam Houston State University Special Collections
    Thornton Papers
Texas Tech University, Southwest Collection
    Allen, Mrs. Samuel E. (Rosa), Papers, 1862–1945 and undated
    Allen, Mr. and Mrs. S. E., Papers, 1870–1978 and undated
University of Houston
    Cullinan, Joseph Stephen, Papers
    Kirby, John Henry, Papers
University of Texas, Dolph Briscoe Center for American History
    Hogg, Ima, Papers
    Hogg, William C., Papers
Walker County Court Records
Young Men's Christian Association Records, Offices, Houston, Texas

PRIVATE PAPERS, CORRESPONDENCE, AND INTERVIEWS

James A. Baker, III
Julie Baker
Lovett Baker (courtesy of John B. Boles)
Malcolm G. Baker Jr.
Stewart A. Baker
Susan Baker
Angela Blanchard
Philip S. Bentlif, MD
Elizabeth Hutcheson Carrell
John T. Cater
Addison Baker Duncan
Barbara Eaves
J. Thomas Eubank
Georgann Johnson
Malcolm Lovett Jr.

Graeme Meyers Marston
Bonner Baker Moffitt
Betty Kyle Moore
James Harrison Moore
Lynda M. Moore
Preston Moore Jr.
Gary Nichols
Roy L. Nolen
James D. Patton
Patricia Honea Schutts
Charles Szalkowski
Francita Stuart Ulmer
Virginia Meyers Watt
Joanne Seale Wilson

NEWSPAPERS

Dallas Morning News

Houston Chronicle

Houston Daily Post

Houston Press

Houstonian

Southern Mercury

Thresher, The (1916–1941)

PUBLISHED SOURCES

Arey, Henry W. *The Girard College and Its Founder: Containing the Biography of Mr. Girard . . . the Will of Mr. Girard.* Philadelphia: C. Sherman, Printer, 1853.

Arnold, Adam Bruce. "Growing with Houston: A Centennial History of the YMCA of Greater Houston, 1886–1986." MA Thesis, Rice University, April 1988.

Aston, B. Rice. *The Promiscuous Breed: The New World.* Houston: n.p., 2005.

Baines, May Harper. *Houston's Part in the World War.* Houston: Author, 1919.

Baker, James A. "Reminiscences of the Founder." *Rice Institute Pamphlet* 18:3 (July 1931).

Baker, James A., III. *"Work Hard, Study . . . and Keep Out of Politics!": Adventures and Lessons from an Unexpected Public Life.* New York: G. P. Putnam Sons, 2006.

Barnstone, Howard. *The Architecture of John F. Staub: Houston and the South.* With Stephen Fox, Jerome Iowa, and David Courtwright. Foreword by Vincent Scully. Austin: University of Texas Press, 1979.

Baron, Steven M. *Houston Electric: The Street Railways of Houston, Texas.* Lexington: Author, 1996.

Beard, Mary Ritter. *Woman's Work in Municipalities.* New York: D. Appleton and Company, 1915; reprinted New York: Arno Press, 1972.

Benda, Ilona B. *Our Community War Service Memorial: Houston and Harris County.* Houston: n.p., 1919.

Boles, John B. *University Builder: Edgar Odell Lovett and the Founding of the Rice Institute.* Baton Rouge: Louisiana State University Press, 2007.

Book of the Opening of Rice Institute, The. 2 vols. Rice Institute, 1914–1915.

Bowie, Walter Russell. *The Master of the Hill: A Biography of John Meigs.* New York: Dodd, Mead and Company, 1917.

Brackenridge, R. Douglas. *Voice in the Wilderness: A History of the Cumberland Presbyterian Church in Texas.* San Antonio: Trinity University Press, 1968.

Bradford, Ernest S. *Commission Government in American Cities.* New York: Macmillan, 1919.

Brown, Lawrence L. *The Episcopal Church in Texas II.* Austin: Church Historical-Society, 1988.

Buenger, Walter L., and Joseph A. Pratt. *But Also Good Business: Texas Commerce Banks and the Financing of Houston and Texas, 1886–1986.* College Station: Texas A&M University Press, 1986.

Carnegie, Andrew. "The Best Fields for Philanthropy." *North American Review* 148 (December 1889): 682–98.

———. "Wealth." *North American Review* 148 (June 1889): 653–64.

Centennial History of the Texas Bar, 1882–1982. Burnet, TX: Eakin Press, 1981.

Chancellor, Paul. *The History of The Hill School: 1851–1976*. Pottstown, PA: The Hill School, 1976.

Chapman, Betty Trapp. "From the Parlor to the Public: New Roles for Women in Houston, 1885–1915." *Houston Review* 15 (1993): 31–44.

———. "100 Years of the Chautauqua Study Club." *Houston History* (Spring 2010): 24–27.

Chung, Monit, Jennifer Levit, and Carole R. Linseisen. "Children's Services in Houston: The First 100 Years (1892–1991) of DePelchin Children's Center." Paper prepared by Graduate School of Social Work, University of Houston, 1996.

Coleman, Alexis J. "Golf in Texas," 92–95. Reprint of article courtesy of Nancy Stulack, United States Golf Association Museum Library.

Comey, Arthur Coleman. *Houston: Tentative Plan for Its Development; Report to the Houston Park Commission*. Boston: Press of Geo. H. Ellis Co., 1913.

Community: Review of Philanthropic Thought and Social Effort, The, vol. 1 (1919).

Cotner, Robert C. *James Stephen Hogg: A Biography*. Austin: University of Texas Press, 1959.

Cram, Ralph Adams. *My Life in Architecture*. Boston: Little, Brown, and Co., 1936.

Crooker, John H., Jr. and Gibson Gayle Jr. *Fulbright & Jaworski: 75 Years (1919–1994)*. Foreword by Judge Thomas M. Reavley. Houston: Fulbright & Jaworski L.L.P., 1994.

Cummins, Light Townsend. *Austin College: A Sesquicentennial History, 1849–1999*. Austin: Eakin Press, 1999.

———. *Emily Austin of Texas, 1795–1851*. Fort Worth: Center for Texas Studies at Texas Christian University, 2009.

Cutlip, Scott M. *Fund Raising in the United States: Its Role in America's Philanthropy*. New Brunswick: Rutgers University Press, 1965.

Davidson, Judge Mark. "The Making of a Judge: 1862, Electing a Judge during the Civil War." *The Houston Lawyer* (September / October 1998).

DeMark, Harry V., ed. *Makers of Houston, 1912*. Houston Biographical Association, 1912.

Eby, Frederick. *The Development of Education in Texas*. New York: Macmillan Company, 1925.

Estill, Harry F. "The Old Town of Huntsville." *The Quarterly of the Texas State Historical Association* 3:4 (April 1900).

Feagin, Joe R. *Free Enterprise City: Houston in Political-Economic Perspective*. New Brunswick: Rutgers University Press, 1988.

Federation of Women's Clubs. *The Key to the City of Houston*. Houston: State Printing Company, 1908.

Fenberg, Steven. *Unprecedented Power: Jesse Jones, Capitalism, and the Common Good*. College Station: Texas A&M University Press, 2011.

Ferguson, Dan. "The Antecedents of Austin College." *Southwestern Historical Quarterly* 53 (Jan. 1950): 238–56.

———. "Austin College in Huntsville." *Southwestern Historical Quarterly Online* 53:387–402.

Ferry, Joan. "Autry House." *The Cornerstone* 13:1 (Winter 2008): 1–7.

Foner, Eric. *Reconstruction: America's Unfinished Revolution, 1863–1877*. New York: Harper & Row, 1989.

Fox, Stephen. *The Country Houses of John F. Staub*. Color Photography by Richard Cheek. College Station: Texas A&M University Press, 2007.

———. "The General Plan of the William M. Rice Institute and Its Architectural Development." *Architecture at Rice* 29, 1980.

———. "Public Art and Private Places: Shadyside." *The Houston Review: History and Culture of the Gulf Coast* 2 (Winter 1980): 39–60.

Fredrickson, Eric L. *Andrews & Kurth L.L.P.: The First 100 Years of Excellence*. Houston: Andrews & Kurth, 2002.

Freeman, J. H. *The People of Baker Botts*. Houston: Baker & Botts, 1992.

Friedland, Martin L. *The Death of Old Man Rice: A True Story of Criminal Justice in America*. New York: New York University Press, 1994.

Frost, Dan R. *Thinking Confederates: Academia and the Idea of Progress in the New South*. Knoxville: University of Tennessee Press, 2000.

Fuglaar, Stephanie. "The Streetcar in Houston." *Houston History* 5 (Spring 2008): 33–42.

Garland, Joseph E. *The North Shore*. Rev. ed. Beverly, MA: Commonwealth Editions, 1998.

Gawalt, Gerard W., ed. *The New High Priests: Lawyers in Post-Civil War America*. Contributions in Legal Studies, 29. Westport, CT: Greenwood Press, 1984.

Gordon, Sallie and Penny Jones. *Images of America: Houston's Courtlandt Place*. Charleston, SC: Arcadia Publishing, 2009.

Greene, Casey. "Guardians against Change: The Ku Klux Klan in Houston and Harris County, 1920–1925." *Houston Review: History and Culture of the Gulf Coast* 10 (1988): 3–15.

Hall, Kermit L. *The Magic Mirror: Law in American History*. New York: Oxford University Press, 1989.

Handbook of Texas Online. www.tshaonline.org/handbook.

Haynes, Robert V. *A Night of Violence: The Houston Riot of 1917*. Baton Rouge: Louisiana State University Press, 1976.

History of Student Life at Rice University, The. Papers ed. by Michael Raphael. Houston: Rice Centennial Celebration Committee, 1990.

Houghton, Dorothy Knox Howe. *One Hundred Years: The Houston Club and Its City*. Houston: Gulf Printing Company, 1994.

Houghton, Dorothy Knox Howe, Barrie M. Scardino, Sadie Gwin Blackburn, and Katherine S. Howe. *Houston's Forgotten Heritage: Landscape, Houses, Interiors, 1824–1914*. Houston: Rice University Press, 1991.

Houston Architectural Survey. Southwest Center for Urban Research and Rice University School of Architecture. Vols. 1–5, Houston: Texas Historical Commission and City of Houston, 1980. Vol. 6, Houston: City of Houston, 1981.

Houston City Directories, 1872–1920.

Houston Country Club. *30th Anniversary Celebration 1908–1938*. Houston: 1938.

———. *Directory, 1940–1941*. Houston: 1940.

Huxley, Julian. "Texas and Academe." *Cornhill Magazine* 45 (July 1918): 53–65.

Hyman, Harold M. *Craftsmanship and Character: A History of the Vinson & Elkins Law Firm of Houston, 1917–1997*. Athens: University of Georgia Press, 1998.

———. "William Marsh Rice's Credit Ratings: 1846–1866." *Houston Review: History and Culture of the Gulf Coast* 6:2 (1984): 91–96.

Jabour, Anya. "'Grown Girls, Highly Educated': Female Education in an Antebellum Southern Family." *Journal of Southern History* 44:1 (Feb. 1998): 23–64.

James, Marquis. *The Raven: A Biography of Sam Houston*. Austin: University of Texas Press, 1929, 1994.

Jayne, Reginald G. "Martial Law in Reconstruction Texas." MA Thesis, Sam Houston State University, May 2005.

Jones, Ralph Wood. *Southwestern University, 1840–1961*. Austin: San Felipe Press, 1973.

Kelley, Mary L. *The Foundations of Texan Philanthropy*. College Station: Texas A&M University Press, 2004.

Kelly, Hugh Rice. "Peter Gray." *The Houston Lawyer* (Jan. 1976): 29–35.

Kilman, Ed. "Work Hard, Study and Keep Out of Politics." *Sunday Houston Post Magazine*, Oct. 3, 1937.

King, Judy. *Except the Lord Build . . .: The Sesquicentennial History of First Presbyterian Church, Houston, Texas, 1839–1989*. Houston: The Church, 1989.

Kirkland, Kate Sayen. *The Hogg Family and Houston: Philanthropy and the Civic Ideal*. Austin: University of Texas Press, 2009.

Kirkland, William A. *Old Bank–New Bank: The First National Bank, Houston, 1866–1956*. Houston: Pacesetter Press, 1975.

Kroger, Bill. "Reconstructing Reconstruction: Stories from the Harris County Court Archives on How the Rule of Law Was Restored after the Civil War." *The Houston Lawyer* (Jan./Feb. 2008): 26–36.

Levine, David O. *The American College and the Culture of Aspiration, 1915–1940*. Ithaca: Cornell University Press, 1986.

Lipartito, Kenneth J. *The Bell System and Regional Business: The Telephone in the South, 1877–1920*. Baltimore: Johns Hopkins University Press, 1989.

Lipartito, Kenneth J., and Joseph A. Pratt. *Baker & Botts in the Development of Modern Houston*. Austin: University of Texas Press, 1991.

Lockhart, John Washington. *Sixty Years on the Brazos: The Life and Letters of Dr. John Washington Lockhart, 1824–1900*. Waco: Texian Press, 1967.

Logan, Bill. *The Houston Heritage Collection of National Bank Notes, 1863 thru 1935*. Houston: D. Armstrong Co., 1977.

Lovett, Edgar Odell. *Edgar Odell Lovett and the Creation of Rice University: The Meaning of the New Institution*. Introduction by John B. Boles. Houston: Rice Historical Society, 2000.

Lundberg, Dr. Robert N. *Bass Rocks Golf Club*. Author, 1995.

Lynch, James D. *The Bench and Bar of Texas*. Nixon-Jones Printing, 1885.

Macon, N. Don. *Mr. John H. Freeman and Friends: A Story of the Texas Medical Center and How It Began*. Houston: Texas Medical Center, 1973.

Mayo, James M. *The American Country Club: Its Origins and Development.* New Brunswick: Rutgers University Press, 1998.

McCants, John Thomas. "Some Information Concerning the Rice Institute, 1955." Pamphlet, Rice Public Relations, Sept. 13, 1971.

Meiners, Fredericka. *A History of Rice University: The Institute Years, 1907–1963.* Houston: Rice University Studies, 1982.

———. *Rice University Historical Commission Newsletter.* Sept. 1978.

Mielnik, Tara Mitchell. "Mary Sharp College." Tennessee Encyclopedia of History and Culture online at http://tennesseeencyclopedia.net/entry/php?rec=843. Accessed Jan. 16, 2012.

Mohr, Clarence L., and Joseph E. Gordon. *Tulane: The Emergence of a Modern University, 1945–1980.* Baton Rouge: Louisiana State University Press, 2001.

Monsanto, Daniel E. *Houston.* Charleston, SC: Arcadia Publishing, 2009.

Montgomery, Julia Cameron. *Houston As a Setting of the Jewel: The Rice Institute, 1913.* Houston: Author, 1913. Reprinted by Rice Historical Society, 2002.

Morris, Sylvia Stallings, ed., and Andrew Forest Muir. *William Marsh Rice and His Institute: A Biographical Study.* Houston: William Marsh Rice University, 1972. Edited and updated by Randal B. Hall. College Station: Texas A&M University Press, 2012.

Muir, Andrew Forest. "William Marsh Rice, His Life and Death, the History of a Fortune." Paper presented to Harris County Historical Society, Sept. 6, 1955. Andrew Forest Muir Papers, WRC.

———. "William Marsh Rice, Houstonian." *East Texas Historical Journal* 2 (1964): 32–39.

Neighborhood Centers Inc. *Heart of Gold Yearbook.* Houston: Neighborhood Centers Inc., 1997.

———. *100 Years: An Enduring Promise.* Houston: Neighborhood Centers Inc., 2007.

Nicholson, Patrick J. *William Ward Watkin and the Rice Institute.* Houston: Gulf Publishing Company, 1991.

Norvell, James R. "The Railroad Commission of Texas: Its Origin and History." *Southwestern Historical Quarterly* 68 (April 1965): 4, 465–80.

Notre Dame of Maryland University. www.ndm.edu.

Nunn, William Curtis. *Texas under the Carpetbaggers.* Austin: University of Texas Press, 1962.

Olmsted, Frederick Law. *A Journey through Texas: Or, a Saddle-Trip on the Southwestern Frontier.* Foreword by Larry McMurtry. Austin: University of Texas Press, 1978, reprint of 1857 edition.

Olson, Bruce A. "The Houston Light Guards: A Case Study of the Texas Militia, 1873–1903." MA Thesis, University of Houston, May 1985.

Parker, Edwin B. "Anti-Railroad Personal Injury Litigation in Texas." Proceedings of the Texas Bar Association, Galveston, July 25–26, 1900. Austin: Texas Bar Association, 1900.

Platt, Harold L. *City Planning in the New South: The Growth of Public Services, in Houston, Texas 1830–1910.* Philadelphia: Temple University Press, 1982.

Pollard, Claude. "A History of the Texas Bar Association." *The Houston Lawyer* (July 1976): 30–41.

"Railroad Consolidation in Texas, 1891–1903." Pamphlet, Woodson Research Center.

Rankin, Melinda. *Texas in 1850*. Waco: Texian Press, 1966, reprint of 1850 edition.

Red, William Stuart. *A History of the Presbyterian Church in Texas*. The Steck Company, 1936.

Rice Institute. *General Announcements*. Houston: Rice Institute, 1913–1941.

Roussel, Hubert. *The Houston Symphony Orchestra, 1913–1971*. Austin: University of Texas Press, 1972.

Settlement Association. *Year Book, 1909*. Houston: Settlement Association, 1909.

Sheppard, Anthony. "The Nineteenth Century Bench and Bar in Harris County, Texas." *The Texas Lawyer* (July 1976): 6–29.

Sibley, Marilyn McAdams. *The Port of Houston: A History*. Austin: University of Texas Press, 1968.

Spratt, John S. *The Road to Spindletop: Economic Change in Texas, 1875–1901*. Dallas: Southern Methodist University Press, 1955.

Standard Blue Books of Texas Who's Who? Houston: Who's Who Publishing Co. of Houston, Texas, 1907.

Steiner, Mark E. "The Origins of the Houston Bar Association." *The Houston Lawyer* (July–August 1988): 13–22.

Stover, John F. *The Railroads of the South, 1865–1900: A Study in Finance and Control*. Chapel Hill: University of North Carolina Press, 1955.

Texas Blue Books: Houston 1900. Houston: Mrs. Corra Bacon Foster, 1900.

Thelin, John R. *A History of American Higher Education*. Baltimore: Johns Hopkins University Press, 2004.

Thomas, William G. *Lawyering for the Railroad: Business, Law, and Power in the New South*. Baton Rouge: Louisiana State Press, 1999.

Trimble, Frances G. *Houston Country Club Centennial, 1908–2008*. Houston: Houston Country Club, 2008.

Tsanoff, Corinne S. *Neighborhood Doorways*. Houston: Neighborhood Centers Association of Houston and Harris County, 1958.

Turner, Elizabeth Hayes. *Women, Culture, and Community: Religion and Reform in Galveston, 1880–1920*. New York: Oxford University Press, 1997.

Turner, Suzanne and Joanne Seale Wilson. *Houston's Silent Garden: Glenwood Cemetery, 1871–2009*. Color Photography by Paul Hester. College Station: Texas A&M University Press, 2010.

United States Census Records, 1860–1940.

Wallace, Frederic A., comp. *Ancestors and Descendants of the Rice Brothers of Springfield, Massachusetts*. Baltimore: Gateway Press, Inc., 2005.

White, Richard. *Railroaded: The Transcontinentals and the Making of Modern America*. New York: W. W. Norton & Company, 2011.

Wind, Herbert Warren. *The Story of American Golf, Vol. 1: 1888–1941*. New York: Callaway Editions, 2000.

Index